Cold War Radio

The Dangerous History of American Broadcasting in Europe, 1950–1989

RICHARD H. CUMMINGS

McFarland & Company, Inc., Publishers
Jefferson, North Carolina, and London

Portions of chapters 1, 2, 3, 6 and 8 appeared as an article in the *Journal of Transatlantic Studies* 6, no. 2 (August 2008); Portions of chapter 1 originally appeared as articles in *The Intelligencer: Journal of U.S. Intelligence Studies*, Winter 1998, Summer/Fall 2007; Portions of chapter 1 originally appeared as an article in *The Falling Leaf* 42 no. 3 (Autumn 1999), the journal of the PsyWar Society: An International Association of Psychological Warfare Historians & Aerial Propaganda Leaflet Collectors; Portions of chapter 1 originally appeared as an article in the *Journal of Intelligence History* (Winter 2001). International Intelligence History Association. 1, no. 2; Portions of chapter 3 originally appeared as an article in *The Intelligencer: Journal of U.S. Intelligence Studies*, Winter 1999; Portions of chapter 3 originally appeared as articles in *Security Intelligence Report*, 9, no. 14 (July 1994), and 9, no. 15 (August 1994); Portions of chapter 4 originally appeared as an article in *The Intelligencer: Journal of U.S. Intelligence Studies*, Spring 2008.

LIBRARY OF CONGRESS CATALOGUING-IN-PUBLICATION DATA

Cummings, Richard H., 1944–
    Cold War radio : the dangerous history of American broadcasting
in Europe, 1950–1989 / Richard H. Cummings.

        p.   cm.
    Includes bibliographical references and index.

    ISBN 978-0-7864-4138-9
    softcover : 50# alkaline paper ∞

    1. Radio Free Europe — History.   2. Radio Liberty — History.
3. Cold War — History.   I. Title.
HE8697.45.E852C86   2009
384.54094'09045 — dc22   2009005006

British Library cataloguing data are available

On the cover: Hands holding hammer and sickle ©2009 Shutterstock; Cold War globe Wikipedia.com

Manufactured in the United States of America

McFarland & Company, Inc., Publishers
    Box 611, Jefferson, North Carolina 28640
    www.mcfarlandpub.com

To everyone who contributed to the greatness
of Radio Free Europe and Radio Liberty

Table of Contents

Abbreviations and Acronyms

AmComLib .... American Committee for Liberation from Bolshevism

AVH .... Allam Vedelmi Hatosag (Hungarian State Security and Intelligence Agency)

AVO .... Allam Vedelmi Osztal (Hungarian State Security Department)

BfV .... Bundesamt für Verfassungschutz (Federal Agency for the Protection of the Constitution)

BND .... Bundesnachrichtendienst (German Federal Intelligence Service)

CIA .... Central Intelligence Agency

CIE .... Centrul de Informaţii Externe (Romanian Foreign Intelligence Center)

CSSR .... Czechoslovak Socialist Republic

DCI .... Director Central Intelligence

DDR .... Deutsche Demokratische Republik (Germany Democratic Republic — East Germany)

DIE .... Directia de Informatii Externe (Romanian Foreign Intelligence Service)

DS .... Drazven Sigurnost (Bulgarian Intelligence Service)

FBI .... Federal Bureau of Investigation

FEC .... Free Europe Committee

FEP .... Free Europe Press

GRU .... Glavnoje Razvedyvatel'noje Upravlenije (Main Intelligence Directorate of the General Staff of the Armed Forces of the USSR)

KGB .... Kommitet Gosudarstvenoi Bezopastnosti (USSR Committee for State Security)

LfV .... Landesamt für Verfassungsschutz (Land Office for the Protection of the Constitution — Land [State] Security Office)

MfS .... Ministerium für Staatssicherheit (East German Ministry of State Security)

OPC .... Office of Policy Coordination (CIA Division)

OSS .... Office of Strategic Services (U.S. intelligence agency in World War II)

NSC .... National Security Council

PPR .... Polish People's Republic

RFE .... Radio Free Europe

RL .... Radio Liberation, Radio Liberty

RFE/RL .... Radio Free Europe/Radio Liberty, Inc.

SB .... Służba Bezpieczeństwa (Poland's security service of the Ministry of Internal Affairs — internal intelligence agency)

Securitate ...... Departamentul Securității Statului (Romanian State Security Department — secret police)

SNB .... Sbor narodni bezpecnost (Czechoslovak national security brigade)

Stasi .... Staatssicherheit (German abbreviation for Ministerium für Staatssicherheit — East German secret police)

StB .... Statni Bezpecnost (Czechoslovak state security service)

Preface

I grew up in the Greater Boston area, never dreaming that I would someday be working in Munich, Germany, in charge of security at an American-sponsored radio station. How I reached that position is a story of fate, or luck.

I recall watching black-and-white television commercials on small screens, ads asking for dollars for Radio Free Europe, especially the one in which Ronald Reagan asked for support for the Crusade for Freedom. There were posters in the subway cars traveling in and out of Boston, asking for contributions in support of Radio Free Europe, to be sent to Mt. Vernon, New York. It seemed that every time I went to a Red Sox game, I saw those posters looking down on me. I did not understand then what they meant, but I found them fascinating.

I also remember sitting on Revere Beach with my friends, discussing the television ad for Radio Free Europe, an ad featuring the song "On Broadway." Then came the air force, unexpected Russian-language training, and assignments in Berlin and Turkey. After my military service, I graduated from Boston University with a degree in Soviet and Eastern European Studies. Before I knew it, in 1972 I was a graduate student in Munich at the Institute for the Study of the USSR and doing research in the Radio Liberty library. I also used to walk through Munich's wonderful city park, the English Garden, looking with curiosity at the long building of Radio Free Europe but not daring to set foot in it. I even applied for a job as a security guard at Radio Liberty but was turned down.

The CIA stopped funding for the institute at that time, and there was no other organization or university willing and able to take over the funding. The institute closed in the summer 1972, and I returned to Boston and began working as a criminal investigator for the U.S. Immigration and Naturalization Service. Through happenstance, in 1980 I met the then director of security for Radio Free Europe/Radio Liberty (RFE/RL), who told me he was going to leave RFE/RL. He suggested that I take over for him. After some hesitation, I applied for the job and was accepted. By coincidence, the day I resigned from the position in Boston, the terrorist "Carlos" and his gang were

1

finishing up detailed planning for a bomb attack on RFE/RL on February 21, 1981.

When I arrived in Munich in November 1980, there was very little security at RFE/RL, as the overall management and staff feeling was that the East Bloc intelligence services would never dare attack RFE/RL in Munich. How wrong they were, as the reader will discover in the chapter on the bombing of RFE/RL, an event that took place within three months of my arrival.

This book is based not only on my unique personal and professional experiences and notes, but also on my research of the previous thirty years of intelligence and security activities at the radio stations. I will detail for the first time the dangerous Cold War world of the radio stations in Munich, true stories of terrorists, spies, threats to émigrés, and political murder. Since leaving RFE/RL for the last time in April 1998, I have been lucky enough to talk about RFE/RL at various academic and security conferences. The reaction has been overwhelmingly positive and has led me to write this book. I have waited until now, as I was director of security at another institution for nine more years and did not have the time to write this book.

For over forty years, Radio Free Europe and Radio Liberty were two Munich-based American-sponsored radio stations which broadcast to countries behind the Iron Curtain. Radio Free Europe and Radio Liberty were also two critical elements of the CIA's early clandestine activities directed against the Communist regimes in Eastern Europe and the USSR. Thousands of persons worked for these radio stations, at a cost of hundreds of millions of dollars. Yet for years their existence remained covered in a Cold War shroud of mystery and intrigue.

Early RFE and RL corporate and U.S. government records no longer exist or cannot be located. Many persons who were responsible for the stations' development have long since died, leaving at best fragmentary documentation. Most archives of American and Eastern intelligence services remain even today classified. That said, the main outlines of the development of the radio stations can be traced from open sources. For example, selected files have been released in the U.S. government's recent declassification program as well as some files of the former Warsaw Pact intelligence services. The Soviet Union's intelligence archives remain draped in a cloak of secrecy.[1]

There will never be a single book to cover in detail the forty-plus years of history of the radio stations. My book is intended to add to the historiography of the Cold War and augment those books based on new documentation and analysis. I focus on security and intelligence problems, leaving the subjects of programming and policy to those more qualified than I am to write such a book. I have tried to remove myself from the stories in the book you are about to read. I do so to maintain objectivity and let the reader focus on the men and women who were the victims or the perpetrators of the crimes of Communism.

The last and only book to make a full study of both Radio Free Europe and Radio Liberty, published in 1983, was *America's Other Voice* by Sig Mickelson, former RFE/RL president. While his book is a good treatment of the history of the stations, Mickelson's book does not cover the exciting period leading up to and including the fall of the Berlin Wall and the breakup of the Communist bloc in Eastern Europe and the Soviet Union. Two the early Cold War books covered only Radio Free Europe: *Radio Free Europe*, by Robert T. Holt, published in 1959, and *Voices Through the Iron Curtain*, by Alan Michie, published in 1963. Both of these books are incomplete insider accounts written while Radio Free Europe was still a CIA covert operation, and the books contain no references to that connection. Other excellent insider books, by Arch Puddington and George Uban, also focus on Radio Free Europe.

Radio Liberty is often overlooked in the studies of the stations. There are two books on Radio Liberty that were published in the 1990s: Gene Sosin's *Sparks of Liberty: An Insider's Memoir of Radio Liberty* and James Critchlow's *Radio Liberty: An Insider's Story of Cold War Broadcasting*. The history of Radio Liberty needs updating, based on information made available after their publication.

I have focused on stories that best represent the history of RFE and RL. Appendix K gives a chronological view of stories that I do not have space to write about in detail. It is not that they are any less important to those who experienced them, but I decided to focus on the ones you are about to read. I leave it up to other researchers to write those stories that I have not detailed, and I hope that those who will write about RFE/RL will find my book a useful foundation for their work on the history of the Cold War and will show them how far an oppressive regime will go to silence those who threaten its existence by exposing its lies and contradictions.

Chapter 1 is a succinct study of the history of the radio stations. I believe this is necessary, to have a good understanding of the years of hostile intelligence activities directed against the stations, especially the staff. Included are extensive, detailed appendices of documents that have not appeared in print before. I did not edit or annotate the documents as that project is beyond the scope of this book. I leave that up to future researchers.

There are important lessons to be learned from this book, which is, I hope, an objective study of how oppressive regimes, whose very existence is threatened with truthful information, will react with hostility. RFE/RL left Munich in 1995 and moved to Prague, where it continues in operation today, even if the means and targets of the information flow have changed. While my book focuses on radio broadcasting, today's communication and information technology is not immune to hostile attacks. Witness the "cyber jamming" of RFE/RL, which started on April 26, 2008. RFE/RL received up to 50,000 fake hits every second in a "denial of service attack," which initially targeted the Web site of RFE/RL's Belarus Service, but quickly spread to other sites. Within hours, RFE/RL Web sites in Belarus, Bosnia, Croatia, Serbia, Azerbaijan, Macedonia, Russia, and Tajikistan) were knocked out or otherwise affected. An editorial in the *Wall Street Journal* published on April 29, 2008, sums up the everlasting problem: "The medium and the means may have changed from days when this legendary U.S.–funded station set up shop to beam news behind the Iron Curtain. But the conflict is no less pitched. Despots live in fear of accurate information and go to extraordinary means to stop it. Welcome to the front lines of the 21st century's information wars."

My job as director of security at Radio Free Europe/Radio Liberty was a dream one. For 15 years in Munich kept my adrenalin flowing, but it was part of a team effort from management and staff. I cannot possibly acknowledge all those with whom I had contact and support in my years at RFE/RL. There are simply too many to list and to exclude anyone would be unfair. They know who they are and do not need to see their names in this book to be reminded of how much I appreciate their help and understanding in my years at RFE/RL. Any successes I might have had running the RFE/RL security program cannot be attributed to me alone. For any and all failures, I accept the responsibility alone. As President Harry S. Truman once said, "The buck stops here."

In 2006, Romanian film director Alexandru Solomon, who was then researching his documentary film *Cold Waves*, interviewed me in Munich. At the interview's conclusion, he asked me before the camera if I had any regrets about what I did at RFE/RL. I told him that I had no regrets and that my experiences are in my blood, even today. I hope that after reading these true stories, you will come away from this book with a full understanding of why I said that. I could be criticized for writing another insider book, but in this case no one else could have written such a book. I was the only director of security at RFE/RL at the front lines in the turbulent Cold War decade of the 1980s.

1. Intelligence Underpinnings
of Radio Free Europe
and Radio Liberty

Genesis

The idea of American radio broadcasting in Russian to the Soviet Union from Germany, rather than from the official Voice of America, was first broached by the U.S. State Department in August 1946. General Lucius Clay, U.S. commander in Berlin, rejected the idea because it was not in keeping with the Four Powers Agreement covering Germany.[1] Instead, he focused on sustaining the German-language radio station Radio in the American Sector (RIAS), for all Berlin and the Soviet-military-occupied zone of Germany, which had started broadcasting in February that year. RIAS successful staff experiences, techniques, and programming became the model for the "surrogate home services" Radio Free Europe and Radio Liberty. The overt U.S. government radio station Voice of America began broadcasting in the Russian language in February 1947.

The Communist "takeover" of Eastern European countries and the Soviet propaganda offensive in the late 1940s served as catalysts for supplementing overt U.S. foreign information programs with covert psychological operations and political warfare, including international broadcasting to the USSR and its Eastern European satellites. Radio Liberty and Radio Europe were described in a secret 1969 Central Intelligence Agency report as "the oldest, largest, most costly, and probably most successful covert action projects aimed at the Soviet Union and Eastern Europe."[2]

The genesis of the international radio stations Radio Free Europe (RFE) and Radio Liberty (RL) can be traced to 1947–48. It was a time of the completion of Soviet domination of Eastern Europe, the Berlin airlift, the Marshall Plan, and the Iron Curtain. Eastern, Central, and Western Europe were physically divided by barbed wire, armed patrols, land mines and guard towers. The Communist Party monopoly and censorship of the domestic media

5

effectively cut off and prevented the free flow of information to the peoples of Eastern Europe and the USSR. U.S. government officials, Congress, and the American corporate world decided to act in a secret private sector–government relationship to bring news and information to the "peoples of the captive nations."

On December 17, 1947, the newly created United States National Security Council reported:

> The USSR is conducting an intensive propaganda campaign directed primarily against the U.S. and is employing coordinated psychological, political and economic measures designed to undermine non–Communist elements in all countries. The ultimate objective of this campaign is not merely to undermine the prestige of the U.S. and the effectiveness of its national policy but to weaken and divide world opinion to a point where effective opposition to Soviet designs is no longer attainable by political, economic or military means. In conducting this campaign, the USSR is utilizing all measures available to it through satellite regimes, Communist parties, and organizations susceptible to Communist influence.[3]

The National Security Council then issued NSC 4-A, which called for the director of the Central Intelligence Agency (CIA) to "initiate and conduct covert psychological operations designed to counteract Soviet and Soviet-inspired activities, which constitute a threat to world peace."[4] One aim of this psychological-war campaign was to create "surrogate" radio stations (home service) that would broadcast to countries under the Soviet control yet not be officially connected with the United States government. These stations could broadcast programs and take positions which the U.S.–sponsored Voice of America could not:

> all activities ... conducted or sponsored ... against hostile foreign states or groups or in support of friendly foreign states or groups but which are so planned and executed that any U.S. Government responsibility for them is not evident to unauthorized persons and that if uncovered the U.S. Government can plausibly disclaim any responsibility for them.[5]

George F. Kennan has been called the "father of containment." Perhaps he was, but he was also a firm proponent of liberation. In 1948 Kennan was the director of the Department of State's policy planning staff and the prime mover in creating Radio Free Europe and Radio Liberty. On May 4, 1948, Kennan presented a U.S. State Department position paper to the National Security Council entitled "The Inauguration of Organized Political Warfare." He defined political warfare as "the logical application of Clausewitz's doctrine in time of peace."[6] Kennan proposed a program of support for "liberation committees, underground activities behind the Iron Curtain, and support of indigenous anti–Communist elements in threatened countries of the Free World."[7]

The purpose of these "liberation committees" would be

> to encourage the formation of a public American organization which will sponsor selected political refugee committees so that they may
>
> (a) act as foci of national hope and revive a sense of purpose among political refugees from the Soviet World;
>
> (b) provide an inspiration for continuing popular resistance within the countries of the Soviet World; and
>
> (c) serve as a potential nucleus for all-out liberation movements in the event of war.[8]

Kennan further described the "liberation committees" as overt operations, which, however, should receive covert guidance and possibly assistance from the government: "It is proposed that trusted private American citizens be encouraged to establish a public committee which would give support and guidance in U.S. interests to national movements (many of them now in existence) publicly led by outstanding political refugees from the Soviet World."[9]

NSC 10/2

In June 1948, after a lengthy debate among various interested government agencies on the questions of overt and covert propaganda, and domestic and international information programs, the National Security Council superseded NSC 4-A with another directive, NSC 10/2. Kennan drafted this directive, which presented more details of planned psychological war with the Soviet Union: "The National Security Council, taking cognizance of the vicious covert activities of the USSR, its satellite countries and Communist groups to discredit and defeat the aims and activities of the United States and other Western powers, has determined that, in the interests of world peace and U.S. national security, the overt foreign activities of the U.S. Government must be supplemented by covert operations."[10]

Covert operations were defined as "all activities ... conducted or sponsored ... against hostile foreign states or groups or in support of friendly foreign states or groups but which are so planned and executed that any U.S. Government responsibility for them is not evident to unauthorized persons and that if uncovered the U.S. Government can plausibly disclaim any responsibility for them."[11]

These activities were then listed as: "Propaganda; economic warfare; preventive direct action, including sabotage, anti-sabotage, demolition and evacuation measures; subversion against hostile states, including assistance to underground resistance movements, guerrillas, and refugee liberation groups, and support of indigenous anti–Communist elements in threatened countries of the free world."[12]

NSC 10/2 specifically dealt with the creation of an Office of Special Projects within the CIA. This new office would, in part, plan and conduct covert operations. The person in charge of this new office would report directly to the director of central intelligence (DCI), and for "purposes of security and of flexibility of operations, and to the maximum degree consistent with efficiency," the Office of Special Projects would "operate independently of other components of Central Intelligence Agency."[13]

In July 1948, U.S. Secretary of State George Marshall sent a telegram to American ambassadors in Eastern Europe and the USSR telling them of the plans to allow political refugees from Iron Curtain countries in the United States to speak in official VOUSA (Voice of USA, later Voice of America) broadcasts to those countries. He asked for their opinions. The ambassadors were unanimous in rejecting the plan. The U.S. ambassador in the Soviet Union explained: "Under present circumstances use of any Soviet refugees on VOUSA would not only be ineffectual but would undoubtedly excite resentment and ridicule against our broadcasts."[14]

This was the final bureaucratic rejection of any remaining idea of using official or overt U.S. radio facilities in the upcoming psychological war. The only alternative for the Truman administration was covert radio operations.

Frank Wisner

If George Kennan could be considered the "father" of the radio stations, one of their uncles surely was Frank Wisner, who was a World War II Office of Strategic Services (OSS) veteran and lawyer, and a main actor responsible for the development of Radio Free Europe and Radio Liberty. In September 1944, he had been sent to Bucharest, Romania, where he controlled an OSS operation that evacuated allied airmen downed behind enemy lines. Wisner remained in Bucharest until March 1945, when he witnessed the arrival of Soviet troops and the tragic aftermath of the occupation.[15]

After World War II, Frank Wisner returned to private practice and joined the Council on Foreign Relations. Former OSS Switzerland chief Allen Dulles was the Council's president. Dulles would turn out to be the third major actor in the development of the radios.[16] In 1947, Wisner joined the U.S. State Department as the Deputy Assistant Secretary of State for Occupied Countries. He became involved with the refugees from the USSR and Soviet-dominated countries in Eastern Europe.

In June 1948, George Kennan placed Wisner at the head of the list for a new CIA position, director of the Office of Special Projects, based on the "recommendations of people who know him." Said Kennan, "I personally have no knowledge of his ability, but his qualifications seem reasonably good."[17] Frank Wisner, still with the Department of State, telephoned Director of Central Intelligence Hillenkoetter on August 4, 1948, and told him that "project for the clandestine radio transmitter " had been approved in principle. A definite approval would only follow once the details were determined regarding "who was to operate the transmitter, to whom the transmissions would be directed, and who would set up the raw material to be transmitted."[18] The philosophical, political, and operational groundwork for the creation of Radio Free Europe and Radio Liberty, using émigrés, had been set.

Origins of Radio Free Europe

The Committee for a Free Europe was ostensibly set up in New York on May 17, 1949, when the articles of incorporation were signed. Directors and officers included future CIA director Alan Dulles and future president Dwight D. Eisenhower. The corporate name was changed to the National Committee for a Free Europe (NCFE) on June 1, 1949. Joseph C. Grew, the corporate chairman, stated its purpose was "to put the voices of these exiled leaders on the air, addressed to their own peoples back in Europe, in their own languages, in the familiar tones."[19]

According to a later U.S. government review of Radio Free Europe, the National Committee for a Free Europe (NCFE) was founded to

1. Create an institution in which the émigrés from the satellite nations could find employment which would utilize their skills and, at the same time, document for the world at large the actions of the satellite governments and Soviet Russia;
2. Utilize the political figures of such emigrations as rallying points and as symbols of unified opposition to communism in this country and abroad;
3. Relieve the Department of State of the need to deal with émigré political leaders whom they could not endorse as "Governments in Exile" at a time when the United States officially recognized the satellite governments; and
4. Generally to "aid the non-fascist, non-communist leaders in their peaceful efforts to prepare the way toward the restoration in Eastern Europe of the social, political, and religious liberties, in which they and we believe."[20]

Let the Broadcasts Begin!

The CIA's Special Procedures Group (SPG) had acquired from the U.S. military small short-wave transmitters for broadcasting to the Soviet Union and Eastern Europe from the U.S. zone of Germany, under the code name "Project UMPIRE."[21] A small, 7.5-kilowatt, short-wave transmitter, nicknamed Barbara, was positioned on a flatbed truck near Lampertheim, Germany.

On July 4, 1950, Radio Free Europe transmitted its first program, thirty minutes in length, to Czechoslovakia as an "audience building broadcast." The press release the day before outlined not only the ideological basis for the programming, but also a cover-up of the true sponsorship of RFE: "Owned and operated by the National Committee for a Free Europe, Inc., a group of private American citizens, Radio Free Europe will broadcast the true story of freedom and democracy to the eighty million people living in Communist slavery between Germany and Russia. Freed of diplomatic limitations, the broadcasts will be hard-hitting."[22]

The inflammatory inaugural message, which set the tone for subsequent broadcasts, was written by Czech émigré Pavel Tigrid, who would become the Czech Republic's first minister of culture, after the 1989 Velvet Revolution:

> Dear Listeners:
> We are assembled in our large studio, all we who work for this transmitter, the proud name of which is Radio Free Europe, the Voice of Free Czechs and Slovaks.
> Today, a terrible enemy rises against all communist informers, agents provocateurs and stool pigeons, all inhuman guards in prisons and work-camps, all judges and members of communist jurisdiction, all propagandists of communist ideology. Radio Free Europe will reveal their names, one by one; all of them will be blacklisted by the democratic world and will be dumped on the rubbish heap of contempt by the Czech and Slovak people.[23]

Ten days later, the NCFE announced full short-wave broadcasting schedules for "hard-hitting" programs for Czechoslovakia and Romania with the following script for the start of these programs:

> You are not forgotten.
> This is the purpose of Radio Free Europe ... to remind you that you are not forgotten ... that you are not alone. To you, chained by tyranny, we will bring a consistent, reliable well of information. We will bring to you the voices of your friends and compatriots ... voices you already know ... voices you come to know.
> We will speak to you freely and without restraint ... we will speak as free

men who believe there is but one foundation for peace ... the freedom of each person, the freedom of each nation to shape its own destiny.

Thus, to speak for freedom, Americans and the democratic leaders exiled from Eastern Europe have united to bring you the voice of Radio Free Europe.[24]

Experimental radio broadcasting began on July 14, 1950, to Romania; to Hungary and Poland on August 4, 1950; and to Bulgaria on August 11, 1950. RFE also broadcast to Albania from late 1950 to September 30, 1953. On May 1, 1951, Radio Free Europe began broadcasting on medium-wave frequencies from the newly constructed transmitter station, nicknamed "Carola" at Holzkirchen, south of Munich. The new transmitter, with antenna towers four hundred feet high, was at that time three times more powerful than any medium-wave transmitter in the United States. Full-schedule broadcasts to Romania began on May 1, 1951, and to Hungary in October 1951.[25]

The first Polish-language program broadcast from Holzkirchen was on May 3, 1952, at 11:00 A.M.:

MUSIC: Bells, interrupted by fanfares.
ANNOUNCER: Radio Free Europe calling — Voice of Free Poland.
MUSIC : Fanfares.
ANNOUNCER : Attention! Attention! On our National Day, on the anniversary of the third May Constitution, you will listen to the inaugurating program of our radio station which will broadcast daily to our countrymen in Poland. In a few moments a solemn dedication of this new radio station will take place.

Attention! Attention! Our voice will reach you from today on new and more powerful antennae.

Attention! Attention! Poles speak to Poles.

We speak to our brothers in Poland thanks to the American National Committee for a Free Europe.[26]

Harold Miller, president of the National Committee for a Free Europe, in a prepared speech translated into Polish, then gave the ideological foundation of RFE broadcasts to Poland, which was to last until the collapse of Communism in 1989:

This superb instrument is to carry the new Voice of Free Poland. Over its pulsing waves, the free Poles hope to make this echo audible to the dauntless people of their enslaved homeland, that you may share with us the knowledge that the people of Poland are not forgotten and that we in America and in the West have faith in Poland and in the certainty of her ultimate victory.

The Polish Station of Radio Free Europe, organized by the National Committee for a Free Europe, is a station run by Poles for their countrymen. It aims at piercing the Iron Curtain with words of truth. It does not propose to tell the people of Poland what to think or what to do. When they know what goes on in the Free World, when they know that their brothers in exile and their friends in the West have not forgotten them, they will be able to draw their own conclusion, and form their own ideas.[27]

Project Troy: Academia and the CIA

Project Troy was a government-academia partnership in the early days of the Cold War. Yet, as in most partnerships, there was disagreement as to how the partners perceived their roles in penetrating the Iron Curtain. The government view was outlined in a memo to the National Security Council:

> Under this project, the Massachusetts Institute of Technology assembled 30 of the nation's top scientists and other experts to explore all means — conventional and unconventional — for penetrating the Iron Curtain. The report endorses the large-scale expansion of radio facilities, already initiated, and calls for even further expansion along lines which should facilitate further piercing the curtain by means which will not interfere with other telecommunications channels (military).[28]

The academic view was different. According to an MIT pamphlet:

> In 1950, as war raged in Korea and the U.S.S.R. tested its atomic bomb, the Soviets were jamming Voice of America (VOA) radio propaganda broadcasts. Undersecretary of State James Webb asked MIT President James Killian to assemble a team to solve the jamming problem.
> Killian and Humanities and Social Studies Dean John Burchard assembled a diverse group (including professors from Harvard and other universities) to address not only the technical issues but also matters of political warfare: what the VOA should broadcast, to whom, and to what effect, once the jamming was circumvented.
> Project Troy had not only led to a solution of the jamming problem, but also to the creation of an interdisciplinary center where scholarly expertise would be applied to foreign policy issues.[29]

One significant part of the Troy Report dealt with "political warfare" and "communication into shielded areas":

> means of communication for piercing the Iron Curtain, mentioning, besides radio and balloons, and other existing ways, the use of direct mail to send professional journals and industrial and commercial publications and ... objects typical of American life, drugs, flashlights, fountain pens, small radio receivers, etc.[30]

"Shouldn't they hear both sides?" Advertising poster used in RFE newspapers and magazines fund requests, from late 1960s (Radio Free Europe/Radio Liberty).

Winds of Freedom: Balloons Over Europe

Another section of the Troy Report dealt with the use of large balloons to send information leaflets over the Iron Curtain:

> An area of a million square miles could be saturated with a billion propaganda sheets in a single balloon operation costing a few million dollars.... If the area of dispersal in such an operation were restricted to 30,000 square miles, which may be practicable, there would be a leaflet laid down, on the average, for each area of 30 by 30 feet ... the dispersion of balloons in flight and the dispersion of leaflets in falling from altitude both lend themselves to saturation operations.
>
> Production specifications should be established now and productive capacity should be located.... The operational testing and production program should be undertaken now. It may cost about one million dollars.... In order to coordinate balloon use with other political warfare operations, organizational planning for the final operations should start now.... A stockpile sufficient for an actual operation should be created now, and the questions of size and type of stock should be reviewed periodically as the program develops.[31]

C. Rodney Smith, director of RFE, left, and General Lauris Norstad, former Supreme Allied Commander, Europe, standing before a map of Europe with Radio Free Europe's target countries, 1950s (Radio Free Europe/Radio Liberty).

By August 1948, under code name Project ULTIMATE, the CIA's Special Procedures Group (SPG) had a printing press and stockpile of meteorological balloons to carry and deliver propaganda leaflets into Eastern European countries in the event of war. In addition, the SPG had acquired from the U.S. military small short-wave transmitters for broadcasting to the Soviet Union and Eastern Europe from the U.S. zone in Germany. On August 4, 1948, Frank G. Wisner, then with the State Department, telephoned Rear Admiral R. H. Hillenkoetter, then director of the CIA, and told him that the State Department, "at the present time," disapproved of the idea of using meteorological balloons to carry propaganda from the American-occupied zone in Germany to Eastern Europe and the Soviet Union. Wisner explained that he had discussed this with Mr. George Kennan, who said that the "time was not propitious."[32]

The Free Europe Committee used the Free Europe Press (FEP) to print millions of propaganda leaflets. The first balloons were launched in August 1951 in an open field only three miles from the Czechoslovak border. Famed American newspaper correspondent Drew Pearson — a major proponent of the balloon-launching program in his newspaper columns, Harold Stassen — prominent Republican politician, and C. D. Jackson, president of Free Europe Committee, launched the balloons "looking like three Statues of Liberty, [holding] high above their heads big rubber balloons. At signal they solemnly let go."[33] After the launching, Harold Stassen said, "We tore a big hole in the Iron Curtain."[34]

The balloons had the Czech word "Svoboda" (Freedom) printed in large letters on the side and the leaflets contained a stirring message:

> A new wind is blowing. New hope is stirring. Friends of freedom in other lands have found a new way to reach you. They know that you also want freedom. Millions of free men and women have joined together and are sending you this message of friendship over the winds of freedom.... There is no dungeon deep enough to hide truth, no wall high enough to keep out the message of freedom. Tyranny cannot control the winds, cannot enslave your hearts. Freedom will rise again.[35]

This test operation was conducted on a stand-alone basis — the balloons were not part of a coordinated programming effort with Radio Free Europe. Each balloon carried about three thousand leaflets, and when the weather was favorable, about two thousand balloons were launched each night. In total, over eleven million leaflets were sent aloft.

The skies of Central Europe from October 1951 to November 1956 were filled with more than 350,000 balloons carrying over three hundred million leaflets, posters, books, and other printed matter. The NCFE constructed three major launching sites in Germany to launch the balloons in round-the-clock operations in good weather. The balloon operations were coordinated with radio programming and had colorful names: PROSPERO, VETO, FOCUS, and SPOTLIGHT.[36]

Operation PROSPERO

PROSPERO was the code name for the RFE balloon program in the summer 1953, when in a timespan of only four days, 6,500 balloons with over twelve million RFE leaflets were launched into Czechoslovakia. The balloon launching started approximately at midnight on July 13 in the small Bavarian town of Tirschenreuth. RFE broadcast word of the launching during the first news broadcasts at 6:00 A.M. This was the first time balloons were launched in conjunction with specific radio programs. RFE was critical of the regime's just installed currency reforms. Included in the leaflets were aluminum replicas of a newly introduced Czechoslovak coin. The Freedom Bell and the inscription, "All Czechs and Slovaks for Freedom — All the Free World for Czechs and Slovaks" were stamped on the coin replicas.

The regime responded to PROSPERO by using military aircraft and anti-aircraft weapons along the border to shoot down the balloons the day after the first launching. In fact, on July 15, the FEP staff saw the military aircraft shooting down the balloons as they first crossed the border into Czechoslovakia. Police cars in Prague and elsewhere used loudspeakers ordering citizens to turn in all the leaflets. Both the Czechoslovak and Soviet media attacked this balloon program. Because of the violent reaction and the media attacks, RFE inadvertently discovered that the balloon program was more successful than first planned. It paved the ground work for even greater balloon efforts with specific programming in the following years. For the first time, PROSPERO proved the value of combining the spoken word of RFE and written word of FEP for effective propaganda.[37]

Balloon Technology

There were different types of balloon techniques. One relatively simple but effective technique, for example, used a remarkable timing device: dry ice. Cartons filled with leaflets were attached to the bottom of the hydrogen-filled balloons. The loosely covered cartons were held upright through the use of envelopes containing dry ice. As the dry ice evaporated, the cartons tipped over, thus dropping the leaflets. To try to hit the intended population target, the launchers developed an ingenious system that calculated the weight of the dry ice, the amount of hydrogen, weight of the leaflets, direction and velocity of the wind.

The Black Book: Regime Reaction

In June 1952, the Committee for a Free Europe published compiled the first of its internal publications entitled "the Black Book," detailing how the various governments of Eastern Europe reacted to RFE's broadcasts. The introduction to "the Black Book" gave the purpose of this publication: "It is always interesting to hear what your enemies are saying about you. Hence, this 'Black Book' of Communist charges has been prepared for internal use by members of NCFE and its divisions."

One representative example was the reaction of a Czechoslovak publication *Dikobras* on November 16, 1952, attacking Pavel Tigrid:

> You tried your best, Paul Tigrid!
> To sing the song of Free Europe!
> But you had to live up to the day
> When a voice as sharp as a dagger is needed.
> Stranksy was kicked out together with Tigrid.
> Whose voice will now be carried across the ether?
> Discard unnecessary unrest!
> Czechs, you need not worry![38]

The following quotation from the second "Black Book" was similar to that of the Eastern European regime attacks in the heat of the Cold War in the 1980s:

> It is not entirely true that the size of this compilation of Communist attacks is an accurate measure of the Committee's effectiveness. But the volume and intensity of the official slander contained herein leaves little room for doubt that the enemy is being hurt and is reacting violently. His temper is not improving, although his vocabulary of abuse has grown measurably since the last edition of the *Black Book* was issued in June 1952. Formerly satisfied with such elementary epithets as "reactionary exiles," we find he has now advanced to more savory expressions: "exile manure," "swamps of prostitution," "American germ murderers" and "slave drivers" and "war arsonists," "treacherous exiles, "liars from Free Europe," "embezzlers," "former SS cut-throats," "furious exile dogs," "disgusting lackeys," and so forth.[39]

America's Cold War Crusade for Freedom

Cold War historians who have written about Radio Free Europe usually point to the origins of the Crusade for Freedom and the "Cold War rhetoric" of the President Eisenhower administration. Yet on October 27, 1948, during his election campaign, President Harry S. Truman proclaimed,

> As an American, as well as your president, I resent the contemptible Republican slur that charges me with being "soft" where Communist tyranny is concerned. Under your Democratic administration, the people of the United States have thrown themselves wholeheartedly into the support of freedom and democracy against the predatory pressures of communism. Our sustained, unprecedented worldwide fight against the spread of communism has brought new hope to people everywhere in the world.... We are engaged in a great crusade — a crusade for freedom, for tolerance, for the rights and welfare of all the people.[40]

On April 20, 1950, President Truman spoke at a luncheon of the American Society of Newspaper Editors on U.S. foreign policy. President Truman called for a campaign of truth in the U.S. information programs:

> The cause of freedom is being challenged throughout the world today by the forces of imperialistic communism. This is a struggle, above all else, for the minds of men. Propaganda is one of the most powerful weapons the Communists have in this struggle. Deceit, distortion, and lies are systematically used by them as a matter of deliberate policy.
> This propaganda can be overcome by the truth — plain, simple, unvarnished truth — presented by the newspapers, radio, newsreels, and other sources that the people trust. If the people are not told the truth, or if they do not have confidence in the accuracy and fairness of the press, they have no defense against falsehoods. But if they are given the true facts, these falsehoods become laughable instead of dangerous.
> We must make ourselves known as we really are — not as Communist propaganda pictures us. We must pool our efforts with those of other free peoples in a sustained, intensified program to promote the cause of freedom against the propaganda of slavery. We must make ourselves heard round the world in a great campaign of truth.[41]

In February 1950, the National Committee for a Free Europe had begun a process to establish, as a separate corporation, the Crusade for Freedom. Allen Dulles was one of the incorporating officers. On April 26, 1950, DeWitt C. Poole, president of the NCFE, announced that General Lucius D. Clay had accepted the position of chairman of the Crusade for Freedom. In Clay's name, a statement of purpose of the Crusade was issued, which read, in part: "The soul of the world is sick, and the peoples of the world are looking to the United States for leadership and hope.... They are looking to us for leadership in a great moral crusade — a crusade for freedom, friendship and faith throughout the earth.... If we are to prove equal to this desperate need, each U.S. citizen must feel a personal responsibility. We cannot leave the job to government alone.[42]

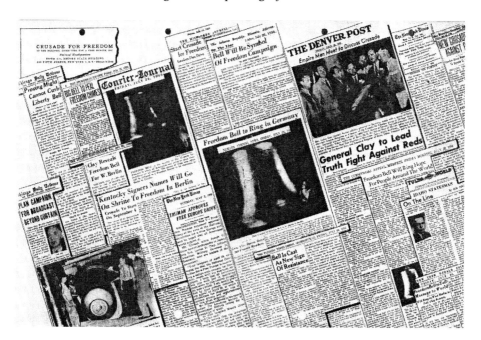

U.S. newspaper coverage of Crusade for Freedom. Note the Crusade's address on upper left corner. 1951 (Radio Free Europe/Radio Liberty).

Also on April 26, 1950, the National Committee for a Free Europe sent a telegram, under the names of General Clay and NCFE Board Chairman Joseph Grew, to President Truman, advising him of the new Crusade for Freedom and its future plans:

> In your speech of April 20, you urged private initiative in expressing the voice of freedom. The National Committee for a Free Europe was organized for this purpose, and particularly to help those who love freedom and, as a result, have been exiled to continue to fight for the restoration of freedom in their countries. We believe that the American people are ready for a crusade for freedom which will not only support the voices of those from behind the Iron Curtain who have lost freedom and home but will augment their voices with an overwhelming expression from free people in this country and everywhere of their faith and confidence that there will yet be a free world.
>
> We recognize the additional responsibility which has been thrust upon us by your challenging words, and we want to assure you that we are proceeding immediately with every resource at our disposal to organize in this country a crusade for freedom which will be a genuine expression of the will of the American people and which, through Radio Free Europe and other facilities, will be carried throughout the world. We have every confidence that the American people will join enthusiastically in this crusade to preserve their heritage, and thus respond fully and promptly to your expression of faith.[43]

President Truman responded with a letter to General Clay and Joseph Grew:

> Your telegram of April twenty-sixth, advising me that the National Committee for a Free Europe is launching a nationwide crusade for freedom, meets with my heartiest approval. I hope that all Americans will join with you in dedicating themselves to this critical struggle for men's minds. I am deeply gratified by your prompt response to my appeal of April twentieth, in which I emphasized the important role of private groups and organizations in this great endeavor.[44]

This correspondence was covered by the nation's press, including the *New York Times*, which, on May 2, 1950, carried the headline "Truman Approves Free Europe Drive."

Eisenhower and the Crusade for Freedom

General Dwight D. Eisenhower passionately called for an American "Crusade for Freedom," in a nationwide radio broadcast on the major radio networks, from Denver, Colorado, on Labor Day 1950:

> I speak tonight about the Crusade For Freedom.
>
> This crusade is a campaign sponsored by private American citizens to fight the big lie with the big truth. It is a program that has been hailed by President Truman, and others, as an essential step in getting the case for freedom heard by the world's multitudes.
>
> Powerful Communist radio stations incessantly tell the world that we Americans are physically soft and morally corrupt; that we are disunited and confused; that we are selfish and cowardly; that we have nothing to offer the world but imperialism and exploitation.
>
> To combat these evil broadcasts the government has established a radio program called the Voice of America, which has brilliantly served the cause of freedom, but the Communist stations overpower it and outflank it with a daily coverage that neglects no wavelength or dialect, no prejudice or local aspiration. Weaving a fantastic pattern of lies and twisted fact, they confound the listener into believing that we are warmongers, that America invaded North Korea, that Russia invented the airplane, that the Soviets, unaided, won World War II; and that the secret police and slave camps of Communism offer humanity brighter hope than do self-government and free enterprise.
>
> We need powerful radio stations abroad, operated without government restrictions, to tell in vivid and convincing form about the decency and essential fairness of democracy. These stations must tell of our aspirations for peace, our hatred of war, our support of the United Nations and our constant readiness to cooperate with any and all who have these same desires.
>
> One such private station — Radio Free Europe — is now in operation in Western Germany. It daily brings a message of hope and encouragement to a small part of the European masses.[45]

Eisenhower asked the United States for financial support and to sign a "Freedom Scroll" with a "Declaration of Freedom." During the publicity trip of the "Freedom Bell" to twenty-six major cities, sixteen million signed the "Freedom Scrolls":

> I believe in the sacredness and dignity of the individual.
> I believe that all men derive the right to freedom equally from God.
> I pledge to resist aggression and tyranny wherever they appear on earth.
> I am proud to enlist in the Crusade for Freedom.
> I am proud to help make the Freedom Bell possible, to be a signer of this Declaration of Freedom, to have my name included as a permanent part of the Freedom Shrine in Berlin, and to join with the millions of men and women throughout the world who hold the cause of freedom sacred.

The World Freedom Bell, a duplicate of the Liberty Bell, was transported to the Schoeneberg Town Hall in the U.S.-controlled sector of Berlin. It was officially dedicated at the Town Hall before hundreds of thousands of Berliners on October 24, 1950, with General Clay as the keynote speaker. Radio Free Europe used four notes of the bell as a program station-break with the words: "That was the Freedom Bell to remind you that you are listening to Radio Free Europe." The "Freedom Scrolls" are enshrined in the Freedom Bell tower vault at the base of the belfry. Visitors to the building can readily see the envelopes and packages containing the scrolls through the vault's glass door.

Americans contributed $1,317,000 to the expansion of Radio Free Europe but expenses for the Crusade amounted to over $900,000, for a net profit of only $400,000. Expenses for the National Committee for a Free Europe

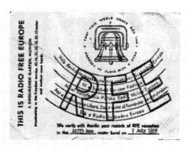

Freedom bell logos used over the years (Radio Free Europe/Radio Liberty).

amounted to $2,300,000, including administrative costs and the acquisition of radio equipment.[46] The vision that the Crusade for Freedom would be able to fully finance Radio Free Europe started to fade.

The 1951 Crusade for Freedom, which ended in early 1952, used the services of actor and future president Ronald Reagan in the televised public-service appeal for contributions to Radio Free Europe:

> My name is Ronald Reagan. Last year the contributions of sixteen million Americans to the Crusade for Freedom made possible the World Freedom Bell — symbol of hope and freedom to the Communist-dominated peoples of Eastern Europe. And built this powerful 135,000-watt Radio Free Europe transmitter in Western Germany.
>
> This station daily pierces the Iron Curtain with the truth, answering the lies of the Kremlin and bringing a message of hope to millions trapped behind the Iron Curtain. Grateful letters from listeners smuggled past the secret police express thanks to Radio Free Europe for identifying Communist Quislings and informers by name.
>
> The Crusade for Freedom is your chance, and mine, to fight Communism. Join now by sending your contributions to
>
> General Clay
> Crusade for Freedom
> Empire State Building
> New York City
>
> Or join in your local community.

The 1951 Crusade brought in brought in more contributions in comparison with the 1950 Crusade, $1,900,000 but the Crusade's expenses were $2,000,000, for a net loss of $100,000.[47]

Negative Reaction in Washington: The Tail Wagging the Dog

The success of the Crusade for Freedom upset the foreign policy bureaucracy in Washington, which saw the Crusade as a threat to the funding of the official government international broadcasting service, the Voice of America. An extraordinary meeting of CIA and the U.S. State Department leadership took place in the private residence of State Department official Edward W.

Opposite: **Night view of Town Hall in Berlin, where Kennedy made his famous "Ich bin ein Berliner" speech in solidarity with the people of Berlin after the Wall was constructed. The Freedom Bell is here, as well as the original Freedom Scrolls for the Crusade.**

Crusade package on display in Berlin (author's collection).

Barrett, assistant secretary of state for public affairs, on the evening of November 21, 1951. Representing the CIA were Messrs. Dulles, Wisner, Lloyd (deputy chief, Psychological Staff Division), and Braden (chief, International Branch, Psychological Division, OPC). During the meeting, Allen Dulles, the director of the CIA, asked questions about the future of the Crusade for Freedom. Edward Barrett gave the State Department position; saying that

> the present type of campaign was harming the total United States effort and making people ask the question whether the Voice of America is really needed. He did not say that to his surprise no serious questions came up in the last Congress concerning the apparent duplication between Radio Free Europe and VOA. Mr. Barrett suggested that instead of the present type of Crusade for Freedom, a low-pressure program should be conducted. He said that something along the line of the tuberculosis seal campaign in magazines, with coupons, and so on, ought to be tried out.[48]

The assembled group agreed on Barrett's proposal. On January 17, 1952, there was another top-level meeting with the CIA, the State Department, NCFE's C. D. Jackson, and Abbot Washburn executive vice chairman of the Crusade for Freedom, to discuss of the Crusade's future.

> Mr. Barrett reminded the group that NCFE had started as an organization to look after and make use of the various Eastern European refugee groups. He recalled that giving these groups a radio voice was something of a later development. He also recalled that the Crusade was established primarily as a cover for the governmental support of the enterprise. Mr. Barrett raised the question of whether or not the Crusade had grown to such proportions that it was now a case of the tail wagging the dog. He also raised the question of whether the two or three million dollars that might be raised in the Crusade might be endangering the $85,000,000 involved in the appropriations for the USIE [United States Information and Educational Exchange] operations. He thought it was important to get back to the idea of just enough of a Crusade to give the minimum necessary cover to NCFE.[49]

The Crusade for Freedom continued until 1960, when its functions were taken over by the Radio Free Europe Fund.

Eastern European Fund and Radio Free Europe Fund

George Kennan's 1948 vision of "liberation committees" reached fruition when, in March 1951, the Eastern European Fund (EEF) was established by the Ford Foundation, with Kennan selected as the first president and Frank Altschul, director of the NCFE, on the board of directors. The purpose of this organization was to "increase the usefulness to free society of exiles from Soviet Power by improving their morale, their mutual welfare, the suitability of their occupation, and their facilities for association and mutual aid, and by helping them to contribute to the general fund of knowledge in this country about Russia and the Union of the Soviet Socialist Republics."[50]

One of the major achievements of the EEF was in 1951 with the creation of the Russian-language Chekhov Publishing House, which published over sixty books in the first year, including novels, short stories, plays and poetry, memoirs, and studies in history and criticism. Publishing continued until 1956. By then over 150 books had been published.

The Eastern European Fund's name was later changed to Radio Free Europe Fund. In 1960 it took over the functions of Crusade for Freedom. The combined organization accepted private contributions and also engaged in public fundraising in the United States. By 1975, the Radio Free Europe Fund had raised a total of fifty million dollars, only a fraction of the true operating costs borne by the CIA in over twenty years of secret funding.

The 1956 Hungarian Revolution

Volumes have been written about the 1956 Hungarian Revolution, and there will be more to come as the historiography of the Cold War evolves. On the occasion of its fiftieth anniversary, numerous international conferences took place in Europe and in the United States addressing the issues surrounding those explosive events. But even with all the associated published information, one of the ever-lasting controversies or myths that has remained alive for over half a century regards the role of Radio Free Europe (RFE) and its broadcasts leading up to and during the Revolution.[51]

The post-revolution Hungarian government issued a white paper on the events of the revolution and clearly blamed Radio Free Europe as one of the main players not only in inciting the revolution but in allowing it to continue longer than necessary, a charge and myth that continues today. The new government needed a bogeyman to blame for the revolution rather than publicly admit to any shortcomings of its political system, and RFE as a universally recognized symbol in Hungary was the ideal candidate.

The white paper included the following charges:

> The subversive broadcasts of Radio Free Europe — backed by dollars, directed from America, and functioning on the territory of West Germany — played an essential role
> - in the ideological preparation and practical direction of the counter-revolution,
> - in provoking the armed struggle,
> - in the non-observance of the cease fire, and
> - in arousing the mass hysteria, which led to the lynching of innocent men and women loyal to their people and their country.[52]

George Urban, former director of the Radio Free Europe Division is one person, perhaps the only one, who listened to all the broadcasts of RFE's Voice of Free Hungary that were taped and are still available.[53] He wrote in his memoirs: "The radio was young and inexperienced. After barely five years of broadcasting, its management was still testing the instruments and boundary lines of the Cold War and was simply not up to the task of responding with clarity or finesse to its first great challenge. Hungary, its baptism by fire, cost it dear."[54]

One 1956 refugee succinctly captured the reaction of those who listened to the live broadcasts:

> No Hungarian is angry at Radio Free Europe. We wanted to keep our hopes alive. Probably we believed too deeply what was not intended by the broadcasters to be taken seriously. The wrong was not with Radio Free Europe. It was partly our fault for trusting in the words. It was partly America's fault for thinking that words can be used loosely. Word like "freedom," "struggle for national honor," "rollback" and "liberation" have meanings. They stand for something. Believe me when I say that you cannot tell Hungarians or Bulgarians or Poles every day for six years to love liberty and then sit back philosophically and say, "But the Hungarians and Bulgarians and Poles mustn't do anything about liberty. They must remember that we're only using words." Such words, to a man in chains, are not merely words. They are weapons whereby he can break his chains.[55]

Origins of Radio Liberty

The beginning of Radio Liberty contrasted dramatically with that of Radio Free Europe. The American Committee for Freedom of the Peoples of the USSR was founded in January 1951, also under CIA sponsorship and policy guidance. The American Committee decided not to raise public funds with a crusade similar to Radio Free Europe's, which would have "aided in providing plausible cover for its true sponsorship."[56]

The CIA had difficulties in uniting the diverse Soviet émigré groups in Germany and in the United States. The American Committee's position was that the most effective psychological war against the Soviet regime would be conducted by former Soviet exiles, who would be united in speaking out against Communism. However, there were difficulties in the way of accomplishing this aim: one was the extreme hostility between Great Russian groups and non–Russian nationalities of the USSR. The other difficulty was the basic political differences between Marxist and non–Marxist exiles, regardless of their nationality:

> In a situation short of war the project can probably make its greatest contribution by de-emphasizing its political activities and devoting its major effort to the improvement of broadcasts from Radio Liberation. This station should use Soviet émigrés in an effort to weaken the Soviet regime and should concentrate on the Soviet military, government officials, and other groups in the population which harbor major grievances against the regime. Present plans call for the provision of new transmitting facilities in Spain. It is important that these or other facilities be developed in order to enable Radio Liberation to reach a wide audience within the Soviet Union.
>
> Pending a final determination of its effectiveness, we believe that the activities of the American Committee should be continued. Because results can be expected in the immediate future only from broadcasting, however, it is recommended that major attention should be concentrated on Radio Liberation. Expenditures on the coordinating center can be reduced but should be maintained at a level adequate to keep the organization in being, without active efforts to broaden the base of the center. If through the efforts of the present membership of the center additional émigré groups can be persuaded to participate, such moves should receive the encouragement and support of the Committee.[57]

Four days before the death of Josef Stalin, "Radio Liberation from Bolshevism" first broadcast from Lampertheim on March 1, 1953, with this announcement: "This is Radio Liberation. Listen to us on shortwave in the 31 meter band." Because of the two low-powered 10 KW transmitters, only the Soviet armed forces in Germany and Austria were targeted. There was no record that the first broadcast was actually heard in the target area. Yet, within ten minutes, the Soviet Union started jamming the broadcasts, and jamming of Radio Liberty's broadcasts would continue uninterrupted until 1988. In May 1955, the radio station made its first broadcast from Taipei, beamed to eastern parts of Siberia and the Maritime Provinces of the Soviet Union.

In keeping with the changing U.S. foreign policy, the station was renamed Radio Liberation in 1956 and finally Radio Liberty in 1959. The corporate name became the Radio Liberty Committee on January 10, 1964, "because of the impact made by its 24-hour-a-day Radio Liberty broadcasts into the

Soviet Union."[58] Former presidents Herbert Hoover, Harry Truman, and Dwight Eisenhower were "honorary chairmen" of Radio Liberty at that time. A Committee press release gave the ideological justification for the existence of Radio Liberty: "Radio Liberty's broadcasts analyze events and developments in the Soviet Union and the acts and policies of the Soviet government from the point of view of the best interests of the peoples of the Soviet Union.... Radio Liberty's writers and speakers seek to give expression to the innermost feelings, thoughts and repressed aspirations of their fellow countrymen."[59]

Howland Sargent, president of the Radio Liberty Committee, also issued a prepared statement giving the main task of the Committee: "To sponsor efforts to communicate with the peoples of the Soviet Union in order to achieve the long-range goal of a fundamental change in Soviet policies and practices which will reflect the will of the Soviet peoples for genuine peace and freedom."[60]

On March 23, 1959, Radio Liberty transmitted its first programs from Playa de Pals, on the Mediterranean coast, north of Barcelona, Spain. Short-wave broadcasting from this site would continue until May 25, 2001. Twenty-seven years after the first broadcast, on March 23, 2006, the huge transmitters, some of which reached 600 feet high, were demolished as Spanish television viewers watched live.

Birth of RFE/RL

A major turning point in RFE/RL's history occurred in 1967 when *Ramparts* magazine publicly revealed the RFE-CIA relationship, which would subsequently lead to a congressional decision that the CIA would no longer finance RFE and RL.

> Within the United States there are many elements, including large ethnic groups with close ties to many of the countries to which the Radios broadcast, for whom cessation of broadcasting would seem a serious and incomprehensible decision, especially in light of the Soviet invasion of Czechoslovakia. The attitudes of the ethnic groups would probably add significantly to the likelihood of adverse publicity attendant on termination, and would lend themselves to domestic political exploitation. Strongly negative Congressional reactions were encountered when the Director of Central Intelligence discussed the possibility of termination with key members of Congress in late 1967. A number of Congressmen are likely to show particular concern for the fate of RFE and RL because of their traditional responsiveness to the interests of domestic European ethnic groups, and because of their considerable knowledge of and belief in the work of the Radios.[61]

On March 20, 1970, there was a meeting in the White House, with President Nixon, Richard Helms, the director of the CIA, and Henry Kissinger, the president's national security advisor. The future of Radio Free Europe was one of the topics discussed. After the meeting, Helms wrote: "With respect to black operations, the President enjoined me to hit the Soviets, and hit them hard, any place we can in the world. He said to 'just go ahead,' to keep Henry Kissinger informed, and to be as imaginative as we could. He was as emphatic on this as I have ever heard him on anything. He indicated that he had had a change of mind and thought that Radio Free Europe should be continued."[62]

In response to this meeting, the CIA wrote a paper entitled *Tensions in the Soviet Union and Eastern Europe: Challenge and Opportunity*. The paper, which was describe as "excellent" by Henry Kissinger in a note to President Nixon, supported the continuation of Radio Free Europe and Radio Liberty, which "represent a 20-year investment of over $400,000,000."[63]

In 1973, a presidential commission under Milton Eisenhower published a report, *The Right to Know*, which formed the basis of legislation to consolidate RFE and RL into a new hybrid organization: a private nonprofit corporation funded by Congress. Final physical and administrative consol-

RADIO FREE EUROPE

THE IN SOUND FROM OUTSIDE

More than half the people in East Europe are under thirty. When they want to know what's happening—they switch on Radio Free Europe. For facts about East Europe and RFE, write: RADIO FREE EUROPE, Box 1969, Mt. Vernon, N.Y. 10551

advertising contributed for the public good

RADIO FREE EUROPE CAMPAIGN
MAGAZINE AD NO. RFE-1128-69
2¼" x 5" (110 Screen)

Radio Free Europe: "The In Sound From Outside," possibly from later 1960s campaign.

idation of the two radio stations took place in 1975–76. RFE/RL remained in Munich until 1995, when it moved to Prague.

Effectiveness of RFE/RL Broadcasts

The effectiveness of RFE/RL can be best understood positively in the words and actions of its listeners. For example, on January 29, 1991, Lennart Meri, then foreign minister of Estonia, nominated RFE/RL for the Nobel Peace Prize with this remark: "I and my fellow Estonians wish to honor Radio Free Europe and Radio Liberty and the people of the United States for forty years of work in helping us prepare for the restoration of our democracy, and we wish to encourage them to continue their important work in the years ahead."[64]

After the power struggle in the USSR in August 1991 and the dissolution of the USSR, Russia's first president, Boris Yeltsin, signed a presidential decree accrediting RFE/RL as a news agency and, for the first time, allowing it officially to open a news bureau in Moscow, saying,

> During the 3–4 days of this takeover, Radio Liberty was one of the very few channels through which it was possible to send information to the whole world and, most important, to the whole of Russia, because now almost every family in Russia listens to Radio Liberty — and that was very important. I think that by virtue of its work and its objectivity, Radio Liberty deserves that the Russian government establish direct contact and invite the management of Radio Liberty to visit us. Of course, I cannot speak on behalf of the Soviet Union, but I can speak on behalf of Russia and say that we must accredit you.

March 1993 witnessed the fortieth anniversary celebration in Moscow of the first Radio Liberty Broadcast. Ex-Soviet President Mikhail S. Gorbachev said, "In the dark years of Communist rule before my own reconstruction reform program (perestroika) began, Radio Liberty told the truth. We hope the radio station will continue in the future. I hope to be present at the 50th anniversary of Radio Liberty."

On July 4, 1994, President Bill Clinton formally accepted an offer from Czech president Vaclav Havel and the Czech government to relocate RFE/RL to Prague. "With this move," President Clinton said, "the radios begin a new chapter in the continuing struggle for democracy throughout the former Communist bloc." President Havel officially welcomed RFE/RL to Prague, September 8, 1995, when he visited the new headquarters building and said, "I am not sure that I would not have been in prison for another couple of years were it not for a certain amount of publicity which I had because of these radio stations."[65]

Romanian President Emil Constantinescu visited RFE/RL in 1997. On

"RFE disc jockeys beam the latest beat and soul hits, as well as interviews with the stars, to East Europe's New Generation." Taken from a RFE pamphlet showing RFE's "disc jockeys," late 1960s or early 1970s (Radio Free Europe/Radio Liberty).

March 11, 1997, he eloquently illustrated the importance of the radio stations in the collapse of Communism in Eastern Europe:

> Communism could not exist, but by lies and lack of information. Communism could be torn apart, not by power of arms, but by power of words and especially of real beliefs. That is why Radio Free Europe has been much more important than the armies, the rockets, the most sophisticated equipment. The rockets that have destroyed Communism have been launched from RFE, and this was America's most important investment against the Cold War.[66]

Newly democratically elected Bulgarian president Petr Stoyanov visited the RFE/RL headquarters in Prague on February 28, 1997. He praised RFE/RL

Radio Liberty QSL card sent to listeners after confirmation of broadcast frequency, used in the 1970s.

role in the Cold War: "We still remember sometimes how, through the inter-ference on the short-wave range, we searched for the radio station we needed, the radio station to give us courage to go through the hardships of everyday life under Communism, Radio Free Europe."[67]

Lech Walesa, Poland's first democratically elected president, responded to a question about the importance of Radio Free Europe, by asking: "Would there be earth, without the sun?"[68]

2. The 1950s:
When the Cold War Was Hot

Famed Cold War novelist John le Carré best captured the émigré community and intelligence activity in Munich in his novel *The Secret Pilgrim*:

> For anybody who has lived in Hamburg, Munich is not Germany at all. It is another country. I never felt the remotest connection between the two cities, but when it came to spying, Munich like Hamburg was one of the unsung capitals of Europe. Even Berlin ran a poor second when it came to the size and visibility of Munich's invisible community.
>
> And now and then frightful scandals broke, usually when one or other of this company of clowns literally forgot which side he was working for, or made a tearful confession in his cups, or shot his mistress or his boyfriend or himself, or popped up drunk on the other side of the Curtain to declare his loyalty to whomever he had not been loyal so far. I never in my life knew such an intelligence bordello.[1]

The Cold War in Munich, Germany, was, in reality, a hot war. The émigré staff at both Radio Free Europe and Radio Liberty faced intimidation and threats of murder and kidnapping, some of which were carried out. Intelligence agents penetrated the stations, and some employees became witting collaborators of the Eastern European intelligence services. All of the intelligence services of the Warsaw Pact operated against Radio Free Europe and Radio Liberty. At times this was centrally coordinated activity, and sometimes the countries ran their own operations. Actions, in this case hostile actions, did speak louder than words in the battle of ideas fought by East and West.

Murder of Abdulrachmann (Abo) Fatalibey

On Monday evening, November 22, 1954, an eighty-year-old Munich landlady was cleaning a small kitchen, which she rented in her apartment. She moved a couch in the corner of the room and noticed something large underneath. Something she had not noticed in the past. She called a tenant in the building to help move the couch. As they moved the couch out from the wall, they saw a man's body lying face down with his hands tied behind his back. Horrified, they ran out of the apartment building and asked a neighbor to return with them. He picked up a flashlight and they all returned to the kitchen to look at body. Then they called the police.

The landlady told the responding police that the dead man was émigré Michael Ismailov, who rented the kitchen but used it infrequently. Only Ismailov had the key, she told the police, and he occasionally used the kitchen to entertain guests. She could not see the face of the man because his coat was pulled up over his head as the police removed the body. She assumed it was Ismailov, and the police accepted her assumption as fact, without further investigating the identification of the body.

The next day the Munich newspapers reported the mysterious murder of an émigré from the USSR, Michael Ismailov. The initial medical report was that he had died of strangulation, after being struck on the head with a hammer. The murderer was unknown. Two days later, the deceased was buried in a Munich cemetery.

Meanwhile, the chief editor of Radio Liberation (as Radio Liberty was then called), Abdulrachmann (Abo) Fatalibey, failed to show up for work and did not call to say he was sick. This was highly unusual. Colleagues went to his empty apartment. They declared him missing to the Munich police and RL management. The Munich media speculated that Fatalibey was the prime suspect in the murder and had disappeared after committing the act.

A rumor started at Radio Liberation a week later that the person buried as Michael Ismailov was, in fact, Fatalibey. RL officials notified the police, who ordered an exhumation. After the subsequent, full examination the Munich coroner said that the body was that of the missing RL employee Abo Fatalibey not Ismailov.

Munich police later reconstructed his last night:

> On November 20, 1954, Fatalibey worked at the station "Radio Liberation" until 4:00 P.M., then went to the US Military Post Exchange at Prinzregentenstrasse and from there to "Cafe Freilinger" at Leopoldstr. There he drank until 7:45 P.M. He then took streetcar No. 22 to Nordbad, where he probably changed into No. 7 in the direction Ostfriedhof-Alpenplatz.
>
> From around 8:00–9:00 P.M., Fatalibey was with Ismailov at the latter's place at No. 6, Alpenplatz, together with Mrs. Ruhland, a tenant of the 2nd floor in the same building. Mrs. Ruhland left at 9:00 P.M.
>
> Around 1:00 A.M., Ismailov was seen alone, and for the last time, in the restaurant "Alpenhof."[2]

Ismailov became the suspected murderer of Fatalibey.

Who Was Abo Fatalibey?

Abdulrachmann Fatalibey was born in 1908 in Azerbaijan, of a Turkic father and Azerbaijan mother.[3] His grandfather had been a cavalry colonel in the tsar's army. He attended various public and military schools in Baku, the capital of Azerbaijan. With the help of local military officer sponsorship, he moved to Leningrad in 1926 to attend the Military Engineering School for the next three years. He joined the Communist Party as a peasant-origin member.

Fatalibey returned to Azerbaijan as a Soviet military officer. He completed more military studies and returned to headquarters of the Leningrad Military District. Fatalibey continued to be active in the Communist Party and Soviet army in both Moscow and Leningrad before being assigned to Kalinin in 1936. Three years later, party leaders finally interviewed Fatalibey in-depth. He was then expelled from the Communist Party for concealment of his "social origins."

When the war with Finland broke out, Fatalibey was sent to the front where he was awarded the Red Star as a Red Army soldier. Fatalibey was accepted back into the Communist Party. When the war with Germany broke out in July 1941, Fatalibey was deputy chief of staff for the Soviet twenty-seventh Army. He was captured by the German army in September 1941 and sent to a prisoner-of-war camp.

Fatalibey was approached by the German military to work on their behalf. He accepted and eventually was sent to Berlin. The Germans formed battalions of nationality groups to fight against the Soviet Army. Fatalibey volunteered for the Azerbaijan Legion and in August 1942 he was sent to the front with the First Battalion, later renamed the Lion Battalion. He was decorated for his action against the Soviet Army and returned to Berlin, where in 1943 he was elected to a high office in the Azerbaijan Congress. According to his biography written for Radio Liberty, in 1944 he was tried in absentia in Leningrad and sentenced to death.

The Lion Battalion was then sent to aid the German war effort in Italy in 1945. Fatalibey was captured by U.S. forces marching through Italy and put in a POW camp. He wrote political letters and pamphlets to U.S. and British political leaders and sent them out of the camp. He avoided repatriation to the USSR. The U.S. military released him, but he had to move to various refugee camps before settling in Rome in 1948.

Fatalibey continued to write anti–Soviet and pro–Moslem pamphlets and drew the attention of the Palestinian religious leaders in Rome. He was invited to Egypt where he became a military advisor for the Palestinian cause—he might even have fought against Israel, according to unconfirmed information. He wrote that he made the necessary battle plans but that they were never put into action. Fatalibey moved into Jordan with some Palestinian leaders. Later he crossed the border into Turkey and settled in Istanbul.

Fatalibey later claimed that when he was in Cairo he had maintained close contact with American and British officials and continued writing anti–Soviet political pamphlets that were sent to Washington and London. He was invited to Munich for a successful interview with RL officials and afterward returned to Turkey to wait for a job offer. In 1950, he returned to Munich to become part of the American Committee for the Liberation of Bolshevism. He also wrote for the political magazine *Azerbaijan*. Fatalibey became known as "the Major" in Munich's active émigré community surrounding RL.

Who Was Michael Ismailov?

Michael Ismailov's background was not fully known. He, too, was born in Azerbaijan and fought in the Lion Battalion in Italy. He deserted the Azerbaijan force and reportedly joined the Italian partisan movement. He spent a few years in various refugee camps in Italy before being released. He remained in Italy, married an Italian woman, and they had two children. He then registered for repatriation to the Soviet Union in 1951. He left his family and returned to the USSR via ship from Naples. He was arrested as an army deserter upon arrival and faced twenty-five years in prison. In 1952 he arrived in Dresden, Germany, where his Italian wife and children were waiting for him.

Ismailov was able to leave the Soviet occupied zone of Germany and arrived in the U.S. zone in 1953. After a few weeks in a displaced persons camp near Nuremberg, he was given permission to move to Munich. Ismailov remained apart from any émigré political activity and was not involved with Radio Liberation.

American Counter Intelligence Corps Espionage Investigation

Almost exactly a year before Fatalibey's death, on November 30, 1953, at approximately 5:00 P.M., two officials of U.S. Army Counter Intelligence Corps (CIC) went to the Munich police and declared that émigré Michael Ismailov was strongly suspected of espionage and that he intended that night to remove important information directly or indirectly from Germany.

Three Munich policemen followed Ismailov that night. At 8:40 P.M. two unknown people gave Ismailov a briefcase, which he took and continued on his way. At the next intersection, Ismailov was arrested. The papers contained in the briefcase were submitted to CIC as well as to the Bavarian Land Office for the Protection of the Constitution, since they were written in a foreign language (presumably Russian-language RL scripts). Both agencies returned the document, with the notation "no interest." Thus, Ismailov's "agent" activities could not be proved. He was therefore only sentenced to two months' imprisonment for violation of passport regulations.

After the murder of Fatalibey, two employees of Radio Liberation declared to the Munich police that they had known all along that Ismailov was an agent for the East and had instructions to do away with Fatalibey and obtain material concerning Radio Liberation. In agreement with the CIC, and presumably Fatalibey, they had tried to establish Ismailov's guilt. They were the ones who had handed the documents to Ismailov in November 1953. Stung by Munich newspaper and Radio Liberty criticism for a poor investigation into Fatalibey's murder, the Munich police responded:

> Had CIC at that time properly informed the German police it might have been possible to convict him not only for violation of passport regulations to two months imprisonment, but also for espionage activities or traitorous connections in violation of other German or Allied High Commission laws and thus prevent him from doing any further harm.[4]

Publicity was anathema to American Committee for Liberation. After the police proved that the body was that of Fatalibey, Radio Liberation succeed in getting two of Munich's newspapers to strike any references to Radio Liberation. The Munich newspaper *Abendzeitung*, however, refused to go along with the request and wrote that Fatalibey worked for Radio Liberation. This was the first newspaper reference in Munich to Radio Liberation. The dam of secrecy had broken and Radio Liberation was publicly exposed. On December 9, 1954, Manning H. Williams, RL's Radio Division director, wrote a long report to the Robert Kelly, deputy to the president of RL. In part, he wrote:

> In view of our established negative policy in regard to publicity, and also in view of police desire to go along in playing the case down, Mr. Moeller, who is responsible for AmComLib press relations in Germany, tried hard to keep the story of our connection with the murder from appearing at all, and has since attempted to minimize the political implications of the murder.[5]

The RL New York Programming Center (NYPC) sent a telex message to Munich on December 2, 1954, about the Fatalibey murder. In part, it read:

> We have reservations re any mention. Treating it, as act Soviet agents would certainly tend increase feeling Soviet omnipotence and hopelessness. Would

discourage potential defectors to know how MVD[6] can reach abroad. Also see possibility some aspects case vulnerable to Soviet counterattacks.

Leave it to you to decide whether possible positive gains outweigh these negative considerations.[7]

At Fatalibey's burial in New Ulm on December 5, 1954, Radio Liberation Deputy Director Robert Kelly read the following morale-building statement to inspire other Soviet émigrés to keep up their struggle:

It is of paramount importance that the Bolshevik leaders know that the anti-communist liberating struggle of the peoples of the Soviet Union — of which Radio Liberation is the voice — are not to be intimidated nor checked by the assassination of its front line fighters. Let us see to it that Fatalibey has not died in vain.[8]

The Radio Liberation program broadcast on December 7, 1954, on the death of Fatalibey, was addressed to "Comrade Soldiers, Sailors, and Officers" of the Soviet Union and ended with this thought: "His murder shows that his recent activities, like the activities of Radio Liberation as a whole, had begun to hurt the dictatorship in a vital spot."[9]

While RL took the cautious route in broadcasting news about Fatalibey's murder, Voice of America (VOA), the official United States government radio station, on December 8, 1954, not only broadcast the allegations about Soviet agent involvement, but also, for the first time in the Russian language, tied in the AmComLib with the support of Radio Liberation. VOA also pointed a finger: "Indications are that he was killed by a Communist agent."

The Kidnapping of Stefan Kiripolsky in Vienna

During the night on July 6, 1951, Stefan Kiripolsky and Helena Neumanova left their village in Czechoslovakia, crossed the Danube River in a small boat to Austria, and then settled in Vienna as refugees. Six months later, Kiripolsky started working as an interviewer at Radio Free Europe's News and Info Service Field Office in Vienna, with a salary of 4,000 Austrian schillings. More ominously, he also started working with the United States Military Intelligence or the Counter Intelligence Corps, helping debrief other escapees from behind the Iron Curtain. Unknown to Kiripolsky, the Czechoslovak Intelligence Service (StB) had an agent in place in Vienna reporting on this activity and started a interest file on him the same month.[10]

In January 1953, the chief of the First Department of the Intelligence Regional Administration in Bratislava, Lieutenant Colonel Pavco, and his second in command, Captain Kroupa, wrote up a plan to kidnap and arrest Stefan Kiripolsky. In order to accomplish this task, a three-member operative group was expected to go to Vienna, and the operation was to be accomplished through cooperation with the Soviet occupation army counterintelligence service in Austria. Deputy Minister of the Interior Prchal did not approve the plan, however, and it was dropped at that time. Nevertheless, surveillance of Kiripolsky's activities continued.

On August 26, 1954, Kiripolsky wanted to go on vacation with Neumanova in the southern part of Austria, which meant he would have to travel through the Soviet occupied zone of Austria via Wiener Neustadt. He mentioned the idea to his supervisor named Williams, who advised him not to go. In spite of the advice, the two left for this vacation.

In Wiener Neustadt, a Russian military officer stopped Kiripolsky and Neumanova at a road checkpoint. The Russian officer seemingly was expecting him to come through that point at about that particular tine. Several other Russian soldiers were present. They took Kiripolsky out of his car to a Russian car, and took him to Baden, Austria, still within the Soviet zone. Neumanova was transported in a different vehicle.

During his first captivity, Russian officers accused Kiripolsky of carrying out espionage activities against the USSR. The Russians interrogated him repeatedly regarding Williams, personnel of the U.S. Army Counterintelligence Corps in Vienna, and about all of his activities for RFE. He remained in Baden for approximately three months and then was transferred to Prague.

Kiripolsky was in the Bubence area of Prague for sixteen or eighteen months during which time the StB as well as the Soviet KGB interrogated him. A former political prisoner once identified this particular area as a restricted area used by the StB, and that all guards were officers with the rank of lieutenant or higher. During the course of his interrogations, Kiripolsky was subjected to various methods of torture, including continuous nightlong interrogations. He was placed in a small cell where he could not sit or lie down. From time to time his cell was filled with extremely hot air, which would suddenly be changed to extremely cold air.

On May 5, 1955, the Czechoslovak attorney general accused Stefan Kiripolsky of the crimes of high treason and espionage. In a trial, which took place on July 27, 1955, at the Military Division of the Supreme Court, Stefan Kiripolsky was condemned to a life sentence and his partner Helena Neumanova to five years prison.

On May 2, 1957, a small newspaper article about prisoners of war in Czechoslovakia appeared in a Swiss newspaper. Stefan Kiripolsky, "former co-worker of the Vienna office of the Munich radio station Radio Free Europe," was included in the names of prisoners. This article caused a stir within Radio Free Europe. On June 12, 1957, Donald Rinker, then RFE security officer traveled to Vienna and met Karl Reinoch, the source of information for this article, in Room 178 at the Hotel Bristol. Reinoch said that he was born in Bratislava, Czechoslovakia, and was presently an Austrian citizen.

Reinoch then explained that he was a secretary in the Austrian consulate general's office in Bratislava, when on September 22, 1950, he was arrested on the street, taken to Prague, and placed in prison for investigative custody. He was accused of espionage and remained there for three months during which time eight different StB officers interrogated him. He did not know their names and stated that up until 1955, StB personnel were known only by a number.

Reinoch was then transferred to Leopoldov prison, where he remained for four months, then was sent to the Bratislava State Prison for six months during which time his trial was held and he was then sent to Ilava prison where he remained until July 3, 1952. Afterward, he was sent to a labor camp at Leopoldov to serve out the sentence of eighteen years. His prison number was 833. After Austrian authorities intervened, he was released on January 31, 1957, and arrived in Vienna.

Reinoch said that he met former RFE employee Stefan Kiripolsky in May or June 1956 in Leopoldov prison. Kiripolsky told him that had been there since the spring of 1956. For three or four months they shared the same cell, and Kiripolsky told him how he arrived there. Kiripolsky said that he had been employed by RFE in Vienna, and that he had an American chief in Vienna named Williams, who was not with RFE but with U.S. military intelligence. Williams spoke Slovak and had a cover name, which Reinoch could not recall.

Kiripolsky told Reinoch that he believed some of his former RFE coworkers in Vienna might have informed on him, indirectly or unwittingly. He remarked that only he and his former coworkers at RFE knew many of the details that were presented at his trial. Kiripolsky also mentioned another person he suspected, but Reinoch could not recall his name. The only thing he could remember about this person is that he had something to do within the offices of the Vienna newspaper *Kurier*.

At that time, some U.S. officials and visitors used offices at the *Kurier*. From time to time when certain Americans came to Vienna they would turn in their U. S. passports at these offices, and this young man safeguarded these passports and assigned rooms to the Americans. The young man had a Slovak name, which Kiripolsky could not remember. At the trial Kiripolsky was shown photographs of some of the passports allegedly turned in at the *Kurier* offices.

Reinoch said that Kiripolsky was particularly bitter against one RFE employee. Kiripolsky told him that during one of their conversations, when they were alone, this employee told Kiripolsky that Kiripolsky thought too highly of the Americans and would some day be disappointed. One day he walked into his office and found the employee sitting at his typewriter. As he saw Kiripolsky come in, he immediately covered the paper in the typewriter. In addition, there were some things discussed at the trial which he recognized as having been discussed previously only with this employee. He also telephoned the employee the day before he was going to leave Vienna on his vacation trip and told him of his plans.

Kiripolsky recalled one specific incident, which might have involved a second colleague. Kiripolsky had obtained the original of the Soviet-Hungarian Agreement pertaining to river traffic, which he had to return. He gave it to the second colleague to have a copy made and then returned the original. A copy of this agreement was shown to Kiripolsky at the trial.

A third colleague gave Kiripolsky the names of two Russian soldiers who had defected to Austria. The names were given to Kiripolsky on a slip of paper at a certain meeting place and Kiripolsky put the slip of paper in his right-hand coat pocket. The StB questioned him about this particular incident and knew exactly how he had obtained the paper and all the details, even the fact that he had placed the paper in his right-hand coat pocket. According to Kiripolsky, the third employee was working for the West German Gehlen Organization (Bundesnachtichtendienst — BND), and said that probably his RFE superior was aware of it.

Kiripolsky also said that he had been accused of sending two agents into Hungary, which he admitted to Reinoch was true. One of them reportedly shot and killed a border guard while crossing the border and thus he was charged with being involved with the murder. Reinoch was asked whether Kiripolsky had ever stated that he had been asked by the StB to cross back to the West to work for them. Kiripolsky told him that while he was in jail in Prague he was told that he would probably be sentenced to death but that they would consider giving him a chance for a prison sentence if he agreed to making a statement against RFE and U.S. intelligence at a press conference.

Kiripolsky agreed and was then taken to another area near Prague, where prisoners were wined, dined, and rested before making a public statement. Those chosen to make statements were well briefed and rehearsed before appearing in public. Kiripolsky said he learned his role so well that he became too mechanical in his speech, and the StB finally decided he would not make a very good impression. They sent him back to his prison in Prague. After this episode he was never again approached by the StB to make a press statement or to work for them in any capacity.

Some of the Czechoslovak redefectors from the West were held in this same area. Two of the redefectors eventually ended up in Leopoldov, but were kept in isolation: only the prison commandant knew their names. As Reinoch was being released from prison, Kiripolsky asked him to report his story to the U.S. military attaché in Vienna, because he did not know whether RFE still had an office in Vienna. Reinoch said that he did not make a report to the U.S. military attaché but directly contacted RFE.

Reinoch then told the following story and requested some possible RFE assistance. Several weeks before the time he was released from Leopoldov prison, Reinoch was approached by Professor Karl Nigrin, a political prisoner and former member of the Prague government in London during World War II. Professor Nigrin was a leading member in prison of a secret committee among political prisoners. The purpose of the secret organization was to discuss the situation of each prisoner, to keep up morale and to plan a course of action if ever there was a sign of collapse within the Czechoslovak regime.

Professor Nigrin outlined a memorandum which he stated he wanted to present to Reinoch in full prior to his release from prison. Reinoch was to memorize this memorandum and, upon reaching Austria, was to take steps to have it written up in proper legal form and then present it to the United Nations and/or President Eisenhower. The memorandum set forth the status of the political prisoners within Czechoslovakia Socialist Republic, listed the conditions in the prison, described the treatment received by the prisoners, and requested assistance on the part of the West. The complete text was to be given to Reinoch on February 2, 1957, but he was released on January 31, 1957, and only received the outline. Reinoch said that he wanted to carry out his promise to Professor Nigrin and his former fellow prisoners, and attempt, if at all possible, to present it as requested. He stated that he himself would appear as a witness at any time and any place, if so requested.

There was no further word on Kiripolsky until Hungarian-born Tibor Karman visited the RFE/RL Vienna office in 1965. Karman was the husband of journalist Andrea Walder, the daughter of a former high-ranking Austrian civil servant. Andrea had met Karman in Hungary, fell in love with him and unsuccessfully tried to smuggle him to the West via Czechoslovakia. All of the persons involved, including Karman and one accomplice believed to be Australian or British, were sentenced to six months in jail. Karman was returned to Hungary. Because of direct intervention of Bruno Kreisky in Budapest, then Austrian foreign minister, in October or November 1964, Karman was allowed to leave the country. Karman said that while he was in the Czech jail at Ilava, Karman met another prisoner, Stefan Kiripolsky.

According to Karman, Kiripolsky looked hale and hearty. Kiripolsky was then working in the Ilava prison hospital to get better food. He told Karman that he had been betrayed, but he did not suspect anyone in the RFE Vienna office. His wife Maria and their daughter Magdalena were last known to be living at Pilarova 6, Bratislava, Slovakia.

The only RFE employment record in Munich was an index that showed that Kiripolsky worked as an interviewer in the Vienna News and Information Service Field Office. He started working on December 1, 1952, and was terminated on August 31, 1954. The reason for termination: "did not return from vacation."[11]

Stefan Kiripolsky was released from prison during the Prague Spring in May 1968. He never contacted the radio stations after the Velvet Revolution. Stefan Kiripolsky died on July 6, 1992, exactly forty-two years after he crossed the Danube River in search of freedom.

Operation Spotlight, Swialto and Radio Free Europe

In December 1953, Jozef Swiatlo, a colonel in the Polish secret police, "defected" in Berlin. Whether or not he was a double agent already under control of the CIA or a genuine defector is a matter of historical debate. For example, according to one report, Swiatlo had been sent to the West with the purpose of silencing Mrs. Wanda Bronksa, a former Polish Communist Party member, who had broadcast over the Voice of Free Poland.[12] Another version is that he was actually a double agent, first for British Intelligence and afterward for the CIA.[13]

Swiatlo was born in Poland in 1915 and attended public school for only seven years. He joined the Communist movement in 1933 for "political reasons and his youthful inexperience" and was twice arrested for his political activities. In 1938, he was drafted into the Polish army. After the German invasion of Poland on September 1, 1939, he was captured by the German army, escaped, and fled to the Eastern Section of Poland then under Soviet army control. He joined a Soviet-backed army and marched westward with the army as a political officer in the Kosciuszko Division that remained in a Warsaw suburb during the uprising in 1944. Afterward, he joined the University of Public Security and became a Polish Security Service officer in 1945.

He rose to the rank of deputy chief of Department 10, which was responsible for protecting the Communist Party from non-party subversive forces and "protect the purity of the Party from within the Party" by screening all appointments and conducting surveillance of party and government officials.

After this defection in West Berlin, the Americans sent him to a CIA defector reception center in Frankfurt, Germany. There he was debriefed by CIA official Ted Shackley, who established his bona fides as a defector and reported his findings to CIA headquarters. He and Swiatlo then flew to the United States in April 1954.[14]

Radio Free Europe was given access to Swiatlo. One staffer interviewed

Swiatlo, wrote the program scripts, which were then recorded by Swiatlo and broadcast over the Voice of Free Poland, from September 28, 1954, through December 31, 1954. Swiatlo was a constant figure on RFE's Voice of Free Poland broadcasts, with over one hundred taped programs and 150 news items, including U.S. Congressional testimony.[15]

Since "Swiatlo" means "light" and listening to RFE was considered a crime, listeners would refer to his programs by asking "will there be any light at your house tonight?" For the next months, RFE's other language services and Radio Liberation used his "revelations." These programs were described as "a brilliant tactical decision that brought unforeseeable strategic gains"[16] and "one of the most successful pieces of radio propaganda ever."[17]

Based on experiences in the previous balloon programs, and to continue with the propaganda barrage, on February 12, 1955, FEP started sending copies of a forty-page compilation of Swiatlo's testimony, "The Inside Story of the Bezpieka (Security Apparatus) and the Party," to Poland. This balloon program was called "Operation Spotlight," and it "was designed as a means of bringing to the Polish people the revelations of corruption and immorality in the hierarchy of the Polish Communist regime."[18] By the end of May 1955, more than 268,000 copies had been ballooned into Poland. The purpose of the Free Europe Press was "to weaken the Communist control apparatus, and through detailed exposure of Communist techniques, to enable the Polish people better to defend themselves against the Communists."[19] RFE engaged in Cold War rhetoric in the foreword to the pamphlet:

> Swiatlo is a man who has drunk from many a filthy well. Does he regret it today? Has he resolved to improve his ways in the innermost recesses of his heart? Does he treat his story of his experiences as an act of contrition or does he regard it as an act of vengeance of his former Party comrades. We have no firsthand information on this matter. We only know that he is to be believed.
>
> This booklet is like a hand-grenade. It may become dangerous should you try to keep it in your possession. It may also be dangerous to repeat the text of this booklet to your neighbor. On the other hand, no harm will be caused to the public good should this pamphlet reach the hands of representatives of the regime.[20]

RFE also put out details about Swiatlo in the March 1955 issue of *News Behind the Iron Curtain*, a monthly subscription journal published by the Free Europe Press. The short introduction explains the importance of the Swiatlo revelations:

> Here is the mirror of what it means to "build a Socialist state," and "what Socialist morality" is truly like. It is a tale of the evils done by the police, Party and Government to their own adherents, and horrible as it is, it is far less horrible than what all of these combined have done to the Polish people.[21]

The Polish regime responded with silence for a few weeks before launching a heavy counter-propaganda campaign of radio commentaries, articles, poems, and newspaper cartoons. Swiatlo's revelations over RFE reportedly caused a major chain reaction in Poland with the dismissal, transfer, and worse, of thousands of Communist Party members and government officials. Perhaps as many as 150,000 persons, according to one estimate, were affected.[22]

The Swiatlo programs also affected Radio Free Europe as the Polish broadcasting service and management were divided on the programs. Robert Lang, the director of Radio Free Europe, wrote an eight-page resignation letter, in which he complained that RFE management in New York had turned down the balloon program and was not consulted before the Free Europe Press started Operation Spotlight. He explained in the letter how the Polish émigrés in the United States were unhappy with the RFE's use of Swiatlo and "the Polish press in this country broke out in rash of angry editorial comment, and, in brief— poof— there went our carefully built up validity."[23]

Lang also revealed in his letter that Swiatlo had once sued RFE for "uncoordinated publishing on his material in *News from Behind the Iron Curtain*" and received $2,000. He threatened to sue again, this time for $10,000, because he was "infuriated — particularly by the introduction which was flown in with his materials in which, among other things, he was labeled a man who has drunk of every shame. We have lost his respect. He won't play any more."[24]

By the 1960s, Jozef Swiatlo, once called "the most successful Western agent in the history of the Cold War," effectively had become a nonperson, and he never surfaced publicly again. CIA Director Allen Dulles's book, *The Craft of Intelligence*, published in 1963, contained only a two-sentence, incorrect reference to Jozef Swiatlo, saying that he had defected in Berlin in 1954, not 1953. His life and/or death in the United States have not been verified through any official acknowledgment or obituary. Ted Shackley, the CIA officer who debriefed Swiatlo in Frankfurt, has written: "[O]nce he had fulfilled his obligations to the U.S. government, he sank quietly into private life as a legal resident of the United States. According to what little I have heard about him, he moved to New York— whether City or State I don't know— and opened a small business. The absence of any news to the contrary gives me confidence that his resettlement was a success."[25]

Operation FOCUS

Operation FOCUS was the name of the balloon program for Hungary that started on October 1, 1954. FOCUS was timed to coincide with November local elections in Hungary and was meant to focus the attention of Hungarian citizens on attainable goals. The leaflets were copies of a "Manifesto and Twelve Demands" (similar to the Ten Demands of VETO) of the "National Opposition Movement." Similar to the VETO operations (see below), small decals with the number "12" were included in the balloon operation and were later found on Communist Party posters. The balloons were launched in the southeast part of Germany close to the Austrian border. Thus, in effect, the balloons had to travel over a neutral country to land in Hungary. With the launching of the balloons, RFE began using its powerful transmitters in Lisbon, Portugal, with twenty hours of short-wave programming each day on the Voice of Free Hungary.

From the first broadcast in Hungarian in October 1951 to just before the FOCUS campaign in 1954, the Hungarian regime and the rest of Eastern Europe ignored RFE's Hungarian language broadcasts. In three years, RFE noted only nineteen media attacks against the Voice of Free Hungary. In the first week after FOCUS started, twenty media attacks were noted in Hungary and other Eastern European countries against FOCUS. By the time FOCUS stopped in early 1955, over one million balloons carrying over sixteen million leaflets had been sent to Hungary.[26]

Operation FOCUS did have an impact in Hungary. In December 1956, for example, the Radio Free Europe Audience Analysis Section commissioned a report of interviews with over a thousand Hungarian refugees. To the question, "From what source did you get news before the uprising?" foreign radio received the highest rating, 86 percent, but surprisingly "balloons — leaflets" had a rating of 21 percent. Another question was "Which source did you rely on most for the news of what was happening inside Hungary before the uprising?" Foreign radio had the highest rating at 80 percent but "balloons — leaflets" received the third-highest rating at 10 percent.[27]

Shortwave Radio Broadcasting to Hungary

The first Radio Free Europe program to Hungary took place on August 4, 1951, when Monsignor Bela Varga, former president of the Hungarian National Parliament, advised listeners "to attempt no futile uprisings at this time. Pending the day of liberation, which will permit them to use their strength effectively ... the free world knows and feels that their own battle is their battle. It is no longer indifferent or neutral. It is wholeheartedly allied to us in this great crusade, which is being waged for world freedom."

Radio Free Europe's Desk X

Famed espionage and intelligence writer Ladislas Farago was employed as a consultant to the RFE Hungarian Desk from October 1, 1950, to January 31, 1952. He used the name John L. Carver, as RFE did not want his connection known to the outside world. He worked out of two hotel rooms, not at the Radio Free Europe office. Thus the name Desk X was used in reference to him. He was paid 700 dollars a month for his consultancy. In May 1951, RFE wanted to drop his services; one manager protested and wrote a memorandum wherein he stated,

> Desk X is responsible for the production of the following series of scripts:
> • Colonel Bell (the military advisor to resistance groups not only in Hungary but was apparently was broadcast to other countries)
> • From Official Soviet Sources
> • The Hungarian Council of Self Defense
> • BODA BALINT
> • P.O.W. Mail

Interestingly, the writer added, "These scripts mark the output of most of our desks and account also most exclusively for whatever effectiveness the Hungarian Desk has — Desk X ... for all practical purposes, *is* the Hungarian program."[28] Yet management was not persuaded and Farago was released from his contract, due to "his penchant for cloak and daggerism," with the word that "his activities were not in FE/RFE's interests."[29]

For the reader to better understand the importance of Balint Boda in the years leading up to the 1956 Hungarian Revolution, here is some detailed information:

> In RFE broadcasts Balint Boda is represented as a man who makes frequent secret trips through Hungary, returning after each trip to tell the Hungarians what he has found out. His audience appeal rests on his daring defiance of the Communists (many Hungarians actually believe that he makes journeys through their country), the uncanny accuracy of his information about the Communists (particularly Communist informers) and the fiery language with which he attacks the people who have betrayed his country.
>
> Hungary is unique — primarily because RFE (Ratio Free Europe) has furnished it with a symbol, "B.B." for Balint Boda, which stirs the imagination and, paralleling the V-sign of World War II, can easily be chalked or painted on walls everywhere. Respondent after respondent from this country recalls having seen the letters "B.B." — or some variant, such as ~"Come Balint Boda," "Balint Boda comes," "Fear and tremble, Balint Boda is coming," "B.B. will take care of the Communists" — "on houses, fences, walls of public and factory toilets, and even on walls of police buildings," or "on fruit stands, bridges, and sidewalks ... AVO men used to scrub them off with wet brushes." Several respondents pride themselves on having shared responsibility for their appearance.[30]

YES—*for just one dollar* . . . a "Truth Dollar"

that fights Communism right in its own back yard—*behind* the

Iron Curtain!

100 words of truth—that's what each dollar you give buys on Radio Free Europe. 100 words of truth beamed right through the Iron Curtain. Truth to smash Soviet lies, give hope and courage to the 70,000,-000 enslaved people behind the Iron Curtain. Truth to stiffen their will to resist, to help keep the Kremlin off balance on its own home grounds.

What better way for you *personally* to do something about Communism?

How Radio Free Europe works

RFE has 29 powerful transmitters this side of the Iron Curtain. Day and night, seven days a week they reach the people of Poland, Czechoslovakia, Hungary, Romania, and Bulgaria. These broadcasts are by exiles in their native tongues.

The Communists use every means to drown out Radio Free Europe—every known device to jam RFE broadcasts, so far without success.

More transmitters needed now

More dollars are needed to get the truth to more people behind the Iron Curtain. Send in your "Truth Dollars" today—one for every member of your family—and fight Communism in its own back-yard. Do it now.

FIGHT
COMMUNISM

with
"TRUTH DOLLARS"

Support Radio Free Europe

Send your "Truth Dollars" to CRUSADE FOR FREEDOM °/° your Postmaster

Contributed in the Public Interest by
SPONSOR'S NAME

"You mean *I* can fight Communism?" Newspaper and magazine ad for Crusade for Freedom fund drive in early 1950s (Radio Free Europe/Radio Liberty).

Colonel Bell

Ladislas Farago has been credited with creating a fictitious figure named "Colonel Bell," the other important fictional character who would later surface in the days of the Hungarian revolution. Colonel Bell was supposedly an ex-military officer and RFE did broadcast some programs on military themes for years before the Hungarian Revolution, not only by "the Voice Free Hungary" but also by other RFE broadcast units:

> One representative script apparently used for broadcasting by Desk X, Carver, under the name Colonel Bell, is one dated September 6, 1951 ... "Colonel Bell's Military Analysis 42: "The Plan in Secret Warfare" (excerpt as written in the radio script):
> This is Radio Free Europe, the Voice of Free _____. Today Colonel Bell continues his review of secret warfare with a discussion of *The Plan* and its significance in preparation for an effective resistance movement.... Colonel Bell's report will be read by a staff member of the _____ Desk of Radio Free Europe.[31]

This fictional character was to resurface in the critical days of October 1956 when two programs were clear violations of Radio Free Europe's Broadcasting Policy and led to the general accusation of RFE's wrongdoings:

> *Program No. 1*
> "Armed Forces Special" #A1 of October 27 [violates] the letter and spirit of policy in effect at the time. The program gives detailed instructions as to how partisan and Hungarian armed forces should fight. It advises local authorities to secure stores of arms for the use of Freedom Fighters and tell the population to hide Freedom Fighters who become separated from their units. It advises the population to provide food and supplies for Freedom Fighters.
> The writer tells Hungarians to sabotage ("disconnect") railroad and telephone lines. It fairly clearly implies that foreign aid will be forthcoming if the resistance forces succeed in establishing a "central military command." The program is cast entirely in the form of advice from the outside; there is no reference to information coming from within the country. The program refers to the "Nagy puppet government" and states that Nagy is relying on the support of the Soviet armed forces. Although the writer is too categorical in his phraseology, his attacks on Nagy are in themselves not out of keeping with policy guidance in effect at the time.
> The program concludes with some rather complex formulations that could be interpreted by listeners as implying help from the outside.[32]

Unfortunately, at the RFE morning policy meeting on the date this program was aired, this programs was misleadingly summarized:

> Laws and experience of partisan war. Without inciting the participants of civil war, we tell them what are the experiences and techniques of partisan

warfare, citing Russian, Yugoslav, etc., experiences. First rule, e.g., is that groups, which are fighting dispersed, should establish contact with one another and establish a political center.

Program No. 2

"Armed Forces Special" #B1 of October 28 gives detailed instructions to Hungarian soldiers on the conduct of partisan warfare. The author states at the beginning of the program that Hungarians must continue to fight vigorously because this will have a great effect on the handling of the Hungarian question by the Security Council of the UN. Without saying so directly, he implies that the UN will give active support to Hungarians if they keep on fighting.

The program is over-optimistic in tone. The opening announcement states: "Colonel Bell will tell Hungarian soldiers how ingenious and smart leadership can counterbalance numerical and arms superiority." The conclusion states: "Colonel Bell has told Hungarian soldiers how to obstruct large forces by small ones and by simple means." In the light of subsequent events the program grossly underestimates the ability of the Soviets to move new troops into Hungary.

Borsanyi implies that the most the Soviets can bring in is about four divisions and that it might take as long as two or three weeks for the Soviets to secure the Danube line if Hungarians fight effectively against them. The program makes a feeble effort at indirect propaganda by recounting a story about how Yugoslav partisans fought against much larger forces of Germans in South Serbia in 1943 and beat them; but the indirectness of this story is completely negated by the obvious comments at the beginning and end of it.

This program of Borsanyi's constitutes a serious policy violation, for the author in no way makes any effort to demonstrate that he is basing his advice on opinions or even information coming from within the country. Here at its worst is the émigré on the outside, without responsibility or authority, giving detailed advice to the people fighting at home.[33]

Similar to "Program No. 1," the summary of this second program, presented at the morning policy meeting of the day on which it was written, was also misleading. It stated only: "We review the success in November 1943 of the 500 Serb partisans who were able to hold back the 13,000-man German troop near the town of Nish."[34]

Poisoning by Atropine?

On November 18, 1975, in Washington, D.C., former Czechoslovak intelligence officer Josef Frolik appeared before the U.S. Senate Subcommittee to Investigate the Administration of the Internal Security Act and Other Internal Security Laws of the Committee on the Judiciary. Here are excerpts from his prepared statement:

The HSR[35] devotes undiminished attention to the RFE radio station, whose very existence is [a] highly irritating factor for the Czechoslovak Government. Although the RFE has always been deeply penetrated by the HSR agent network and networks from other intelligence services of the communist bloc, it constantly evokes fits of anger among the leading representatives of communist regimes. The effort by Major Jaroslav Nemec, alias Nekola, the Czechoslovak vice-consul in Salzburg, to execute a mass poisoning of the workers of RFE, is only a small sample indicating the extent to which this anger can escalate.

During the second half of the 1950's, Minister Rudolf Barak was actively involved with plans to blow up the RFE facility. Whatever voice may be raised against RFE in political place in the United States is considered by the Czechoslovak intelligence service to be a voice of active alliance against the RFE and the intelligence service is immediately tasked with utilizing this voice and supporting it actively with its resources.

It is a sad fact that, for example, the Czechoslovak émigré movement never represented and does not now represent any political force and, with the exception of the few individuals who are reporters for RFE, VOA, or employed by the Council for a Free Czechoslovakia, it is fragmented into small political groups or nonpolitical clubs, as is evident from émigré and expatriate publications.

The most active attention is paid to people who, after arriving in a foreign country, have become reporters for one or another of the radio stations which the regime hates (RFE, Deutsche Welle, Radio Vatican, Voice of America, BBC) or who have entered into the armed forces or perhaps the civil service, or about whom it is anticipated that they are in contact with enemy intelligence or counterintelligence defectors.

Senator Thurmond: Mr. Frolik, would you expand on the penetration of Radio Free Europe by Czechoslovakian agents, as well as the attempted poisoning of RFE workers in Germany?

Frolik: Yes. Radio Free Europe from the beginning was the main target of the Czech intelligence effort only because Radio Free Europe exists. It is an irritating factor to the Czech government and to all Communist governments in the East. They tried to penetrate it, and they penetrated it very successfully.[36]

Operation VETO: A Combined Political Warfare Operation

In April 1954, the Free Europe Committee and the Free Europe Press started Operation VETO as an integrated balloon and broadcast campaign over the Voice of Free Czechoslovakia, aimed at achieving eventual "liberation from Communism" in Czechoslovakia. RFE developed a strategic plan of integrating the radio programming with the balloon-leaflet campaign.

RFE's objectives were to build up the moral strength and action potential of an internal force that would lead to the liberation of Czechoslovakia. This would only occur when both external and international political developments would demonstrate to the Soviet Union that it would be more costly to intervene than not to intervene. This time would not come in 1968 with the Prague Spring but only in 1989 with the collapse of Communism in Eastern Europe.

RFE spoke directly to the people of Czechoslovakia and told of the existence of a intangible people's opposition movement. According to RFE, this was not a formal underground organization and there was no headquarters or material basis for it. Every Czech and Slovak who was opposed to Soviet domination belonged to this spiritual movement.

RFE had spent months piecing together a picture of complaints collected from refugee statements and intensive review of the Czechoslovak media. The leaflets listed a nonviolent political program of ten demands, including "Housing for families, not the state" and "Better pay — less talk." Small decals were included that could be concealed in a closed hand; these depicted only the number "10." Later they were pasted on Communist Party posters as a symbol of opposition. From May to August 1954, over forty-one million leaflets were sent into Czechoslovakia via balloons during Operation VETO.[37]

Balloons being carried through snow before launching, early 1950s (Radio Free Europe/Radio Liberty).

Testimony of Josef Frolik Continued

FROLIK: Another operation against Radio Free Europe was in the mid–1950s, roughly 1955, during the time Radio Free Europe sent balloons with leaflets over the Czechoslovakian territory; one of the balloons hit a plane, a commercial liner and the plane crashed. And the craziness: which this created in government circles...

SENATOR THURMOND: This was a Czechoslovakian plane?

FROLIK: Yes. And the plane crashed. All the people perished in the plane. Barak at the time planned to blow up the transmitters of Radio Free Europe as retaliation for this act, or this accident. Radio Free Europe didn't plan to send a balloon to crash a plane, it was an accident.

In 1957 — but I am not sure — or 1958, one of the Czech intelligence officers who was stationed under the cover of the vice consul at Salzburg, Austria, whose name was Jaroslav Nemec, this man had an agent in Radio Free Europe. It doesn't matter what his name was, but the man was an agent of the CIA also, and he gave an order to this agent to put atropine salt into shakers in a cafeteria of Radio Free Europe.

SENATOR THURMOND: What is the significance of the atropine salt?

FROLIK: It can create hallucinations and, in large quantities, death of people.

SENATOR THURMOND: And the agent to whom he gave the order to was in actuality a CIA agent?

FROLIK: A double agent.

SENATOR THURMOND: A CIA agent.

FROLIK: Yes.

SENATOR THURMOND: And he thwarted the plan, you say?

FROLIK: He gave the plan to the CIA, and therefore it didn't happen. Nemec was persona non grata after that in Austria. The Austrian government issued an arrest warrant for Nemec. The chief of the Czech station in Vienna, Molnar, attempted to locate Nemec and warn him of the warrant. But he was unable to find him. Nemec was somewhere in the Alps and when Molnar finally found him, he put him into the trunk of a car and carried him back to Czechoslovakia.[38]

Code Name "Jachym" and Attempted Poisoning

One of the so-called double agents mentioned by Frolik at RFE, code named "Jachym," started working for the Czechoslovak Intelligence Service in 1953. He was sent to West Germany through a faked escape across the border the next year. The faked escape was meant to establish his bona fides within the Czech émigré community and then lead to a permanent job with RFE. He had been trained in radio codes, secret writing and other craft. He had at least fifty-nine meetings with the StB in Austria, Holland, Switzerland, and Germany. "Jachym's" intelligence tasks in Germany involved the Czech emigration, U.S. military intelligence, and Radio Free Europe. He provided extensive and valuable documents, and he was involved in "active measures."

At one point in the operation, the StB believed that "Jachym" was a double agent of the CIA. The StB had other agents in RFE, code named "Alex" and "Kytka," for example. The StB first thought Alex was a CIA double agent, but then they became convinced that "Jachym," who had to be a double agent, had deceived Alex. Jachym once saw Alex meet the StB control officer, and he reported it to his CIA control officer. This CIA connection was not known within RFE's management, which would not have sanctioned it. RFE's long-standing policy was not to allow employee involvement in intelligence activity, even in double-agent operations involving the security of RFE. All meetings with the CIA took place clandestinely outside RFE, without RFE's knowledge or approval.

In October 1963, "Jachym" sent a coded message asking why the StB was not in contact with him. The StB department made another damage analysis and decided it was a mistake to suspect him. They resumed personal contact for a few more years. As it would turn out, the StB's original suspicions were correct in both cases. The StB eventually dropped him as a source of information — presumably after the StB again began correctly assuming that he was a double agent.

In the early 1990s, when he was confronted with the spying allegations, "Jachym" for the first time admitted that he had lied to RFE on his employment application: he had not escaped to Germany but had been sent on an espionage assignment. He acknowledged being part of the 1959 StB plot to put atropine in the RFE salt shakers, but he said he was under control of the CIA from the beginning, again without RFE's knowledge and approval. Under CIA control, he gave Nemec one salt shaker that he had purchased at a local department store. This one would have to be a little different from one normally found in the canteen, for easier identification if atropine were in it. "Jachym" did not actually place the salt shaker in the canteen, but one or two other RFE employees ("Alex" or "Kytka") possibly did so — he saw one of them pocket two salt shakers, presumably to give to Nemec. Neither is alive today to give details of their involvement.

The U.S. government directly or indirectly contacted the Austrian government, and Major Nemec was declared persona non grata. The Austrian government issued an arrest warrant for Major Nemec. The chief of the Czech intelligence station in Vienna, General Bohumile Molnar, drove to Salzburg to warn Nemec of the arrest warrant. When Molnar finally found Nemec in a ski-resort town in the Austrian Alps, he put him into the trunk of a car and drove him across the Austrian border to Czechoslovakia.

In March 2004, the Czech Republic Ministry of Interior made this report (punctuation left intact):

The intention of revenge against the RFE on account of the accident of the Czechoslovak plane caused by a balloon of the RFE: This is an interesting idea, on 22.01.1956, the plane crashed in the Tatra mountains. There were 22 dead persons (but not all of the passengers died). First references to the intention of a destructive action in the building of the RFE in Munich by using explosives were mentioned in April 1957 — the action having a cover name BOROVICE (Pine Tree). The action was confirmed (April–August 1957), however not executed, the agent of the Intelligence Service, appointed to fulfill the action, agreed at first, but refused at the end. Only partial knowledge concerning the action BOROVICE has survived and therefore it is impossible to confirm a direct connection of the plane crash and the project of the destructive action. But it might well be possible. Frolík accepts the allegation that the plane crash was caused by the collision of the plane with the balloon of the RFE, which is most probably not right, and the real cause of the plane crash was a navigation mistake by bad weather.[39]

The Kidnapping of Dr. Aurel Abranyi in Vienna

Dr. Aurel Abranyi was a graduate of Budapest University, a lawyer, and an editor/writer for two Budapest newspapers before World War II. He escaped from Hungary in 1949 to Austria. He settled in Vienna, stated practicing as a lawyer, and became an Austrian citizen in 1953. He maintained continual contacts with friends, relatives, and other persons, for information about Hungary. He could have been the prototype for Le Carré's "the Professor" in chapter 6 of his novel *The Secret Pilgrim*.

He was never an employee of RFE, but for about three years Dr. Abranyi was a source of reliable information about events in Hungary to the RFE Vienna office, identified by RFE as "Marc." RFE would later identify one of his contacts as "a known intelligence swindler and fabricator." During a political trial in Budapest in the summer 1956 he was falsely identified by Hungarian media as the Foreign Director of RFE's so-called "espionage ring." This caused a stir within RFE's Security Office, as they had no knowledge of Abranyi or his relationship with RFE.

During the chaotic early days of the 1956 revolution, Kalman von Konkoly and other RFE employees crossed into Hungary. Konkoly went into a Hungarian intelligence monitoring station and took documents and reels of taped telephone conversations.

After the failed Hungarian revolution in October–November 1956, RFE management reviewed all connections to Hungary, including RFE's relationship with Dr. Abranyi. This relationship officially stopped in December 1956, but not his story. Abranyi unsuccessfully sued RFE on a breach of contract. In 1957, Abranyi and Konkoly published a brochure in Munich based in part on some of the documents Konkoly had removed from Hungary.[40] Konkoly reportedly was fired for his unauthorized trip into Hungary, and for making RFE materials available to outsiders.

On October 12, 1961, at 4:00 P.M., Dr. Abranyi left his law office to visit Lazlo Geroe, a Hungarian-born businessman living in Vienna, who had telephoned, inviting him over for a visit. The next day, Abranyi's wife called the Viennese police to report that he had not returned home. The police forced open the door of the businessman's apartment and found evidence of a violent struggle, including spent hypodermic needles.

Both Abranyi and Geroe were now missing. The police later determined that Geroe had left his apartment at 8:00 P.M. and had driven across the Czechoslovak border on October 12, 1961, at 9:00 P.M. A few days later, after further police investigation, an arrest warrant for issued for Geroe on suspicion of kidnapping and murder.

In December 1961, Geroe wrote a letter from Budapest to Austrian authorities, denying any involvement with Abranyi's disappearance. About two years later, a lawyer representing Geroe appeared in Vienna and suggested that his client would return to Austria to face the charges. There is no record that Geroe ever returned to Vienna to answer the allegations.

In November 1987, a Hungarian newspaper printed an article entitled "Untangling an Enigmatic Crime," that contained information about the kidnapping of Abranyi. According to this article, when Geroe, with Abranyi in the auto's trunk, approached the border from Czechoslovakia into Hungary, a gate in the Iron Curtain opened. Hungarian military officers and other officials were obviously waiting for Geroe. Abranyi, still unconscious, was placed in a rug and dragged across the border into Hungary. The gate closed and all traces of what happened were cleaned up. Geroe then drove alone through the official border crossing to Budapest.

Abranyi was reportedly imprisoned, harshly questioned for months and was forced to sign a confession. A military court found him guilty of treason.

A visitor to RFE's Vienna office in 1963 said that he had seen Abranyi in a Hungarian prison and that he was being kept in reserve for possible use in an upcoming propaganda campaign. This did not happen and sometime afterward, the death sentence apparently was carried out. This has to date not been confirmed by Hungarian officials. For many years afterward his wife failed to get information about his whereabouts. She tried to get the Austrian courts to declare him dead. The courts refused as his "death was not proved." In the post–1989 years, his sister and other relatives failed to convince the Hungarian government to release details of his kidnapping and death.[41]

3. Piccadilly versus the Tramp: The Murder of Georgi Markov

In her wildest dreams Agatha Christie couldn't have conjured a more bizarre murder and a more bizarre murder weapon than the one that killed a Bulgarian writer named Georgi Markov who, while living in exile in London, wrote commentaries for Radio Free Europe. — Ed Bradley, *60 Minutes,* CBS Television, October 20, 1991

In February 1991, former dissident and Bulgaria's first post–Communist president Zhelyu Zhelev made a six-day visit to England. During the visit, he had lunch with Queen Elizabeth and met with numerous British business and political figures. He had decided to also do something more personal on his last day in England: leave London and drive to a cemetery in Whitchurch, in Southwestern England. There he participated in a short memorial ceremony conducted by a Bulgarian priest, walked over to one flower-covered grave, stood quietly and read the epitaph:

IN MEMORY OF
GEORGI IVANOV MARKOV
NOVELIST & PLAYWRIGHT
MOST DEARLY LOVED BY
HIS WIFE ANNABEL
AND DAUGHTER SASHA
HIS FAMILY & HIS FRIENDS
BORN SOFIA 1.3.29
DIED LONDON 11.9.78
IN THE CAUSE OF FREEDOM

President Zhelev then bent over and placed a wreath on the grave. After a few seconds, he stood up and turned to the small crowd, including Georgi Markov's widow and daughter, who had gathered around. Full of emotion, he said, "I am hopeful that Bulgarian authorities will soon reach some conclusions on who was responsible. The killing has shamed Bulgaria and mars its reputation abroad."

Who was Georgi Markov? Why is he buried in England? Why would the president of Bulgaria attend a memorial service, place a wreath on his grave and make such a provocative statement? How did he die "in the cause of freedom?" He was a victim of ultimate censorship: political murder. His death proved how far a totalitarian regime would go to protect itself from the truth.

Who Was Georgi Markov?

Georgi Markov had been a successful literary figure in Bulgaria.[1] His first book, *The Night of Celsius*, was published in 1957. His novel *Men* was published in 1962 to rave reviews in Sofia and won the Union of Bulgarian Writers annual award. The novel was then translated throughout Eastern Europe and made into a film. Other novels were published, including *Portrait of My Double* (1966) and *The Women of Warsaw* (1968). He entered the privileged world of the Bulgarian literary and intellectual circles and joined the officially approved writers' union.

Markov started a new career as a successful dramatist in 1963 with the play *The Cheese Merchant's Good Lady*. He then entered the cultural life of leading performers of the Bulgarian State Theater. Communist Party leaders, who mingled within the theater and literary circles, also accepted Markov into their fold. Georgi Markov attended parties with them and knew the intimate details of their personal lives that were carefully hidden from the public. This "insider knowledge" would lead to his death abroad.

A roof, then under construction at a huge party showpiece steel factory, collapsed, killing and injuring workers. The party failed to inspire or lead workers in the search for victims. Years later, Markov wrote a novel entitled *The Great Roof,* which he saw as an "allegory and document of the moral degradation" of Bulgarian socialist society: "In the fall of the roof, I perceived a symbol of the inevitable collapse of the roof of lies, demagogy, fallacies and deceit which the regime had constructed over our country."

Markov failed to get the "censorship committees" to approve the novel for publication. His literary career took a turn for the worse. On June 15, 1969, his play *The Man Who Was Me* was previewed before a general audience and party officials. While the audience enthusiastically responded to the play, the party members did not. The play was stopped. A close friend warned him to leave Bulgaria. As part of his preparations to leave, he burned his diaries of fifteen years. Using a passport and visa issued three months earlier, Georgi Markov defected to the West, crossing into Yugoslavia. He saw Bulgaria for the last time:

> I looked back towards Bulgaria and it seemed to me that even its natural beauty sharpened the feeling of how unbearable it was to have to live the ugly life, which I and many others like me were forced to endure.

The very act of living in the country represented an endless chain of compromise. Even the struggle against compromise was not without compromise.[2]

For a time, he lived in Bologna, Italy, with his émigré brother Nikola. In 1971, Georgi Markov settled in England, where his continued his literary career. As a defector, he was branded a traitor by the Bulgarian media. Five years later, Bulgarian authorities tried Markov in absentia, sentenced him to six and a half years of imprisonment, and confiscated all his personal property.

In 1974, his adapted play from Bulgaria, *Let's Go Under the Rainbow*, was first staged in England. *The Archangel Michael*, his first new play as a defector, won an award at the Edinburgh Festival. The play was set in Central Europe and was a dialogue between a policeman and a doctor who were looking for refugees wounded during an insurrection.

Markov Joins Radio Free Europe

Georgi Markov also became a broadcast journalist for the British Broadcasting Company (BBC), and a freelance scriptwriter for Radio Free Europe (RFE) in Munich. Markov's first freelance contribution to the RFE Bulgarian Service, on June 8, 1975, was called "The Debts of Contemporary Bulgarian Literature." For the next three years, he wrote more than 130 prime-time Sunday-evening programs in a series he called "In Absentia, Reports about Bulgaria." These programs were informative on the cultural life in Bulgaria, and revealed the otherwise-hidden life of Communist Party leaders, especially Todor Zhivkov. Markov's Radio Free Europe programs posthumously were collected and translated into English as *The Truth That Killed*.[3]

The theme of censorship was central to many of Markov's RFE broadcasts. His play *Let's Go Under the Rainbow* was stopped after thirteen performances in Sofia. In "Where are You Dear Censor?" Markov explained the use of "one of the most characteristic" words in socialist reality: "stopping," the synonym for censorship or banning. He added, "The regime can, I think, be very proud of its dialectical conjuring trick — the shifting of the functions of censorship from an outdated, historically compromised and ineffective institution to a multitude of private voluntary censorships established inside individual people.[4]

In another of his programs, "The Dialectic of Censorship," Markov details the absurdity of the Bulgarian censors: "During the 1960s Bulgarians were subjected to censorship of Soviet works which Bulgarian dialecticians

Sure I want to fight Communism —but how?

With "TRUTH DOLLARS"–*that's how!*

Your "Truth Dollars" fight Communism in it's own back yard—*behind* the Iron Curtain. Give "Truth Dollars" and get in the fight!

"Truth Dollars" send words of truth and hope to the 70 million freedom loving people behind the Iron Curtain.

These words broadcast over Radio Free Europe's 29 transmitters reach Poles, Czechoslovakians, Hungarians, Romanians and Bulgarians. RFE is supported by the voluntary, cooperative action of millions of Americans engaged in this fight of good against evil.

How do "Truth Dollars" fight Communism? By exposing Red lies revealing news suppressed by Moscow and by unmasking Communist collaborators. The broadcasts are by exiles in the native

tongues of the people to whom they are beamed.

Radio Free Europe is hurting Communism in its own back yard. We know by Red efforts to "jam" our programs (so far without success). To successfully continue these broadcasts, even more transmitters are needed.

Every dollar buys 100 words of truth. That's how hard "Truth Dollars" work. Your dollars will help 70 million people resist the Kremlin. Keep the truth turned on. Send as many "Truth Dollars" as you can (if possible, a dollar for each member of your family). The need is now.

FIGHT COMMUNISM

with "TRUTH DOLLARS"

Support Radio Free Europe

Send your "Truth Dollars" to CRUSADE FOR FREEDOM *c/o your Postmaster*

Contributed in the Public Interest by

SPONSOR'S NAME

"Sure I want to fight Communism — but how?" Newspapers and magazine ad for Crusade for Freedom fund drive in early 1950s (Radio Free Europe/Radio Liberty).

found insufficiently 'Soviet.' Soviet films dealing with this or that not particularly praiseworthy aspects of Soviet reality or deviating from the clichés of 'socialist realism' were released in the Soviet Union but not shown in Bulgaria."[5]

Markov had a very large listening audience among the adult population, although Radio Free Europe's Bulgarian language broadcasts were heavily jammed. One broadcast frequency deliberately was not jammed so that a unit of Bulgarian State Security could monitor and prepare reports on the broadcasts.

Communist Party Secretary Todor Zhivkov was very well informed about Radio Free Europe broadcasts. He daily received a highly classified report and transcript of RFE's broadcasts, prepared by the Bulgarian State Security "Directorate for Struggle Against the Ideological Subversion." This unit cooperated closely with the infamous sixth Directorates for Internal Counter-intelligence, External Intelligence, and the Engineering Division, which operated the local jamming transmitters on Bulgarian soil and coordinated the "skywave" jamming with the Soviet Union.

Zhivkov received another classified report called "Anti-Bulgarian Propaganda Bulletin" that included selected program transcripts of RFE, VOA, BBC, Deutsche Welle, and Vatican Radio. The Bulgarian Press Agency produced and distributed this report to the Communist Party Central Committee and chief editors of the central press, radio and television.

In 1977, Georgi Markov's father was dying of cancer. Georgi asked the Bulgarian regime for permission to return to Bulgaria or have his father visit him in the West. The regime denied both requests. His father died in June 1977. Georgi wrote, "I received news that my father had died in Bulgaria. And it was the sorrow over his death and my inability to be with him during his last days that showed me, quite clearly, the main reasons for my departure, which I have tried to describe with so many words, but which can be summed up quite simply as the feeling that things were unbearable."[6]

In the next month, Zhivkov signed a Politburo decree proclaiming, "All measures could be used to neutralize enemy émigrés."[7] Markov received various warnings and anonymous threats to stop broadcasting his inside knowledge of Zhivkov and the obsequious circles of Bulgarian intellectuals and government officials. Markov persisted and peeled away the artichoke leaves of lies and corruption in Bulgaria until his death.

The tone of Markov's programs over Radio Free Europe changed. His biting satirical series of eleven programs from November 1977 to January 29, 1978, were now called "Personal Meetings with Todor Zhivkov."[8] This program series was relentlessly critical of Zhivkov's aristocratic and hypocritical life and exposed a side of Zhivkov's personality and lives of the Bulgarian intelligentsia previously unknown in Bulgaria. The cult of personality was the rule in Bulgaria. No one told the emperor he was naked. Because Markov's programs were so popular with his listeners — even with jamming — his revelations radically and dramatically changed Zhivkov's mood.

In one of his broadcast scripts, Markov wrote,

> I have stressed over and over again that the principal evil in the life and work of Bulgarian writers, painters, composers, actors ... was interference by the Party.... And behind the Party's interference stood its chief organizer and executive — Todor Zhivkov.... [A]s a result of Zhivkov's general, arbitrary and often quite unwarranted interference, Bulgarian cultural life became permeated by an atmosphere of insecurity and chaos.[9]

Zhivkov reportedly was upset by Markov's plans to publish a book of interviews and other material included in his Radio Free Europe program series. Zhivkov was concerned with the rise of the Bulgarian dissident movement "Declaration 78" that appeared in spring 1978. "Declaration 78" had put out six demands, including " an end to violations of human and civil rights" and "the abolishing of privilege in all spheres of public life."[10]

Markov's Fate Decided in Moscow

In Moscow, early in 1978, Georgi Markov's fate was decided during a meeting in a third-floor office in the KGB main headquarters building, "the Center." Those in attendance were Yury Andropov, chairman of the KGB, Vladimir Kryuchkov, then chief of intelligence (First Administration), his first deputy, Vice Admiral Usatov, and General Oleg Kalugin, chief of foreign counterintelligence.[11] Kryuchkov had been a long-time confidant of Andropov: he served in the Soviet embassy in Budapest during the Hungarian revolution in 1956, when Andropov was ambassador to Hungary.

Kryuchkov received an "urgent" telegram from Sofia, presumably through the KGB resident, and invited Kalugin to the meeting. The meeting in Andropov's office started with routine discussions of normal operational KGB matters. Kryuchkov then told Andropov about the highly classified message, presumably sent by the KGB resident in Sofia, from Bulgarian minister of internal affairs, General Dimitir Stoyanov. Stoyanov was asking the KGB to help kill Georgi Markov. Kryuchkov explained that Georgi Markov had escaped to the West and for the last few years had been working for the BBC and Radio Free Europe. He added that Markov had become an open and very outspoken opponent of Communist Party Secretary Todor Zhivkov. He had been close to Zhivkov's family, friends, and prominent Communist Party members and knew many "kitchen secrets" of their private lives.

Zhivkov personally asked the USSR for help, and Minister Stoyanov simply passed the request through his KGB intelligence contact, according to Kryuchkov. Because Minister Stoyanov had sent the message requesting KGB assistance and not Zhivkov, Zhivkov was in a position to deny direct knowledge of KGB assistance in the killing.

After Kryuchkov finished speaking, Andropov rose and slowly paced around the office. He paused and then emphatically said, "I am against political murders! I am against political assassinations!" He sternly added: "The days when this kind of thing could go unpunished are gone. We can't turn back the clock. I repeat, I'm against it. We are being dragged into all sorts of situations. This is their problem; let them solve it on their own."

Kryuchkov politely interrupted Andropov, who continued standing behind his chair: "Yury Vladimirovich, please understand, if we refuse the Bulgarians, we will put Minister Stoyanov in an awkward situation. Zhivkov will think that Stoyanov no longer has respect in the KGB. That the attitude toward Bulgarian comrades is changing in the U.S.S.R., in the leadership here. In short, this may not be the best thing in terms of consequences for the development of our relations and, particularly, for Minister Stoyanov who helps us in everything."

After some silent and tense moments, Andropov sat down and finally agreed, on condition that there would be no direct Soviet participation in the killing itself: "All right, you have my consent to participate, on the technical side only — no personnel involvement. Send an instructor; give them appropriate technical means and equipment. Let the Bulgarians themselves resolve this problem. That is all. This is as far as I am prepared to go." Andropov also was in a position to deny any direct KGB involvement in the death of Markov.

After this meeting, Kalugin and Kryuchkov returned to the Foreign Intelligence Headquarters outside Moscow. Kalugin went to his office and called two of his KGB subordinates: General Sergey Golubev, chief of the Security Service and specialist on "murder," and another KGB officer. He repeated this version in various television interviews he gave in the immediate years following the collapse of Communism in the USSR and Eastern Europe. He would later change this in his memoirs published in London.

General Sergey Golubev had a distinguished career abroad: he had been assigned to New York in 1961, Washington in 1963–64, Cairo and in 1967–1969, and was one of those hundreds of KGB officers expelled en masse from Great Britain in 1971. Kalugin reportedly told Golubev, "We have an assignment, a job to do. You have to get in touch with the Scientific Division that will provide you with the necessary poisons and weapons. We will give you instructions, and you then will go to Sofia to help the Bulgarians."

At the KGB Center, Sergey Golubev went to a secret research lab, Laboratory No. 12, which was a part of the KGB Operational Technical Support Directorate. Laboratory No. 12 was referred to in intelligence circles as the "Chamber," or "Kamera." KGB General Viktor Chebrikov, one of Andropov's closest subordinates in the KGB, was then the director of the "Chamber." The "Chamber" developed, among many technical devices, chemical substances used to incapacitate political enemies and antidotes to these substances, if western intelligence agencies used them against KGB agents. For example, Laboratory No. 12 successfully developed the "spray gun" and poison used to kill two Ukrainian nationalist anti–Soviet activists in Munich in the 1950s: Ivan Rebet and Stefan Bandera.[12]

Golubev received operational instructions in the "Chamber," and the next week he flew to Sofia with Ivan Surov. Surov's job was to give the Bulgarian Intelligence Service practical training in the use of special poisons, which could not be traced after the victim's death. Golubev and Surov discussed with the Bulgarians intelligence officers the various options of killing Markov. They worked out one plan to use a poison that could be surreptitiously dissolved in tea, coffee, and any liquid that Markov might drink.

In January 1978, the Radio Free Europe Security Office received the first warnings that Markov would be killed. Nikola Markov, a successful stamp dealer in Italy, called and said he had been warned in a very brief telephone call that his brother would be killed. He said the warning came from a close political associate of Zhivkov who opposed the order to kill Markov. Nikola Markov said he could not identify the informant because it would endanger him. This highly placed source told Nikola Markov that additional information would come from a third party, a Bulgarian émigré living in Western Europe.

Warnings to Markov

Georgi Markov contacted the RFE Bulgarian Service Director and said that a Bulgarian émigré named Popov (a pseudonym) had visited his brother and told him that "the Bulgarian Intelligence Service ... planned to kill Georgi Markov in Munich in the middle of January." Popov said that Georgi would fly to Munich on January 16, 1978, and two Bulgarian intelligence agents were already in Munich. They planned to kill Georgi by "depositing in his food or drink a harmful bacteria that would lead, in a matter of days, to his death." Georgi dismissed this possibility as harassment intended to discourage him from publishing his planned book on Zhivkov. Markov postponed his visit to Munich.

The deputy director of RFE was told of the Markov threat. He said that he had received word from the U.S. embassy in Sofia that Markov's programs were very effective and the Bulgarian regime was irritated with the programs dealing with his relationship with Zhivkov.

Nikola Markov later said in a 1991 interview with RFE that between January and the end of July 1978, a highly placed source repeatedly told him, "Georgi Markov's days are numbered." Nikola passed along every warning to Georgi, whose reactions changed from disbelief to defiance and finally to resignation. Georgi Markov did not, at first, believe the Communists would harm him. Georgi had been a friend of Communist Party Secretary Todor Zhivkov. As time passed and the warnings persistently continued, Nikola says his brother remained convinced that the Communists would not harm him because it would create a "world scandal."

Popov later told Nikola Markov that two Bulgarian agents had been in Munich in January and attempted to learn full details of Georgi Markov's trip: where he would live, sleep, eat, etc. Popov told Nikola that he should not question him about his continuing association with the Bulgarian Intelligence Service. He should simply accept this association as it was. Popov advised Nikola that the Bulgarian Intelligence Service had definitely "planted" someone within Radio Free Europe and was fully informed of all its activities.

In the spring of 1978, Popov added another reason why Markov was being targeted: the Bulgarian regime believed Georgi Markov was implicated in the defection of veteran Bulgarian journalist Vladimir Kostov in Paris in July 1977. Kostov had been the Bulgarian News Agency's Paris correspondent and an experienced intelligence officer. He had sought and received political asylum for himself and his family.

After a second postponement of his planned trip to Munich, Georgi Markov arranged to fly to Munich in May 1978. He telephoned RFE on May 10, 1978, and said he would keep his upcoming trip to Munich confidential. He planned to arrive on Friday, May 19, and disclosed this to no one except a few trusted friends in Munich.

On Saturday, May 20, Markov intended to visit RFE and another editor at RFE, who then was seriously ill in a Munich hospital. Then Markov intended to fly back to London. The RFE Security Office notified Munich police and other German authorities of Markov's impending visit. Munich police decided not to interview Markov or provide protection, since the threats were too vague. Markov returned to London after the uneventful trip.

Yet according to former KGB General Kalugin, the attempt to kill Markov was made during one Markov's trips to Munich in the spring of 1978. One Bulgarian agent was to put a poison pill in Markov's drink in Munich during a party in his honor. The plan failed for reasons unknown. The Bulgarians and the KGB decided to try something else.

Ricin

Golubev returned to Sofia to work out a new plan to kill Markov. The KGB decided to use a camouflaged weapon. A folding umbrella was adapted with a firing mechanism and silencer to shoot a small pellet at close range, one and a half to two centimeters (about one inch). Golubev requested that the KGB residency in Washington purchase several U.S.-manufactured umbrellas and send them to the Center. The "Chamber" then adapted the umbrella tip to enable it to shoot the victim with a tiny metal pellet containing ricin, a highly toxic poison derived from castor oil seeds. Reportedly ricin is seventy times stronger than cyanide, and one ounce of ricin could kill as many as 90,000 persons.

The KGB was not the only intelligence agency interested in ricin as a toxic weapon. In the 1970s, the CIA publicly revealed that a U.S. Army team called the Special Operations Division (SOD) at Fort Detrick, Maryland, had developed biological and chemical weapons for the CIA under a top-secret project that would last almost twenty years. This project, MKNAOMI, was practically unknown at the CIA, due to the extreme sensitivity of its mission. Few written records were kept. CIA personnel working at Fort Detrick used the cover of Special Support Staff of the Department of Defense.

But a KGB agent at the Soviet embassy in Washington could have easily discovered that on October 23, 1962, the U.S. Patent Office granted patent 3,060,165 to four persons "as represented by the Secretary of the Army." The patent was first filed on July 3, 1952, Serial Number 297,142, for the use of ricin as a biological weapon. The strikingly honest descriptive language used to apply for this U.S. patent, in 1952, is revealing:

> Ricin is a protoplasmic poison prepared from castor beans after the extraction of castor oil. It is most effective as a poison when injected intravenously or inhaled ... a very fine particle size was necessary so that the product might be used as a toxic weapon.

In addition to the development of lethal biotoxins, the U.S. Army's Special Operations Division developed special weapons for the CIA, which could be concealed in commonly obtainable items. One adapted pistol developed by the SOD reportedly could accurately shoot a miniscule dart at a distance of 200 yards.

Golubev then took the KGB-converted umbrellas to Sofia to instruct the assassin on how to use this weapon. The pellet was supposed to penetrate the clothing and be lodged in the upper skin layer. The selected Bulgarian agents first tried the poison on a horse. A dose of only one milligram was sufficient to kill the horse. After that success, the Bulgarians decided to shoot a prisoner who had been condemned to death, simulating "field conditions." A Bulgarian intelligence officer approached the prisoner, and shot the poison pellet into the victim. The prisoner cried out with fear and the pain of the shot. To their surprise, several days later he was still alive, with no sign of ill health. Why he hadn't died was unclear.

The agents decided on another plan: they knew that Markov and his family would vacation on the beautiful Italian island of Sardinia in early summer. They planned to kill Markov during the vacation. Kalugin believed they wanted to put some sort of poison on the car door handle, or on the walls of a room where he was staying. However, this plan also failed as the agents, during their surveillance of Markov, realized that Markov's wife or daughter might also be poisoned. The Bulgarian intelligence agents decided to postpone the operation until they perfected the umbrella weapon. Soon after this decision, the Bulgarian Intelligence Service agents assigned to the Bulgarian embassy in Sofia intensified their surveillance of Markov.

Even though he was under death threats, Markov continued to supply creative scripts to RFE. On July 3, 1978, he enthusiastically started a new series of Sunday-night twenty-minute programs: *Markov Speaks*. His first program in this series was "The Mind under House Arrest." These broadcasts would continue throughout the summer. One critic called the program series "a miniature classic of the genre ... describing his reflections on listening to Radio Sofia broadcasting."

Markov last visited RFE/RL in August 1978. For the first time, he openly admitted to RFE that about four months earlier he had received a telephone call in London from a man who advised him to stop writing for Radio Free Europe. The anonymous caller bluntly told him that if he did not stop these programs, he would be killed. The threatening calls continued sporadically. When previously threatened, Markov's response to the caller was to point out that his assassination would only make him a martyr. His murder would confirm the truth of his broadcasts: his death would demonstrate to the world the depth of corruption of the Bulgarian regime.

Markov received his last threat just before he flew from London to Munich. This threat was different from the others he had received. Because of the menacing tone and emphasis in the voice on the phone, he was deeply bothered by this threat. "Not this time," said anonymous caller. "This time you will not become a martyr. You will simply die of natural causes. You will be killed by a poison that the West cannot detect nor treat." To ensure that Markov fully understood, he emphatically repeated the murder threat.

After the phone call, Markov said he slept poorly. In the morning, he went to work at the BBC and told only his closest colleagues about the new threat. The brothers met at Heathrow, and Nikola told Georgi again of the threat information. This time, according to Nikola, Georgi said he was fed up with hearing about the murder plot and told Nikola to leave him alone.

"If they want to kill me, they can do it." This was the last time the brothers saw each other. Then, as the days passed and nothing happened, he became preoccupied with other matters and pushed aside the threats.

Murder Attempt in Paris

In August 1978, when Georgi Markov met his brother in London to discuss the various death threats he had received, he did not and could not know that a killer was on his way to carry out Zhivkov's wishes. First, however, the assassin had a little job to do in Paris.

Vladimir Kostov describes in his memoirs, *The Bulgarian Umbrella*, what happened to him in Paris at about 2:00 P.M. on August 26, 1978:

> There were crowds of people in the Metro corridors. A few seconds before stepping off the escalator, I felt a sharp pain in the small of my back, just above my waist. At the same moment, I heard a sound like the rattle of a stone hitting the ground. Natalya (his wife) heard it, too, without suspecting that anything had happened to me. My first thought was that I had been struck by a stone slung with great force, as though from a catapult.[14]

Two hours later, Kostov and his wife went to the Nanterre Surgery and were examined by the doctor on duty. He told them, "I can't feel any lump in the place where you think you were hit. I suppose some insect — a wasp perhaps — got in under your shirt.'" Kostov asked about the possibility that someone had deliberately attacked him. The French doctor skeptically said, "It's quite obvious that you have not been shot or stabbed. As for poison, it's more than two hours now, so you'd either be dead or critically ill. Go home. If it gets worse, come back and see me."[15]

In the next forty-eight hours Kostov's conditioned worsened, he had a high fever and the right side of his back was very swollen. Monday, he was still in pain and went to another hospital and another doctor told him that his wound was not an insect bite but the cause was unknown. The swelling went down and the pain stopped. Kostov put the matter in the back of his mind and went on with his life.

Attack on Waterloo Bridge

Thursday, September 7, 1978, was Zhivkov's sixty-seventh birthday. Georgi Markov worked a double shift at the BBC. After working the early-morning shift, he went home for rest and lunch. Afterward, he drove from home to a parking lot on the south side of Waterloo Bridge. It was his habit to then take a bus across the half-mile bridge to the BBC headquarters in the large building known as Bush House.

After parking his green Citroen in a parking lot near the Bridge, he climbed the stairs to the bus stop. As he neared the queue of people waiting for the bus, he experienced a sudden stinging pain in the back of his right thigh. He turned quickly and saw a man bending to pick up a dropped umbrella. He was facing away from Markov and simply said to Markov, "I'm sorry," in a foreign accent, according to Markov. This unknown man then hailed a taxi parked nearby. Markov later described the man as heavyset and about forty years old.

Though in pain, Georgi Markov continued to work. The pain continued and Markov noticed a small blood spot on his jeans. Markov told some colleagues at BBC what had happened to him and showed one friend a pimple-like red swelling on his thigh. He finished his shift, went home that night and developed a high fever.

His wife called a colleague at BBC, who took Markov to a London hospital, where he was treated for an undetermined form of blood poisoning. His condition worsened and did not respond to doctors' efforts. The next day he went into shock, and for three days, his body fought the poison. The medical teams were unable to diagnose the cause of his illness.

Sunday night, September 10, 1978, as Markov lay dying in the hospital, RFE broadcast the eleventh program in his series, *Markov Speaks*. The title of this program was "Day of Freedom and Day of Militia." But this was not to be the last of Markov's RFE programs.

Markov Dies

Monday, September 11, 1978, at 9:45 A.M., after days of delirium, pain, and suffering, Georgi Markov died at age forty-nine. The preliminary diagnosis indicated that Markov died of "septicemia, a form of blood poisoning caused by bacterial toxins, possibly a result of kidney failure."

After the attack, Nikola Marko had telephoned the hospital and spoken with Georgi who complained of being poisoned. According to Nikola, when he later told Zhivkov's associate of his brother's death, the man was not surprised. Nikola Markov believed the warnings from this source were motivated by respect and friendship for his late brother, not political or personal profit. He then stopped the contacts with Nikola Markov.

Bulgarian intelligence agents afterwards visited Georgi Markov's mother in Sofia. They told her that Georgi Markov had been killed because his work for Radio Free Europe had made him an enemy of the state.

Scotland Yard Begins Investigation

Various newspapers in London carried the story of Markov's death as front-page news, with embellished headlines: "Poison Brolly [umbrella] Murder Riddle" and "Defector Riddle or Death by Dart." Markov's colleagues at BBC notified Scotland Yard that they suspected murder. Scotland Yard began an investigation into Markov's death.

Doctors performed an autopsy Tuesday morning, at Wandsworth Public Mortuary. One doctor removed large blocks of tissue from both of Markov's thighs for comparison, including the area from the right thigh that had an unexplained two-millimeter puncture wound. As two other doctors were examining the tissue on a porcelain autopsy table, they found a tiny metal pinhead in the puncture, which they assumed had been placed there to mark the location of the wound. When they attempted to extract the "pin," a tiny pellet moved across the tissue and fell onto the table. They examined the pellet closely under a microscope and saw holes. One doctor then called Scotland Yard and gave their findings.

A police team went to the mortuary, retrieved the pieces of Markov's thigh and the tiny pellet, and took them to the Chemical and Microbiological Warfare Establishment at Porton Down, commonly called the "germ warfare center." There, a team of the England's foremost specialists in forensic medicine, and reportedly Dr. Christopher Green of the Central Intelligence Agency, examined the tissue and the pellet.

They found that two 0.34 mm holes had been drilled, possibly using a high-technology laser, at right angles to each other, producing an X-shaped cavity in the pellet. When the pellet was examined, the holes were empty. Thus, the medical specialists had no evidence as to what type of poison was used. The medical team estimated that only 0.2 milligrams of an unknown poison was used. A police spokesman announced that Markov had "not died of natural causes." British Anti-Terrorist Squad (BATS) detectives then joined the Scotland Yard investigating team.

On September 15, 1978, a British police inspector visited the Radio Free Europe London office and requested translations of all the scripts broadcast by Georgi Markov, especially the last six. He also wanted any Markov scripts that had not been broadcast. The scripts were in Munich, and the police inspector asked that they be placed on a plane for London. The RFE Security Office gathered the scripts and put them on a plane to London that night.

While there was wide publicity in the weeks following Georgi Markov's death, one article was remarkably accurate in guessing the cause of Markov's death. *Newsweek*, September 25, 1978, reported:

[Markov] had written a recent series of broadcasts for Radio Free Europe in which he documented corrupt practices and indiscretions in the Bulgarian regime.... [A]fter his father died of cancer in June (1977) without having been allowed out to the West, Georgi became much more vitriolic in what he was saying on RFE.... He was really smearing mud on the people in the inner circle ... a Bulgarian agent may have employed one of the traceless poisons developed by "Kamera" (Chamber), a section of the Soviet KGB's Department V.

A Second Pellet Found

The day Markov died, the RFE Bulgarian Service in Munich called Vladimir Kostov in Paris and told him the tragic news. The following day he called a friend at BBC who told him that Scotland Yard was investigating. Kostov learned that as Markov lay dying, he repeatedly said that agents of the Bulgarian Intelligence Service had poisoned him. Because of his intelligence background, Kostov maintained contact with French intelligence officers. He called French intelligence authorities dealing with political incidents, the Directorate of Territorial Security (DST), which then started an investigation to determine if the attack on Kostov and the attack on Markov were related. DST immediately assigned him twenty-four-hour protection and contacted other interested French government agencies, as well as British authorities.

On Monday, September 25, 1978, George LeVaye, then assistant director of security for RFE, went to Paris to meet Kostov and assist the French police and the Scotland Yard team that had flown to Paris. The two investigating teams decided that Scotland Yard would assume full authority to investigate the crimes because the British investigation was weeks ahead of the French.

Kostov told George LeVaye that authorities had arranged for an exploratory operation Tuesday morning. They would remove a small foreign object that had shown up on X-rays, and a small portion of the skin around the still-inflamed perforation on his back. Doctors told him that a local anesthetic would be used, but that he could leave the hospital almost immediately afterward.

Kostov, accompanied by his wife, arrived at the hospital the next morning. The two Scotland Yard representatives and at least four visible DST persons, in addition to their regular escort, accompanied them. The Scotland Yard detective had photographs of what appeared to be a hollowed needle tip. He said that the hollow tip might originally have contained a toxin that could have slowly leaked out of the tip to poison the system.

Immediately following the operation, another Scotland Yard detective flew back to England and submitted to the British forensic laboratories the small metallic object and skin sample that had been removed from Kostov's body. The pellet from Kostov matched that taken from the body of Markov. Using a high-powered scanning electronic microscope, the investigating team determined that the pellet was a minute, jeweler's-watch bearing, made of an alloy of 90 percent platinum and 10 percent iridium. There was still a minute amount of a yet unknown substance left in the pellet shot into Kostov.[16]

Three weeks after Markov died, Vladimir Simeonov, a colleague of Markov's at the BBC, failed to show up for work. A coworker went to his home and found his body sprawled face down on a staircase. Thirty-two-year old Simeonov had defected in 1971. There was media speculation of a Bulgarian assassination squad using bacteriological weapons against Bulgarian émigrés. Police tests and reconstruction of his death concluded that he "accidentally fell down the stairs, broke his nose, and suffocated by inhaling blood while unconscious."

On October 20, 1978, a memorial service for Georgi Markov was held in London. The service included selected Bulgarian folk music, singing of Psalm 30, and readings from both the New Testament and Dostoevsky's *The Brothers Karamazov*.

RFE Rebroadcasts Markov's Programs

On October 29, 1978, RFE started rebroadcasting selected programs of Georgi Markov. The first was originally broadcast in June 1975 as an introduction to his series, "In Absentia: Reports about Bulgaria." Most of these programs were later translated into English and published in 1983 as *The Truth That Killed*.

Markov Was Murdered!

One plausible reason the KGB purchased umbrellas in the United States was to simulate "evidence" of a CIA plot to kill Markov — thus deflecting suspicion away from the KGB and Bulgarian secret services. In 1975, the U.S. Senate Intelligence Committee held hearings into CIA activities. One published report referred to CIA-sponsored Army Special Operations Division (SOD) research into weapons that could be concealed and fired from different devices. One weapon developed by the Special Operations Division was named M-1 and could be concealed in a pistol, "a fountain pen, a cane, and even an umbrella." Reportedly, a fountain pen had been developed to shoot darts in a plot to kill Fidel Castro. After Markov's death, Bulgarian press stories alleged that "Markov was a an agent of Western intelligence." Having been squeezed by the CIA, the CIA had disposed of Georgi Markov in such a way as to incriminate the Communists, according to one Bulgarian press report. After weeks of research and experimentation, in January 1979 a coroner's inquest in London ruled that Georgi Markov had been murdered by use of the poison ricin. One medical researcher said, "Ricin is twice as deadly as cobra venom and has no antidote." Ricin was injected into a pig that developed the same symptoms as Markov and died twenty-four hours later, according to another witness. A Scotland Yard detective said that the investigation team had traveled to France, Italy, Germany, and the United States, yet there were no suspects. The coroner, Gavin Thurston, ruled that Markov had "been unlawfully killed."

Fall of Communism in Bulgaria 1989

The Markov case reached an impasse and lay dormant until after the overthrow of Todor Zhivkov in December 1989; he had been in power since 1954. The following month, Bulgaria's ambassador to England announced that authorities in Bulgaria had reopened the Markov murder investigation. This announcement did not meet with an enthusiastic response at Bulgarian intelligence headquarters.

The spokesman for the Ministry of Interior, who had worked in the intelligence field for over thirty years, declared: "The idea that Bulgaria's secret services caused Markov's death is a very elementary and unprofessional construction that appeared in the British press.... It is like a detective novel.... It sounds more like a plot from Conan Doyle."

During the following months, officials from Bulgaria visited England, and Scotland Yard officers visited Bulgaria. The official Bulgarian investigation was opened on October 21, 1990, under the leadership of then Internal Affairs Ministry official General Leonid Katsamunski.

Markov Files Destroyed

In March 1991, Bulgarian authorities announced that the official files in the Markov case had been destroyed by General Vladimir Todorov, then chief of Bulgarian Intelligence. Reportedly, seventeen volumes of about 200 pages each had been destroyed. The files were restricted to only eight persons. Todorov said that the files "did not contain anything important. Most of it was a press clipping."

Deputy Interior Minister General Stojan Savov admitted that he had instructed the chief of the state archives to hand over the files to Todorov. Shortly after this announcement, Vassil Kotsev, who was once the chief of Bulgarian foreign intelligence, the First Main Administration, and identified as the person in charge of the Markov and Kostov operations, died in a questionable automobile accident. Todorov had succeeded Kotsev when he retired from the Bulgarian Intelligence Service.

Todorov unexpectedly flew to Moscow in May 1991, presumably to avoid arrest. His family said he flew to Moscow for medical treatment for heart problems and diabetes. In Moscow, he gave an interview in which he said he destroyed the files as "regular routine cleaning of archives."

Yet there is another and, perhaps more plausible, reason for Todorov's flight to Moscow. Two Scotland Yard detectives flew to Sofia in early June 1991 to meet with the Bulgarian investigators. Todorov would have been forewarned of the upcoming arrival of the Scotland Yard detectives. One could easily draw the conclusion that he fled Sofia to avoid being questioned by Scotland Yard. Some government officials in Sofia believed he took the Markov files with him to Moscow rather than destroy them. He returned to Sofia in the fall of 1991, after the Bulgarian government had strongly protested and had officially asked for his extradition. He was placed under house arrest immediately after his arrival.

In a very interesting newspaper interview in November 1991, Todorov said, "The statements in the press about my having direct or indirect participation in Georgi Markov's death are, to say the least, preposterous, irresponsible and lawless. The more so as up until this moment I have not been interrogated in connection with the investigation to clear the causes of the writer's death, neither as a defendant, nor as a witness."[17]

Regarding the attempt on Vladimir Kostov in August 1978, Todorov said, "There was never an attempt on Kostov's life. Everything is a frame-up and could be explained by the emigrant writer's wish to present himself as being persecuted by his ex-superiors from the Bulgarian Intelligence Service, and by the regime in Bulgaria in general. Until that moment, Kostov's voice was rarely to be heard on Radio Free Europe. Only after, he became a permanent commentator in the Bulgarian section."[18]

General Stojan Savov committed suicide on January 6, 1992, two days before the trial of Savov and Todorov was to begin. Todorov's trial continued. In June 1992, the court found Todorov guilty of destroying the files in the Markov case. He was sentenced to fourteen months imprisonment. The sentence was later reduced and he was freed in February 1993.

Secret Agent Markov?

A strange twist in the Markov story came in August 1991, when George Tambuev, a Bulgarian parliamentarian, alleged that Markov was an agent of the Bulgarian secret service. He said that by using computer analysis of all known material, he had reached this conclusion. Tambuev was chairman of a parliamentary commission investigating police files on Bulgarian deputies. Tambuev said in a newspaper interview that Markov had been sent to London as a spy. He claimed that Markov's real identity was uncovered later by the British intelligence services. He did not explain who killed Markov or why.

Markov's mother-in-law publicly rebutted this allegation: "Nobody would have used him as a secret agent. There was nobody who was more indiscreet. He was a very open, lively, and funny man. The idea of his being an agent is laughable. In addition, who would have murdered him then, if he were an agent? The reason he was murdered was that he was a good writer and he was making fun of the regime."

KGB General Kalugin Goes Public in 1991

In 1991, former KGB General Kalugin appeared to be omniscient and omnipresent in the news media concerning Markov. For example, in March 1991, he was interviewed on Bulgarian television and said that Bulgaria's former Communist leader, Todor Zhivkov, asked Soviet agents for help killing Georgi Markov in 1978. Former general Dimitir Stoyanov, interviewed by a Bulgarian newspaper in March 1991, denied the accusation: "I never asked for assistance from Yury Andropov or Kryuchkov for the assassination of Georgi Markov."

The KGB then issued an official press statement in response to the charges that they had assisted in killing Markov. The KGB accused Sofia's mass media of "damaging friendly relations with an unseemly campaign" and said that "insinuations and the search for a new external enemy in the Bulgarian mass media harm the traditional friendly ties between our states and sow mistrust and suspicion."

In addition, in March 1991, Radio Liberty broadcast an interview with Kalugin, in which he repeated his charges against the KGB. He was especially critical of the chairman of the KGB, Vladimir Kryuchkov. The KGB again strongly denied Kalugin's allegations and the Soviet news service TASS made the following Russian-language report for the international audience: "A TASS correspondent has been informed at the USSR KGB public relations center that allegations of KGB involvement in the so-called 'Markov affair' are a crude invention. There was absolutely no appeal from the Bulgarian special services to the USSR KGB regarding this 'affair.' The KGB reserves the right to appeal to appropriate Soviet bodies regarding calling Kalugin to account for slander." Kalugin was later interviewed on Hungarian TV and repeated his charges. More Kalugin interviews followed in newspapers and magazines in the former Soviet Union and other countries.

Le Carré vs. Kalugin

Famed novelist John Le Carré visited Moscow in 1993 and wrote an article about this visit in the *New York Times*, including an evening in Oleg Kalugin's apartment. He and Kalugin discussed the Markov case, among other topics. Le Carré wrote,

> It was a disgusting, vindictive murder, but that is not how General Kalugin sees it.
> "People ask me, 'Did you have anything to do with Georgi Markov's assassination?' 'Listen,' I tell them, 'we're not children. I was the headman for all that stuff, for Christ's sake! Nothing operational could be done unless it went across my desk, O.K.? Markov had already been sentenced to death in his absence by a Bulgarian court, but the Bulgarians were terrible. They couldn't do a damn thing. We had to do it all for them: train the guy, make the umbrella, and fix the poison.' Listen, all we did was carry out the sentence. It was completely legal, O.K.?"
> Feebly, I protest that I don't think Markov a good topic of conversation. But, to my shame, I am inhibited by a tangle of absurdly British considerations: my Russian friend who procured the introduction is sitting with us at this moment; I am General Kalugin's guest; his wife prepared all these hors d'oeuvres.
> Somehow I make our excuses and we leave, and the fresh Moscow air has never tasted so good to me.[19]

Oleg Kalugin took exception to this article and wrote a letter to the *New York Times*, giving his recollection of the meeting with Le Carré:

> In his wording, it looks as if I condoned the murder of this man and have no remorse over what happened. In fact, when we discussed the affair I referred in broad terms to the problems existing in different countries in regard to dissidents, spies and traitors. I said that some prefer character assassinations or the electric chair, while others do away with their real or imagined enemies by sentencing them to death in absentia. Right or wrong, that's how different political and legal systems operate, and we have to face it squarely.
> As to the substance of the Markov affair, my record is known and clear. I did not participate in the planning, discussion or execution of the plot. I did

not train either Russians or Bulgarians, nor did I hand over to them the lethal weapon.[20]

John Le Carré wrote a response to the Kalugin letter:

> And I am sorrier still, not for Communism's winners, among whom I count the general, but its losers. For which reason the general will perhaps allow me a little compassion for the surviving family of Georgi Markov, whom his former service murdered and who even in death is being hounded by the Bulgarian regime, which now cynically and untruthfully brands him a former K.G.B. double agent. And when the general speaks of my venom, I would prefer him to call it plain anger at the notion of a former K.G.B. luminary making a party piece out of his involvement in the murder of a brave opponent of a disgusting regime, however much he now wishes to explain it away.[21]

Code Name Piccadilly

In March 1993, Bulgarian newspapers announced that Markov's killer was still alive and living in Western Europe. Then Bulgarian Presidential National Security Adviser Rumen Danov told the daily paper *24 Hours* that investigators had traced the killer of the dissident, Georgi Markov. "He is alive but I cannot say any more as I could complicate the investigations." Danov added, "Markov's killer knows the hunt [is] closing in." Articles in British and Danish newspapers followed this announcement.

Danish TV identified the man as Francisco Gullino, code name "Piccadilly." Gullino was born in Italy in 1946 and was a Danish citizen. He was identified as being involved in organized crime in Europe, especially dealing in forged art and antiques. Bulgarian police reportedly had arrested Gullino as he attempted to smuggle drugs through Bulgaria to Western Europe.

In 1972, he agreed to work with the Bulgarian Intelligence Service and signed a "loyalty statement" confirming such cooperation. One could speculate that Gullino was involved in the July 1973 mysterious kidnapping of prominent Bulgarian defector and publisher Boris Arsoff in Denmark. Arsoff was put on trial in Sofia in September 1973 and sentenced to fifteen years imprisonment. One newspaper in Sofia praised "the timely intervention of Bulgarian State Security which put an end to Arsoff's activities." He died shortly thereafter in prison.

Bulgarian investigators said that Gullino was in possession of four false passports containing his photo. In addition, they found receipts in the intelligence files signed "Piccadilly." Gullino was interviewed by Danish intelligence service (PET) officers, on suspicion of being a Bulgarian intelligence agent. Because he had admitted signing the loyalty statement to a "foreign intelligence service," a minor offense, Danish authorities charged him with breaching Denmark's espionage laws.

In 1993 Scotland Yard detectives flew to Denmark and interviewed Gullino for six hours in Copenhagen. A Bulgarian investigator joined them in the interrogation and gave Scotland Yard and Danish investigators details from Bulgarian Intelligence files. "Piccadilly" had been in London at the time of Markov's murder and had received 2,000 British pounds from Bulgarian intelligence, according to the Bulgarian investigator. Gullino abruptly left Denmark after being interviewed.

In July 1993, Bulgarian Chief Prosecutor Ani Krouleva publicly complained that western media press leaks had forced "Piccadilly" to flee Denmark for Hungary. She reportedly said, "Recently published details on the murder investigation could not have been made by sheer accident," adding, "this leads me to believe that agencies other than the Bulgarian Secret Service could have had a stake in the Markov murder.[22]

Yet Krouleva's senior investigator Bogdan Karayotov made a statement to the Bulgarian media, saying that Bulgaria had given Scotland Yard proof that Gullino had been arrested for drug trafficking back in 1971, recruited by State Security, and cooperated with Bulgarian Intelligence Service in the drug area. Karayotov added, "Since 1976 Gullino was set to work exclusively on killing Georgi Markov." His only source of income for living and traveling around the world was the money he received from the Bulgarian Intelligence Service, according to Karayotov. On July 13, 1993, RFE broadcast a twenty-two-minute program that aired the contradictory interviews of Karayotov and Krouleva.

In November 1993, Anthony Georgieff, one of RFE's Bulgarian Service editors, located Gullino in Karoly Vary, Czech Republic, apparently using a cover address in Budapest, Hungary. Gullino had an answering machine in Budapest and Georgieff left a message. Gullino called back the next day and the editor asked for an interview. Gullino was noncommittal. Georgieff then faxed a letter offering Gullino confidentiality. He called Gullino the next day and left another message on the answering machine. Gullino returned the call and said he had received the fax. He asked for time to think about it, saying that it had all been such a long time ago. That was the last contact RFE had with Gullino.[23]

A Danish television crew visited RFE and interviewed Kostov, not only about his knowledge of the Markov murder, but also about what had happened to him. At this time, RFE/RL learned that Gullino was not only a suspect in the Markov murder, but also for some similar activity in Rome. The RFE/RL Security Office received a message from Sofia that Karayotov wanted to come to Munich to review the RFE/RL security files on Markov.

Kalugin's Arrest in London

The Markov story took another strange turn when on October 31, 1993, British police held Oleg Kalugin on his arrival at London's Heathrow Airport. The anti-terrorist squad took him to police headquarters and questioned him about the Georgi Markov murder. While in police custody, Kalugin was visited by the Russian consul general in London, German Dorokhin. Later an embassy spokesman told reporters, "Mr. Kalugin said he has no connection with Mr. Markov's case." He added, "He met the Bulgarian president in 1992 and gave him all the evidence he had about the case. The Bulgarian government was completely satisfied. He is completely innocent." The Russian embassy demanded Kalugin's immediate release. London police released Kalugin and he was not charged with any crime.

In his published memoirs, Kalugin decided to minimize his role in the Markov murder: it was not Kalugin who had ordered Golubev to help the Bulgarians kill Markov, it was Kryuchkov. After his arrest in London, he apparently realized that he had been admitting his complicity in murder for years. He took pains to change that and minimize his role. He wrote: "In all my years in the KGB, I have only once been involved in what we call in the business a 'wet job'—an assassination. It occurred in 1978, and though I didn't have a pivotal role in the killing, I nevertheless did not try to talk my superiors out of the plot to kill the Bulgarian dissident Georgi Markov."[24] In an interview for a CNN television series on the Cold War, "Inside the KGB," aired in March 1999, Kalugin said:

> The Bulgarians were given a choice of weapons, and finally they picked up this umbrella as a cover to shoot the man with a poisoned pellet. It was not supposed to be uncovered, because the pellet would dissolve in his body within 24 hours, if I recall correctly. I did not conceive, I did not plan, I was not involved in any execution, but I was aware. In addition, I always say that knowledge does not imply a misdeed, does it? Do you suppose I would go over to the United States or U.K. and announce publicly? I would hang myself.

Trial of Todor Zhivkov

Todor Zhivkov, at age seventy-eight, stepped down as head of the Bulgarian Communist Party on November 10, 1989, and a few weeks later he resigned as president of Bulgaria. He was later indicted on charges of embezzlement and placed under house arrest. In September 1992, Zhivkov was sentenced to seven years imprisonment for embezzlement, and in January 1994 the Bulgarian Supreme Court upheld the conviction and sentence. Zhivkov's lawyers managed to persuade the chief prosecutor's office to agree to a two-month postponement, during which the court would determine if Zhivkov would survive the jail sentence due to the state of his health.

In late 1993, Zhivkov was also indicted for having organized the forced assimilation campaign against ethnic Turks from 1984 to 1989, as well as for having diverted several million dollars of state funds to Third World leftist and terrorist organizations. Minister of Interior Stoyanov was also indicted in the forced assimilation campaign, including the order that forced ethnic Turks to change their names to fit Bulgarian standards.

At the time of this writing, the murder of Georgi Markov remains officially unsolved. No one has been brought to trial for the murder. Yury Andropov left the KGB in 1982 to assume the pinnacle of power as chairman of the Communist Party of the Soviet Union. He died in 1984. Viktor Chebrikov succeeded Andropov as chairman of the KGB in 1982 and held this post until 1988. In 1985 he had assured Mikhail Gorbachev's victory by providing compromising materials on his two leading political opponents.

Viktor Kryuchkov replaced Chebrikov as KGB chairman in 1988 and remained in that position until August 1991, when he was arrested for attempting to overthrow Mikhail Gorbachev. Kryuchkov and thirteen other top Soviet officials were put on trial in November 1993. He testified that he and the other thirteen officials has attempted a coup d'état in August 1991 to thwart plans by western governments to impoverish and dominate the Soviet Union. Kryuchkov said he had "received reports that NATO had divided the Soviet Union into 'spheres of influence' should it collapse and that the West planned to reduce the Soviet population from about 280 million to 150 million within 30 years."[25]

Double Agent Markov?

The Bulgarian Intelligence Service continued the anti–Markov campaign in September 1994 when two writers traveled to London to announce their new book about Georgi Markov. The authors of the book, *The Umbrella Murder*, published in Sofia, Vladimir Bereanu and Kalin Todorov, said they had spent four years researching the murder and had interviewed a Bulgarian diplomat, now living in Sofia, whom they said was the killer. They added, "Markov was not a dissident. He was an agent for the Bulgarian secret service." The authors also claimed that Georgi Markov had been killed because he had been recruited by the British Secret Service and was working as a double agent.

Markov Died Naturally?

The campaign to discredit Georgi Markov continued. About a year after Markov's death, an émigré named Dinioi Dinev was arrested and tried in Paris for working for Bulgarian intelligence. One of his tasks had been to report on the activities of Vladimir Kostov before the murder attempt. In December 1979 he was found guilty and sentenced to three years imprisonment. Almost fifteen years later, in October 1994, Dinev was interviewed on Bulgarian television and said, "Markov died naturally of his third heart attack and British intelligence services made up the story of the attack." He added:

> The pellet is a contraption, and I expect, before too long, a man in London will confess in his memoirs that he constructed it. The same applies to Vladimir Kostov. No one's ever seen the pellet. I worked with Markov on two films in Bulgaria. He was a colleague of mine in the DS. That was natural. It was impossible for anyone to travel abroad without working for DS. No one wanted to harm Markov. There were far more dangerous émigrés, and he wouldn't have entered the hit list.

Dinev's credibility is more than suspect: the Bulgarian TV program *168 Hours*, quoting a French magazine as a source, stated that Dinev and a Russian named Sergei Gorshkov were allegedly at the center of a $2.5-million money-laundering operation. Dinev was quoted as saying that Russian mafia gangs used him because he had "a reputation of an honest, balanced and correct man. I travel all the time between Paris, Moscow, Sofia and USA. In Moscow I have two bodyguards with Kalashnikovs and two with semiautomatic rifles as backup."

Fifteen KGB Agents?

In January 1995, Foreign Office minister of state Baroness Chalker told the House of Lords that Britain had requested information from the Russian government the year before. She said, "We have asked them for an explanation of why it is taking so long.... Whether they are seeking to avoid responding, I cannot tell you for certain at the moment." She added that a list of fifteen suspects, all KGB officers, had been compiled by Scotland Yard's antiterrorist squad and sent to Moscow. She then added, "We have asked the Russians to establish the whereabouts of these persons and whether or not they will willingly talk to the police." The fifteen people were given special awards in Russia, signed by Zhivkov in February 1979, purportedly for their involvement in the Markov murder, "with the '9th of September 1944 Order of the First Degree' with a Coat of Arms for ... cooperation and help in the promotion of the fraternal cooperation between the KGB and the Bulgarian Internal Ministry."

Fourteen Bulgarian intelligence officers received confidential awards in October 1978 for "superb performance, operational alacrity and high responsibility in identifying, documenting and intercepting persons serving as agents of foreign intelligence, and for bringing to an end the anti-state activities of Bulgarian nationals."

Kostov Returns to Bulgaria

After the fall of Communism in Bulgaria, Vladimir Kostov — former intelligence officer, journalist, and the first victim of the umbrella weapon — was pardoned by a presidential decree in November 1990. He had been found guilty by a military court in 1978 and sentenced to death for "defecting and for discussing his state security service." He resigned from Radio Free Europe and returned to Bulgaria. In 1995, he was firmly established as the chief editor of a socialist newspaper in Sofia.

Bulgaria Denies Involvement Again

On March 20, 1995, the Bulgarian government issued a "White Book on the Country's Situation." Chapter 11, part 1, deals with the "State of Bulgaria's Foreign Relations." The white book blames the previous liberal and democratic governments for "the self-denigrating confession of involvement in crimes such as the attempt against the Pope, at a time when even the foreign authors of this version have reneged on it, and the concurrent link of the name of Bulgaria with the tragic demise of Georgi Markov, without a final and unequivocal explanation of the incident."

With the publication of this report, it appeared that the Bulgarian government under a neo–Communist party — renamed a socialist party — was retrenching.

In September 1995, the seventeenth anniversary of the death of Georgi Markov, three former KGB officers visited Sofia. In a macabre show of solidarity with those involved in the Markov murder, former KGB General V. N. Fyodorov met with former Bulgarian Intelligence Service generals Todorov and Stoyanov. Fyodorov also paid his respects to former general Savov by visiting the gravesite.

When then British Foreign Secretary Malcolm Rifkind visited Sofia in January 1997, he pledged to provide Sofia with "all the support and cooperation

Britain could muster to help shed light on the 1978 death in London of Bulgarian communism's arch enemy."

Newly elected Bulgarian president Petr Stoyanov said he was prepared to do "everything that the constitution allows" to reveal why Markov died and who ordered his sinister execution. Speaking to BBC on the twentieth anniversary of Markov's death, President Stoyanov optimistically said that authorities would continue to investigate the case even though the former secret service in Bulgaria had destroyed evidence. Stoyanov added that "the assassination of the dissident writer Georgi Markov was one of the darkest moments in the history of the former communist regime."

On October 21, 1998, authorities in Bulgaria officially closed the Markov murder case when the chief prosecutor of Sofia, Nestor Nesterov, said that the case had been abandoned because the time limit for investigating the killing had expired. The same day Bulgarian President Stoyanov told visiting British Foreign Minister Cook, "It is painful for every Bulgarian democrat but, leaving the scene, communism has taken to its grave also some secrets, such as the files about the murder of Georgi Markov." Cook said, "The communists didn't leave their files, it was unlikely that sufficient evidence would ever come to light."

In November 1999, Markov investigator Bogdan Karayotov told the Bulgarian private radio station Darik Radio that Georgi Markov had never been used by any secret or intelligence service, Bulgarian or foreign. Bogdan Karayotov was forced on November 24 to retire as head of the Capital Crimes Division at the National Investigative Office. The formal reason to retire him was that he was already several years beyond the retirement date. The real reason, according to Karayotov in the radio interview, was that in one of the investigations Karayotov had discovered that the head of the National Investigative Office, Boyko Rashkov, had close private contacts with a "suspect in a sensational murder case." Rashkov had allegedly attempted to impede the investigation to the benefit of the suspect.

Karayotov told Darik Radio that the legal time limit of investigation in the Markov case had expired the previous September, and that the "case was now waiting to be officially closed but we know whom the killer was." Bulgarian law provides a thirty-year statute of limitation for first-degree murder. Thus, theoretically, if the case is not reopened and if an indictment is not issued by September 10, 2008, the killer may publicly say "I did it," without fear of prosecution.

On Thursday, December 28, 2000, Georgi Markov was honored in Sofia, Bulgaria, when President Stoyanov presented Annabel Markov with Bulgaria's highest honor: the Order of Stara Planina. The order's citation spoke of Markov's "remarkable contribution to Bulgarian literature and of his opposition to the

Communist authorities." Stoyanov said, "I decorate the writer Georgi Markov for his work and the bravery with which he advocated the anti-communist cause when he lived abroad. I decorate him, because I think that Georgi Markov served as an example of courage, self-renunciation and bravery."[26] However, President Stoyanov did not admit that Bulgarians killed Markov. Annabel was quoted as saying,

> Thank you, Mister President. I feel very sorry that my husband is dead and cannot receive his award in person, even though I would like to thank you all for this opportunity, to thank you who are here and remember him. It is unfortunate that his awful murder has not been revealed, but I consider this event as the beginning of his recognition in Bulgaria as a patriot and great writer. Thank you.[27]

In July 2001, Bulgarian President Stoyanov made another official visit to England. Shortly before he departed London, Stoyanov visited Annabel Markov. At her request, the meeting between them took place in private. He brought her a file with documents from the State Security archive concerning the murder; the contents were not made public.

Bulgarian investigative journalist Hristo Hristov spent over six years trying to open the Bulgarian intelligence and government archives on Georgi Markov. In 2005, his book *Kill the Tramp: The Murder of Georgi Markov and Bulgarian and British Government Policy* was published.[28] He furnishes details of Francisco Gullino, including the possible use of Gullino until 1990. However Hristov was frustrated with the lack of cooperation from Bulgarian authorities and even after the publication of his book he was making appeals and lawsuits to get the closed files that still exist opened to the public.

In 2006, the PBS television station in New York broadcast a program on Georgi Markov and then made its findings available on the Internet, including a re-enactment of the murder, photograph of the pellet, video clips, and an interactive "Teacher's Toolbox" for educators and students to "examine the evidence."[29] Also included in the program was an interview with Dr. Christopher Green, CIA specialist, who said,

> We had pretty much all of the story from a forensic point of view. We had the body, the thing in the body that he was hit with — the pellet — and the stuff from the pellet. We knew that the material used to kill him, ricin, had been under development by a foreign service linked to the incident. We also knew that he had been a target of assassination attempts in the past. The story of him being a target was very well known. Therefore, we had information on the means, motive, and the opportunity.[30]

With 20 percent of the destroyed Bulgarian intelligence service files missing or destroyed, the death of Georgi Markov appears destined to be one of the unsolved mysteries of the Cold War.

The Stefan Sverdlev Story

One of the saddest casualties of the Cold War has to be former Bulgarian Intelligence officer Stefan Sverdlev. His life would have been insignificant, except that the western media and others used him for their own purposes during the Cold War. He was truly a hapless pawn in the Cold War game. He once was portrayed in the press as a top-level Bulgarian Intelligence Service officer and one of the most important Cold War intelligence defectors. However, this short, overweight, homely man was definitely not James Bond.

In 1971, Colonel Stefan Sverdlev of the Bulgarian Border Police took his wife and five-month-old boy, and fled Bulgaria, illegally crossing the border into Greece. From his training, he knew exactly how, when, and where to cross the border. He supposedly took over five hundred classified documents with him. The family was given asylum in Greece. For a few years they were apparently happy in Greece. Then their fortunes changed. The Greek Socialist Party won the national elections and assumed power. Sverdlev was no longer welcome in Greece. In 1977, he and his family traveled to Germany, where he was granted asylum. His daughter, who had preceded him to Greece, remained behind.

The disparate Bulgarian émigré community in Munich is small but very active. Because of its small size, an émigré's personal life was known by every other émigré. In December 1978, Stefan Sverdlev was described by some émigrés as being in urgent need of financial aid. A few RFE/RL Bulgarian Service employees said that they wanted to take up a private collection for him at RFE/RL. They said that since both U.S. and German authorities had debriefed Sverdlev at great length, he was no longer of great interest to them. The employees explained that any intelligence information he could supply was considered outdated, and that Sverdlev was now ignored or forgotten.

He picked up an occasional odd job as a laborer in Munich, and the family received some financial assistance from both the city of Munich and the Bulgarian émigré community. Sverdlev remained quietly in the background of émigré life in Munich until April 1979, when BBC television filmed a documentary program on the life and death of Georgi Markov. Though he could not have had any knowledge of the murder, he was the highest-ranking former Bulgarian Intelligence Service officer in the West. For the BBC program, Sverdlev was interviewed about the Bulgarian Intelligence Service. He said, "It is Bulgarian in name only. Soviet advisors control the entire operation.... It is inconceivable that this murder could have been done without the Russians knowing about it. According to the program's commentator, the KGB had decorated Sverdlev for "outstanding services in the protection of the frontiers of socialism."

Speaking publicly for the first time since his escape from Bulgaria in 1971, Sverdlev said, "I knew of kidnapping and assassination of Bulgarian exiles by Bulgarian agents." Sverdlev's status in the West changed because of this program. He became the West's expert in Bulgarian intelligence matters.

He again faded back into the obscure world of Bulgarian émigré politics, until the attack on Pope John Paul II in 1981. On February 4, 1983, an interview with Sverdlev appeared in the French magazine, *Le Figaro*. He was interviewed on the subject of the attack on the pope. On February 9, 1983, Sverdlev again was interviewed on this subject in the Zurich newspaper *Weltwoche*. A photo of his DS Service identification card alongside a current photo appeared with the article.

The November 1983 issue of *Reader's Digest* contained an article that detailed Bulgaria's alleged involvement in the international drug trade. Senior Editor Nathan Adams, who had interviewed Sverdlev in Munich, wrote the article. Adams emotionally described Sverdlev's defection on February 10, 1971:

> Clutching his five-month-old son in one powerful arm and leading his wife and daughter by the other, he slipped into the frigid chest-deep current. Within 15 minutes, the family had reached a Greek border outpost. In Sverdlev's possession: some 500 sensitive KDS (Komitet Darzhavna Sigurnost — DS for short).
>
> News of Sverdlev's defection sent shock waves all the way to KGB headquarters in Moscow. In the months ahead, Bulgarian networks in Greece began to collapse as Sverdlev talked and analysts pored over the top-secret documents.

With remarkable detail, Sverdlev publicly revealed to Adams a secret 1970 Bulgarian intelligence directive that would implement a 1967 Warsaw-Pact plan to destabilize and corrupt the West through the influx of narcotics. Supposedly, this was one of the five hundred documents Sverdlev brought with him when he defected in 1971. Though he had given the written information to the Greek government twelve years before, he was still able to remember details from the directive, including its number and date of issuance.

Sverdlev's Family Kidnapped?

Sverdlev's wife and child returned to Bulgaria in November 1983, under still questionable circumstances. His wife Pavlina had received a letter from her mother on or about November 4, 1983. According to the letter, her mother would be in Vienna with a Bulgarian tourist group November 12–14. They would stay at the Hotel Fuchs. Paulina was supposed to reply if she could meet with her mother. Her mother was then eighty years old, and Sverdlev's wife apparently thought that this would be the last chance for her son and her mother to meet. She agreed to the meeting and apparently telephoned her mother in Bulgaria. Hotel reservations were made for both Mrs. Sverdlev and her son. She then apparently traveled to Vienna with her thirteen-year-old son, Sergei.

Sverdlev called the hotel on November 12, 1983, at about 6:00 P.M. He asked his wife to make sure everything was in order. He was told that his wife and child had not checked in yet. The next day, Sverdlev told members of the Bulgarian Service of RFE that he had not heard from his wife since she had left for Vienna. He said that both his wife and son had possibly been kidnapped in front of the Hotel Fuchs. Some Bulgarian Service employees decided to get in touch with members of the press to give publicity to the case.

Meanwhile Sverdlev's friends were able to get his story in the western press. *The New York Times*, United Press International, *Die Presse* in Vienna, and some Munich newspapers carried the story. The media reaction in Sofia was not long in coming. Bulgaria's official news agency (BTA) reported from Sofia that Pavlina Sverdlev and her son had returned voluntarily to Sofia. She returned under amnesty of the twenty-year prison sentence she had received in absentia. Most of Sverdlev's friends believed she returned to Bulgaria simply because she was tired of their poor and futureless life in Munich.

Death Threats to RFE/RL Employees

In November 1983, the Rome-based American journalist Claire Sterling interviewed Sverdlev in the entrance hall of RFE/RL. Afterward she wrote an article for the *Wall Street Journal* in which she described the "kidnapping" and added previously unknown details of a Bulgarian-language letter mailed to émigré circles in Germany. This letter supposedly contained a regime "hit list" of four persons: Sverdlev, RFE/RL employees Vladimir Kostov and Velicko Peitchev (in that order), and a former Bulgarian intelligence officer. Peitchev, who was a friend of Antonov, had been invited to Rome by the investigating magistrate and had met Antonov in jail. Both Kostov and Peitchev afterward broadcast extensively about the trial in Rome. Ms. Sterling described the letter as having "a costly engraved letterhead bearing Bulgaria's coat of arms."

On January 22, 1984, Sverdlev was living at another friend's apartment when a Bulgarian truck driver arrived in Munich for a visit. The truck driver was introduced to Sverdlev and proceeded to tell him the following:

The day before the wife and son returned, or shortly before they returned to Bulgaria, she was visited by six men, one of whom was her brother. The five men were to physically take her and the boy to Czechoslovakia and then fly them to Sofia if she refused to return the way they set it up, i.e., by train through Vienna. She apparently agreed and they left together to Sofia.

In one to two months, a colonel of the Bulgarian Intelligence Service will arrive in Munich. His mission is to set up some sort of operation in order "to clear some accounts with some people." The names of RFE/RL employees Peitchev and Kostov were mentioned. RFE's Bulgarian Service broadcasts about the Antonov arrest and trial as an accomplice in the attack on the pope were too critical of the Bulgarian regime.[31]

Sverdlev then asked the truck driver if he was working for Bulgarian intelligence. The truck driver reportedly answered yes, as this was the only way he could travel outside Bulgaria. Sverdlev then called a friend of his who had once been employed with Greek intelligence. This contact verified that he had sent the truck driver to Sverdlev to warn him about the future operation and to tell him about his wife. Apparently the truck driver worked for both Greek and Bulgarian intelligence, according to Sverdlev.

Senior management decided that it could not simply dismiss the threats to its employees, because of the bombing of RFE/RL in 1981 and other hostile activity. On February 15, 1984, a detailed summary of what RFE then knew was sent to the political officer at the American consulate, Munich:

> Attached for your review is a summary of information received concerning a possible Bulgarian Intelligence Service operation against RFE/RL employees Peitchev and Kostov. The name of the truck driver is unknown but he is said to have connections with both Greek and Bulgarian intelligence officers. Sverdlev defected in Greece in the late 1970s and one of his former contacts in Greek intelligence purportedly sent the truck driver to Sverdlev to warn him. We have no supportive information to back up his story.[32]

In addition, copies of various newspaper articles concerning Sverdlev, Peitchev and Kostov and the Antonov arrest and trial were attached.

A week later, the political officer in Munich advised that he put together a telex based on what he had received. He said he had forwarded the plan to Washington and the U.S. embassy in Sofia, Bulgaria, with the recommendation that the Bulgarian regime be contacted concerning the possible upcoming action against RFE/RL—and to "knock it off." He added that the Bulgarian officials who would be told this would most likely deny it. But least they had been put on notice that the U.S. government was aware of their planned action. No one was threatened or harmed, and the matter quietly fell in the background of other pressing problems.

Sverdlev Redefects?

Sverdlev continued to live on the edge of extreme poverty in Munich for years until August 23, 1988, when he also returned to Bulgaria from Greece, by reversing the route he had taken in 1971. Since Sverdlev had constant contact with RFE/RL Bulgarian Service employees, management anticipated that he might be forced to testify on Bulgarian TV or radio and denounce both RFE/RL and its staff.

Sverdlev borrowed a lot of money from several people in order to publish a documentary on Bulgaria. One estimate was that over the years he borrowed over DM 250,000 from RFE/RL employees and other émigrés in Munich. Munich police were called about the possible redefection or kidnapping of Sverdlev. Using a court order, the police entered Sverdlev's apartment and discovered that he had taken everything of value with him. The apartment was not disrupted. The RFE/RL police contact said Sverdlev had voluntarily gone back to Bulgaria. However, they were trying through INTERPOL to contact the daughter in Greece for more information.

Sverdlev Returns to Munich

Some months later, Sverdlev reappeared in Munich. He said that he had remained in Sofa, hiding in an attic for three months, before sneaking out through Yugoslavia to Italy and back to Germany. The émigré community did not trust him and ignored him. German authorities questioned the fidelity of his story about returning to Bulgaria and then back to Germany. However, the investigation produced no evidence that he was acting as an agent of Bulgarian Intelligence Service, and the investigation was closed. Nevertheless, Sverdlev had other problems just as serious.

Because of unfulfilled promises to pay off his large debts or use the money to publish a book, Sverdlev spent some time in jail in Munich on fraud charges. Adding to Sverdlev's tragic life, his wife divorced him in 1990. The following year his son died after accidentally falling from an eight-story window, although there was no evidence of wrongdoing. The official Bulgarian police report was that the son had tried to rob a taxi driver and fell while trying to escape. Sverdlev believed it to be the work of a Bulgarian intelligence service.

Sverdlev Commits Suicide

In March 1994, Suerdlev applied for a visa to visit his daughter who was still living in Greece. The Greek government denied the visa request because he was an "undesirable person." On or about October, 20, 1994, after years of being alone, still penniless, and facing problems with his continuing claim to asylum in Germany, former Bulgarian Intelligence Colonel Stefan Sverdlev committed suicide in Munich by taking an overdose of sleeping pills and anti-malaria drugs. His death was a sad ending to a sad story of a small pawn in the big Cold War game.

4. Carlos the Jackal and the Bombing of Radio Free Europe/Radio Liberty

The thing about a myth is not whether it is true or not, nor whether it should be true, but that it is somehow truer than truth itself.— Thomas Keneally, *Schindler's List*

On November 30, 2001, at a formal ceremony in Bucharest, Romania, honoring fifty years of Radio Free Europe/Radio Liberty (RFE/RL) broadcasts, Romanian President Ion Iliescu decorated RFE/RL President Thomas Dine and five veteran journalists of the Romanian Service with different orders. Iliescu said that the ceremony represented "a sincere, though perhaps belated acknowledgment of the fact that Romania's history in the years of the totalitarian regime cannot be written without emphasizing the role played by the station on our lives under the conditions then prevailing." He added that RFE/RL had been Romania's "window to the normal world outside," and a source of "adequate and pluralist information." President Iliescu also recalled the "darker side" of Romania and RFE/RL's history:

- The February 21, 1981, terrorist bomb attack on RFE/RL in Munich
- Physical attacks on other Romanian journalists working for RFE/RL
- The still-unclarified circumstances surrounding the deaths of three directors of RFE/RL's Romanian Service.

Dine responded, in part:

Mr. President, your specific statement today, publicly acknowledging the role of Communist Romania's Securitate carrying out an act of terrorism against RFE/RL twenty years ago, is doubly significant and very much appreciated.

The bombing of RFE/RL's headquarters in Munich in February 1981 was a deplorable act. Its violence illustrated how deeply Radio Free Europe's broadcasts affected the authoritarian communist regimes. It served and serves as a timely reminder of the power of ideas and truth against brute force and deception.[1]

The bombing of Radio Free Europe/Radio Liberty on February 21, 1981, was Carlos the Jackal's only known American target, and one for which he has never publicly claimed credit. German police and court documents, reports from the former East German, Hungarian, and Romanian intelligence agencies, give overwhelming evidence that he directed the bombing from his base of operations in Budapest, Hungary, beginning in 1980.

Who Was the Man Known as Carlos the Jackal?

Before he was known as Carlos, Ilyich Ramirez-Sanchez was somewhat successful in the terrorist field in the early 1970s.[2] One deadly example of his early style was his murderous hand-grenade attack at the upbeat and fashionable Le Drugstore cafe in Paris on September 15, 1974. Two innocent persons were killed and more than thirty were injured.

The next year Ramirez-Sanchez was living in London and Paris under assumed names. On June 27, 1975, three French security officers, investigating recent terrorist attacks against the Israeli El Al airlines at Orly Airport, went to his apartment for routine questioning. He was not a suspect in the attacks, and the French officers were not armed. At one point in the questioning, he excused himself, went to the bathroom, and retrieved a hidden pistol. He returned from the bathroom, shot and killed two of the unarmed and unsuspecting French officers; one survived. He also shot Michel Moukharbal, his close aide, whom he assumed was the police informant. Seventeen years later, a French court tried Carlos in absentia and sentenced him to life imprisonment for the murders.

Ramirez-Sanchez had been previously living in London under the assumed name of "Carlos Andreas Martinez-Torres," ostensibly from Peru. After the shooting and publicity in Paris, British journalist Peter Niesewand of the *Guardian* received a tip that Carlos Martinez-Torres might be the one involved in the Paris murders. Niesewand, a creative and ambitious journalist, went to an apartment of Carlos's one-time girlfriend and found weapons and explosives in a bag he had once given to her for safekeeping. Niesewand then saw a copy of Frederick Forsyth's novel, "The Day of the Jackal," the suspense novel about an assassin hired to kill French President Charles DeGaulle. Niesewand coincidentally had just read the novel. Although the book belonged to someone else, Niesewand decided that Carlos had used it as his terrorist handbook. He filed the story on "Carlos the Jackal" for the *Guardian*, and then called the London police to report his findings. The myth of Carlos was born. Niesewand might have been impressed with Ilych Ramirez Sanchez, but the novelist Frederick Forsyth was not impressed with the mythical Carlos the Jackal. After the arrest of Carlos in 1994, Forsyth wrote:

With one exception, Carlos' career is a litany of cowardly acts on extremely soft targets. So, what is it about this essentially unsuccessful and exceedingly brutal little man from Venezuela that fascinates the West? I believe it lies in three factors, all flawed.

- First, Carlos has always loved publicity.
- Second, he had a reputation, sedulously nurtured, of being a ladies' man.
- Third, and here one must give him credit; he was a human chameleon, moving through Europe unspotted time and again.[3]

Carlos enjoyed the sudden international media attention and exploited it. He led a successful kidnapping of influential Arab oil officials in Vienna, shortly before Christmas 1976. He introduced himself to his captors by arrogantly exclaiming: "My name is Carlos. You may have heard of me." With each successive terrorist act, Carlos's image as a successful and dangerous terrorist grew internationally. The myth of Carlos fascinated the western media, yet the man known as Carlos became inactive and went into seclusion for the next five years.

Carlos Chose Eastern Europe

In 1978, Carlos was asked to leave Iraq but, before doing so, Iraqi intelligence officers gave him an envelope containing $200,000.[4] After testing the waters in some Eastern European countries, mainly Bulgaria, Carlos chose Hungary in 1979 for his base of operations because of "favorable communications, liberal border controls, and good relationships with the Foreign Ministry and other government and security organizations."[5] Carlos formed organizations called "Organization of the Armed Arab Struggle — Arm of the Arab Revolution" (OAAS) and the "Organization of International Revolutionaries."

Ramirez-Sanchez mostly used the name Michel with his group, not Carlos. His group consisted of terrorists from the Basque separatist group ETA/PM (Politico Militar), the Swiss terrorist group Prima Linea, the Red Brigades from Italy, the People's Front for the Liberation of Palestine (PFLP), former members of the Revolutionary Cells in Germany, and others yet identified. English was the common language used by the group. Nevertheless, there was no group agenda, no strategic political plan, no manifesto or logo.[6]

Carlos had created a myth and exploited it when dealing with Hungary and East Germany (DDR). For example, on April 2, 1980, Carlos wrote a letter to Hungarian Communist Party Chairman Janos Kadar, explaining why he chose Hungary:

Dear Comrade Janos Kadar:
  The Socialist countries permit our combatants to freely pass through their

territory, and now a palpable trend is appearing toward building relations with our organization.

We have been struggling for a year, for the realization of our revolutionary objectives, enjoying the security advantages provided by socialist Hungary. From Hungarian soil, we have developed our international relations, making contact with the revolutionaries of every nation, without the Hungarian authorities hampering us in this.

Revolutionary greetings,

Carlos, on behalf of the Organization of International Revolutionaries.[7]

The East Germany Intelligence agency commonly known as Stasi used the code name "Separat" for the Carlos group. One revealing Stasi document, dated February 10, 1981, gives a remarkable overview of the plans and intentions of the Carlos group with Eastern Europe:

The group still considers itself a revolutionary organization, whose struggle is aimed against imperialism of all kinds. They are predominantly concentrating on the support of national liberation movements, as they are convinced that these groups are the most efficient in their revolutionary struggle.

The group considers the socialist states to be its strategic allies; it is interested in maintaining a friendly relationship with them, but expects material and logistical support in return.

Currently, the group does not intend to put much emphasis on its own terrorist activities. Based on their recent activities and statements it is reasonable to assume that the group increasingly tries to grow into the role of a coordinator or mediator between various national terrorist forces.

The "Carlos" group wants to strengthen its influence on other terrorist groups by providing weapons, financial means, and passports, which it obtains in other countries, or produces itself at its bases, and by other logistical support.

Now, the leadership of the "Carlos" group is of the opinion that it is not possible to establish its own, stable bases in the group's operational areas.

In the long-term (a period of about 10 to 15 years), it thus intends to establish bases in Socialist States with the aim to use them for meetings, for updating their technical equipment, and for recreation. The headquarters should be situated in Budapest.

In the case of potential problems with some of the socialist countries, the group intends to accept the Rumanian offer to move its headquarters to Bucharest.

In the case that, for one reason or another, Romania will have to be abandoned, "Carlos" intends to switch to Syria. Preparations are thus underway to create a base in Syria, reportedly with the help of the Syrian intelligence service.[8]

The two German terrorists in the Carlos group, Magdalena Kopp and Johannes Weinrich, were known respectively as Lilly and Steve. Kopp was then Carlos's girlfriend and the group's expert on forging passports. She and Carlos had traveled together to Damascus, Syria in February 1980, and met with top Syrian intelligence officials. They received Syrian diplomatic passports, weapons and the use of two houses and automobiles. The Syrian government also ordered the Syrian embassies in East Germany, Hungary, Czechoslovakia, and Bulgaria to assist Carlos, when he requested it.

Beginning of an Uneasy Relationship

On July 16, 1979, the South Yemen embassy in Berlin sent a notice to the Hungarian embassy in Berlin requesting a one-month stay for one Adil Favaz Ahmed (Carlos), who was due to arrive the next day, traveling on a diplomatic passport.

On August 20, 1979 at 6:30 A.M., Carlos went to Budapest police headquarters to file a complaint that three men in a green Opel automobile with West German license plates, WES YE 359, were following him. The police told Carlos they would investigate.

Shortly before the arrival of West German Chancellor Helmut Schmidt, a German consulate officer named Metger went to the Interior Ministry on August 23, 1980, and said that an anonymous letter had been received at the German embassy in Vienna the day before. In this letter, Carlos was identified as living in Budapest under the name Adil Favaz Ahmed. The Hungarian official promised to look into it.

On August 29, 1980, Carlos picked up Magdalena Kopp at the airport after her arrival from Berlin. On their way to their apartment, Carlos saw another suspicious automobile, stopped, jumped out of his vehicle, and shot four times at the suspicious one. No one was injured. Carlos continued on to the apartment, called Johannes Weinrich in Berlin to tell him to remain there, as German or Italian intelligence agents were following him. Carlos went back to the Budapest police headquarters and insisted on meeting Hungarian intelligence officials. One official later said that they agreed to meet Carlos on August 30, 1980, in order to quiet him down. Carlos requested security protection and offered to work with the Hungarian intelligence agency.

The next day, Hungarian intelligence agents told Carlos that it was indeed possible that West German agents, due to the upcoming visit of Chancellor Schmidt, were following him. They told Carlos it would be better if he and others of the group agreed to leave Hungary before Chancellor Schmidt's arrival. He and Magdalena Kopp flew to Sofia, Bulgaria, on September 1980. The next day, West German consulate officer Metger called the Ministry of Interior, requesting an update of the risk of terrorism in Hungary during the Schmidt visit. He was told that there were not any German or other terrorists in Hungary. Chancellor Schmidt visited Hungary September 4–6, 1980, without any problems. Carlos remained out of Hungary until the end of September 1979.

Carlos and the Romanian Securitate

In July 1978, General Ion Mihia Pacepa defected to the West by walking into the U.S. embassy in Bonn, West Germany. He was a close advisor to Romanian President Nicolae Ceausescu and acting head of the Romanian foreign intelligence service, Directia de Informatii Externe (DIE). Pacepa was a true insider, who knew the secret lives of top Communist Party officials that were carefully hidden from the public. The next month he was sentenced to death in absentia for "treason, defection and refusal to return to his country." The Romanian foreign intelligence service contacted an unlikely person to carry out this death sentence: Ilych Ramirez Sanchez — the terrorist known to the world as Carlos the Jackal. Pacepa could not have known or even dreamed that his actions would ultimately lead to Carlos's bombing of RFE/RL.

The Romanian intelligence service made the initial contact with Carlos through the brother of Palestine Liberation Organization chief Yasser Arafat in August 1979. That month, two Romanian foreign intelligence officers from unit UM 0620, Sergiu Nica and Ion Deaconescu, flew to Prague to meet Carlos, who was visiting the city. Their purpose was to offer Carlos $10,000 to kill Pacepa. Nica and Carlos spoke in English. The deal did not go through and the two officers returned to Bucharest.

During the time that Carlos was using the safe house in Budapest, before and after the bombing, he had continual telephone contact with Lt. Col. Sergiu Nica, who used the code name Andrei Vitescu with the Carlos group. For a yet unknown reason, exactly nine years after the bombing (February 21, 1990), Nica hand wrote a report concerning his knowledge of some Romanian intelligence activities:

> In 1978, when PACEPA betrayed us, I was working in Bucharest in the military unit U.M. 0620 and was in charge of the intelligence service and, among other duties, personally concerned with the informative action against the international terrorist "CARLOS." Our country was threatened from various angles (attack at the Otopeni airport, indications as to attacks of various embassies in Bucharest, etc.) with no possibility to localize the terrorist.
>
> Thanks to a foreign source, I was able to determine in 1979 that "Carlos" was living in socialist countries; ... "Carlos" was interested in establishing contact with the Romanian authorities, as well. I passed on this information and, after several meetings with the "informants" Colonel BLAGA, Stefan and General VLAD, Iulian, the management of the State Security Service, i.e.

POSTELNICU, Tudor himself, decided to send me on a business trip abroad in order to verify statements concerning "Carlos'" identity, to determine his attitude towards Romania and, also, to get me interested in a possible collaboration with him, with the aim to neutralize the traitor PACEPA.

Between 1981 and 1982, General PLESITA met "Carlos" and other members of his organization several times. With these meetings he intended to:

• Have "Carlos" refrain from taking terrorist actions against Romania
• Support him in a certain way (meetings in Bucharest with his mother, as well as with terrorist elements active in South America)
• Get "Carlos" to support us with the neutralization of the traitor PACEPA.

As far as I know nothing was attempted with PACEPA because they did not have any people in the U.S.A. Nevertheless, we could be sure at that point that no terrorist attacks would be taken against Romania.[9]

In January 1980, Carlos sent Magdalena Kopp instead to Bucharest, where she remained for three days. Carlos was not pleased with the results of the Bucharest meeting. He and Weinrich then flew to Bucharest for further negotiations. The Hungarian intelligence service monitored the Carlos group's telephone calls in Budapest, using code name C-79, for their surveillance operations against Carlos.

As early as February 4, 1980, the Hungarians knew about the plans to kill a Romanian émigré working at Radio Free Europe, but at that time the potential victim was not identified by name. After many telephone calls between Carlos and Sergiu Nica, both he and Johannes Weinrich flew to Bucharest in August 1980 to meet with the Romanians.

On August 18, 1980, the Romanian Ministry of Interior approved Action Plan Nr. 225/f.9/0025323 against RFE/RL's Romanian Broadcast Service director, Noel Bernard. This action plan has the only known direct reference to the planning of the eventual bombing of RFE/RL six months later:

Apply special measures in order to paralyze the activity of RFE. In addition, neutralize some employees by damaging and destroying buildings and facilities of the radio, homes of staff, their cars, as well as by producing physical harm to the most active employees and contributors of RFE.

Through defectors Riva, Protopopescu, Kraus, Barta Geza, and others, we shall study
• The buildings and installations of the Free Europe radio station,
• The guard and security system,
• Vulnerable points etc.,
with the aim of finding ways and concrete solutions to damage and destroy the buildings and installations of the Free Europe radio station, by planting explosives, causing fires etc.[10]

Carlos and the Bombing of Radio Free Europe

A top-secret summary report on October 3, 1980, by Department III/II-8 of the Hungarian Interior Ministry, based on monitored telephone calls between Carlos and Sergiu Nica, identified RFE/RL Romanian Service employee Emil Georgescu, Romanian King-in-Exile Michael, Paul Goma, and other émigrés as targets for Carlos.[11] The attack on Emil Georgescu was supposed to be accomplished by an attack on the Romanian Section of RFE and then possibly the terrorists would take "secret" documents from the building.[12] In addition, Carlos received the assignment of breaking in or destroying RFE/RL's monitoring station outside Munich in Schleissheim and obtaining "secret" documents that were erroneously believed stored there. In return, the Romanians gave Carlos thirty-four Italian, German, French, and Austrian passports, plus Romanian diplomatic passports for Carlos, Weinrich, and Magdalena Kopp.

A few weeks before his thirty-first birthday, October 14, 1980, Carlos reportedly chaired a planning session in Budapest. The Hungarian intelligence

Aerial view of RFE/RL headquarters in Munich, from evidence used in trial of Johannes Weinrich in Berlin.

service electronically monitored this and other meetings. Swiss terrorist Bruno Breguet, code named Luca, had joined the group in September 1980, participated in the meeting, and possibly detonated the bomb at Radio Free Europe. This was his first action with the Carlos group.[13] The Carlos group discussed existing surveillance reports that detailed how the RFE/RL appeared on a Saturday night. Someone had obviously had already observed the RFE/RL Headquarters Building at 9:00 P.M. and 1:00 A.M. The surveillance report showed that about 40 percent of the rooms had lights on, and the observer estimated that 20 percent of the employees worked at 9:00 P.M. When the bomb exploded Saturday night at 9:50 P.M., only forty employees were in the building, out of a staff of almost one thousand. Their surveillance report was wrong in the estimated numbers of employees. Nevertheless, it shows that Carlos's intent was to bomb the building with a minimum amount of casualties. Carlos decided that his team would go to Munich in November and wait for the explosives, weapons, and other logistics necessary to carry out the attack. Further surveillance also would be required. Carlos, Weinrich, and Kopp then traveled to Bucharest on October 29, 1980, for a week's stay.

On December 19, 1980 in Budapest, Carlos and Johannes Weinrich had a heated discussion about the bombing. Carlos said wanted to do it Christmas Eve or on Christmas Day because no one would expect a bomb attack on those days. Weinrich agreed in principle, but said that they were not ready, as they did not have the cars they required, and suggested New Year's Eve.

Weinrich then told Carlos that when he and the Swiss terrorist Bruno Breguet were doing surveillance of RFE/RL earlier that month he had stopped to urinate against one of the trees on the RFE/RL grounds. Two guards were walking in his direction and saw him, but they did not say anything and kept going around the building. He noticed that one guard had a bunch of keys in one hand and a flashlight in the other. Because he had been seen, Weinrich told Carlos that he needed a new coat or the same guard might recognize him when they returned to bomb the building. Weinrich said he would not shoot the guard first. Carlos asked, "Why not?" Weinrich answered that the shooting would draw unnecessary attention to them, and that a lighted Christmas tree blocked the view of guard anyway. Weinrich told Carlos that even if the bomb were discovered before it exploded, if anyone tried to move it, it would explode anyway, and the CIA would know just how professional their work was.[14]

The original time for the bombing was scheduled to be 10:15 P.M. Weinrich told Carlos that he had plotted out that he and Bruno Breguet would need twelve minutes to get to the train station and head off from Munich in different directions. If they were discovered on the train, they would have alibis. Breguet would take the train to Nuremberg, where he would change to

Aerial view of RFE/RL headquarters showing Munich skyline, from 1950s (Radio Free Europe/Radio Liberty).

a train that would arrive from Switzerland on the way to Berlin. He would exchange tickets with a helper who was on that train, and Breguet would than continue to Berlin as if he had been on that train the whole time. Carlos told him that this was a great idea.[15]

Carlos and the others in the Group left Budapest on January 30, 1980. Taking advantage of the terrorists' absence, Hungarian counterintelligence officers entered Carlos's apartment the next day and discovered new documentation about the bomb preparation. Included in the documentation that had been brought to Budapest by the Euskedi Ta Askatasuna (ETA) terrorist Luk Edgar Groven ("Erik"), were sketches of RFE/RL. But it was not clear from this document when the bombing would take place.

Carlos set February 14, 1981, as the date for the bombing. Carlos went to Bucharest at the end of January 1981 and remained there until February 3. Due to the fact that the ETA could not provide the necessary vehicles for the Valentine's Day bombing, the attack was postponed for one week. Carlos called "Andrei" in Bucharest on February 13, 1981, and in guarded terms told him that there was a delay in "Steve's" activities: "Steve cannot travel to Bucharest this weekend but will travel a few days later."

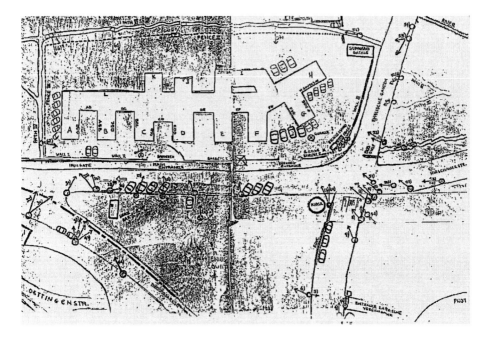

Copy of drawing Carlos the Jackal used to bomb RFE/RL (author's collection).

On February 19, 1980, Weinrich telephoned Carlos and told him that the bombing would now take place on Sunday, February 22: "I am having bank transfer problems but that should be resolved by Sunday morning." The next morning Carlos called Nica and told him of the new date and time of the bombing: "Steve will come to Bucharest Sunday morning. He will telephone at 10 A.M. with the exact time."[16]

Bombing Details

There was very little physical security at RFE/RL; because of Munich city restrictions, only three 50-watt light bulbs illuminated the building's exterior. Munich's regulations prevented exterior lighting from disturbing the neighborhood. On the night of the bombing, only a few offices were lit, so the terrorists' route along the building's perimeter was in shadows. The office lights in the immediate area illuminated the exact location where the bomb was placed.

There were two external contract security guards employed then at RFE/RL: one acted as a parking lot attendant, the other did infrequent patrols around the building. The RFE/RL security guard worked as a receptionist in the building. The external security guard's patrol lasted at least eighteen minutes and only occurred once an hour. His last patrol in the exact corner of the building where the bomb was placed was at 9:18 P.M. He did not notice anything unusual. The bomb attack on RFE/RL was the only physical attack in over forty years of history of the building. There had been no warning or threats, so the guards were not on high alert.

On Saturday night, February 21, 1981, the temperature was below freezing in Munich. Snow covered the grounds around the sprawling two-story building. All evidence points to four members of Carlos's gang physically involved in the bombing:

- Johannes Weinrich (code-named Steve) from German terrorist group Revolutionary Cells
- Bruno Breguet (Luca) from the Swiss terrorist group Primea Linea
- Jose Maria Larretxea (Schep) from the Basque terrorist group ETA
- A yet unidentified woman (Secretary) from ETA.

No one observed the men as they left their car parked in the shadows directly across from the target. The bomb was placed securely against the one of the wings of the largely empty building. The three men quickly left the building grounds, returned to their cars, and drove away.

Just above the area where the terrorists placed the bomb, three employees of RFE's Czech Language Service were busily preparing a news program scheduled for 10 P.M. that would never be aired. At 9:50 P.M., one employee picked up the ringing telephone and said, "Hello." No one answered. The employee again said, "Hello." The room suddenly exploded into rubble. How the bomb actually exploded, whether through a timer or through a radio transmitter, is not known. Police investigators later were unable to determine just how it was done, due to the total destruction of the bomb. The time was later confirmed by a German agency used to monitor earthquakes. The bombing was so powerful it had registered on the equipment.

Part of the large building was in shambles. Earthquake monitors didn't hear the screams of the injured employees. The two Basque terrorists stopped about three hundred yards from the damaged building and changed cars. They left behind a 1968 white Ford with French license plates that had been stolen in the night of February 20–21, in Strasbourg. Six months later, Munich police towed the car as abandoned. When they opened the driver's door, they discovered five Soviet Koveshnikov F-1 hand grenades in the console between the front seats. These grenades were of the same type used by Carlos in the 1970s in Paris.

Breguet made his way to Berlin via a train from Munich and Nurnberg, where he switched trains and was given a ticket purchased in Switzerland to give him an alibi at the time of the bombing. The German terrorist Johannes

Author's photograph of February 1981 bomb damage.

Weinrich took the train to Switzerland, and the two ETA members also left Germany. Months of careful preparation in Budapest, Hungary, had paid off.

The bomb's concussion caused extensive damage and terror in the immediate area: windows were shattered in 50 percent of RFE/RL's office building (more than 170) and in buildings more than one hundred yards from RFE/RL headquarters. The sound of the bomb blast was heard throughout most of Munich. Damage to the building exceeded two million dollars. Two persons in the neighborhood and four RFE/RL employees were seriously injured. One female employee's face was blown away in the blast; over subsequent years, she had over twenty operations to repair her face. She died in 2003, permanently scarred both physically and emotionally because of the injuries she suffered.

On Sunday, February 22, 1981, Nica called at 9:21 A.M. and asked Carlos if there was anything new and when would Carlos next be coming to Bucharest. Carlos answered that everything was in perfect order but that he had not slept the whole night and that he would call back as soon as he confirmed with "Steve" that everything was okay.

That evening at 6:00 P.M., ETA leader Luc Eric Groven (code-named "Erik") called Carlos, happily congratulated him, and said that Schep and the

Top: External view of 1981 bomb damage (author's collection). *Bottom:* External view of 1981 bomb damage (author's collection).

Internal view of 1981 bomb damage, showing Czech broadcast office where the three staff members were seriously injured (author's collection).

Secretary were safe and healthy. Carlos told him to pass on his greetings to them. "Erik" told him he could personally do that when Carlos met them the next time. Carlos said that the bombing had taken too much of his time recently and that he'd had to postpone other matters. But it was now over. He noted that the twentieth-six Communist Party Conference in Moscow was coming up and said that the bombing would give them something to think about.

Afterward, Weinrich called Carlos from Switzerland and said, "I met my family yesterday and everything is fine.... Everything is in order. All members of the family [have] returned from their short vacation and are home."

On March 6, 1981, Carlos flew to Bucharest, where Colonel Sergiu Nica, and others of the dreaded Romanian intelligence service, reluctantly toasted him with champagne for his performance, even though, according to their wishes, he was not successful. Nica was visibly upset but Carlos did not seem to notice it. Nica raised a glass of champagne and ironically toasted Carlos, "Usually I kill for money but this time I kill for nothing. Narok!" (Cheers!)[17] Carlos smiled throughout the toast, as he did not get the irony. Nica apparently knew about the story of Carlos and one of his friends in the 1970s. Carlos had visited a friend one morning and, holding a gun to his head, said:

"Do you remember the movie where the cowboy says 'I kill you for money, I kill you for a woman, and I kill you for nothing because you are my friend.'" Carlos then put the gun down and hugged his friend. He was only joking.[18]

Carlos did not have an ideological or political reason to bomb RFE/RL. His motivation was pragmatic: Romanian financial and logistical support. Carlos had apparently become a hired gun for Romanian dictator Nicolae Ceausescu.

After a few weeks of rest and recreation in Bucharest, Carlos returned to Budapest to face difficult times with his Hungarian hosts. Swiss-born Georgio Bellini, listed by Stasi as one member of his gang, had been arrested in Germany before the bombing, and one Stasi officer wrote: "He had been informed about the preparation and execution of the attack against Radio Free Europe. Should he reveal what he knows, great dangers for the Socialist States as well would follow." He did not reveal anything, and there was no cause to keep him in jail in connection with the bombing, so he was released and returned to Switzerland. Years later he denied any knowledge of the bombing in sworn statements to Swiss and German prosecutors. Magdalena Kopp backed this up in her own sworn statements to both prosecutors.

Lilly and Luca Arrested in Paris

Almost one year to the day after the bombing of RFE/RL, Magdalena Kopp and Bruno Breguet were arrested in Paris, presumably on their way to another tango. In the trunk of the car in which they were arrested, police found five kilograms of explosives and a map of Paris. Carlos threatened the French government with retaliation if the two were not released within thirty days. To prove he was serious, Carlos carried out his threat with a bomb attack on the Paris-Toulon Express train. Five persons died. The current French President Jacques Chirac had been scheduled to ride on that train but had canceled his reservations shortly before the train's departure. The day the trial of Kopp and Breguet began, a car bomb in Paris exploded, killing one and seriously wounding sixty-three persons.

Officially, the French court was not intimidated and sentenced Kopp to four years imprisonment and Breguet to five. Yet, after Carlos's arrest, controversy broke out in France over the question of whether they were given lesser sentences because of Carlos's bombing attacks.

Carlos and his group continued their terrorist activity against French interests in December 1983: a suitcase bomb exploded at the Marseilles railroad station, killing two persons and wounding forty-five. That same month, a bomb exploded aboard the French "bullet train," killing three and injured four. The next month, a bomb blast at the French Cultural Center in Tripoli, Lebanon, killed one person.

Magdalena Kopp and Bruno Breguet were released from French prison in 1985. Breguet returned to Switzerland where he apparently gave up the terrorist life. Magdalena Kopp first went to Germany and then to Venezuela to stay with Carlos's family.

Discord between Carlos, Romania, and Other Socialist States

Because of the RFE/RL bombing, Carlos had become a liability for the socialist countries. He was called to the Hungarian Ministry of Interior where he was warned that western secret services and Interpol were actively seeking him and his group. For these reasons, Carlos was told that he and his group should leave Eastern Europe within the next two to four months. He would be allowed to export his weapons, explosives, and other materials. Carlos's residence permit in Hungary was withdrawn. His group would be allowed to move from Hungary and only stay for short periods in Budapest.

On April 24, 1980, Colonel Varga, the Hungarian liaison officer with the Carlos group, traveled to Berlin to see the bombing of RFE/RL. On April 29, 1981, Stasi officers wrote a top-secret summary report. The cover sheet, also top secret, was a memo from Major General Neiber, Stasi Deputy Minister, to GDR Interior Minister Mielke. Neiber wrote:

> Enclosed I present to you the report of Department XXII on the consultation held in Berlin on 24–25 April 1981 with Comrade Lieut.-Col. VARGA, head of Department 8 in Main Administration No. 2 in the fraternal organ of the Hungarian People's Republic, concerning the "Separat" operation.
>
> Comrade VARGA handed over "Documentation on the preparation of an attack by 'Separat' on Radio 'Free Europe' in Munich, whose contents were surreptitiously acquired by the Hungarian comrades."
>
> On our part, consultations are going to continue to be held, as regards further proceedings, with the Cuban comrades and with the KGB of the USSR. It is intended to examine with the Cuban comrades whether a perspective in Latin America, acceptable to the members of "Separat," can be offered to them.[19]

The Interior Minister returned the report with a hand-written note on the cover page: "Agreed. Mielke." On May 4, 1981, a copy of the six-page Varga report was sent to the head of Division X, with this cover letter:

> Comrade Major-General Neiber has instructed that you be given a copy of the report of Division XXII on the consultations held on 24–25 April 1981 with Comrade Lieutenant-Colonel Varga of the Hungarian fraternal organ.

The Comrade Minister received the original; he has given his agreement to the proposal of the Hungarian comrades not to hold multilateral consultations now concerning the "Separat" problem, or further consultations with the Cuban comrades and the KGB of the USSR, either.

It is intended to investigate, with the Cuban comrades, whether a perspective in Latin America, acceptable to the members of "Separat," can be offered to them.

The documentation handed over by the Hungarian comrades concerning the preparation of an attack on Radio "Free Europe" in Munich has been evaluated by Division XXII and filed with the "Separat" operation.[20]

The Hungarians had asked for a "multilateral consultation" with other Warsaw Pact countries on this issue. In May 1981, a joint-intelligence decision was made to "investigate, with Cuban comrades," whether or not they could convince the Carlos group to move his base of operations to Cuba; he refused. The Stasi files show that the various intelligence services decided to act cautiously, because of a fear that Carlos and his group would seek revenge or move over to "the enemy camp."

One participant of this high-level meeting was Major Helmut Voigt, chief of Department XXII/8 of the Stasi — the department responsible for terrorism in the former East Germany. Voigt played a liaison role in the activities of the Carlos group in the early 1980s, using the code name Helmut. After the fall of the Berlin Wall in November 1989, Voigt first went underground in Germany and then fled to Greece, where he was eventually arrested and extradited to Germany for successful prosecution by the German government.

The Czechoslovak Intelligence Service (StB) and the Soviet KGB agreed with the Hungarians, and Bulgarian intelligence service approval came later. The Cuban security organ representatives in Budapest also were told about the planned measures.

Carlos was called to the Hungarian Ministry of Interior where he would be confronted with disclosure of the violations of Hungarian law he and his group committed. Carlos would be warned that western secret services and Interpol were actively seeking him and his group. The two-hour meeting with Carlos and Weinrich was recorded with a hidden camera. Unfortunately, only a few minutes of this meeting somehow survived and that was of poor quality. The sometimes-heated discussion was in Russian. At one point, Carlos was handed a forged Interpol report identifying Carlos and his group in Budapest. Carlos reportedly asked the Hungarian counterintelligence officers to provide him with "information about where and why the western secret services [were] searching for him and his men."[21]

Andras Petresevitis, Hungarian Counterintelligence deputy director told him,

I cannot say more than this at the moment. According to my judgment, my briefing, your situation is assessable. What's more, it can also be understood why we have arrived at this decision, that the Budapest headquarters base must be liquidated. Because you should not direct, organize the activity of groups. You are not safe here. If you are discovered, the actions too are endangered. I think you feel responsibility for all your people, for yourself. I hope this is clear. Should you continue from here, your group would be endangered. At the same time, it harms the interests of the Hungarian's Peoples Republic if we get involved. Therefore, we are informing you about the decision. You must liquidate your base. Thus we emphasize once more, our request is that you liquidate your base.

I emphasize that you will still be able to transmit, travel through Hungary. You may stay here for short periods. We do not limit your movement, activity. We do not interfere.[22]

Petresevitis described Carlos as "schizophrenic, full of fear and paranoia. However, at the same time it must be said that he is not stupid, or untrained. However, he is a very dangerous fanatic who is ready for anything out of vengeance." Carlos was told he and his group had to leave Eastern Europe within two to four months, but first he would be allowed to export his weapons, explosives, and other materials. Carlos was also told that, in 1990, Hungarian state television had broadcast a film shot secretly at a meeting between Carlos and Hungarian security agents in 1980. The agents told Carlos that the Hungarian authorities were displeased that he was amassing an arms stockpile. Carlos said: "This is only one-and-a-half tons. I had ten tons in Romania."[23]

During a televised interview in 1990 with the former director of counterintelligence, Miklos Redei, a reporter asked him, "Why did you not arrest Carlos? Why did you not liquidate him?" Redei replied,

To tell you frankly, it would have been very easy to arrest him, even at the expense of causalities. But we knew for certain that should proceedings or extradition of Carlos, or any other member of his group [have taken place], we would have provoked by this decision, and by the confrontation following our decision, the vengeance of the whole terrorist group — made up of more than a few members — against Hungary. This would have meant that they would have bombed any of our foreign embassies, that they would take hostages, bomb our planes, etc.[24]

Interestingly, before Soviet Communist leader Brezhnev's visit to West Germany in November 1981, Stasi officials asked Carlos not only to refrain from any terrorist action, but also to influence all other terrorist groups he had contact with, so that there would be no terrorist activity that might negatively influence the Brezhnev visit. This was not the first such instance. In February 1981, Stasi learned that neither Carlos nor other terrorist groups in

Europe planned terrorist activity during the twenty-sixth Congress of the Communist Party of the Soviet Union. Further, Stasi officials asked Carlos to use his influence with the leadership of the Armenian Liberation Front to tone down its anti–Soviet activity; he told the Stasi officials that he did so. A Stasi document sums up this episode:

> In the context of its political and intelligence operations aimed at the struggle against and gathering of information about terrorist forces, groups, and organizations, the MfS (the Ministry for State Security) did not learn about plans or intentions of terrorist groups to act against the interests of the Soviet Union and particularly against the preparations and the carrying out of the XXVI party congress of the Communist Party of the Soviet Union (CPSU).
>
> According to the information of the MfS, there is currently no proof of efforts by imperialist intelligence services to use their moles in terrorist organizations to plan and implement anti-soviet activities, or activities directed against the party congress.
>
> Thorough operational checks of extreme-leftist terror organizations, such as the "Red Army Faction," the "Revolutionary Cells," the "Group of International Revolutionaries" (called: "Carlos" group), the "ETA," and the "Movement 2 June" revealed no such activities.
>
> As to the so-called "Armenian Liberation Front" which has carried out anti–Soviet activities in the past, we have no information. It was only possible to learn that "Carlos" personally maintains contact with the organization; he made it clear in a discussion with leading members of the organization, that he succeeded in reducing the anti–Soviet attitudes of the organization.[25]

Weinrich told Carlos in one letter that his financial situation was so critical that he seriously considered asking his parents in Germany for a loan of 50,000 to 100,000 DM. Financial problems also continued to haunt Carlos in August 1983, as he wrote to Weinrich:

> I will use the French intervention in Chad as a pretext to restart cooperation (with Libya). I have not waited any longer, because all my money is finished with Feisals's trip (he takes $2000 for you and $500 reserve). There is left only the $15,000 reserve.... Also cut down unnecessary movements.

In the same letter, Carlos gives further details of his Romanian connection:

> Get from Bucharest all the papers and photographs regarding the old Jewish woman in Rome who you once phoned. I think we should engage ourselves in this affair next month after her return from holidays.... Please remember that this is a one million dollars business!
>
> Regarding Andrei: 2 days after your leaving Bucharest, Andrei phoned me here himself, to warn us from the Saudis; he spoke in a way nobody else could understand: "the Saudis are very angry (with us), they are searching very well all vehicles and luggage coming into the country, specially from Lebanon, we must be very careful...." When I asked him why he did not inform you, he answered that he had just received the information.[26]

Bombing in Berlin

On May 31, 1983, Weinrich flew from Bucharest to East Berlin using a Syrian diplomatic pass with the name Heinrich Schneider. His baggage was searched and 24.3 kilograms of the Romanian plastic explosive Netropinta were found. A computer check of Weinrich showed his connection to the Carlos group. A Stasi officer came to the airport and released Weinrich, but not the explosives. For the next weeks, Weinrich unsuccessfully tried to get Stasi to release the explosives. He stayed at the Intercontinental Hotel in East Berlin until June 10, 1983, when he flew back to Bucharest; it is not known when he returned to East Berlin. The plastic explosives stayed under the control of Major Helmut Voigt of Department XXII who as "Helmut" was the Stasi contact man for the Carlos group.

Even though papers found on Weinrich in May indicated that an attack was planned on the French Consulate and Cultural Center in West Berlin, after months of further discussion between Voigt and Weinrich the explosives were released to Weinrich on August 16, 1983. He in turn gave them to Nabil Shritah, the third secretary of the Syrian embassy, for safekeeping. A week later, Weinrich went to the embassy and retrieved the explosives.

The explosives were then carried to West Berlin in a car driven by Abul Hakam, the Arab nations contact man of Carlos's group. In West Berlin, the driver met a Lebanese member of the Carlos, named Ahmad el–Sibai. El-Sibai placed the explosive in a building next to the French Cultural Center and on August 25, 1983, at 11:50 A.M., the bomb went off. Damage was estimated to be in excess of 2.5 million DM; one person was killed and 23 were injured.

Abul Hakam flew to Budapest and El-Sibai flew to Damascus the next day. Weinrich remained in East Berlin for one day and then flew to Belgrade, Yugoslavia. There he wrote a 27-page letter in English to Carlos, wherein he described the bombing of the French Cultural Center in Berlin:

> Belgrade 29 August 83
> Dearest Michel
>   1) OPERATION BERLIN
>   Regarding Helmet, it is clear that we could trick them, mainly on behalf of the help given by Nabil. By the way: he knows about the Operation but as he told and suggested me, not officially.... Because he gave me the hand in keeping explosives without informing the Ambassador, who was absent, but came back before the Operation. So officially, Nabil doesn't know about the Operation, only the fact that I brought a bag and took it later.
>   Helmet was always warning us, not to have an operation in West going directly from East and returning. We always denied and kept the cover of only transporting the bag to the West. They seemed to me on Friday — last meeting with them — not to be sure, if we have done it or the ASALA [Armenian

Secret Army for the Liberation of Armenia]. In addition, I kept the story: telling them in a way that ASALA never claimed an operation, if not carried out by them.

We did what we wanted, they have tried to sabotage all the time but surely there was no way out.

They will learn (perhaps) their lesson, when they get the news about official confirmation that it was ours. Moreover, mainly: I do not intend to use Berlin for a very, very long time, which will be the best lesson for them.

I did not intend to report on that in such length, but I think, you can grasp the picture and will agree with the conclusion to plan everything in a way, that we can avoid Helmet.

The Operation itself had bigger impact than I've expected. I sent you the pictures for showing to Omar — if you want — but please send them back by next occasion.[27]

Weinrich, obviously, understood the necessity of keeping the Carlos myth alive, when he wrote that someone

has asked me if it is true what he heard that recently you and me had a kind of disagreement and split the organization. I only laughed as an answer ... denying it by saying: it is good for us that the rumors ... are growing unlimited.

Obviously there are rumors ... going around.

Think about it, if we can play with it, for example, on behalf of our position regarding socialist countries ... to confuse them ... we will talk about it....

They do think you are in Bucharest.... My reply was, we are everywhere and nowhere in the same time, one can find us only in the underground.[28]

Operation Tourist

On June 10, 1986, Carlos flew from Budapest to Prague, using the name of Wattar Walid. Accompanying him were Magdalena Kopp, who was then pregnant, using the name of Maria Aziz, and Johannes Weinrich, who used the name Radwand Farid. They carried Syrian diplomatic passports and Czechoslovak visas valid for three days. The Czechoslovak regime wanted Carlos to leave the country and set up a surveillance operation called Operation Tourist. Czechoslovak intelligence officers confronted Carlos in a hotel. According to one officer who later was interviewed by a Czech magazine:

Carlos came back with a case from the safe. He opened it and without a problem started counting the money in it. For the first time in my life, I saw what a million dollars looked like in one hundred dollar bills.... Later it was found that it had been a reward from Ceausescu, for "work" performed by Carlos.

A certain agreement, a status quo, existed between people of his kind and our (Party) leadership if they didn't cause trouble and were spending hard currency, they were free to rest here for a while. I think "Carlos" was trying to find a quiet spot where his girlfriend could later give birth.[29]

As a ruse, the Czechoslovak intelligence officers told Carlos that French intelligence was after him because of his activity in Paris, and that their men were already in Prague. Carlos, Kopp, and their Palestinian bodyguard were quickly escorted onto a waiting airplane scheduled for Moscow. All three were heavily armed and allowed to carry their weapons on the plane, because of their Czech intelligence officer escort who later described what happened:

> One final unpleasant incident took place on the plane. As Carlos' bodyguard was bending down for the suitcase, his gun fell out. I noticed it and so did the flight attendant. She nearly fainted. It's easy to talk about it now but back then I had a split second decision to make. I realized that if I tried to hand the gun back to him he might interpret this as an attack and use the other to knock me off—these people can be fast when it comes to this. So I said: "Look, you dropped something." "Sorry" he replied, picked up the gun and hid it. I told the stewardess that it was only a dummy, that it had been arranged and that she should keep it to herself.[30]

Carlos and Kopp transited Moscow with their weapons and flew to Damascus, Syria, where their child was born. For the next five years, they were apparently inactive in the international terrorist scenes. Magdalene flew to Venezuela with their child and stayed with Carlos's family. Some journalists even speculated that Carlos had died in Libya. The German intelligence service, BND, routinely intercepted Kopp's mail and telephone calls to her family in southern Germany. So her location was not a secret. Reportedly Weinrich proudly drove a Mercedes in Damascus and had it serviced regularly at the Mercedes dealership. He regularly attended parties given by prominent German citizens in Damascus.

Arrest of Carlos

Syria, submitting to international criticism as a government involved in state-sponsored terrorism, somehow convinced Carlos to leave in 1990. He had apparently become persona non grata with his former sponsors. Carlos had problems settling in a friendly country. Both Iraq and Libya, also under intense international pressure, refused him refuge. Carlos settled in southern Yemen with his wife and child. Civil war erupted in Yemen in 1993, and Carlos learned that Palestinian factions protecting and supporting him would be transferred to Gaza and Jericho to take part in the Palestinian autonomy preparations. Carlos decided to seek refuge in the Sudan.

The Sudan was listed for years by the U. S. State Department as one country that harbored international terrorists. But in 1994, Carlos had become expendable for the Sudanese officials. The Central Intelligence Agency located Carlos and French officers arrested him in Khartoum in August 1994 and transported him to Paris.[31] In December 1997, Ramirez-Sanchez played out his role as Carlos, the professional revolutionary, and shortly held center stage during his trial in Paris. The jury was not swayed with his histrionics and revolutionary rhetoric: he was found guilty and sentenced to life imprisonment for killing two French secret agents and their Lebanese informer in 1975. Carlos buzzed around like an autumn fly before he faded irretrievably into the history books.

Magdalena Kopp and their daughter were living in Venezuela with Carlos's family. She flew to the Sudan and paid Carlos's outstanding bills. She took possession of his personal belongings and returned to Caracas. In December 1995, she voluntarily returned to Germany.

Johannes Weinrich was arrested in a suburb of Aden, Yemen, and extradited in June 1995 to Germany. The details of Weinrich's arrest were shrouded. One Yemeni official said he had been arrested "several months after the end of the civil war in Yemen in July 1994." He was using a Somali passport in the name of John Saleh. He also had a passport with the name Peter Smith. German authorities, on the other hand, said he had been arrested on June 1, 1995, after a long German-led investigation.

Hungarian Investigation

On July 7, 1991, Hungary's supreme state prosecutor suspended a year-long investigation of possible formal Hungarian support for the international terrorist Carlos, who used Hungary as a base between 1979 and 1985. Hungarian media reported that the investigation was suspended "because it would be necessary to question members of the 'Carlos' group in order to clarify if any Hungarian officials acted as accomplices or abettors in terrorist activities. The whereabouts of 'Carlos,' who has been implicated in several major terrorist acts, is uncertain."

Even though the media reports showed that the Hungarian government halted its investigation in July, on September 24, 1991, RFE/RL wrote the following letter to Dr. Gyoergyi Kalman, chief prosecutor of Hungary, with a copy to the Hungarian Minister of Interior Dr. Peter Boross:

> In July 1990, your office publicly announced an investigation into the activities of the terrorist group "Carlos" in Hungary. Inter alia, the investigation was to examine evidence that, while they were in Budapest, the "Carlos" group planned the 1981 bombing of RFE/RL. In addition, money, arms, and

explosives were reportedly given to the "Carlos" group before their traveling to Munich, and the group returned to Budapest after successfully bombing RFE/RL.

In May 1991, it was announced that the investigation was completed. Since RFE/RL was extensively damaged, and several employees were seriously injured, I am respectfully asking you for the results and details of your investigation.

Kalman's answer to RFE/RL, dated November 15, 1981, was clear:

On 28 June 1991, we suspended our investigation in the case of Ramirez Ilyich Sanchez ("Carlos") and accomplices suspected of several attempted murders and other crimes, because the suspects are abroad and the steps taken to locate them had not been successful.

The suspicion that the bombing of the building of RFE/RL had been carried out by "Carlos's terrorist group could not be proved or disproved in the course of the investigation. We have informed the German authorities accordingly.[32]

Partly for this reason, and partly because we are not supposed to divulge information to private persons, I am afraid I cannot let you have the unconfirmed data.[33]

Kalman's letter later sent to the Bavarian state prosecutor was more detailed:

The operative investigation findings, made during the stay in Hungary of the tourists "Carlos" and his life partner Magdalena Kopp ("Lily"), whose name is also on your files, contain data indicating that the "Carlos" team carried out the attack aimed against "SZER" respectively by members of other terrorist organizations connected with them.

"Carlos" and "Lily" were staying in Budapest on the days before and after the attack. Their comrades directly involved in the attack called "Carlos" on the telephone and informed him about the execution of the attack and the escape route. Accordingly, the attack, planned by "Carlos" was led at the scene of the crime by Johann Weinrich ("Steve"), citizen of the FRG; Bruno Breguet, Swiss citizen and member of the Swiss terrorist organization "Prima Linea," detonated the explosive device. Cooperating in the provision of the means necessary to the explosion were also: Lud Edgar Groven ("Erik"), Belgian citizen, Lopez de Monteverde ("Santiago"), Spanish citizen, both members of the militant division of the Basque terrorist organization "ETA," as well as additional terrorists.

The tapes recorded during the tapping of the telephone calls mentioned are unfortunately no longer available, since after a certain lapse of time they were erased and reused as ordinary recording tapes.

It was not possible either to substantiate or to contradict the operative material that came to light in the course of the investigations conducted by us and disclosed above. Therefore, the data mentioned cannot be used as authentic evidence in a criminal procedure.[34]

RFE and SRI

After RFE/RL sent the September letter to the Hungarian prosecutor's office, one was sent to the prosecutor general of Romania, with copies to the director of the Romanian domestic intelligence service, Servicivi Roman de Informatii (SRI), Virgil Magureanu, and the Romanian interior minister:

> In February 1981, there was a bomb attack directed against Radio Free Europe/Radio Liberty. Employees were injured, and damage to the building was extensive. It has been reported that this was a terrorist act sponsored by the former Romanian President Nicolae Ceausescu. Media reports purport that Nicolae Ceausescu paid one million dollars to the terrorist known as "Carlos" to bomb RFE/RL, and commit other acts of terrorism against both the corporation and employees of Romanian origin.
>
> We are not yet free from the fear of the repetition of terrorist acts.
>
> Therefore, we are asking you to kindly investigate the above-mentioned case, and to find out
>
> 1. whether this attack was carried out in collaboration with the Romanian secret services, and
> 2. if there were any employees of RFE/RL who delivered information to the former Romanian secret services.[35]

A partial answer came in a phone call from SRI Director Magureanu to the then director of the RFE/RL Romanian service, Nicolae Stroescu. Magureanu told him that he believed Ceausescu was behind the bomb attack on RFE/RL in 1981. He added that RFE/RL and he were "partners," and that the bombing must be investigated. Moreover, he would lead an investigation into it and "as soon as possible" send the results of his investigation.

RFE/RL waited nine months for his answer. Because of the long delay, RFE/RL sent Magureanu another letter in June 1992: "According to information received from Hungarian, Czechoslovak, and former East German government sources, the famous terrorist named 'Carlos' was supposedly paid one million dollars or was promised one million dollars in August 1979, to silence the Romanian 'Opposition' in the West."

Two months later, SRI Director Magureanu sent RFE/RL an answer, which read in part:

> After the death sentence, in absentia, was passed on ex-general Mihai Pacepa, formerly deputy head of the General External Information Department, with the rank of State Secretary of the Ministry of Internal Affairs, in 1979, the terrorist Iliych Ramirez Sanchez, alias Carlos, was contacted and approached to help in carrying out the sentence.
>
> Carlos did not offer definite assurances beyond stating that "he would study the problem."
>
> The emissaries who contacted him in Prague were carrying $10,000, but because of the opulence displayed by Carlos, they considered the amount of

money they possessed much too modest to tempt a terrorist, and more they could not promise.

2). Although the Securitate External units had the task of neutralizing the most active members of the station, there is no indication that the former Securitate was involved in the attack of February 21, 1981 against RFE.

STASI documents, in your possession, which give evidence that the Ceausescu regime had been involved in that attempt might simply be the result of the habit of attributing to one of the most reactionary regimes in Eastern Europe all crimes that had taken place during that period.

In fact, in these crimes or criminal attempts, regimes were involved that when compared to the one in Romania, appeared more liberal, given the limits of Communist regimes.[36]

In October 1993, there was a meeting between RFE/RL representatives and Virgil Magureanu. Among the topics of discussion were Carlos and the bomb attack on RFE/RL. With Magureanu were three of his top aides, one of whom had a "Carlos" file with him. He presented three volumes of the Securitate files entitled "Carlos," dossier number 110 486, for the years 1977, 1978, and 1988 (ending on June 10, 1988).

The files for the years 1977 and 1978 were about an inch and a half thick. The 1988 files were about two and a half inches. There were numerous newspaper articles about Carlos and some reports. The SRI colonel adamantly insisted that there was no evidence that Carlos was ever in Romania. There was summary report of Carlos's activities up to 1988, but that contained only sketchy information. There was no mention of the bombing of RFE/RL in the Carlos files — or any mention of RFE/RL at all in these files.

The SRI colonel insisted that these were the only known files on Carlos. He did admit the possibility of other files in the CIE archives, Communist Party archives, or Ceausescu's personal files, but these have not yet been discovered. He said that it was possible that Carlos did visit Romania, but under disguise and under another name. The colonel said they thought that the Carlos gang was impenetrable, and therefore no one could have known their activities. RFE/RL had previously sent them a copy of a letter from the Stasi files on Carlos where there was mention of the "one million dollar contract with Romania." He said SRI experts had analyzed this letter and determined it was a forgery. He was told that it was not believable that the former Stasi would have a complete file on Carlos, and include forged letters as disinformation against Romania. The colonel just shrugged his shoulders and ended the discussion.

After returning to Munich, RFE/RL faxed Magureanu, thanking him for his hospitality but complaining:

> The three officers ... were apparently not ready to ... to have an honest discussion about the past activities of the Securitate and the External Service. This is not to say that they were not professional in their attitude and behavior —

they were and should be commended. But, much of their information contradicted some of the information you had presented earlier — for example information about "Carlos" in Prague in 1979. However, there was an agreement that the investigation into past Securitate and External Service activity directed against RFE/RL would be continued, and perhaps these contradictions will be resolved in the near future.[37]

Two weeks later, RFE/RL sent Magureanu another message:

One more pawn to sacrifice in our chess game: some details.
From the former Stasi files about "Carlos" and the connection to the former "Securitate."
I am sure you can find someone in the SRI to give you exact translations. But before
you get the translations; let me share with you a few very important points:
1. "Carlos" and his girlfriend Magdalena KOPP ("Lilly") had continual contact with a "Securitate" officer named Andre VICESCU, Bucharest Telephone number, 111 969
2. "Securitate" offered sanctuary to the "Carlos" group (Code name "Separat") and provided weapons and false documents
3. "Carlos" himself was in Bucharest in February 1981 and in November 1981 — he used telephone number, 136 469
It is clear to RFE/RL and others interested in this problem, that the Ceausescu government at the highest level not only encouraged "Carlos" in his terrorist activities but also acted together with other members of the Warsaw Pact to see that "Carlos" was successful.
If actual documentation (physical files) have been destroyed, most "Securitate" files were put on microfilm or made part of a computer data bank — perhaps one of the reasons why the "Carlos" file contained no information (or very little) for the years 1980 to 1986.
With all due respect to you, and knowing your other priorities, it is now your move.[38]

Magureanu promised to continue looking for more file information on Carlos. Magureanu resigned as director of the SRI in April 1997, without concluding his investigation.

Angela Nicolae, a spokeswoman for the public prosecutor's office in Bucharest, Romania, said in January 1998, "Prosecutors have started investigations into Carlos' connections with the Securitate." Switzerland sent intelligence information about Carlos and his gang to Romania, including videotapes of a meeting between Carlos and Weinrich.

In November 1998, Romanian Military Prosecutor Dan Voinea announced that a bank account number 47 11 210 350 2 in the Romania Bank of Foreign Trade had been discovered for Carlos and Magdalena Kopp, using the names "Michael Mallios" and Anna Louise Toto-Kramer respectively. Magdalena Kopp later wrote in her memoirs that Sergiu Nica broached the idea of opening an account for her and Carlos. She did so with a deposit of $1,000. According to Magdalena Kopp, the account never had more than that amount of money.[39] Also in November 1998, in a radio interview with Germany's international radio station Deutsche Welle, Voinea said that Carlos had received one million dollars for the bombing attack on RFE/RL. Voinea said that among Carlos's contacts in Romania were former Securitate chief General Iulian Vlad, former chief of the Securitate's foreign intelligence service General Nicolae Plesita, as well as former Romanian Interior Minister Tudor Postelnicu.

Where Are They?

In March 2003, the trial of Johannes Weinrich for his role in the bombing of RFE/RL began in Berlin. Magdalena Kopp was called as a state witness but refused to testify. However, in her various sworn statements to German prosecutors before the trial, she clearly identified Romanian intelligence involvement in the bombing of RFE/RL and confirmed that Carlos was praised in Bucharest after the bombing. She said that she was given the task of going to Bucharest in January 1980 to set up the relationship between the Romanian "secret police" and Carlos. She added that the group had received weapons and explosives, part of which went to the ETA. Because of her apparent cooperation with the German prosecutor's office, her legal status changed from "suspect" to "witness" in the bombing of RFE/RL. The presiding judge decided not to continue with the trial for the bombing as Weinrich was already serving a life sentence.

Jozsef Varga was the Hungarian intelligence officer who was the official liaison with Carlos. In sworn statements to both Hungarian and German investigators for the Weinrich trial, and in television interviews, he admitted meeting Carlos twenty to twenty-five times, mostly in the Wild Rose restaurant in Budapest. He said that he'd never discussed the bombing of RFE/RL, before or afterward, with Carlos or Johannes Weinrich. Interestingly, in one television interview, Varga said that the Hungarian officials notified their Soviet counterpart with the pre-bombing information. The Soviet officers in Budapest then said that they would pass the information on to the French to show goodwill and improve Soviet-French relations. Varga added that this information exchange was never confirmed.[40]

The myth about Bruno Breguet continued when one story surfaced in a usually reliable publication in late 1996 that Breguet was in French custody in post–Communist Budapest. He was being confronted with witnesses and documents, particularly concerning the implication of high French authorities in arms traffic to Algeria. This traffic supposedly involved high French ministerial officials and high regional officials in Nice. Reportedly, French DST (Direction de la surveillance du territoire) counter-espionage found him in Croatia and passed the information to the DGSE (Direction Générale de Sécurite Exterieune) foreign intelligence service that sent member of its Special Forces to capture Breguet and take him to Budapest. Breguet apparently cooperated with French intelligence and justice officials and has not publicly appeared since then.[41]

In a film documentary on the Romanian Service of Radio Free Europe released in November 2007 in Romania, Carlos in a telephone interview denied involvement in the bombing of RFE/RL: "We had nothing to do with that. That is not our level. If we had worked as agents, I think it would have been better to work for Saddam or the president of Libya, who had millions, right? The Romanians had nothing."[42]

Romanian Communist Party leader Nicolae Ceausescu, Securitate Code Name "Chief Architect," waged a vengeful personal war against the RFE Romanian Service. His side fought with intimidation, threats, and physical attack; the RFE/RL countered with the truth in the programs broadcast to Romania. The bombing of RFE/RL did not halt the broadcasting.

According to media reports in January 1998, General Nicolae Plesita, who directed the Romanian Foreign Intelligence Service between 1980 and 1984, acknowledged to the Romanian prosecutor's office that Carlos had been in Romania from 1980 to 1982. However, Plesita afterward refused to talk to reporters, telling them "Carlos is an issue too big for you." In 1996 and 1997 General Plesita was interviewed by German prosecutors who had traveled to Bucharest. He disclaimed any knowledge of the bombing and pointed his finger to Sergiu Nica as the one who would have been most involved with Carlos, because Nica had exclusive authority to deal with him. In other sworn statements to both Romanian and German prosecutors, Plesita could not recall meeting with Carlos. But Carlos remembered meeting Plesita. In an exclusive film interview, Carlos had this to say about Plesita:

> He was a nice guy. I like him a lot. He drank like a sponge, you know. We decided we could talk freely, the two of us. We walked in the park, where there were no microphones. Our conversation was difficult, as he did not speak Russian very well. But I considered him a nice guy. He offered me a gift for my birthday. He gave me two Soviet-made shotguns. I liked that a lot. It was like Che Guevara. We offered each other presents. It was the Latin spirit. It felt like home, it was good.[43]

5. Revenge of the Chief Architect: Ceausescu's War Against Radio Free Europe/Radio Liberty

> *To the despair of the communist regime, Radio Free Europe was indeed what it set out to be—the speaking newspaper for Romanians everywhere. I do homage to the memory of Ghita Ionescu, Mihai Cismarescu, Noel Bernard and Vlad Georgescu, men who fought with altruism and passion for the knowledge and utterance of the truth. I extol Monica Lovinescu and Virgil Ierunca, who, while physically in exile, continued to live every day for the Romanian people, keeping awake, through their unforgettable Free Europe broadcasts, the moral conscience of Romanians.* — Traian Basescu, President of Romania[1]

The Bastard: The Mysterious Death of Vlad Georgescu

Vlad Georgescu was a prestigious historian and dissident, who had a long history of trouble with the Securitate. Starting in 1974, the Securitate harassed him for criticizing the Ceausescu regime. He was accused of treason in 1977 and was jailed for writing several anti–Ceausescu essays and passing them on to the U.S. embassy for publication abroad. Because of U.S. government interest in his case, Vlad was allowed to leave Romania and travel to Washington, where he asked for and received political asylum. Shortly afterward, he became a contributor to RFE's broadcasts. Two years later, he was appointed associate director of RFE's Romanian Service and then became the department director based in Munich.

Nestor Ratesh, his eventual successor as director of RFE/RL's Romanian Service, best described Vlad's significance for RFE/RL:

> The Securitate had no illusions about his directorship. Right from the beginning, it started to prepare the conditions for his complete neutralization. The phrase appears the first time in a four-page plan of action dated June 25, 1982. It meant "liquidation." Numerous informers were sent to Munich to investigate Vlad's situation:

- his physical and mental health,
- his relationships within and outside the radio,
- his family circumstances and marital relations,
- his daily routine,
- where and how he was spending his free time and other such operational particulars,
- his ground-floor apartment, deemed to present security risks,
- the exact position of each piece of furniture, principally Vlad's desk, usually in conjunction with the windows and doors.
- The informers were to bring back detailed descriptions and sketches.
- Threatening telephone calls and letters, including some to his 8-year-old son, came in frequently.[2]

In December 1987, Vlad Georgescu (Securitate code name "Bastard"), then director of the Romanian Service, RFE/RL, loaned the RFE/RL security office his copy of the recently published book, *Red Horizons*, by Ion Mihai Pacepa. The book was highly critical of the cult of personality surrounding Romanian Communist Party leader Nicolae Ceausescu and his wife Elena. Pacepa, a former general of the Romanian external intelligence service (DIE), defected to the United States. Pacepa claimed in his book that he had inside knowledge of activities of the Romanian intelligence service against RFE/RL. These included

- bomb threats against RFE/RL,
- attacks and threats against RFE/RL Romanian Service employees, and
- the use of a secretary in the office of the director of Central News, Agent "Balthazar."[3]

Vlad Georgescu's sister-in-law, who lived in Romania, was due to visit Vlad. He aired his first review of the book on a Saturday in November. She was called into the Romanian intelligence service (Securitate) office on the Monday following the broadcast. The Securitate officer castigated Vlad for reviewing the book. He then told her that if Vlad allowed a reading of the book itself to be aired, he would be killed. She was allowed to leave Romania in order to give Vlad Georgescu this threatening message. Vlad was not intimidated and decided that the Romanian Service would begin broadcasting a reading of the book starting the week of January 5, 1988. The RFE/RL security office sent a risk report to senior management advising them to take this threat against Vlad Georgescu, and indirectly against RFE/RL, seriously.

On December 18, 1987, RFE/RL President Gene Pell expressed considerable concern about the broadcasts. He was even thinking about canceling the series: if RFE/RL canceled the book series, this would have been a political decision, rather than because of RFE/RL backing off due to the threats.

On December 29, 1987, the *New York Tribune* published a long article headlined "Book Exposing PLO-Romanian Intrigue and Scandals Said Targeted by Terrorists." The journalist wrote that the FBI was investigating a possible terrorist plot designed to disrupt distribution of the Pacepa memoirs. He went on to say there were at least three known death threats to those associated with the book, including RFE/RL employees. "Agents of the PLO are principal suspects in the threats against the book publishers and Radio Free Europe, the government defector says." This was the first information that the Palestinian Liberation Organization might be involved in any threats against RFE/RL.[4]

The Romanian Service broadcast the first of four programs on January 4, 1988. A week later there was a meeting in Vlad Georgescu's office to discuss the recent Romanian programs and what steps RFE/RL was taking regarding any security problems he and his staff might face. Four more programs were broadcast that week and four programs were broadcast the following week, for a total of twelve programs. After the broadcasts, Vlad Georgescu told the radio listeners: "If they kill me for serializing Pacepa's book, I'll die with the clear conscience that I did my duty as a journalist."[5]

FBI Investigation

On January 14, 1988, the legal attaché's office at the U.S. embassy in Bonn confirmed to RFE/RL that the FBI field office in Washington, D.C., was investigating the possibility of a PLO terrorist plot against the publisher of the Pacepa book. There was no confirmation that the FBI was investigating any PLO threat against RFE/RL or its staff.

The legal attaché's office sent off a report to the field office concerning the individual threat to Vlad Georgescu. The legal attaché said that RFE/RL would be kept informed, either directly from Bonn, or indirectly through the U.S. consulate in Munich (depending on the sensitivity of information). The general opinion of both the legal attaché's office and FBI headquarters was that the PLO had the means and, if given the opportunity, they would carry out the threats.

On January 25, 1988, Vlad Georgescu sent the following note to the RFE/RL Security Office:

> A previously unknown organization, called "Group in the Service of the Marshal" (Antonescu) in New York decided to sentence to death the ex-king Michael. The text and photographs were sent to him and to a member of the RFE/RL Romanian Research Section. More death sentences will follow, claims the leaflet, since "there are still many traitors running around." This was not the first time that similar threats were sent using the name of a rightist émigré organization. But, I had few doubts that the real address is in Bucharest."[6]

The letter had been postmarked in Paris. There were two color photographs of King Michael and his wife included. These were identical, except that one had been painted to show a bullet hole in the King's head with blood dripping down over his face; the other had been painted over to show blood on the King's hand. Michael had become King of Romania at age nineteen, after his father Carol II had abdicated during World War Two. In 1944, King Michael helped lead a coup against the pro–Nazi government. King Michael abdicated and fled Communist-ruled Romania in December 1947. While living in Switzerland, King Michael broadcast an annual Christmas message to Romania over Radio Free Europe. A copy of the letter with those of the photographs were given to the Munich police.

Threat Letter to RFE/RL

Tuesday, January 26, 1988, was Nicolae Ceausescu's seventieth birthday. He had been in power for twenty-three years. The cult of personality was in full force. Romania had only two hours of television per day. On this day, the two hours were devoted to adulation of the Ceausescu couple. "Choirs of factory workers and school children, in sunshine and bright costume, sang hymns of gratitude for his existence," according to Charles T. Powers, a *Los Angeles Times* reporter. The Romanian state media published glowing notes of congratulations from foreign leaders, including Britain's Queen Elizabeth, King Baudoin of Belgium, King Juan Carlos of Spain, and King Carl of Sweden. The notes were frauds. Notes of official protest followed the notes of congratulations.

The next day, a letter written in Arabic script was mailed in a typical international airmail envelope from Frankfurt, West Germany to "Mr. PELL, FREE EUROP (sic) RADIO, MUNCHEN." An airmail envelope was not required for mail within Germany. The director of RFE/RL's Radio Free Afghanistan broadcast service provided this translation:

> We are the Lights of the Islamic Revolution
> We are announcing that we [have] just started to eliminate workers of
> American Imperialism and Zionism
> And the first one was Siegfried Wielspuetz
> who we have already finished; and now comes your turn, and the
> turn of those guilty servants, who are running the different
> nationalities of your radio.[7]

Siegfried Wielspuetz, the third secretary of the German embassy in Paris, had been found shot to death on a footbridge by the Seine River in Paris on Monday, January 4, 1988. Police found a leaflet in one of his pockets, written by the Kurdish National Liberation Front, one arm of the Kurdish Worker's Party (PKK) based then in Damascus, Syria. The note detailed Kurdish complaints of mistreatment in West Germany. Two days before the death of Wiel-spuetz, a German charter plane crashed off the coast of Turkey. An anony-mous telephone caller to a news agency in London claimed both acts in behalf of the PKK. But, a spokesman of the PKK denied any responsibility and denounced the murder as a "cowardly act." German federal criminal police and French police conducted an investigation into his death. Though polit-ical motives were not completely ruled out, the police later theorized that Wielspuetz had built up heavy debts over eighteen months before his death and might have committed suicide. We did not know why the letter mailed to Gene Pell referred to Wieslpuetz.

Emil Hurezeanu then received his first direct telephone threat: "If you do not behave by mid–February, we will take care of you." This threat had been prerecorded and was automatically repeated several times.

Monday, February 1, 1988, the RFE/RL London News Bureau sent another translation of the letter by a British terrorist expert. There was a major difference from the original translation: the name of the group claim-ing responsibility for the letter:

> We, the EAGLES OF THE ISLAMIC REVOLUTION,
> announce that we have set out eliminating
> agents of American and Zionist Imperialism.
> Siegfried Wielspuetz was the first we got rid of.
> And now it is your turn, and the turn of the agents,
> who direct the nationalities section of your
> broadcast system.[8]

The term "Eagles of the Islamic Revolution" was similar to that of a known terrorist group called "Eagles of the Palestinian Revolution," a Syr-ian-backed Palestinian group, that claimed credit for the September 1973 ter-rorist action when terrorists boarded a train transporting Soviet Jewish emigrants at the Austrian border and held three of them hostage until the Aus-trian government agreed to close the Schoenau Castle transit facilities for Russian Jews. The group also took credit for the bombing of a synagogue in Vienna in April 1979. Two days later, German border police arrested two sus-pects on the German–Austrian border. Police then found more than one hun-dred pounds of explosives, time fuses, and eleven passports in their rented car. German authorities believed they were on their way to Hamburg, Ger-many, to bomb an Israeli ship in the harbor.

At the same time, on the German-Dutch border, border police arrested two more men, identified as Arabic, in a car with French license plates. The men had two forged Iranian passports they admitted they intended to give to the suspects in the synagogue bombing in Vienna. Police later identified the four men as Lebanese. A German court found them guilty of engaging in terrorist activities and sentenced them to jail. The last known terrorist act of "the Eagles of the Palestinian Revolution" was a 1985 bombing attack against moderate PLO members and supporters of Yassir Arafat in Western Europe.

The State Department political officer then telexed the new translation of the letter, with a request for a further opinion. On February 3, 1988, RFE/RL contacted Dennis Pluchinsky, then U.S. State Department's top expert on terrorism. His first reaction was that "there is no [such] known group. The death in Paris was reported to be suicide. There is no known, or apparent, reason for any "Islamic" group to go after RFE/RL or its personnel." He was told about the PLO threat to the publisher of the Pacepa book and threats to RFE/RL for broadcasting. He said that it could be an attempt by Romanian intelligence to divert attention away from any connection back to the Romanians, in the event that there was an attack on Mr. Pell or RFE/RL. Therefore, the danger was there.

On Wednesday, February 3, 1988, RFE/RL's Soviet Audience and Opinion Research (SAAOR) director in Paris gave French authorities a copy of the threatening letter, with a request for any information on the group and possible connection to the German diplomatic officer's death.

The RFE/RL post office was instructed to screen carefully all mail addressed to Mr. Pell, or to the president's office; any mail so addressed without a return address should immediately be brought to the RFE/RL security office for inspection.

The Munich police then gave RFE/RL a translation into German of the Arabic, which cast doubt on the group's claim that it killed the German diplomat in Paris. The German translation indicated only that he was no longer needed ("der wir nicht mehr gebrauchen"). There was no mention in the German translation of threats to nationalities, but it was a general threat letter against all RFE managers ("diejenigen, die Radiostation betreiben"). But the police still believed that Mr. Pell remained directly threatened.

On Wednesday, February 10, 1988, Herr Hartmann of the Munich police said that there was nothing new to report. He advised that his office continued to believe that the threat was to be seriously taken. On Friday, February 19, 1988, Herr Hartmann and two other Munich police officers arrived at RFE/RL. Hartmann said that the investigation had been turned over to the Bavarian State Prosecutor's Office. Two complaints were filed: one on the threat to Pell, and the other on the threat to RFE/RL employees. Otherwise, there was nothing new to report.

On Monday, February 22, 1988, the U.S. legal attaché in the American embassy in Bonn called. He requested more background information on the Pacepa book threats.

The Munich police agreed to continue the neighborhood patrols around

RFE/RL until the end of the week, when they would stop, pending a new threat letter or other information that suggested that the police patrols should be renewed. The police did not have any new information on the threat.

On Tuesday, March 1, 1988, the regional security officer at the American consulate called and stated that the FBI had accepted jurisdiction of investigation. He requested the original threat letter. He was told that it was probably with the Bavarian state prosecutor. Friday, March 4, the legal attaché called and requested a copy of whatever reports there were about the letter and threat. He also requested the original threat letter. He then asked for and received the telephone number of the Munich police section that was investigating the threats. The most up-to-date report on the death threat was sent to him.

On March 11, the SAAOR director in Paris advised:

- The police had no record of an organization called the Eagles of the Islamic Revolution. The Eagles of the Palestinian Revolution are another matter. Their leader was killed in Paris in 1978 under circumstances that remain unclear. The group does not appear to be very active now, due in part to the French authorities' recent success at penetrating a host of Palestinian and Iranian organizations.
- There is no evidence locally of Palestinians and Romanians working together. Neither the Romanians nor the Palestinians have shown any interest in the RFE/RL presence in Paris recently. The Romanians have been quiet in France lately.
- He is quite willing to help identify the authors of the threat letter. To do so, he needs a copy of the original. Comparing it with documents from their massive Palestinian and Middle Eastern archive could turn something up. He will move on the matter when he receives a copy.[9]

On Friday, April 29, 1988, the Bavarian State Prosecutor's office sent a letter to RFE/RL, officially stating that the investigation into the threats against Gene Pell and RFE/RL was closed, with no results or prosecution contemplated.

On May 5, the RFE/RL SAAOR director in Paris sent the following message:

On the letter in Arabic, they ran a computer test with all the letters in Arabic they had. No corresponding information. Also, they checked all documentation in Iranian student milieu and found nothing. The case went all the way to the Minister of the Interior, so it was thorough and had high-level backing. Conclusion is that this must be some small local group in Germany aimed at the radios. There was no connection to France. They will continue to monitor this against anything that they get in the future in Arabic.[10]

A month later, the legal attaché came to RFE/RL to go over the information known. He received a photocopy of the letter, with the relevant passages from the Pacepa book. On July 19, two U.S. State Department security officers visited RFE/RL. One was the regional security officer in Bonn, the other was a temporary duty (TDY) security officer at the U.S. consulate in Munich. They said that the TDY officer would be responsible for counterintelligence matters affecting RFE/RL, threat assessments and reporting of threats to American businesses. They then asked with what other agencies the RFE/RL had dealt. They said that they were now responsible for the investigations.

They were told that the legal attaché's office was sending someone down to meet with Vlad Georgescu on the threat to him. One of the State Department men then asked to use the phone to call the legal attaché's office in Bonn, because they had reached an understanding that the Security Office and not the legal attaché would be involved. He called Bonn, spoke with the legal attaché's office and said that the security officer from the consulate would be sitting in on the meeting with Vlad Georgescu. They then left the building to walk to the consulate.

Five minutes after they left, the legal attaché called. He advised that they were the only agency responsible for the investigation, and that they had requested advice from Washington on how to proceed. He said that the meeting with Vlad might be called off pending clarification of whom does what with whom.

The political officer at the consulate telephoned on July 20. He said that it appeared that both sides were right, but he wouldn't adjudicate between them. He added that the meeting would take place as scheduled, but that only the legal attaché's representative would be at RFE/RL. If the State Security officer wanted to speak with Vlad, it would be at the consulate another time. But the next day a representative of the legal attaché's office met with Vlad Georgescu, with a State Department security officer present. Both gentlemen afterward mentioned that the respective headquarters in Washington were arguing about which agency had responsibility for the investigation into the threats against Vlad Georgescu and RFE/RL. Shortly afterward, Vlad Georgescu went to the United States for an operation to remove a brain tumor.

On September 1, 1988, journalist Anatole Lieven of the London *Times* telephoned RFE/RL and said he was writing an article about cancer cases in the Romanian Service. His article appeared on September 3, 1998. He wrote about the deaths of three Romanian Service employees after bouts with cancer and speculated that they were killed by "cancer-inducing radiation — the rumored Plan Radu."

Earlier in November, Hurezeanu also received a threatening phone call with the following text:

> Hello, I'm a friend of Harry's. If you won't ease your tone, you will be killed. Mr. Emil, we won't hesitate to carry out the final solution. You'll be next on

the "black list," after Vlad. If you don't believe me, look out the window ... then why are you so silent?

Hurezeanu did not look out the window and hung up the phone. He later said that the use of the term "Harry" clearly showed that the Romanian Securitate was behind the phone call. He explained that when he was leaving Romania, a Romanian intelligence officer said, "My name is Harry, and you should remember me." Hurezeanu was also threatened earlier that year, as he began reading excerpts from the Pacepa book. The telephone caller then referred to "Harry," too.

On November 15, 1987, a group of about 5,000 workers had demonstrated in Brasov, Romania, against the general living conditions. Reportedly, police arrested one hundred of the group and transported them to Bucharest, where they disappeared. Leading émigrés planned an anniversary march and demonstration throughout Europe on November 15, 1988.

Many prominent Romanian exiles who were participating in the preparation of the demonstrations received threatening letters with the same letterhead, purportedly sent by the "Sons of Avram Iancu." The motto of the group was "Only with the sword can we decide about our destiny." It was named after Avram Iancu, a Romanian lawyer and patriot who became famous in the 1848 for his revolutionary activity against the Austro-Hungarian Empire then controlling Romania. He was also a symbol for the right-wing extremist group "the Iron Guard" during World War Two.

Emil Hurezeanu heard about the threatening letters and broadcast a program about the "Avram Iancu" group on November 11, 1988. He challenged them as a front for the Romanian Intelligence Service, Securitate. A week after he broadcast the challenge, Hurezeanu received this letter postmarked in Baden, Austria.

> You committed an error. You consciously falsified our organization's name. Your speculation concerning our identity doesn't bother us. The most important thing is that we exist. But we are very angry that you falsified our name, and you did it on purpose. Because you wanted to falsify the real character of our actions, we don't know you Mr. Hurezeanu. We don't call ourselves Avram's Sons but "Avram Iancu Sons." You are scared to call us "Avram Iancu Sons," because you know this name is a national hero equal with national pride. That is true. We started a crusade against Attila's Bunches who conquered and wasted our land, who want now to enslave us again. And those are the persons you sold yourself to. Would you like the flag carried (see photos, i.e., Hungarian flag) to wind up on the roofs of the Cluj you don't like? You and your Hungarian friends are not patriotic Romanian character embodied in the personality of "Avram Iancu." The name "Avram Iancu" is a Saint's name and ... because you falsified it ... you insulted the entire Romanian people. Your time will come surely! We put you name on the list as well.[11]

Hurezeanu said that the wording "Attila's Bunches" was a well-known expression of the Romanian Intelligence Service. The photos were taken in Berne, Switzerland, and were of a famous Hungarian Romanian dissident who was expelled to Hungary and then living in exile in Berne. That same week, four Romanian émigrés living in Berlin received a threatening letter with the same letterhead message.

A few days later Huruzeanu decided to demonstrate to the Securitate he was not intimidated, when he broadcast a program giving some details of the threats he had recently received:

> Now a word about the Sons of Avram Iancu, the radical organization of the Romanian exiles that has addressed me, in writing and personally, reproaching me that I modified their name to The Sons of Avram. They also write that "your speculations about our true identity are natural and do not affect us. After all, what is important is that we exist." I stated, just as the entire West German press, that the Sons of Avram Iancu are probably not the false successors of the great patriot but the ... "stooges" of the Securitate. Now the Sons have threatened me, tell me that they have also put me on the list of the final accounts. They also sent me two photographs taken during the demonstrations in Budapest last June, on which poet Geza Szoecs can be seen carrying a Hungarian flag. The photos were probably taken from the Romanian Embassy building there. The Sons want to confirm that they have, indeed, no connection with Avram Iancu, but, probably, with Tudor Postelnicu, the present Minister of the Interior and longtime former head of the Securitate. The fact that they now [have] sent threats also to RFE's address adds an aggravating element to the entire intimidation campaign of recent times. But nobody should indulge in illusions; the threat with the sword will be answered with the word every time.[12]

Death of Vlad Georgescu

Vlad Georgescu had experienced digestive problems in the first months of 1988. In July 1988, doctors discovered a brain tumor. He had surgery to remove a malignant tumor. He flew to Washington to undergo unsuccessful experimental treatment at the National Institutes of Health. In early November, he returned to Munich where he died a week later on November 13.

The next day, RFE/RL President Gene Pell issued the following staff announcement:

> It is with profound regret that I must report the death of Romanian Service Director Vlad Georgescu. Mr. Georgescu died last evening at Bogenhausen Hospital in Munich following a valiant fight against cancer. He was 51. Vlad Georgescu was appointed Associate Director of the Romanian Service in 1982,

and named Director the following year. He was a brilliant intellectual, a highly respected administrator, and a kind and gentle man.

He suffered much persecution, abuse, and imprisonment because of his unflinching belief in freedom and human rights, before he was finally allowed to leave Romania in 1979 after persistent protest and intervention by the United States Government and the Western academic community. He never ceased fighting for those principles or for his people and his country. Romania has lost a stalwart patriot. RFE/RL has lost a dedicated servant of the cause of liberty. Most important, his wife Mary Luiza, and his son Tudor Vlad have lost a loving husband and father.

I know you will join me in sharing in their grief and in mourning the loss of a true friend and colleague.

On November 18, 1988, the U.S. legal attaché visited RFE/RL concerning the death of Vlad, the general Romanian threats, and other matters. At the end of November, a FBI special agent went to the RFE/RL Washington office and questioned a Romanian Service employee about the circumstances of Vlad's illness and death. Vlad Georgescu had taught at the FBI academy before moving to Munich. The agent was especially interested in the threats Vlad had received before the broadcasting of Pacepa's book. He also wanted to know different details of his lifestyle, the physical setting of his office and car. The agent also asked about the threats others had received. He said he would discuss Vlad's diagnostic with the FBI pathologists. Then he asked about the latest threats that some of the staff had received, mentioning in passing a letter in Arabic addressed to Mr. Pell.

In the middle of December, RFE/RL contacted the U.S. legal attaché's office in Bonn regarding the *U.S. News and World Report* article on the death of Vlad Georgescu. His answer was that the U.S. Department of Justice had not yet authorized any investigation into the allegations of "murder through radiation." Therefore, any report that the FBI was conducting any such investigation or would investigate was premature. Activity by the legal attaché's office in West Germany was put on hold, because of "some flap" about the unauthorized visit of a FBI agent to the RFE/RL Washington office.[13]

The LKA (Bavarian State Police) decided that there was no cause to investigate the death of Vlad Georgescu.

In Washington, on December 27, 1988, an article by Bill Gertz appeared in the *Washington Times*. He quoted Pacepa in an interview as saying that he believed four Radio Free Europe officials had been killed with a radiation device designed by Romania's Intelligence Service, CIE, with help from the Soviet KGB. He added that he warned U.S. officials about the weapon during debriefing sessions in the late 1970s. In his book *Red Horizon* Pacepa wrote: "In the spring of 1970, Service K added radioactive substances provided by the KGB to its deadly arsenal. Ceausescu himself gave the procedure the code name "Radu." ... The radiation dosage was said to generate lethal forms of cancer." Gertz quoted Pacepa as saying, "I don't know anything for sure, because I was no longer in Romania when these events occurred. But I have no doubt this was not coincidental. I believe Ceausescu wanted these people killed with Radu."

According to Nestor Ratesh, "The intelligence file on Vlad Georgescu is huge, covering five volumes and over 1,600 pages. However, close to 300 pages are missing, including almost all that pertained to Vlad's last year of life."[14]

On December 28, 1988, RFE/RL's Romanian Service broadcast former Romanian King Michael traditional year-end message to Romania. He called for an end to "criminal, diabolic activities of the irresponsible [Romanian] government." He called on Romanians to take part in peaceful resistance.

1989

In March 1989, RFE/RL's Romanian Service broadcast an open letter signed by six major Romanian Communist leaders, including the father of Mircea Raceanu, in which they attacked Nicolae Ceausescu. Five days later, Mircea Raceanu, former Romanian political officer and deputy chief of mission of the Romanian embassy in the United States in the 1970s, was detained by police in Bucharest while on his way to the American ambassador's home to watch a movie.

The broadcasting of this letter was very important for RFE/RL. Two hundred forty-one Romanian respondents, interviewed by RFE/RL between April 20, 1989, and June 16, 1989, were asked: "Have you heard about the letter addressed to President Ceausescu by the six former Romanian Communist Party leaders?" Sixty percent of the listeners said that they had. All those who were aware of the letter were also asked what they thought its impact and importance would be and what would result from it. About a third were optimistic about the impact of the letter, about a third were pessimistic, while the remaining third had mixed opinions.[15]

Some western newspapers called this letter the most challenging event to the Ceausescu regime in over twenty years. The broadcasting of this letter was important for another reason. The day after the "letter of the six" was broadcast, the Romanian General Prosecutor's Office announced that it had charged Mircea Raceanu with treason and having been recruited in 1974 by a foreign spying service (read CIA) and providing "secret data and intelligence" afterward. There was no mention of the letter in the Romanian press. Raceanu later described what happened after his arrest:

The interrogation went on for 11 months. What they wanted from me were three things: that I was recruited, that I received money and that I passed documents. I opted to protect the group of my father. The whole file is by me. I wrote it and they accepted it. You will find in that file a brilliant story of all that, but it is not the truth. I considered it my duty to use all means against that system."[16]

Raceanu was sentenced to death in July 1989, but in September Ceausescu commuted the sentence to twenty years in prison. On December 23, 1989, he was released under an amnesty as the last political prisoner of Communist Romania, and eventually moved to the United States.

On St. Patrick's Day, March 17, 1989, the American consulate political officer sent RFE/RL the following information, from a recent Romanian Intelligence Service defector:

> During 1988 an active, perhaps very active program was considered for eliminating certain persons in the West, especially persons who disliked the Ceausescu family and regime. Attacks on Ceausescu and his family received priority attention in Romania. The most visible people attacking Ceausescu were those working for Radio Free Europe (RFE). Ceausescu was very discontented with the measures taken by the Romanian Foreign Intelligence Service (CIE) during the past seven or eight years.
>
> Last summer [1988] the chief of the service dealing with RFE was obliged to retire from the CIE and the new chief began a completely new operation to infiltrate the Romanian section of RFE. His explicit orders were to eliminate those who attacked Ceausescu daily. Previous RFE attacks on Ceausescu were very sober. Now they are very clever and portray him in a joking manner, which has him dancing on his nerves. The broadcasting is very entertaining and RFE has a large audience in Romania.
>
> The defector could not comment on the use of radioactivity in carrying out the elimination, but felt that chemical means were much more logical. Given the long time of exposure to radioactive materials required to produce cancer, and the delectability of radioactive materials, it would be easier to accomplish the task using a chemical carcinogen. The prime requirement for such a chemical would be that it was not instantly lethal, thus non-alerting to authorities and allowing the perpetrator time to get away.
>
> It was possible that the CIE was considering radu, radium or radon because they were very common and slow acting. Again, the delectability of the substance was great and it would persist for a long time. Also, whoever was to emplace the substance was in jeopardy just by handling it.
>
> The defector remembered hearing discussions in the CIE about a natural substance originating in Latin America being considered as a poison. This was not curare as it was too lethal too quick. The CIE needed something that caused death but appeared to be from natural causes.[17]

That seemed the end of the case, until July 1989 when the BND (West German Foreign Intelligence Agency) advised that a Romanian intelligence service officer had defected to West Germany on July 17. Two days before his defection, a friend who was also an officer in the Securitate told him: "Because of a series of RFE broadcasts in March this year dealing with a letter signed by six former leading members of the Communist Party to Ceausescu, a killer team was sent to West Germany to murder RFE employees Hurezeanu and Nicolae Munteanu.[18]

Both Hurezeanu and Munteanu were advised that they should be extra cautious for a few days. Hurezeanu said that he had received a strange phone call from an anonymous male caller who said he was in Belgium. He told Hurezeanu that a team of killers had just been sent from Romania to kill Ion Ratiu, a prominent Romanian dissident living in England. Munteanu had just interviewed Ratiu. Hurezeanu had previously interviewed him in 1988. Ratiu was the president of the World Union of Free Romanians (loosely translated) and was actively involved in the fate of Romanian refugees living in Budapest.

The team reportedly consisted of two women who were chosen and sent by Mrs. Ceausescu. The caller said he was going to send a photograph to Hurezeanu of some women in Romania and would circle the two that were on their way to England. Hurezeanu said that such a letter should arrive in a day or two.

The letter arrived with a photograph of nine women. Two women were marked as those who were reportedly underway to London to kill Ion Ratiu. The original envelope, letter, and photograph were handed over to the German police. In August, the Bavarian Prosecutor's office closed the investigation into the most recent threats against RFE/RL and Emil Hurezeanu.

Later the same month, police in Geneva, Switzerland, announced that former Romanian King Michael had received a series of death threats in phone calls and letters mailed in Western Europe and the United States. Some letters bore the signature "Sons of Avram Iancu."

The RFE/RL's German government contact advised that in October 1989 he had learned, from a reliable defector, that Nicolae Ceausescu personally ordered "the use of the killer commando." He gave the assignment to an experienced Securitate officer. He ordered the officer to travel to the Federal Republic of Germany and try through a "local-activation" of a contact in Munich to assign the plot to a person living in the West. Then the Securitate officer would observe the action from the background. If this plan failed, he was supposed to hire a professional killer to fulfill the assignment. The following persons reportedly took part in the discussion of the mission: Elena Ceausescu, two more Securitate officers in the small Ceausescu circle of supporters, and a lieutenant colonel in Ceausescu's personal body guard.

Nicolae Ceausescu and his wife Elena would live only two more months as they were tried and executed during the pre–Christmas revolution in

December 1989. The threats against RFE/RL and its Romanian Service employees stopped. The circle was closed on December 29, 1989, when the Bucharest daily *Romania Liberia* started serializing Pacepa's book *Red Horizons*.

Code Name Jackal: Action Plan Against Noel Bernard

For sixteen years, Noel Bernard was a highly respected director of RFE/RL's Romanian Broadcast Service. Nestor Ratesh, who was one of Bernard's successors, succinctly captures Bernard's popularity in Romania:

> He not only managed the service, but was also its main editorialist. His almost daily commentaries were balanced, reasoned, civil, elegantly written and delivered in a clear, imposing voice. It was radio journalism at its best. He was a hero in Romania, an almost fabled character. One anecdote that made the rounds in the 1970s went like this:
> Ceausescu decided one day to make an impromptu visit to a remote village. The villagers seemed rather unimpressed by his presence. Intrigued, he stopped a couple of peasants and asked them whether they knew who he was. "No," came the answer.
> "But wait, it can't be, you certainly do know me," said the visitor. "I am the one who speaks to you quite often, who tells you everything you should know. Here in your village, you can hear me on the radio."
> "Don't say, good gracious! Of course we know you. Welcome to our village, Mr. Noel Bernard."[19]

Noel Bernard died of cancer on December 23, 1981. His widow, Ioana Magura-Bernard, who also worked in the Romanian Broadcast Service, was convinced that Noel was murdered through some form of radiation. In the summer of 1982, the Romanian Service Director's offices were searched for radiation traces. No trace of radiation was found. However, in the summer of 2007, the Romanian external intelligence service (SIE) released a copy of a top-secret, ten-page report dated August 18, 1980, which gives prima facie evidence that Romanian agents, in fact, planned to murder Noel Bernard (code name the Jackal).[20]

Even more incriminating documents are reports from intelligence officers in Germany to the headquarters in Bucharest regarding Noel Bernard. For example on October 22, 1980, the Romanian embassy in Germany sent a report to CIE headquarters with the following notation: "Concerning the compromising and liquidation of N. Bernard.... Through the means available to us steps have been taken in order to perform the action documented by the Chief Architect.[21]

Another report, dated March 1, 1981, after Noel Bernard's illness, became public knowledge:

(Subject) Noel Bernard convalescent (attached is the article translated from German).

(From) Comrade Colonel Bogdan,

The data published by B.I.R.E. confirm that the measures take by us started to show effects. We should intensify measures to compromise Emil Georgescu and Ioana Magura so as to intimidate them and have them removed from the radio.[22]

On June 11, 1981, the U.S. State Department informed the Board for International Broadcasting of a report from a recent defector of stepped-up Romanian regime interest in Noel Bernard. There was no reason to believe and no indication that physical violence or foul play would be involved, but RFE/RL was told that he could experience some type of harassment activity.

Threat Letters from Madrid

A prominent Romanian historian named Nicolae Iorga was apparently murdered by elements of the fascist party *Iron Guard* in 1940. An article appeared in the newspaper *Tribuna Romaniei* paying tribute to Iorga, without mentioning how he had died. RFE/RL broadcast Emil Georgescu asked in a broadcast on November 27, 1980 why there was no mention of the *Iron Guard* in this particular newspaper article published in Romania but distributed in the West. On December 1, 1980, the Romanian Service aired a second program that was critical of the *Iron Guard*. Two weeks later, Emil Georgescu received two threatening letters: one from Paris, the other from Madrid. The one from Paris was signed GRUPUL V and dated December 9, 1980. Both referred to broadcasts about the *Iron Guard*.

In December 1980, Noel Bernard also received two letters; one from Paris dated December 16, 1980 and signed GRUPA V. The other was received on December 30 and signed "V." Both letters made mention of recent RFE broadcasts critical of the *Iron Guard*. On January 2, 1981, Noel Bernard sent the following memorandum:

> Further to the letters recently received by Emil Georgescu, I, too, have now received two similar letters, one from Paris, the other from Madrid. I enclose the original letters and translations thereof. I attach no special importance to these letters. The fact that the Iron Guardists left Romania during and just after the war, and that the letters now received use the new Romanian autography introduced in Romania long after they had left, leads me to believe that the authorship should be looked for in Bucharest.

(Translation of first letter)

Paris, December 16, 1980
Esteemed Mr. Noel Bernard,
Until recently we had the impression that you succeeded in adopting in the
section which you direct an independent line toward the Romanian exile. At
present, with regret, we note that the situation has changed fundamentally
and that the radio station has begun to be increasingly preoccupied with
insults against the Iron Guard movement.
Now there can no longer be any doubt that you have joined forces with
the communists whose game you are playing at the present, with the aim of
giving the broadcasts to hit our comrades in Romania. When you stated that
our comrades still occupy leading functions in various fields in Romania, you
probably forgot that your kikes occupy many more such functions in Romania.
We believe that in this way you acted in a very imprudent manner. For all
this the Iron Guard will not forgive you
(Signed) "Group "V"

(Translation of second letter)
Mr. Bernard,
We have established that the radio station which you direct and more
recently you personally are attacking with increasing violence the Iron Guard
movement. Why do you do this? In whose pay are you and who's [sic] game
are you playing? Are you perhaps imagining that your degenerate minds that
the force of the Iron Guard has decreased? You are very wrong. If until now
you have not become aware of our power, be sure that you will not be able
to escape wherever you may hide. You should know that we are not joking.
Long live the Iron Guard and its Commander!
(Signed) "V"[23]

On January 27, 1981, three letters were posted and mailed to RFE/RL's
Romanian Service broadcasters. Two letters were posted in Linz, Austria. One
was received by Noel Bernard on February 3, and signed GRUPA V and
referred to Bernard's medical condition, and made threats against Bernard and
his wife. The other was sent to Romanian Service employee Cunea and made
reference to Bernard's condition and threatened Bernard. The third letter was
posted in Neuburg A.D. Donau, West Germany, and mailed to Vlad
Georgescu, then living in Washington, D.C.

I listened to the 3rd January broadcast of RFE, comprising of a so-called
commentary regarding the Iron Guard movement, which you pretend to have
written. I must admit that you have the typical impudence of the stinking
Jew, unashamed and lacking the most elementary commonsense. Without
having any professional or political merits, you started to pose as the umbili-
cus of the earth, the teacher, the man of culture, the historian and from these
positions you observe the world and defame the Romanian nation.
You pronounce severe sentences, indulge in anti-national appreciations,

and defame the true Romanians who sacrificed everything for the cause of the fatherland and nation. With what right do you indulge in this dirty game? Everybody knows that you a common agent; that you have been an inform-ant in Romania, and that you have learned the profession of being a squealer. Now you have been recruited by Noel Bernard and work for that cesspool. You hope to make a career and obtain money; you have become a Judas, a Pharisee who does everything for a handful of lentils, who smears with mud the fatherland, the nation and all that is Romanian. You have become more Jewish than the Jews: you are a beast full of cancer and venom and are try-ing to gain the confidence of the Americans through the Jews of RFE. You could have gone about it honestly, without insulting the Romanian nation. Don't forget you will be punished for all you do against us. In your life's last hour you should awaken. You should do this at least for your family.

(Signed) "Group V" 24

Khrushchev Book Bombs from Madrid

On February 3, 1981, parcel bombs were delivered to the homes of Romanian exiles Paul Goma and Nicolas Penescu, sometime RFE freelancers living in Paris. Penescu was the former Romanian interior minister and it was reported that he received serious injuries as a result of the explosion. Goma was unhurt, but a French policeman was hurt when the police attempted to defuse the bomb. The following day, Romanian Service freelancer Serban Orescu, living in Cologne, was slightly hurt when he opened a package and it exploded. All three of these men were prominent in the Romanian exile community and leading members of the Romanian Human Rights Cam-paign. All three had been in Spain attending the Madrid Conference on Secu-rity and Cooperation in Europe in December 1980. All three parcel bombs were packed inside hollowed-out books containing the works of Nikita Khrushchev, and all were mailed from Madrid.

Ms. Moschuna, secretary to Noel Bernard, said that Nicolae Penescu, a prominent exile, was apparently injured as he tried to open a small package sent from Spain. She explained that the wife of Penescu called RFE/RL in order to inform Noel Bernard of what happened. Mrs. Penescu stated that her husband had just returned from the Madrid Conference on Human Rights where he was a participant. A package arrived from Spain and he had tried to open it. The package exploded and he was injured. The full extent of his injuries was not known; however, he had been taken to a hospital.

Ms. Moschuna added that she did not attribute the injury to Penescu because of any connection to RFE/RL but to his contribution to the Roman-ian émigré community in Paris, and elsewhere, as he was very well known in exile circles.[25]

Code Name Cobra

In September 1984, Constantin Constantinescu, a code clerk of the Romanian embassy in Bonn, defected to the West. To establish his credentials, he presented a copy of a thirteen-page physical surveillance report that was written by Romanian intelligence service (CIE) officer Ion Constantin sometime between October and December 1983. Constantinescu indicated that he was able to "save" a copy of this report from destruction as he saw its significance, and there was a breakdown in the normal destruction process thus allowing him to retain it. A summary of the subsequent debriefing of Constantinescu about his knowledge of this surveillance report was made available to the RFE/RL Security Department.

Of extreme interest was the physical description of the wall of RFE/RL along the main street Oettingengtrasse and analysis of the working of the entrance and exit gates of RFE/RL. This report was not necessarily accurate in this regard. Nor was it regarding the location and use of the CCTV cameras on the building, thus leading one to the conclusion that the surveillance conducted at the front of the building was limited due to fear of detection.

The summary of the debriefing also mentioned that the surveillance report contained references to "certain offices on the first floor." Presumably these "certain offices on the first floor" referred to the Romanian Service of RFE/RL.

Constantinescu said he believed that the headquarters in Bucharest "was collecting information on the radio station to carry out intimidating acts against the personnel in the station's Romanian section." And he did not believe that there was interest "in having the facility seriously damaged."

Also of interest in the debriefing summary, was the mention of the headquarters group in Bucharest responsible for organizing "physical attacks on anti–Romanian personnel abroad" and the words "usually hires foreigners to carry out the operations themselves." Constantinescu lacked other knowledge of contemplated action against RFE/RL other than the surveillance report and conversations with Ion Constantin. In other words, he had not seen any other telex information or other written reports on RFE/RL or on individual Romanian Service members of RFE/RL.

In December 1983, one or two days before leaving for temporary duty to Bucharest, Ion Constantin handed Constantinescu a package of material for destruction. Normally, the destruction of the material should have been carried out by both him and Constantin, but Constantin was in a hurry and left the material for Constantinescu to destroy. When Constantinescu saw the report on RFE/RL, he immediately realized the report's importance and retained it. He did not see any other materials on the topic, whether cables or operational letters. He did not hear anyone besides Constantin discuss this topic at the Romanian missions in Cologne and Bonn.

Constantin's thirteen-page report and sketch, which the defector brought out, was a physical surveillance report on the RFE/RL target. It described the

- traffic in the area,
- traffic signs and parking,
- the facility and wall surrounding it,
- the different entrances/gates,
- certain offices on the first floor,
- the presence of certain security personnel, and other installations in the immediate vicinity.

Constantin concluded his report by noting that he had collected a number of different city plans, tour books, and postcards which covered the target and its immediate surroundings, which items he was to attach to the report in an appendix which would also contain twenty-four photos of the target and its immediate surroundings (the Hilton Hotel, Bavarian Bank, Isar River, etc.). Constantin stated in his report that he personally had walked through the entire area.

From discussions with Constantin, the defector learned about a group at CIE Headquarters, designated C-428, which deals with such "diversionary" acts as physical attacks on anti–Romanian personnel abroad. C-428 depended on CIE residencies abroad to collect information in support of its plans, but usually hired foreigners to carry out the operations themselves. Constantin had received instructions, presumably originally from C-428, to collect detailed information on the RFE/RL facility in Munich, referred to by the code name "Cobra." Constantinescu recalled that Constantin remarked: "They want to place bombs at the Radio Station."

Constantinescu learned that similar surveillance reports on the RFE/RL facility had also been submitted to C-428 by Constantin Ciobanu, the CIE resident, and Dan Mihoc, a CIE officer, both at the Romanian embassy in Bonn. In December 1983, while in Bucharest, Constantin was given two days of briefing by C-428 and was shown the reports from Ciobanu and Mihoc. Even though his own report had been evaluated "good," Constantin was asked to obtain additional information of interest (Constantin did not elaborate on this) In 1984, Constantin made two more trips to Munich, where he asked one of his collaborators to help him in this project.

Constantinescu's personal opinion was that the CIE was collecting information on the radio stations in order to carry out intimidating acts against the personnel in the stations' Romanian Section. He did not believe, however, that the CIE was interested in having the facility seriously damaged.[26]

In November 1984, the German government ordered the expulsion of the above-named "diplomats." Media coverage was intense. For example, the German newspaper *Die Welt*'s detailed article on the expulsion contained this ominous reference to Dan Mihoc: "His superiors in Bucharest ordered Mihoc in January this year to buy a set of specialist medical works about poisons that could not be traced by autopsies and he sent the volumes to the Romanian capital."[27]

The Bavarian State Counterintelligence Agency's 1984 Annual Report contained this remark:

> When an intelligence officer of the Romanian Embassy in Bonn defected to the West in 1984 important information was obtained on the activities of the Romanian Intelligence Service on the territory of the Federal Republic of Germany. The defector presented evidence of the preparation and the actual carrying out of criminal activities with a political background by the Intelligence Service, represented by officers of the Romanian Foreign Intelligence Service CIE who had diplomatic status with the Romanian Embassy in Bonn.[28]

RFE/RL and SRI (Serviciul Roman de Informatii)

On June 10, 1992, RFE/RL requested information from the director of the domestic intelligence service (SRI), Virgil Magureanu:

> According to information received from Hungarian, Czechoslovak, and former East German government defectors, the famous terrorist named "CARLOS" was supposedly paid one million dollars by Nicolae CEAUSESCU in August 1979, or was promised one million dollars in August 1979, to silence the Romanian "Opposition"" in the West. Among the criminal acts carried out by "CARLOS" were
> 1. The attack on Radio Free Europe/Radio Liberty on 21 February 1981.
> 2. Book bombs, Khrushchev's memoirs, sent to dissidents in Paris, France (GOMA and PENESCU) and Cologne, Germany (ORESCU) in early 1981.
> 3. The knife attack on Emil GEORGESCU in July 1981 by two Frenchmen named LAYANI and COTTENCEAU.
>
> **Questions:**
> 1. What is contained in the Romanian Securitate files about the bombing of RFE/RL?
> 2. The book bombs?
> 3. The attack on Emil Georgescu?
> 4. The deaths of Noel Bernard, Michael Cismarescu, and Vlad Georgescu?
> 5. Who within the Romanian Service of RFE/RL supplied the Securitate with information?
> 6. Who was sent to the West with the goal of infiltrating RFE/RL?

Two months later, SRI Director Magureanu sent a report with a short but very interesting answer to question number 4: "In addition, concerning the cause of death of Noel Bernard, Mihai Cismarescu and Vlad Georgescu, nothing else is known beyond what was established in the medical death certificates."[29]

Former General Nicolae Plesita and Five Romanian Diplomats Accused of Acts of Terrorism

Almost twenty-three years after the expulsion of the diplomats, on November 7, 2007, the Institute for the Investigation of Communist Crimes in Romania filed a "penal notification with the High Court of Cassation and Justice regarding the acts of terrorism committed by Nicolae Plesita and five former diplomats ... namely Dan Mihoc, Constantin Ciobanu, Ion Constantin, Ion Lupu and Ion Grecu."

The IICCR press release, in part, read:

> The facts incriminated by the IICCR's penal notification, most of which regard acts of terrorism, are extremely serious, and they aimed [at] elimination [of] some of the communist regime's adversaries, and also to inducing a state of fear and panic among opponents or potential opponents of the regime.
> Among the crimes committed at the time, one could mention
> - first degree manslaughter,
> - attempt of murder,
> - kidnapping,
> - both physical and psychological abuse,
> - violation of the laws regarding the use of explosive materials,
> - forgery and use of forgery in official documents,
> - association in committing crimes.
>
> The evidence used in supporting this penal notification are ... official documents, testimonies from different sources, press articles, etc. They all offer information about the placement or placement facilitation in February 1981 of explosive devices. This devices were disguised as parcels and sent by mail to three well-known communist regime contestants (Paul Goma, Nicolae Penescu and Serban Orescu) with the intention to cause their death or serious body injuries. The evidence also sustains their implication in other terrorist attacks, toxic gas assaults or the kidnapping and assassination of other persons.[30]

The Ether Group

In June 1980, the Securitate set up a special operations group with the code name Ether (ETURUL): "The Ether was not merely a preventive measure, springing from the Securitate's excessive zeal, but a retaliation: the secret police noticed the Romanians' trust in the Western news, and finally reacted in a systematic, organized way, by treating the offence of listening to Radio Free Europe as a political crime *per se*, which called for a severe punishment."[31]

Some of the activity of the Ether group included surveillance, placing of microphones in residences, and intercepting mail of relatives of Radio Free Europe employees, generally to prevent the relatives from providing information to RFE that could be used in its programs. At one point in the Ether program, the Securitate officers had fifteen days to identify the sender of a letter that was broadcast over Radio Free Europe. If the sender was identified, the Securitate put a sixty-day plan in operation, including surveillance of the sender and his or her family, intercepting all letters and monitoring of telephone calls. The Securitate employed stages of "persuasion" to the sender, which started with an admonishment. If the person responded negatively to this, the next stage was "positive influence." If that failed, an "official warning" followed in the Securitate offices, usually in a hostile environment:

> The offender was forced to sign a written engagement that he or she [would] put an end to the offence, and the document was kept in the personal surveillance file. Just the mentioning of the reason for the "official warning" brought about a social and professional stigma: the admiration for Radio Free Europe could cost you the job or at least the promotion, the access to the housing facilities (namely, the privilege of being a tenant of the state), not to mention the passport or membership of the Romanian Communist Party. Unfortunately, the most serious consequences were not and could not be written, due to their illegal character, even under communist standards.[32]

Were someone to continue to listen to Radio Free Europe, the ultimate punishment would be imprisonment. Annual reports of the Ether group were limited to one top-secret copy. The 1985 annual report, "Concerning the Stage of Fulfillment of Tasks within the ETURUL Program," gives an insight into the workings of the operational group:

> *1.— Identification of the contact means and ways of the foreign radios and prevention of information data reaching them,*
> To this effect, we acted to develop the information potential, which lead to an increase of 21%. At the same time, better instructions were secured and, as a consequence the transmission abroad of over 3000 materials, data and information, meant for the reactionary radio-stations were traced and stopped ... through combined actions, at influencing and disinformation, some hostile elements of the Romanian emigration were persuaded to renounce the sending of slanderous materials to RFE.
> *2.—The enforcement of a more efficient information control on people maintaining or intending to establish links with foreign radios.*
> More firmness was shown in the case of elements intending to contact, or

those who had established contact with the foreign radios, by using diversified measures. Principally, with the assistance of competent authorities, measures were used to positively influence elements involved and persuasion to give up their plans of contacting or maintaining the link with the foreign reactionary propaganda agencies. In 44 cases fines were used, according to Statute 23 of 1971 and in others, more outstanding cases, arrests were imposed by the Prosecutor's Office and the Militia, on the basis of Decree 153 of 1970.

More attention was also focused on identifying and neutralizing hostile activities by people listening and spreading news, of harmful contents, broadcast by foreign radios, to this effect over 30 groupings, in their initial phase of existence, were dispersed among young people and, in a wider field, over 1,200 people were officially warned. In most cases these measures were efficient, and those involved gave up their hostile intentions and preoccupation.[32]

In total there were over fifty-five volumes, totaling 16,000 pages, produced by the Ether program before the collapse of Communism in Romania.[34]

6. Code Name Iago:
The Murder Attempts
on Emil Georgescu

The name Emil Georgescu is practically unknown in the West, outside of a few Romanian émigrés who remember him from his broadcasts over RFE/RL. He always was impeccably dressed: dark suit, white shirt, conservative tie, and high-glossed black shoes. Emil was short, stout, and a chain smoker who continually coughed during our first meeting and every meeting we had afterward. His skin color seemed to be always gray, even in summer. He gave everyone the impression that he was a sick man. Yet with his listening audience he was one of the most popular broadcasters for the RFE/RL Romanian Service.

His daily program, Domestic Bloc, a mixture of news and satire, was very highly rated with Romanian listeners, according to RFE/RL's audience surveys. His commentaries were especially biting in his personal criticism of Communist Party leader Nicolae Ceausescu and his wife — both of them ruled Romania with an iron fist. No one criticized the Ceausescus without suffering some type of adverse reaction.

In the halls of RFE/RL, one heard the apocryphal story about Georgescu's popularity:

> One Romanian asks, "What time is it?"
> The other Romanian doesn't look at his watch but looks out the window and says, "It must be 11 o'clock. The shutters are closed. Emil has started his daily commentary."

Emil Georgescu was born in Romania on December 7, 1929. He graduated with a law degree from the University of Bucharest in 1952. Afterward he was a prosecutor and then, according to our files, a defense lawyer. In 1965, Georgescu became a member of the Romanian Communist Party. He and his wife arrived in Germany in 1973. After a few months in a refugee camp, they obtained political asylum, based on his wife's ethnic German background; they settled in Munich. He started working for RFE as a freelancer, and, after proving he could work as a journalist, he was permanently employed in October 1976. He was a colorful character, even if not universally liked at RFE.

On April 29, 1979, and May 1, 1979, RFE's Romanian Service broadcast a 31-minute interview with then bishop Valerian Trifa. Trifa was at the time under investigation by the U.S. Department of Justice as a World War Two German collaborator — he was eventually deported from the United States. Two staff members responsible for the interview were dismissed for having arranged the program. They appealed and the case was investigated. In a report for RFE/RL's oversight board, Board for International Broadcasting, the authors summarize Emil Georgescu's status within RFE's Romanian Broadcast Service:

> On Monday, April 30, at the regular morning editorial meeting when the day's programs are announced and discussed, the programs for May 1 — a holiday in Europe — were also reported. A major segment is called the Domestic Bloc, whose Editor is Emil Georgescu. Bernard announced that for the Domestic Bloc, he had decided on using the Trifa interview.
>
> Georgescu asked if he should preface the interview with a playing of "Long

"Radio Free Europe: A free flow of information and ideas promotes international understanding." Possibly from late 1960s campaign (Radio Free Europe/Radio Liberty).

Live the Iron Guard"— the official hymn of the Romanian Legionnaire — or
Iron Guard — movement. His comment was greeted with general laughter and
understood to be ironical. Some private conversations took place simultaneously in which Trifa's past and current status in the United States was discussed. Nothing that anyone at that editorial meeting said can be considered
a protest against broadcasting the Trifa interview. In fact, the April 30 meeting was representative of many others like it — Georgescu wisecracking as others engaged in a buzz of private conversation.[1]

1976 Automobile Accident

In October 1976, Georgescu and his wife were en route home one evening when a car twice rammed his automobile and forced it off the road. The
other driver silently abandoned his car and started walking toward the
Georgescu vehicle. When he saw that other persons had stopped to look at
what had happened, the unknown driver jumped into another automobile and
sped away, leaving his damaged vehicle behind. Georgescu was not injured,
drove home, and reported the "accident" to the police.

Munich police afterward told the RFE/RL security office that their investigation showed that someone named Rene Scheibling, from France, had
rented the abandoned vehicle. Scheibling had registered at the Deutsche Kaiser
Hotel in Munich. Interpol had searched French records but found no further
trace of Scheibling, and the Munich police closed the case.

The next month, Victor Pfeiller, whom Georgescu described as an émigré friend living in the same suburb of Munich, telephoned him at home. He
told Georgescu that he had just received an anonymous telephone call from
a man speaking Romanian. The caller said he was calling from Frankfurt and
knew that Pfeiller was a friend of Georgescu. The caller said the Romanian
regime had arranged Georgescu's recent accident. He added that the regime
had arranged for another automobile accident in Germany that had occurred
a few weeks previously. In that accident, a Romanian priest named Zaparzan
and his aide, named Leonties, were killed.

The caller told Pfeiller, "Georgescu should not drive his car after dark,
or step into a stranger's car, and he should not eat anything unless his wife
[has] prepared the food." The caller then hung up without identifying himself.

The next day, Georgescu received a telephone call from a man who
identified himself as Alexander Pana. He warned Georgescu that the Romanian regime had sent someone to Germany to murder him, and that his car
"accident" was the first attempt. Pana added that the person sent to kill him
was Vasile Coman. Coman, according to Pana, was then seeking asylum in

Camp Zirndorf, a refugee center near Nuremberg. He said Coman was sent here to murder Zaparzan, Leonties, Georgescu, and one other person, whose name Georgescu couldn't recall. Pana finished, "All these details are known to German authorities."

Munich police later confirmed to Georgescu that the entire matter was indeed known: the police knew about Pana and Coman, who apparently was being held in custody for suspect intelligence activities. Coman had told police that he was working for Romanian intelligence and had been sent to the West to create disturbances for three Romanian exiles in the West: one in Madrid, one in Paris, and Georgescu in Munich.

Munich police then told Georgescu that the auto accident that occurred October 19, 1976, had no connection with Coman or intelligence activities. The police had contacted Interpol, but had anticipated no early reply. Georgescu was advised to use reasonable caution always, but thus said that they could not provide him physical protection or a weapons permit as he had requested.

Death Threats

In early November 1980, *Stindardul*, the Romanian language right-wing émigré newspaper in Munich, published an article denouncing Emil Georgescu. This was the first *Stindardul* effort directed against the RFE/RL Romanian Service for some time. Noel Bernard, then director of the Romanian Service, was mentioned several times in the article, but not necessarily in the same derogatory way as Georgescu, who was criticized for his "anti–Iron Guardist views."

On November 27, RFE's Romanian Service broadcast a program dealing with the death of a prominent Romanian historian named Nicolae Iorga, who had apparently been murdered by elements of the political group Iron Guard in 1940. An article had appeared in the Romanan newspaper *Tribuna Romaniei* paying tribute to Iorga, without mentioning how fact he had died. On December 1, 1980, the Romanian Service aired a second program that was critical of the Iron Guard.

Securitate Reaction

On 8 December 1980, the Romanian Foreign Intelligence Service (CIE) sent an urgent telegram to its Paris officer:

Strict Secret

Copy One

TELEGRAM

Sender: AB/ L-498   Urgent   Destination Paris

Date: 08 XII 1980

Comrade Tudor,

Take measures in order to mail from France a threatening letter as coming from the Legionnaires in France, addressed to Emil Georgescu, an employee of Free Europe, who has attacked the Legionnaires in programs broadcast lately by the station.

The letter will have the following content:

"Emil Georgescu, we learned that you have started to attack the Legionnaires. We thought you were a Romanian although we heard that your wife is a friend of the Jewess Ioana Magura. Now you have unmasked yourself as a traitor to the Romanian folk. We have no further doubts that you have sold out to our enemies, the Jews and the Communists. We have not forgotten the fact that in Romania, as a prosecutor, you condemned many innocent people. You scoundrel, you defected from Romania neither because of hard times nor out of political conviction. The Day of Judgment has come. Our revenge will find you even in a snake pit, and neither will the Jews, the Communists and those from Free Europe be able to save you. We will not rest until we see your bullet-riddled corpse. GRUPUL V."

The letter, typed on a domestic Romanian typewriter, will have as addressee: Emil Georgescu — 8013 Haar — Munchen, Am See 12, RFG, and will be sent under the rules of a qualified action.[2]

Two weeks later, Georgescu received two threatening letters: one from Paris, the other from Madrid. Both referred to recent broadcasts about the Iron Guards. The one from Paris was dated December 9, 1980, contained the exact text of the telegram above, and was signed "Grupul V."

Georgescu wrote a memorandum concerning them to Noel Bernard, the director of the Romanian Broadcast Service, who in turn sent it to the RFE/RL security office:

> *To the special attention of Mr. Noel Bernard, with the*
> *request to be submitted to the top management of Radio Free Europe.*

Yesterday, the 15th of December, I received two letters [at] my home address, one from France, the other from Spain.

The contents of both letters entails threats against my life (Enclosed, please find two letters).

They state to be [from] the "Iron-guard" — the former Nazi organization in Romania.

Despite this statement I'm convinced that this is a surreptitious maneuver of the Romanian Secret Service.

I'd like to remind you that on the 19th of October 1976 two non-identified men organized a car accident in order either to kill, or to intimidate me.

Through the investigation of the German police and Interpol the two participants had used false French passports and could not be identified.

At the same time I received a menacing letter from Belgium. The content of this letter was intended to convey the impression that it had been written by Romanian emigrants.

I couldn't possibly believe that Romanian emigrants were capable to devise such plans without being easily discovered by Interpol.

I want to point out the following:

1. In 1976 I was disappointed of the German Police efficiency regarding this above mentioned case.
2. I work for the American ideals and consequently I expect to have the necessary protection which my delicate position demands.
3. Despite the fact that our Radio is located in German Territory I expect to be protected by the American Security Force.
4. I would not be surprised if I were told that C.I.A. had detailed information about the occurrence in 1976.
5. I request to have the facts of the occurrence of 1976 as well as these two letters broadcast. I'm convinced that this broadcasting could be a means for my own protection.
6. I have entitled a lawyer to publish in the newspapers all this material as well as my comments in case these threats become reality.[3]

The vulgar letter posted in Madrid on December 10, 1980, read:

You freak,

We have heard that you have begun to bark at us, you mangy Judas. While you were on the other side of the Iron Curtain you bit as much as you could, you imprisoned many sons of the Iron Guard and other true Romanians. Now you are howling against us, you have sold out to the Masons and the Jewish Mafia at Radio Free Europe, you lick the stinking ass of the Jew Bercovici.

If you don't shut your Jewish trap, we'll see to that you will be gripping clay underground, on the other side, you pestilent beast.

Be careful, viper, we will cut out your venomous tongue.

Tell your Jews to prepare wreaths for you, and you yourself should make your last will, you kike.

Long Live the Legion and the Captain[4]

During a meeting in the RFE/RL security office on December 18, 1980, Georgescu said the letter from Spain contained three explicit, but unnecessary, references to the exiled organization the Iron Guard, that had groups in Paris, Madrid, and in Munich. The first was the symbol of the Iron Guard. The second was the green color of the ink used for the symbol — the Iron Guard wore green shirts as opposed to the Nazi brown shirts. The third superfluous detail was the closing phrase: "Long Live the Legion and the Captain." He added that the Iron Guard did not write the letter, because it was just too obvious; that is, there was no need to use these signs when writing to him. He concluded that the Securitate wrote the letter, using the cover of the Iron Guard.

He explained that groups of the "neo-fascist" Romanian Iron Guard were in Spain, France, and Munich. Nevertheless, "it was known within émigré circles that the Romanian Intelligence Services had infiltrated these groups." His only comment about the second letter was that he was not sure of the meaning of "GRUPL V,"; he thought at the time it was probably just some meaningless term the Securitate created.

Georgescu said that November 27, 1980, was the fortieth anniversary of the fascist Iron Guard assassination of the famous Romanian historian Nicolae Iorga. During his three-minute introduction to the historical program that day, Georgescu referred to an article in the November issue of *Tribuna Romaniei* newspaper, which the Romanian regime issued in Bucharest for Romanians living in exile. Iorga was a professor at the University of Bucharest, chairman of the Royal Academy, and royal councilor to King Michael. This article only referred to the historian Nicolae Iorga without saying that Iron Guard members had killed him. Georgescu asked whether the Romanian regime wanted to shield former Iron Guard members who live in Romania or abroad. He was attacking both the Romanian regime and the Iron Guard.

Georgescu added that the second relevant broadcast took place on December 1, 1980: he aired his views that day on the reunification of Transylvania with Romania in 1918. Nevertheless, another RFE/RL employee, according to Georgescu, had repeated the references to the assassination of Iorga, after Radio Bucharest acknowledged the role of the Iron Guard. Georgescu again insisted that the Romanian Secret Police, the Securitate, wrote the letters to intimidate and terrorize him.

Ceausescu's Birthday, 1981

The next important event in the Emil Georgescu story took place on January 26, 1981, which happened to be Romanian dictator Nicolae Ceausescu's sixty-third birthday. A then unknown assailant beat Emil Georgescu on the head. The man who attacked Georgescu did not identify himself and did not threaten Georgescu during the attack. He only said in German, "*entschuldigen Sie mich bitte*" (excuse me). As Georgescu walked by, the stranger turned and hit him four or five times in the head with a closed fist. When he called the police, Georgescu told them that he had only been hit once with an open hand. No official police report was made of the incident.

On January 30, 1981, the assailant, using the code name "Helmut," made an inaccurate report to the Bucharest intelligence headquarters:

Received by: Lt. Col. Macau
Source: "Helmut"
Date: Jan. 30, 1981   Highly confidential
Copy no. 1

Starting Jan. 21, 1981, and until the evening of Jan. 26, 1981 (Monday), the source has been shadowing Emil Georgescu around his residence. For 3–4 hours, the source was accompanied by the Italians Giovanni (Gioni) and Vincenzo. Emil Georgescu went for a walk with the dog twice, but the first time he was accompanied by his wife, and the second time by Mircea Pompy [!] Cojocaru.

In the evening of Jan. 26, 1981 (Monday), at about 21:00 (20:30 ?), Emil Georgescu left the building alone to walk his dog. At that moment, the source moved the car to a predefined place, and Vincenzo and Gioni got out and followed Emil Georgescu. Vincenzo's part was to beat him up, and Gioni's to screen him from possible outside action.

Emil Georgescu was approached in front of the shrubs next building. After a series of punches to his face, he fell yelling "Hilfe" (help). While on the ground he got several kicks. His yelling made people from the building step out onto their balconies. The Italians ran away in opposite directions and all three met at the car. According to Vincenzo, Emil Georgescu is seriously tattered, with evident facial lesions and the left arm broken.

If in the radio broadcasts there is no reference to this event, this means that one is waiting that it transpires from other sources, which might open up ways to identify the author of the attack.

Concerning Emil Georgescu, the problem of attacking him personally has raised serious problems for the source, because of his uniform, even existence. Through these Italians, the source is able to eliminate anybody for a reward of 10,000 DM.

I emphasize that these statements should be considered credible and that the conditions and conjuncture of the source's activity be taken into account.

The source doesn't know Emil Georgescu's home, except for what could be glimpsed from outside over so many days of look-out. The apartment is in a super luxurious block of flats in Munich's Haar suburb (Haar am See 12). Telephone: 46.79.07. Emil Georgescu lives on the ground floor, on the right side of the main entrance. Outside there is an engraved metal plate with a lawyer's firm. The apartment is made of 5 rooms — a long corridor, 2 rooms on the right, 2 on the left, bathroom and kitchen on the right after the entrance, from a small corridor. His study (as can be seen from outside through the balcony door) is in the last room on the left. Each evening, his wife shows herself in an armchair in front of the big window of the balcony (actually it is not a balcony, rather a small garden surrounded by hanging plants). The apartment is surrounded by a fence of shrubs. The block of flats has a ground floor and three floors with 4 apartments each, left-right.
"Helmut"[5]

On the right-hand margin of this telegram was the ominous note of the Securitate officer:

> The emerging situation is forcing us to use a different approach, different tactics, circumstances and means for accomplishing the action of annihilating Iago.[6]

The next day, January 27, 1981, was a very interesting day, though not all the events may have been connected. On this date, three threatening letters were mailed to RFE/RL Romanian Service employees.

- One of two letters posted in Linz, Austria, was sent to Noel Bernard, then Romanian Service director. He was suffering from cancer when I met first him. The threatening letter arrived on February 3 and was signed "GRUPA V." This letter referred to Bernard's medical condition and contained threats against both Bernard and his wife.
- The other was sent to another RFE/RL employee and also mentioned Bernard's condition and threatened Bernard.
- The third letter was posted in Neuburg A.D. Donau, Germany and mailed to Vlad Georgescu in Washington, D.C.

Vlad Georgescu was then employed as a journalist for RFE in Washington and one of his programs had been broadcast on January 3, 1981, and attacked the Romanian émigré organization the Iron Guard. The threatening letter Vlad received was signed with another variation: "GRUPUL V." The text of the letter was just as vicious and vulgar as the ones Emil Georgescu had received in December 1980:

> Now that you have been recruited by Noel Bernard and work for that cesspool ... you have become a Judas.... You are a beast full of cancer and venom and are trying to gain the confidence of the Americans through the Jews of RFE.[7]

Emil Georgescu quietly continued working. On the morning of February 18, 1981, a suspicious young man followed him, and he looked similar to the one who has attacked him January 26, 1981. Emil later explained that he and his wife had been walking their dog around 8:15 P.M. when they noticed a young man lurking in the bushes who then followed them for some distance before approaching them. The man apparently never spoke to either of them. At this point Mrs. Georgescu reached into her pocket and pulled out a "gas alarm" that emitted a very shrill sound, and the man ran in the other direction. The Georgescus returned to their apartment and called the RFE/RL guard supervisor.

After the Carlos-directed bombing of RFE/RL on February 21, 1981, Georgescu's problems took on secondary importance to RFE/RL management.[8] For the next months after the bombing, days at RFE/RL were full of meetings, surveys, etc., with both German and American officials, on how to add security to a building that previously had none. In addition, Georgescu said that he was maintaining direct contact with the Munich police concerning the death threats he had received. The bombing of RFE/RL and getting back to a normal work environment was on everyone's mind, including Emil Georgescu.

Georgescu Meets His Killer

The problems surrounding Emil Georgescu remained in the background at RFE/RL, due to the reconstruction of the building after the bombing in February, until April 27, 1981: Emil Georgescu that evening received a phone call from a then unidentified male, speaking Romanian, who stated that he had been paid 10,000 DM to kill Emil and another Romanian émigré, Victor Frunza, then living in Denmark. The caller said that he was not a killer and was calling only to warn Georgescu. He advised Emil not to answer the phone during the night. He would tell the other man, the one who had sent him, that Georgescu was not home; this was the reason he couldn't kill him. He added that he would turn himself in to the American authorities in the morning, when he would meet with Georgescu at RFE/RL. The caller also said that he had a pistol with a silencer, and that he would surrender that, too, in the morning. After repeating that he would be at RFE/RL in the morning, he ended the phone call.

The meeting between Georgescu and his "killer," which was to take place at RFE/RL, turned out to be a ploy. The next day Mrs. Georgescu was assaulted during the lunch hour, and Georgescu returned to his apartment to see what happened. About thirty minutes later, Georgescu and his wife arrived at RFE/RL. Mrs. Georgescu explained that her second-floor neighbor had noticed a bearded young man taking photographs of the Georgescu apartment, and she had called Mrs. Georgescu. Mrs. Georgescu left her apartment and went outside to watch what this man was doing. At first, she couldn't find him and went to the garage area where she found him taking Polaroid photographs; he was waiting for one to develop. After a few seconds, he noticed her and started to walk away. At this point, she went up to him and asked in German what he was doing there. He answered in broken German that he was taking pictures for a Romanian friend. She then asked him in Romanian for the pictures, and he answered in German: "Warum?" (Why?) She then took hold of his arm, tried to pull him toward the apartment, and yelled that she was going to call the police.

There was a brief struggle; he broke loose and started to run away. She called for help, and three men started to run after this man. Nevertheless, he eluded them and got away. Mrs. Georgescu, then obviously upset, called Munich police to report the incident. After this call to the police, she telephoned the Romanian embassy in Cologne. She asked for the reasons the Romanians were doing this and what would it take for them to stop it. A spokeswoman replied that she didn't know what Mrs. Georgescu was talking about. Mrs. Georgescu then said that they were going to hold a press conference and that she had the license plate number of a yellow car from Cologne that had been seen leaving the area just after the bearded man assaulted her. Georgescu had reported that two "federal authorities from Cologne" had earlier visited him. They asked him many questions about the recent threats, the bomb explosion in Cologne and many questions about the Romanian Service on RFE. Georgescu added the men were familiar with the internal politics of RFE's Romanian Service. One of the men told Georgescu that he was involved in the espionage affair that involved Germany's ex-chancellor Willy Brandt.

After Mrs. Georgescu called Herr Hartmann of the Munich police, she returned to the garage area to see if the young man had dropped anything during their brief struggle. She found a cigarette package on which was written "15 Archus." She gave the package to Herr Hartmann when he arrived. Archus is the city in Denmark where RFE/RL freelancer Victor Frunza then lived.

Radu Rusch

At 7 P.M. Georgescu said in a telephone call that the man who had told him that he had been sent to kill him had again called. In addition, this man had assaulted Mrs. Georgescu. He said that he would explain everything when he surrendered to the "appropriate American authorities." Georgescu arranged that he and this yet unidentified man would meet in the reception area of RFE/RL at 8 P.M.

Shortly before then, Mrs. Georgescu was standing outside the building with three Munich policemen. Mrs. Georgescu said that her husband was in the RFE/RL guardroom with the man who had said he was going to kill him. She added that Georgescu would not let the police in the room. He had told the police that this man had saved his life, and Georgescu promised that he would help him.

In the guardroom, Georgescu and a man were deep in conversation. Georgescu then stood up and happily said, "This man saved my life. He can prove everything." He said that he was the one who had frightened Georgescu in October 1980 (see below). He introduced the man, who was about 6'2" and muscular, as Radu Rusch. He towered over Georgescu and could have seriously injured him without a weapon. Rusch had long curly hair, a full beard, and a wild look in his eyes. Rusch was asked for the pistol he reportedly was carrying. Rusch stated that he had given it to his "boss," and that he was unarmed. He was wearing a brown leather jacket and jeans. He handed over his passport and wallet. Rusch said that he refused to talk to the German police, and Georgescu insisted that the Munich police be kept out of it.

Georgescu was very excited and kept thanking Rusch for saving his life. He then offered to take care of him, to give him money. Copies of the passport pages were made. The police officers nervously waited another fifteen minutes outside the room and then insisted that they had to arrest Rusch. Rusch became very nervous and begged that he not be turned over to the police because Romanian intelligence had a source in the police. A Munich police supervisor arrived and Georgescu pleaded on his knees with the police supervisor to hear Rusch's story and to let him stay at RFE/RL to speak with the "Americans." The police supervisor told Georgescu that he lacked the evidence to arrest Rusch and agreed to leave Rusch at RFE/RL. Georgescu and Rusch then went to the RFE/RL security office and a long night began.

The Story of Radu Rusch

Rusch began his story by saying that he had been born with the name Radu Dochioiu in 1952, and that his name later has been changed to Radu Rusch. He said the first time he saw Georgescu in person was in late October 1980. Previously, in Nuremberg, Germany, he had seen "hundreds of photographs of Georgescu, including those of Georgescu entering and leaving the RFE/RL building. Rusch said that he knew the layout of Georgescu's apartment. He knew approximately when Georgescu took his dog for a walk at night, and in what direction he left the apartment. The first night in October 1980, he had waited around the corner from Georgescu's apartment where he knew he would be walking. Two other Romanians, named Mihai Corneliu Vulcu[9] and Aurelian Totoescu, were about 200 meters away, sitting in a car. Rusch was only to rough up Georgescu, not kill him. He saw Georgescu approaching and he went toward him. He got to within a few feet of Georgescu and changed his mind, as he looked at Georgescu's face and decided that he couldn't hit him. He asked Georgescu for a light for his cigarette. Georgescu gave it to him and Rusch said thanks. Georgescu went on his way and Rusch went back to the car and told the men that he had just missed him. Georgescu walked back to his apartment.

Rusch and the others drove back to Munich, and he stayed at the

Muenchner Hof hotel. The next night they drove back to Georgescu's apartment in Haar and repeated the process: he went to the prearranged spot and the other two men waited in their car. Georgescu came out of his apartment and walked his dog in same direction as the previous night. When Georgescu got to the same spot, Rusch walked out from behind some bushes and again approached Georgescu. As before, he did not attempt to strike Georgescu but just asked him for a light. This time Georgescu's dog acted nervously, as did Georgescu, and Rusch left in a hurry.

He offered the same excuse to the other two men as he did the previous night: Georgescu was too fast in returning to his apartment. Vulcu and Rusch drove back to Munich and Vulcu gave him 3,000 DM for his services. Rusch paid off the money he owed on a car and bought some gifts for his family in Romania. Vulcu told him that they would be in touch with him again in two or three months, when they would try it again.

Rusch was asked to explain how he had been recruited to do this against Georgescu. He said that through word of mouth in Frankfurt, it was known in Romanian émigré circles that he needed a job. One day a Romanian named Totoescu asked him to help fix one of his cars. For ten days, he helped Totoescu and earned 1,600 DM. Totoescu offered to sell the car, a Renault Alpine, for 1,600 DM. From his earnings, Rusch paid 600 DM as a down payment. Rusch was then told one day that he could earn 3,000 DM: "I've got a deal for you where you can get easy money, and it won't be dangerous." He was then introduced to Vulcu who told him how Georgescu and RFE/RL Freelancer Victor Frunza had cheated on a business deal worth about 300,000 DM and now Georgescu had to be taught a lesson. There was no talk of any political motive for beating up Georgescu. In fact, Rusch stated that at this time he did not know that Georgescu worked for RFE/RL.

Rusch returned to Romania where he remained for a few months, arriving in West Germany again in March 1981. He was working in a pizza place in Schweinfurt, and Vulcu, who had recruited him earlier, came into the place one day. He told him that he could make a lot of money and that it would be easy to earn it. He didn't explain at this point how he could earn the money. Vulcu just told him to pack his bags. They then took the train to Nuremberg. On the train, he was told that they were going to Denmark to beat up Victor Frunza. After arriving in Nuremberg, Rusch was then told that they were going to kill Frunza. If he did not do it, Rusch's family in Romania would be killed.

Rusch and Vulcu then drove from Nuremberg to Denmark, crossing the border at 7 A.M. on April 24, 1981. They arrived in Copenhagen before noon and rented a room in the Hotel Memo. They talked more about guns in Copenhagen, near the train station. At a restaurant that evening, Vulcu met a Danish prostitute and they went to a cafe. The pistol was in a false bottom of a rucksack and was equipped with a silencer. When Vulcu was in the cafe, he told Rusch to take the pistol, go to the address of Frunza in Copenhagen and kill him. Rusch went to the address about 10 P.M. and discovered that the address was part of an office complex. He noticed a plaque with "Radio something" on the outside of the door leading into the building.

He returned to the cafe and told Vulcu what he had found. Vulcu was upset and angered that they had the wrong address. Rusch and Vulcu then took the Danish prostitute and made some Polaroid pictures of the address, using the prostitute as a model in front of the building. Vulcu explained that they would show these pictures to the others to prove that they were in Denmark. He did not identify who these "others" were. The three returned to the hotel. Vulcu and the prostitute slept in the room, while Rusch slept in the hallway.

The next morning they took a taxi to a bridge along a river and started to look for Frunza, using the address they had. Vulcu gave the gun and bullets to Rusch. In addition, Rusch said they had "toxic gas bullets" to use against the police, if they shot Frunza and the police tried to capture them.

They left Copenhagen and drove around looking for the city Archus, a few hundred miles northwest of Copenhagen. They gave up the search, took some more Polaroid pictures in Copenhagen and Denmark to prove that they had tried to find Frunza, and then they left Denmark.

On Sunday morning, April 26, they returned to Nuremberg and that night they took a train to Munich. They walked to a prearranged spot near the main train station where they found a green Lada or Fiat, with Munich license plates. Vulcu had the keys for the car. They then drove to Haar. Vulcu told him it would be easy to stand on the terrace and shoot Georgescu through the window.

They arrived between 9:30 and 10 P.M., and noticed that the shutters were drawn. Vulcu stayed in the car in a parking lot next to a bank near the apartment building. Rusch went for a walk around the building and returned to the car, telling Vulcu that all the lights were out in the apartment. Vulcu didn't believe him, and both returned to Georgescu's apartment building. Because the apartment was dark, they drove back to Munich where Rusch stayed with a friend at the Muenchner Hof hotel. Vulcu told Rusch told not to say anything or, repeating an early threat, his family in Romania would be killed.

Monday, they met about 10 A.M., across from the main train station, and returned to Haar. Vulcu handed the gun over to Rusch and told him to kill Georgescu Monday night. Vulcu drove back alone to Munich.

Rusch spent most of the time in a small cafe near Georgescu's apartment.

At about 8 P.M., he went to the Haar S-Bahn station (public transportation) and then called Georgescu at about 9:30 P.M. It was then that he told him that he was sent to kill him, but he couldn't do it. He was supposed to call Vulcu's wife in Nuremberg and say: "I've bought the shirts" if he killed Georgescu. If he had not he was to say: "I couldn't find the shirts." After calling Georgescu that evening, he called Vulcu's wife and told her, "I couldn't find them."

Tuesday morning Rusch met with Vulcu who took the pistol and said he would do it himself as Rusch couldn't do anything right. They bought more Polaroid film and drove to Haar.

Vulcu waited in the car in front of the apartment building where Georgescu lived while Rusch took the pictures of the apartment. Then is when the struggle with Georgescu's wife took place. After the struggle, Rusch ran from the scene. Vulcu noticed what happened, got out of his car, and went into the cafe. He waited a few minutes and then drove in the direction where Rusch had run and eventually picked him up. At this point, they noticed that a yellow Opel was following them. There were two men in the Opel and the passenger was continuously talking into a microphone or a telephone. After a few minutes, Rusch and Vulcu stopped the car and took some pictures. The yellow Opel also stopped. The passenger spoke into a microphone or telephone and then quickly drove off in the other direction.

Rusch and Vulcu got back into their car and drove into Munich, arriving about 2:30 P.M., Rusch got out at the Munich main station, and Vulcu apparently left for Nuremberg. Vulcu said he would return Saturday or Sunday, and that they would try it again. He told Rusch that he would get in touch with him somehow.

Never in Rusch's story did he mention that the attempt on Georgescu was a result of his working for RFE/RL. In fact, Rusch told us that he didn't know that Georgescu worked for RFE/RL, until he called to tell Georgescu that he was sent to kill him. He said that Vulcu never mentioned that the Romanian Secret Service directed the action against Georgescu.

Rusch said he knew nothing about the bombing of RFE/RL on February 21, 1981. He thought that Vulcu had a list of others to be killed, but he was not sure. He never saw any names of anyone else that might work for RFE/RL.

At one point, Vulcu said that after they killed Georgescu and Frunza, they could make big money by going to France, Spain and the United States and killing others.

The entrance and exit visa stamps in his passport confirmed Rusch's dates of arrival and departure in Germany and Denmark.

Rusch said that if he didn't kill Emil, another team would be sent to do

it. Rusch finally finished his story. Georgescu appeared at the police headquarters at 8 A.M. Rusch also went to Police Headquarters and gave the police
a written statement. Afterward, Rusch left Munich and returned to Romania.

Vulcu was subsequently arrested in Nuremberg. Photographs of Emil
Georgescu along with diagrams of his apartment were in Vulcu's possession.
Afterward, he was released and, while facing possible prosecution, he hastily
left Germany for Romania.

Murder Attempt on Emil Georgescu

Georgescu and the Munich police apparently were working very closely,
and some events, such as letters or phone calls, were not reported to us but
directly to the Munich police. In late July, two Frenchmen went to his apartment at 11 P.M. They said they were looking for a lawyer and asked to meet
him. Georgescu refused to let them into his apartment, and they quickly left,
only to return the next morning.

On July 28, 1981, shortly before 8 A.M., Georgescu left his apartment to
go to work. He walked down a flight of stairs to the garage entrance. At the
bottom of the stairs, a man was standing there. He asked Georgescu in French
if he were Emil Georgescu. Georgescu started to yell for help; the man attacked
with a knife and stabbed him. Georgescu tried to defend himself with an
attaché case, but the man continued stabbing. Georgescu was no match for the
attacker who was well over six feet tall; Emil Georgescu was about 5'5". Emil
Georgescu was stabbed over 25 times. At one point, Georgescu managed to
ask in French, "Why?" and the attacker answered, according to Georgescu, "So
you will never write again."

Georgescu's wife heard his screams, left the apartment, and ran down
the stairs calling out for help. The attacker then tried to open a locked door,
turned around, and pushed Mrs. Georgescu out of the way. He ran to a waiting car. Mrs. Georgescu ran up the stairs, again calling out for help, and followed the man. She saw the car and part of the license plate. Neighbors called
the police. Medical help and the police quickly arrived. Mrs. Georgescu gave
the police a description of the car and license plate number.

The medical team decided that Emil Georgescu was too seriously injured
to be transported by ambulance, and a special medical helicopter flew him to
a Munich hospital. The knife with which the attacker had stabbed Georgescu
had a relatively short blade, and this possibly saved Georgescu's life.

Mrs. Georgescu telephoned RFE/RL with the news. Police had by then
already arrested two Frenchmen, Claude Cottenceau and Freddy Layani, as
they were driving towards Austria. Mrs. Georgescu left with the police to

identify the attacker. RFE/RL president Glenn Ferguson posted the following message to RFE/RL staff on the murder attempt:

> At approximately 8:00 A.M. this morning, Mr. Emil-Valer Georgescu, a Supervising Program Editor in the Romanian Broadcasting Service, was stabbed in the abdomen and chest in the basement garage of his apartment house. An operation has been performed at the Neuperlach Hospital, and he has been taken to the intensive care unit. We do not have any definitive word concerning his condition.
>
> The police have apprehended two suspects, and positive identification of the assailant has been made. We have not received any report from the police concerning a motive for the attack. When additional information has been received, we will notify you immediately.[10]

Georgescu remained hospitalized in critical condition for many months. On February 1, 1982, Emil Georgescu returned to work and made his first broadcast over RFE/RL. Then RFE/RL president Glenn Ferguson notified the staff of Georgescu's return with the following message:

> We are pleased to inform you that Mr. Emil Georgescu, a senior member of the staff of the Romanian Service of RFE/RL, has fully recovered from the serious injuries, which he received in an attack on his life on July 28, 1981. It is expected that Mr. Georgescu, a Supervising Program Editor, will be able to resume his duties shortly.
>
> Mr. Georgescu discharged an important role in the Romanian Service. We are happy to learn that his physical condition will allow him to return to work. While we remain deeply concerned by the attack on Mr. Georgescu, we have confidence in him, and we commend him for his loyalty and commitment to RFE/RL.[11]

Emil Georgescu and his wife were then under 24-hour police protection, including a police escort to and from work. He and his wife were given weapons permits, and after some police training they purchased pistols. Nevertheless, he was not allowed to carry the pistol into the RFE/RL building. In his first broadcast, he detailed what has happened to him the previous July and what led up to the actual attack. He mentioned the Radu Rusch episode, and what Rusch allegedly had told the police about his involvement in a plot to kill Emil.

In March, the political officer at the U.S. consulate said that Rusch went into the U.S. embassy in Bucharest, Romania, and complained to the officials at the embassy that Georgescu's program was too critical about him. Georgescu aired a second program about Rusch, and in April 1982, the U.S. Consulate in Munich informed RFE/RL that Rusch again had gone into the U.S. Embassy in Bucharest.

Prosecutor's Evidence

According to the prosecution's report dated March 15, 1982, the two Frenchmen gave sworn statements full of contradictions; they continued to maintain that they had nothing to do with the attack, and that they were innocent. The prosecution's evidence included statements of Georgescu, his wife Lydia, policemen, and people from the hotels where the Frenchmen stayed while in Munich. There were over six hundred pages of evidence, statements, and documents. The two Frenchmen remained separated in jail after their arrest in July 1981.

One of the planned defense witnesses was one Boris Rubin, who had an extensive arrest record in Germany for, among other things, weapons sales. Rubin made a full sworn statement implicating himself and the Frenchmen in stolen jewelry schemes. He said that he was involved with one Frenchman regarding more than DM 100,000 of stolen jewelry, meeting at times in Paris and in Munich. In December 1980, Rubin explained, he had been in prison in Paris where he met one Pierre Utreh. Utreh then introduced Rubin to Jean Claude Cottenceau, the man who is alleged to have driven the car after the Georgescu attack. Cottenceau offered to sell stolen jewelry to Rubin. In January 1981, Cottenceau flew to Berlin and met Rubin. Rubin met Cottenceau at the Hotel Thober in January 1981 and paid him DM 50,000 for stolen jewelry.

Rubin continued with details of his travels and contacts: in February he had flown to Paris and met again Cottenceau and Utreh. He only stayed one day. Utreh subsequently flew to Berlin and gave Rubin a diamond ring. Rubin flew back to Paris around Eastertime 1981 and paid DM 35,000 to Cottenceau. He also met the actual attacker Freddy Layani and possibly six others. After May, he met Cottenceau and Layani in Berlin. Shortly after this meeting, Cottenceau called from Paris and offered more stolen jewelry to Rubin. In June he flew to Paris and again met with Cottenceau and Layani.

Never in Rubin's statement was there any mention of Georgescu working at RFE/RL. Rubin' s statement implicated himself and the Frenchmen in criminal activities in Berlin and in Paris. One had to be careful in taking his statement as completely truthful or accurate. As will be shown below, the Frenchmen were in Munich more than once and at times asked for directions to Haar, where Emil Georgescu lived.

After the attack on Georgescu, a woman working at the Hotel Paris in Munich recognized the two Frenchmen from photographs in the newspapers, and she called the police. She called the police because the two Frenchmen registered there under other names. She gave a statement to the police wherein she said that the Frenchmen stayed at the hotel and asked her for directions to Haar. She either gave them a map with instructions on how to get there, or they had a map and she made some notations on the map. They returned to the hotel a week later and made reservations for July 28, 1981, the day Georgescu was attacked. This woman recalled that the two Frenchmen had said that they either were traveling to Berlin or were in Berlin before that date.

A Munich police report about Radu Rusch was also included in the prosecutor's file, including Totoescu's statements. Totoescu reportedly said that Rusch was caught trying to smuggle refugees across the border from Hungary to Austria. He was returned to Romania. It was not known how he was returned, or if he decided to work for either the Hungarian or Romanian intelligence services. For some unknown reason, Radu Rusch's sworn statement was not included in the Munich police reports.

Georgescu Press Conference

Emil Georgescu gave a press conference in May 1982. About one hundred people, including invited guests who would support his position, press reporters, a TV crew, and, the Munich police-protection team were there. Half the audience consisted of Romanians, including some RFE/RL staff members. Georgescu's support consisted of Paul Coma, the famous Romanian dissident in exile in Paris, Victor Frunza from Denmark, Romanian priest Father Pop, and RFE/RL employee Serban Orescu. Goma and Orescu were victims of the book bombs in February 1981—see Chapter 4 for more details.

Georgescu distributed a two-part, forty-page written statement to the audience shortly before the conference got under way. He opened the press conference with extensive excerpts from that statement. Twice Georgescu departed from his written text. He issued a stinging protest, delivered in dramatic tones and theatrical gestures, as only he could do, against representatives of "American intelligence" and RFE managers. He charged that they had deprived him of friendly witnesses in the trial by spiriting away to the United States the two Romanians (unnamed) who had confessed that Romanian Securitate had hired them to murder him.

Georgescu then vehemently denied charges that he made undue or illegal profits from his activities on family-reunion cases. He said he made only 100 DM per case he handled. Georgescu spoke partly in German, partly in Romanian. With him was a Romanian-German interpreter who performed poorly, and Georgescu and those in the audience constantly corrected his German.

The press conference collapsed into confusion. The remarks of Victor Frunza and Father Pop, particularly those of the Father Pop, were personal and at times irrelevant. It appeared that the two wanted to draw attention to themselves and their self-importance, rather than to the Georgescu case. They stood in front of the other participants to steal the spotlight for themselves. Frunza spoke in Romanian, with the benefit of the same interpreter, while Father Pop spoke in German.

RFE/RL employee Serban Orescu's contribution was limited to a brief account of how he had been the victim of a parcel-bomb attack in February 1981. His remarks were sober and factual, and he deliberately refrained from discussing the controversial aspects of the case. He spoke in an academic tone and with personal restraint, in marked contrast to the emotional style and speculations of the other participants. Goma was pushed aside from the beginning (he was simply cut off by Father Pop), and he was silent for most of the press conference. The local press the next day contained some details of the press conference, but the results were not ones for which Georgescu had hoped.

Chaotic Trial in Munich

The trial itself became controversial. Some days before the trial was to begin on April 19, 1982, the still mysterious "Group V" made written bomb threats to Georgescu's lawyer and the courthouse:

> We have read in the newspaper *Die Welt am Sonntag* that the trial against our friends and comrades Layani and Cottenceau is to be opened on April 16, 1982, and that you, sir, are to represent the traitor Emil Georgescu.
>
> We have to warn you that we will blow up both the court building and your house in case our two friends are sentenced, and that you will not have long to live.
>
> Emil Georgescu is a crook. He has cheated his country and he continues to swindle millions of people through that dirty radio station RFE, millions who listen to his commentaries. We haven't yet settled our accounts with him. He will have to die like a traitor because he sold himself to the American imperialists for hard currency.
>
> Group V[12]

Because of this threat, Georgescu's lawyer withdrew from the case, and extra police were added around the courthouse. The trial of the two Frenchmen opened, on schedule, on April 19, 1982. Georgescu was not only the prosecutor's the main witness, but also a "co-prosecutor" who was allowed to question witnesses. There was extensive press coverage about the opening day of the trial and for some days afterwards. All the contradictions and confusion of the trial were published.

The defendant Layani, the younger Frenchman, admitted that he had stabbed Georgescu. However, he said he was recruited in Paris to only "beat Georgescu and return with money and jewelry." He said that he had stabbed Georgescu only in self-defense. He had been told that Georgescu was armed and said that when he first confronted Georgescu, Georgescu had jumped at him and because of the struggle he'd had to defend himself. He also gave details about prostitutes and criminals in Paris, and his mother and ex-wife testified in his behalf. Cottenceau refused to testify.

Georgescu testified that he believed that the Romanian secret police was behind the attack. He reviewed the history of what had happened to him after he'd started working for Radio Free Europe. He said that Layani had told him while he was being stabbed that he wouldn't write anymore. Layani denied it: he said that he did not stab him in the hand and that he'd never said anything to Georgescu in the struggle. Georgescu denied that he jumped at Layani, and he pointed out that the Frenchman was much bigger than he was. The defense lawyers then subjected Georgescu to a rigorous cross-examination: he was questioned in depth about his clients and fees, for example.

Mrs. Georgescu testified about what she had seen and heard. Other prosecution witnesses included policemen, workers at the hotel where the Frenchmen stayed, and a taxi driver who had witnessed Mrs. Georgescu chasing after the Frenchmen after the attack. At times, she was very emotional and would interrupt any witness she thought was attacking her husband's credibility.

The court decision was returned on July 21, 1982. Although the prosecutor had demanded life sentences for attempted murder, Layani, then twenty-five years old, was sentenced to eleven years for attempted manslaughter by stabbing Georgescu 22 times. Cottenceau, then thirty-four years old, received four and a half years for causing serious bodily harm. The judge said he believed that a third party, possibly the Romanian Secret Service, was involved. However, he added, "There was no evidence to show which third party was behind the knife attack."

The 1982 German interior minister's official annual report, published in 1983, contained this interesting information:

> Only through prompt assistance could the severely wounded victim be saved. The perpetrators were arrested and sentenced to several years in prison. They stubbornly refused to give any information on who had hired them. After the failure of this assassination attempt, other persons from the Romanian intelligence service were given the assignment of liquidating the Romanian émigré once and for all.[13]

A Defector's Story

In August 1982, police protection for Georgescu was reduced and eventually stopped. That same month, a defector from Romania had walked into the U.S. embassy in Bonn. The man, Adrian C., told a story about how the

Romanian Intelligence Service (Securitate) forced him into working for the Securitate, or go to jail if he refused. He explained that he had been recruited in Romania in order to infiltrate the Iron Guardists there. Before meetings of the Iron Guard, he was fitted with microphones so the conversations could be recorded. In addition, he had planted transmitters in various locations for recording purposes.

In March 1982, one Colonel Tudor of the Securitate had approached him and given him the chance to work for the motherland. Adrian C. was to provide a list of friends and relatives living in the West, and he would later meet with a foreign affairs specialist of the Securitate. In April or May 1982, he met with this foreign affairs specialist and Colonel Tudor. He was told at that time to prepare to immigrate to West Germany and he was given the assignment of killing an unidentified "bandit" working for the Romanian Service of RFE/RL. He was to receive the name of the victim later, presumably after arriving in West Germany. After completion of this assignment, he would then return to Romania and complete his education by attending law school at the expense of the Securitate. He never intended to kill anyone. Adrian C.'s story, that Colonel Tudor had recruited him, was plausible: a Colonel Tudor was known in the Securitate. His story was questionable, however: he was not given any previous training in how to kill someone and he had never held a steady job in Romania before the recruitment.

Adrian C.'s aunt lived in West Germany and he made all arrangements for obtaining a visa. After arriving in Germany, he went to the U.S. embassy in Bonn and "surrendered" because his real intention was to emigrate to either the United States or to Canada. RFE/RL told him how to legally emigrate to the United States as a refugee, if he still wanted to do so, and he was turned over to German authorities who would further debrief him and give him protection.

Adrian C. arranged with Emil Georgescu to give a broadcast interview concerning his assignment. The interview was conducted, but Adrian C.'s story was changed to say that he had been recruited to actually kill Emil Georgescu. He told Emil that he had given this information to the U.S. officials in Bonn and later to German officials. He added that he had found Emil's name and address in the Munich phone book and then written to him. He met with Emil and told Emil that he recognized him from the photograph that the Securitate showed him while he was in Romania. Emil then apparently arranged to have Adrian C. give his testimony to the Munich criminal police and the state prosecutor.

An official at the U.S. embassy said that Adrian C. had told the debriefer in Bonn that he was not given the name of the "bandit" at RFE/RL. Also that during the initial debriefing he had been asked directly about Emil Georgescu, and that he'd answered only that he knew that Emil broadcast over RFE/RL, and that there had been an attempt on Emil's life. He repeated that he had not been given the name of Emil as the one he was assigned to kill. There was no explanation given for the discrepancies in his stories. Adrian C. quietly disappeared and his interview with Georgescu was not broadcast.

Emil Georgescu Resigns from RFE/RL

Emil Georgescu was never again the same broadcaster he was before the knife attack. His programs were not as effective, his popularity decreased, and he was even reprimanded for plagiarizing a previously broadcast program. In June 1984, Georgescu wrote a twenty-five page emotional appeal to be relieved from duty. He gave one professional reason:

> I must however confess that I am at the same time deeply disappointed with the fact that I have failed to move the people of my land to action, to follow the example of the Hungarians in 1956, or that of the Polish people during these last years.
>
> This makes me believe that I either do not fulfill my duty efficiently, or that the nation I come from is a nation of cowards and that they are not worth the risk to my life.

He added his personal fear:

> I have to confess that my own shadow scares me out my wits, that I am terribly afraid: afraid of being killed, afraid of having to bear again the terrible pains that I experienced once. I sometimes regret not having let myself be killed on that fateful day, July 28, 1981. This nightmare might have ended then.[14]

His health deteriorated into lung cancer. He and RFE/RL reached a mutual agreement that he would resign from RFE/RL. Emil Georgescu died on February 1, 1985 and was buried in Munich. Yet his story did not end with his death.

General Ion Pacepa

Someone living in the West who could have provided Judge Kraemer the "political background" at Georgescu's trial was General Ion Pacepa, former chief of the Roman Foreign Intelligence Service who had defected to the United States in 1978. In his book *Red Horizons*, which first appeared in the United States in 1987, Pacepa wrote about the following incident, which took place in 1976:

"We just had another telephone discussion with Emil Georgescu in Munich," Luchian started off, as he shook my hand with his enormous bear paw. "Soon I'm going to bring Georgescu to his knees." He slapped a fat gray file with his huge palm.

On the evening of August 22, 1976, the eve of Romania's national day, the minister of interior, the then chief of the DIE and I had been summoned for a walk in Ceausescu's rose garden.

"Emil Georgescu must be silenced forever," Ceausescu ordered. "He should have his jaw, teeth, and arms broken, so that he will never be able to speak or write again." He added that foreign criminal mercenaries should do the job without any possible connection with Romanian authorities, and that no written record be kept of this conversation and the operation against Emil Georgescu.

Through DIE sources in France, West Germany, and the United States, as well as through signed and anonymous letters sent to Radio Free Europe, the DIE insinuated that Georgescu had received illegal moneys from Romanian émigrés and had been involved in dishonest fur and jewelry deals. Several scare letters were sent to Georgescu himself, threatening that he would be killed and his home burned down if he resumed his activity for his "Jewish masters" at the radio. These letters were written as if from a terrorist wing of the illegal Romanian fascist organization in exile the Iron Guard, and were signed "Group V." The DIE created group V out of whole cloth.[15]

There were some problems with Pacepa's analysis. He had left Romania in 1978 and was therefore not part of foreign intelligence operations in 1980 and 1981, when the letter writing campaign started. Why he remained silent so long about Georgescu is still an unanswered question. As in the "Balthazar" case above, he could have been a very important and effective witness. Nicolae Ceausescu had condemned him to death, and he feared for his life. He was under the protection of the CIA and apparently, his safety in Germany could not be guaranteed.[16]

After the fall and execution of Ceausescu in December 1989, RFE/RL contacted the newly appointed director of the Romanian Intelligence Service (SRI), Virgil Magureanu, for information on the Emil Georgescu case:

> According to information received from Hungarian, Czechoslovak, and former East German government sources, the famous terrorist named Carlos was supposedly paid one million dollars by Nicolae Ceausescu in August 1979, or was promised one million dollars, to silence the Romanian "Opposition" in the West. Among the criminal acts carried out by Carlos was ... the knife attack on Emil Georgescu in July 1981 by two Frenchmen named Layani and Cottenceau.

Magureanu answered in the obtuse Romanian Intelligence writing style:

> On the attack of the former RFE Romanian Service employee, Emil Georgescu, no information was obtained to invalidate those generally known

and accredited: the action was undertaken by the French citizens Layani and Cottenceau, as revenge for the swindle in which the victim was involved.

There are a few known cases in which persons, who became employees of RFE, had, before their departure abroad, been informers of the Securitate — including Emil Georgescu, who continued his informing activity by communicating via an unknown channel even after his employment with RFE/RL.[17]

Emil Georgescu was a victim of the Romanian External Intelligence Service not only physically, but also as an object of disinformation. Former RFE/RL Romanian Service director Nestor Ratesh succinctly summarized this hostile activity when he wrote,

> The Securitate staged a large and sophisticated campaign of mystification, purporting to prove that Emil Georgescu had been involved in shady businesses, the attempted murder being nothing but a settling of scores between dishonest partners. In Emil Georgescu's Securitate file (three volumes containing more than 1,000 pages) I saw many copies of forged letters that were sent to RFE/RL management and broadcasters, newspapers, German authorities as well as to the CIA and FBI directors, to members of Congress, and even to the president of the United States. They were meant to expose Emil as a crook and even as a Securitate agent. Many officers, spies and informers were involved in this effort, which for a while scored an undeserved success.
>
> An important document from Georgescu's Securitate file dating from late 1982 set as a task for the next phase to continue to gather "timely data on his situation and activity at the office and in his private life necessary for undertaking the measures for his neutralization."
>
> Agent "Helmut" reappears in the picture in mid–March 1983, surveying Georgescu's home and the RFE surroundings, setting for himself several benchmarks and succeeding in taking a few pictures. Four months later, agent "Konrad' brings the news that the guards (at Georgescu's home) had been withdrawn, although he continues to carry a pistol.
>
> On August 8, 1984, a key document cites an informative-operative combination by which Georgescu "was contacted directly by a trusted foreign source of ours." The document concluded somewhat cryptically, "We will watch with due attention the reactions to the measures undertaken and the way the personal situation evolves."[18]

7. Aggression in the Ether: Oleg Tumanov and Other KGB Agents

Valentine's Day Present 1986

Soviet intelligence officer Viktor P. Gundarev defected to the West in Athens, Greece, on Friday, February 14, 1986. The first media reports of Gundarev's defection appeared a week after his defection. He was about fifty years old and identified as a colonel in the KGB. Reportedly he defected with his seven-year-old son and a woman identified as a teacher who was taking care of his son.

The following night, Athens police detained four men from the Soviet embassy because they apparently were staking out the U.S. embassy to prevent his departure to the United States. Media reports said they were "armed to the teeth" with automatic weapons and hand grenades. The four men claimed diplomatic immunity and were released from custody. Gundarev's presence in the United States was confirmed by the State Department on February 22, 1986. According to the State Department spokesman, Charles Redman, Gundarev had been working since 1983 in Athens under cover of "head of the maritime section of the Soviet commercial mission" and had been granted asylum in the United States.

That day, John Bothwell, a retired U.S. Navy officer, was arrested at Heathrow Airport in London for "violating Britain's official secrets act." Reportedly he spent six months a year in Athens, and the other six months in Britain. His arrest was directly attributed to Gundarev's defection and debriefing in the United States. One media report quoted unidentified sources as saying that "confederates warned Bothwell of Gundarev's defection, but not in time."

His defection, though interesting in many respects, did not at first glance affect RFE/RL. However Gundarev's defection and the arrest of Bothwell unleashed a chain of events that led to the unmasking of KGB agents in Radio

171

Free Europe/Radio Liberty. Apparently fearing arrest, RFE/RL Russian Service employee Oleg Tumanov, one KGB agent at RFE/RL, fled Germany. Tumanov first was reported missing on Wednesday, February 26, 1986. The Russian Service Director called the security office and said that Tumanov had not reported for work that morning. He added that the RFE/RL "news budget" for Oleg Tumanov was piled in front of his apartment door, and that there had been no word from him for over twenty-four hours.

Tumanov Background Information

According to information listed on his RFE/RL application form, Oleg Tumanov was born in Moscow on November 12, 1944. His father was Alexander V. Tumanov, identified as a retired officer — branch unknown — born about 1903. His mother was Evdokina A. Tumanov, a retired civil servant, born about 1910. His last address in Moscow was listed as Leningradsky Prospect 14. Rumors in the RFE/RL Russian Service included ones that his father was a retired intelligence officer and that his uncle was a colonel in the KGB. His brother Igor Alexandrovich still lived in Moscow, but his occupation was not known. Tumanov attended elementary and secondary school in Moscow until 1961. He then attended a "trade school for draftsmen" until 1962. In 1963 he joined the Soviet merchant marine and served until 1965, when he supposedly jumped a ship outside Libya, swam to shore, and asked for political asylum. American authorities were notified and Tumanov was flown to West Germany. He was then processed at the U.S.-controlled refugee center known as Camp King near Frankfurt, Germany, as a defector, including a polygraph test. Officials at Camp King notified Radio Liberty about a young Russian prospect. A Radio Liberty manger went to Frankfurt and interviewed Tumanov, who was then invited to Munich and successfully passed the written and spoken Russian language tests. Tumanov joined Radio Liberty in June 1966 as a news writer trainee.

Tumanov had received permanent residence for Germany in Frankfurt on April 14, 1966, and was given a German travel document. His travel document issued in 1981 interestingly shows a different birth date of February 12, 1944. He never acquired German or U.S. citizenship.[1]

On the night when he was missing, the news budget was still piled against his door. The next morning, there was more news budget against the door; he had not returned to his apartment. In the afternoon, a Russian Service employee went into the apartment with a small suitcase that she was returning to the apartment, with some of Tumanov's clothes that she had washed for him. She didn't know that he was missing.

The apartment was in disarray. Unwashed dishes, glasses and other utensils were piled high in the kitchen. A few dishes on his living room table had spoiled food on them and were beginning to smell. His clothes closet was empty, except for a few ties and old jackets. It was obvious that some paintings had been removed from the walls of his apartment. He was known to be an avid photographer, but there were no cameras or photographic equipment in the apartment. Tumanov also was known as a serious stamp and coin collector; empty stamp and coin albums were left on one desk in the hallway. There were no suitcases to be found.

According to the Russian Service employee, Tumanov was at her apartment Sunday night, February 23, 1986. Someone she only knew as "Alexei" telephoned. She said that "Alexei" spoke to her in broken German with a heavy Russian accent.

She didn't listen to their telephone conversation. Oleg afterward told her that "Alexei" had a stamp collection of Russian and Soviet stamps worth about DM 6,000 that he wanted Tumanov to see. She recalled that Tumanov had earlier spoken with "Alexei," perhaps two weeks previously, about stamps. He identified "Alexei" as living in the West for about ten years. Tumanov told her that he'd agreed to a meeting at 3:00 P.M., Tuesday, February 25. "Alexei"

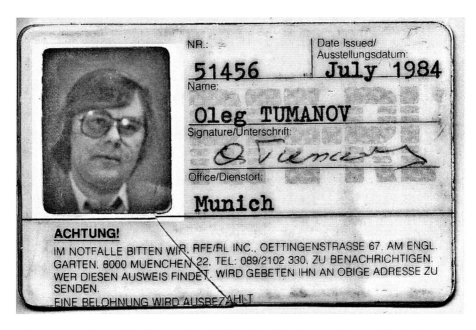

Former employee Oleg Tumanov's RFE/RL identification pass in 1984 (Radio Free Europe/Radio Liberty).

reportedly said that he had to leave earlier to go to a stamp auction or meeting in Vienna, so the meeting was moved up to 11:00 A.M. Tumanov then left her apartment shortly before 8:00 P.M. Sunday night and returned about 1:00 A.M. He did not explain his absence.

Little was known about Monday, February 24, except that Tumanov signed in a visitor at RFE/RL at 11:50 A.M., and spoke with him about a job possibility at RFE/RL. Tumanov left work about 1:00 P.M., stating that he was sick.

Tuesday morning, February 25, he called his supervisor, stating that he was still sick but that he could be expected to return to work Wednesday.

Thursday, February 27, his Russian Service girlfriend filed a "missing persons" report with the Munich police. Tumanov's ex-wife also had filed a missing persons report with the Munich police earlier that morning. Tumanov was then officially listed as missing. The following day, one of RFE/RL's contact officers in the political section of the Munich police called and said that he was looking into the matter of Tumanov. The lock to his apartment was changed and the keys were retained in the security office.

On Monday, March 3, 1986, Bavarian State Police (LKA) were advised that one of our employees was missing. The next day a police officer called and asked if he and another LKA officer could enter the apartment. They did and it appeared that nothing had been changed in the apartment or had been removed from it.

The German travel documents issued, found in his apartment after Tumanov's disappearance, showed extensive travel throughout Western Europe, especially to Vienna. From Vienna he had flown through East Berlin to Denmark, against RFE/RL travel restrictions then in effect. Both men made a preliminary search of the apartment for any clues as to what might have happened to Tumanov. Since most of the papers in the apartment were in Russian, it was hard for them to make sense of the various books, videotapes, and papers, in the apartment and they selectively asked for translations.

There were various bank statements from the Deutsche Bank, including one showing that someone named Vladimir Krysanov had a bank account in Munich using Tumanov's name and address. Krysanov lived in Sweden and apparently defected in 1966. Krysanov and Tumanov apparently "accidentally met" at Camp King after both defected under similar circumstances. Krysanov was turned down for employment with RL in 1971, as his qualifications were never really established.

It is possible that Krysanov was a member of the émigré group known as NTS and operated an antique bookstore in Stockholm. He was known to have assisted the NTS representative in Stockholm, Timofeev, until Timofeev's death. Tumanov did not join NTS, though he maintained a close relationship with various Munich members of NTS.

According to later police information, Tumanov went to his local bank on Monday, February 24, and requested a withdrawal of his money. The next morning, he received DM 20,000 in cash from the bank. The bank official would not give out more information without a court order.

One interesting document found in Tumanov's apartment was a receipt from Munich's Russian-language bookstore, Kuban & Sagner, for books purchased from 1982 to 1986. The receipt shows that Tumanov paid a bill of DM 4,400 on February 17, 1986, one week before he disappeared.

The first newspaper articles about Tumanov started appearing on March 4, 1986. Then the *New York Times* correspondent in Bonn, James Markham, telephoned and asked for some background information on Tumanov. His article, "Russian Station Editor Missing," appeared in the *New York Times* and *International Herald Tribune.* Afterward, numerous articles appeared in the western press, speculating that the KGB had kidnapped Tumanov or that he was a KGB agent in Radio Liberty. The *New York Daily News* ran one article headlined "Was This Teddy Bear Really a Mole?"

The initial results of these articles were immediate: on March 4 two telephone calls were received at RFE/RL. One call was placed to the London office, the other to Munich. The call to London was in very clear British English, with the caller saying, "He is back in Moscow, alive and well. Thank you." The telephone message to Munich, in broken English, was difficult to understand but the meaning was clear: Tumanov was in Moscow. From the beginning, the U.S. consulate had been kept abreast, through personal meetings and telephone calls, of the Tumanov case developments.

Tumanov's KGB Connection Revealed

On April 1, 1986, RFE/RL first received some of the details of Oleg Tumanov's KGB background, when the RFE/RL security office learned from a very reliable source that Oleg Tumanov was indeed a bona fide defector to the West and not sent by the KGB with a mission to infiltrate Radio Liberty. Within a year of his defection, however, KGB officers had located Tumanov in Munich at Radio Liberty. KGB Headquarters Directorate "K" (counterintelligence) then ordered the respective KGB subordinate unit in East Berlin–Karlshorst, to approach Tumanov for recruitment as an intelligence agent. Within a year, KGB officers had located Tumanov in Munich. KGB Headquarters Directorate "K" (counterintelligence) ordered an approach to Tumanov by the KGB Representation in East Berlin, Karlshorst. A KGB officer contacted Tumanov and handed him letters from his father and mother. Tumanov's father was apparently a well-connected man who pleaded with his son to cooperate or take responsibility for ruining his father's career. Tumanov agreed to cooperate with the KGB.

By 1972, Tumanov was fully recruited and reporting about Radio Liberty. He was handled via personal meetings with his KGB case officers in East Berlin, Vienna and Helsinki, but never in West Germany.

Tumanov stole personnel lists and background information on Radio Liberty Russian Service personnel. By 1974, he had contributed twelve or thirteen volumes of information. A Soviet propaganda film about Radio Liberty, *Radio Divisiant*, appeared in 1974 and some of the documents Tumanov supplied were shown in the film. Of continuing interest to the fifth Chief Directorate (Ideology and Dissidents) was the relationship between Radio Liberty and the Frankfurt-based Russian émigré association known by the initials NTS.

In 1974, Gundarev became the acting chief of his section, with continuing responsibilities for the Tumanov case. His defection to the West dramatically affected Tumanov: after Tumanov learned of Gundarev's defection, he hastily flew to Berlin to ask for KGB advice on his exposure and possible arrest. After the KGB's preliminary damage assessment, he was told to return to Munich and continue working at RFE/RL. When the arrest of John Bothwell, because of Gundarev's revelations, became public knowledge, this was apparently too much of a risk for Tumanov, as well as for the KGB. He again requested to return to the USSR as soon as possible. This time the KGB agreed and quickly put Tumanov's exfiltration plan into effect.

KGB Agent Number Two, "Kit"

RFE/RL also received information from the same source about a second KGB agent, code name "Kit," identified as a naval officer, who had defected to the West from a Soviet reconnaissance warship off the coast of California.

"Kit" was Yuri Mikailovich Pyatakov, born on October 15, 1929 in Irkutsk, where he attended elementary and high schools. In 1948, he entered a military school for foreign languages, specializing in Korean. Later he attended the Institute of Foreign Languages in Irkutsk, specializing in English. He served eleven years in the Red Army, reaching the grade of captain. At the time of his defection on February 18, 1966, he was serving on the Soviet radio intercept trawler *Deflektor*, approximately twelve miles off California. From the trawler, he jumped overboard and was picked up by a U.S. destroyer, which was then engaged in surveillance of the *Deflektor*. He was debriefed until March 1966 and reportedly furnished reasonably valid information on Soviet monitoring. Because his credentials appeared to be excellent, and a polygraph examination tended to confirm his credibility, he was granted permanent residence in the United States under Public Law 110 in July 1966. He now used the name Yuri Michael Marin.

The KGB operation began when Marin was in Washington. He was spotted and recognized by a Soviet officer from the Soviet embassy. Apparently there were difficult "control problems," either surveillance or in finding Marin's residence and place of work. The KGB headquarters ordered the KGB residency in Washington to make a direct approach to Marin.

The first contact took place in a Washington D.C. art museum. Marin agreed to continue the contacts. By the third or fourth meeting, a counterintelligence officer was meeting Marin at his residence. Afterward they moved the relationship to clandestine meetings that lasted for about a year. He was then given the code name "Kit."

In September 1967, Marin was hired by the U.S. Army Russian Institute in Garmisch, Germany, about an hour's ride south of Munich. In his briefings by U.S. Army personnel, Marin reportedly said that he was warned that he faced execution if he ever returned to the Soviet Union. To his army colleagues, he appeared to accept this as fact and was not intimidated by it. From Garmisch, he made frequent trips to Munich for personal reasons.

In May 1970, he became considerably upset when he learned that he would not be granted U.S. citizenship in 1971 after the five-year period normal for regular applicants. His former membership in the Communist Party of the Soviet Union made it mandatory that he wait ten years before naturalization. He requested that a special private bill in his behalf be introduced in Congress, but that was refused.

He was hired by Radio Liberty in June 1971 as an announcer and occasional writer. A year later, he married a Radio Liberty employee. Sometime in 1973, he sought to work at the Russian Institute in Garmisch, but this time he was turned down for unknown reasons. At the KGB direction, Marin continued working for RL.

The KGB's Directorate "K" Headquarters 4th Department in Moscow reportedly supervised its Radio Liberty and Radio Free Europe operations from 1972 to 1974 and handled the "Kit" operation. By then Marin was being run in place at Radio Liberty by the KGB representative in East Berlin–Karlshorst. His initial reporting requirements were similar to those of Tumanov: obtain information about the staff, steal or make copies of important Radio Liberty documents.

"Kit" Objectives Changed

In early 1973 Directorate "K" changed Marin's objective to "active meas-ures" to expose Radio Liberty as a CIA "tool." Gundarev's section also began planning the escape (redefection) of "Kit" to USSR, via Austria and Budapest. Gundarev was supposed to meet Marin in Budapest as part of the Headquar-ters' reception team, but was replaced by his section chief, Fedor Zryanov, who wanted to go to Hungary. Gundarev stayed in Moscow to prepare a staged press conference, scheduled after Marin's arrival in Moscow.

Marin was scheduled to be transferred to Radio Liberty in New York in November 1973 but instead he departed Munich in his own automobile on October 14, 1973, for a then unknown destination, which turned out to be Budapest.

Even though the KGB was apparently prepared for Marin's return to the USSR, for some unknown reason, the initial staged press conference was delayed until sometime in 1975. Following several more press conferences, a book about his life as a KGB agent in Radio Liberty was published under his name but was actually written by someone in the KGB's Service A — Active Measures department. Articles appeared in the Soviet press under his name, wherein he exposed various "CIA spies" at Radio Liberty. Photographs of employees and photocopies of various Radio Liberty memoranda also appeared in the Soviet media — presumably supplied by Tumanov and/or Marin.

Yuri Marin was well paid for his services. The KGB set up a Moscow bank account for him and paid 3,000–4,000 rubles monthly into it. On his way to Moscow, he sent his wife a money order drawn on the National Bank of Hungary. He thereafter communicated with his wife using various addresses in the USSR. By the end of the 1970s, Marin reportedly resettled in Latvia or Estonia and was not seen or used in any propaganda campaign afterward.

Agent "Alex"

RFE/RL also learned about a third KGB agent identified with code name "Alex" in the early 1970s, who also was under the control of Directorate K, 4th Department. Alex was a "bona fide Berlin wall-jumper" and Red Army deserter. He was of the same generation as Tumanov but had an enlisted rank and lesser education. He had also resettled in West Germany. Similar to Mar-ian and Tumanov, he was recruited after his defection and was not a KGB agent with the task of infiltrating Radio Liberty. It was believed that Tumanov or Mar-ion spotted him for the KGB. His successful recruitment and subsequent han-dling were directed from the KGB representative in East Berlin–Karlshorst.

Gundarev guessed that perhaps Tumanov or "Kit" originally spotted him for the KGB. His recruitment was directed from the KGB representative in East Berlin. The inducement was passing him letters from his ailing mother in USSR who pleaded with him to cooperate in return for medical attention. KGB headquarters and KGB East Berlin planned a reunion for Alex in East Berlin with his ailing mother.

Alex reported information on other RL employees, independently of both Marin and Tumanov. Alex was employed at RL from 1961 until he was terminated for cause in 1972. He had had a history of problems at RL, including drinking and fighting with other employees. He was a chauffeur for RL. He was suspected of being involved in criminal matters and after his termination he was suspected of being a KGB agent.

After his termination from Radio Liberty, Alex became a truck driver who made periodic trips transporting goods to Italy, Spain, and other European countries. In early 1974, Kazachyuk, Alex's control officer, and the 4th Department Directorate "K" supervisor, Fedor Zyryanov, talked of—but rejected—a plan to use Alex as a "courier" for the more valuable and timely reporting from Tumanov. The plan was to take advantage of Alex's transport trips outside Germany for more frequent delivery of Tumanov's reports to the center in Moscow.

In April 1976, Alex arranged for an RL employee to travel to Berlin to try to get her mother to emigrate from the USSR. He introduced her to a "young Russian" named "Nikolayev" who told her to not to tell anyone about the meeting. She and Alex spent one night in West Berlin, flew to Copenhagen the next day and took the train back to Munich. There were no other known contacts afterward with the Radio Liberty employee, except one incident when he bruised her arm in an attempt to enter her apartment.

First Signal from Moscow

In early April 1986, a Russian Service employee met his distant cousin in Salzburg, Austria. The cousin was the director of the Moscow Experimental Factory of Musical Instruments. In this capacity, he was allowed to travel to the West on "business," mostly to Central America. After Tumanov's disappearance, this Russian Service employee received a phone call at home wherein his relative asked him if he was allowed to travel to Austria, as he was going to travel there. "It would be nice for relatives to meet," he said. The Russian Service employee answered that he could travel freely and he would like to meet him.

During the first week of March 1986, the cousin called again and said that he would be in Vienna with a group and then they would go to Salzburg and perhaps they could get together there. He added that he would call from Vienna as soon as the group arrived.

On or about April 10, the relative called from Vienna and said that he would be spending the weekend in Salzburg with the group he was traveling with. Our employee and his daughter took the train to Salzburg where they met the cousin. Most of the first day was a "family-reunion" day, as they had lunch and supper and walked around, enjoying the sites and sounds of Salzburg.

Our employee put his daughter on a train back to Munich at about 9:00 P.M. and he and his cousin returned to the hotel. Then the cousin made his pitch. He said, "The homeland needs you." And, he said that the KGB had "made a mistake" by the way he was treated in the Soviet Union, after he made his decision to emigrate. He added that "we" know that "you are working for Radio Liberty."

The cousin then asked if Tumanov was still being sought. Our employee answered, "Perhaps you have him. The cousin shrugged that remark aside and said, "That is another matter." There was no further discussion of Tumanov. Tumanov's disappearance had not been mentioned in the Soviet media, implying that the cousin knew about it from KGB circles.

What was interesting was the fact that the RL employee was first contacted in February, around the time of Tumanov's disappearance, and that Tumanov's name came up in the conversation in April. This meant either that the KGB was attempting to replace Tumanov at RFE/RL and the RL employee was being sounded out as a recruitment possibility, or, on the other hand, that Tumanov's replacement was already in place and this was nothing but disinformation showing that the KGB did not have anyone in RFE/RL. The latter seem more plausible, as the approach to the RL employee, while classical, was very clumsy in its execution.

Tumanov's Television Debut

On April 28, 1986, the Soviet news agency TASS announced that Oleg Tumanov had returned home and considered it "his civic duty to reveal plans hostile to the peoples of the world — the plans of those who inspire a 'crusade' against the USSR and supervise wide-scale psychological warfare." Tumanov appeared at a 3:00 P.M. press conference in the Press Center of the Ministry of Foreign Affairs in Moscow. However, the ninety-minute conference did not go as expected. Foreign correspondents did not buy his story. After he read a prepared statement, simultaneously published by TASS, the floor was opened to questions from Soviet and foreign correspondents. The next day British newspaper the *Guardian* best summed up the chaotic press conference:

The slick new Soviet publicity machine suffered its first public humiliation yesterday when a carefully staged press conference in Moscow for yet another dissident returning to his homeland virtually collapsed in ridicule.

Clearly nervous, sighing deeply, and at times mumbling almost incoherently, Mr. Tumanov refused to give any details about when or how or why he had decided to return to the Soviet Union.

The Soviet news agency TASS reported:

Oleg Tumanov, former acting editor-in-chief of the Russian service of Radio "Liberty" [RL], spoke at a press conference at the Press Center of the Ministry of Foreign Affairs of the U.S.S.R. today. He told newsmen how after defecting to the West more than 20 years ago he had found himself in an anti–Soviet trap set up by the military intelligence service and the Central Intelligence Agency of the United States.

"My road back home has been tortuous," Oleg Tumanov said in conclusion.

"I wouldn't wish anybody to experience this kind of 20-year-long road. I am now at home and it would seem the easiest thing to say that everything I have lived through has been a nightmare dream. No, a dream it hasn't been. Everything I told you here has been a reality, a nightmarish reality. Only perhaps it is not everybody that can see this reality objectively. I could and so the road back to my homeland was for me the natural and logical one. At a difficult time, and the world is going through a difficult time now, every honest person should be with his own people. This is why I am here."

That night, in prime time, Moscow Television Service, Vremya, broadcast excerpts from the press conference and focused on the Soviet journalists' questions. For example,

SECOND CLASS CAPTAIN NIKITIN, OBSERVER FOR *KRASNAYA ZVEZDA*: You spoke about the links between the radio station and CIA. Are there such links with the Pentagon and what is their nature?

TUMANOV: The fact is that different services, special services, of the United States, both the CIA and military intelligence, make wide use of the research materials, let's say, at the centers of the two radio stations. They are also involved in research in the military field. People who leave the Soviet Union normally undergo debriefing by military intelligence and by the CIA. They collect material ... [corrects himself] this material is collected, and returns in part to the radio station in a summarized form, and in full form, I say that it often also contains military information, so to say, that goes both to the Pentagon and to Langley.

It is well known that in cases, let us say of some military action, both radio stations pass under the jurisdiction of the Pentagon, since they both have a staff of translators, and all sorts of other data, which is essential for psychological and propaganda warfare.

The television announcer concluded, "The participants in the news conference answered other questions from journalists." The same night, Radio

Sofia and Radio Warsaw briefly reported on the press conference and both quoted Tumanov that Radio Free Europe and Radio Liberty were "branches of American special services, a convenient cover for secret operations against the Soviet Union and other Socialist Countries." Radio Prague carried brief items in the afternoon newscasts, and Czechoslovak television carried a long report on Tumanov in its prime-time evening news program. In addition, that evening, Radio Budapest broadcast a long report from its correspondent who attended the press conference.

After the April 28, 1986, press conference, Tumanov was contacted by a member of the Russian Service. He wrote a letter in return and called her. He said he was still living at his parents' address in Moscow, was working, and he hinted that his book about Radio Liberty would be published soon.

Espionage Investigation Started

In the first week of May 1986, an officer of the Bavarian State Police, LKA received the keys to the Tumanov apartment and sealed the apartment. Then he made a search of Tumanov's desk in the Russian Service of RFE/RL. It was more-or-less pro forma, as he showed me a copy of a request from the federal prosecutor's office indicating that an investigation had been initiated into the possibility that Tumanov was an agent of the KGB while working for RFE/RL. This investigation was a direct result of Tumanov's press conference in Moscow and appeared to be a routine reaction on the part of the federal prosecutor's office.

The Soviet propaganda campaign continued as Tumanov briefly appeared on Soviet television on May 11, 1986, and repeated his earlier charges.

A week later, Tumanov appeared at a round-table press conference attended by pro–Soviet journalists, on May 19, 1986. This time they were more successful, as the questions were prepared in advance. It aired on Soviet television June 2, 1986, with the title: "The Truth about the Corporation of Lies." Tumanov gave extensive details, some factual but mostly fictional, of Radio Liberty's operations and personnel. The RFE/RL security department was mentioned several times for how it handled people visiting Yugoslavia, "bugged" employees' telephones and apartments, opened mail addressed to employees, and conducted background checks on applicants.

The Soviet news agency TASS international and Radio Prague broadcast programs that night that quoted Tumanov:

> Radio Liberty, founded under the patronage of the CIA, continued working under its direction. Nobody could be employed by Radio Liberty without a screening from the American Secret Service. Richard Cummings, a staff mem-

ber of the CIA, headed the Security Department of RFE/RL in Munich. Radio Liberty has close contacts with the U.S. Military Intelligence, which has in Bavaria two schools for the preparation of espionage cadres.

On June 23, 1986, Radio Moscow started a series of six "interviews" with Tumanov, broadcast in the Romanian language. The thrust of these broadcasts was to inform the Romanian listeners abut RFE's interference in Poland.

Bothwell Trial

In late June, John Bothwell, who had been arrested in London on charges of spying for the KGB, was released and the trial halted as the evidence produced by the defense proved that "the accused was feeding the KGB disinformation in return for money and continued good business relations." He was involved in trade with Eastern Europe and the USSR and he had to produce "secrets" for the KGB to keep up his trade. He apparently fed the KGB rehashed articles from the British press as authentic information. Bothwell had, apparently, successfully fooled Gundarev and the KGB.

On June 30, 1986, Tumanov's German travel documents, which were previously given to the German counterintelligence agency for review, were returned. They were in turn forwarded to the German Federal Police (Bundeskriminalamt) for analysis. His travel documents had covered his travels during the period from 1966 to 1984. The documents were returned, along with written analysis. Nothing new was learned. However, whereas no evidence was contained in the documents to confirm his travels to Eastern Europe or the USSR, the possibility could not be discounted.

The LKA returned the keys later, and the apartment was cleaned up on July 29, 1986, with Mrs. Tumanov taking what she claimed was hers. The court in Munich then confiscated all remaining items for payment against any outstanding Tumanov debts. There was no further word through the U.S. consulate concerning other employees of RFE/RL who might have worked with Tumanov for the KGB, or who might be his successor.

Two reliable non–RFE/RL sources, unknown to each other, reported that Oleg Tumanov's return to the USSR in February had been met with derision and skepticism within the Soviet populace of Leningrad and Moscow. In Leningrad, he was considered a "double traitor" and in Moscow he was considered a "double agent for the West."

Electronic Spy Reunion

In August 1986, a very interesting "reunion of spies" took place over
Radio Prague, which carried a broadcast about RFE/RL with statements by
three former employees, Andrzej Czechowicz (Poland), Pavel Minarik
(Czechoslovakia) and Oleg Tumanov:

- Tumanov said in a recorded statement that was carried by Soviet radio earlier that year: "RFE/RL was compiling intelligence information above all
  with the purpose to intensify the effectiveness of Radio Liberty."
- Czechowicz said that after six years of experience he was confident to say
  that RFE was an institution fully paid, managed and controlled by CIA.
  Czechowicz also described his view on how RFE/RL gathered information,
  and said, "RFE/RL has permanent informers in Poland. We have succeeded
  to detect at least the most important ones."[2]
- Pavel Minarik said he had worked at RFE for seven years and had returned
  to Czechoslovakia in 1976. Minarik said also that U.S. Senator James W.
  Fulbright had in 1971 described RFE as a relic of the Cold War that belonged
  to the dustbin of history. Minarik sad he was able to confirm that nothing
  had changed in RFE/RL's general Cold War attitude and that the CIA still
  maintained its position in their set-up.[3]

In February, Minarik, as chief editor of the Czech-language magazine
SIGNAL, published a Tumanov interview:

MINARIK: Did the fusion of RFE and RL change anything in the operation
of these stations?
TUMANOV: Nothing at all. BIB was created officially for the purpose of better control of both stations but this is very formalistic. Already the methods
of audience research remain extremely dubious. Accidental tourists and/or
new émigrés are asked about the work of RFE/RL, although it is clear that
none of them is in the position to evaluate it properly.
MINARIK: More than 10 years ago, BIB confirmed that RFE alone had 14 CIA
officers in employ. What experience do you have about it?
TUMANOV: I want to talk primarily about RL. I could name a whole bunch
of people there who [have] been cadre workers of CIA. Some had to leave
temporarily when the position of CIA within the US political system weak-
ened, but more than one have come back under Reagan's administration. For
instance, both RL director Vasileff and Russian service director Galskoy are
members of American military espionage service. In addition, we ought not
to forget Nicholas Petroff, assistant director in the Russian service, who coop-
erates closely with CIA and in this function assures contacts with American
consulate in Munich.
MINARIK: Since RFE and RL are organizations with quite special compe-
tences, are not the Americans there afraid of their own employees?
TUMANOV: Not only afraid, they just do not trust any Eastern European
employee, especially new ones. Each émigré is constantly under control by

the security department, which keeps closely in touch with the West German police organs. Security uses denunciators between RFE and RL employee as well as among émigré groups. If you want to achieve something in RFE and RL, you need to be a good denunciator. Nevertheless, between you — an émigré from [the] East — and the Anglo-American employer, a deep gap will always remain.

MINARIK: How do both stations cooperate with émigré groups?

TUMANOV: Outwardly there are efforts to hide this cooperation, but for instance RL keeps supporting financially the émigré organization NTS, which collaborated during the Second World War with fascist Germany. Formerly quite a number of NTS members even worked in the Russia Service of RL but later on several had ... various reasons to go. Nevertheless, direct contacts between RL and NTS continue. A quite typical case occurred during the Polish events of 1981 when it was possible to produce at English Garden Nr. 11 leaflets that later appeared in Poland.

In addition, there exist also secret members of NTS. These are used for trips to USSR as tourists. Recently for instance traveled there Aljona Kozheshnikov who took some money and words about moral support to certain people in USSR. When she returned, her organization claimed that she brought back important samizdat documents. These were then speedily produced by NTS and delivered to RL, which was informed in advance.

MINARIK: Do you know any concrete cases of RFE/RL ideological diversion being realized with the help of western journalists?

TUMANOV: The method is such: RFE and RL never broadcast first any information they want to plant. In such cases, they use their contacts with various journalists and selected media. They deliver the so-called information to them and when normal media publishes it, RFE and RL pick it up and start their propagandistic cannonade.[4]

Tumanov's Wife Arrested in Germany

On October 5, 1987, RFE/RL learned that there was an investigation being conducted on Tumanov's ex-wife, who allegedly was working for the Soviet military intelligence GRU against the U.S. military Russian Language Institute in Munich and Garmisch.[5] Allegedly, she tried to recruit an employee of the Russian Institute to report on the U.S. Army students, who studied Russian in Munich. Names, assignments, and other personal data were given to the GRU. The unnamed employee traveled to East Berlin and met her "control officer." She had previously reported the recruiting attempt by Tumanova to military counterintelligence officers, who then ran a joint investigation with the Bavarian counterintelligence agency.

RFE/RL later was told that Tumanova reportedly acted as a go-between with the GRU and the woman who traveled to East Berlin under instructions from Tumanova. She was paid about DM 1,500 and given instructions by the

GRU officer she met. Tumanova told her that she had been working for the GRU for ten years, after being coerced by threats against her parents. Tumanova was arrested, put on trial, and sentenced to probation — presumably because of the KGB coercion.

Tumanova was subsequently interviewed by German authorities about her intelligence activities. At one point, she admitted meeting with two men in East Berlin she presumed to be GRU officers. They apparently asked her about the background of certain employees at RFE/RL. There was some publicity in the German media over this case in the first week of October 1987.

On Monday, July 17, 1989, Svetlana Tumanov telephoned the Radio Liberty News Bureau manager in Paris. He reported that she wanted to meet him. He had met her once with Oleg Tumanov socially many years ago. After some initial harmless chitchat about mutual friends and acquaintences, they agreed that they would meet in the RFE/RL office that afternoon. At 3:00 P.M., she entered his office. She kept looking carefully at his radio behind him, and he thought that maybe she was thinking that the conversation was being recorded. He suggested going out of the office to a local cafe. She agreed, and they left the office.

In the cafe, she said, "Greetings from Oleg." He asked her when she last saw him; she answered, "About 2 weeks ago in Moscow." Their conversation continued: "How's he doing?"

"Okay. However, he is drinking too much. He is working for ABN news agency and is responsible for matters concerning RFE/RL. Why don't you make a trip to the Soviet Union?

"Oh, maybe sometime, but I will need an entry visa and they will probably not give me one."

"Don't worry about that. Oleg can help. But, of course, you cannot go as an accredited journalist with Radio Liberty, but you can meet whom you want after you get there. I am working in joint ventures with the Soviet Union on trade matters."

"What about Oleg? I don't think he was a spy, but he left like Philby, or Burgess and MacClean in the middle of the night. And working for Novosti. Everyone knows that the KGB runs Novosti."

"So what; the KGB is running everything anyway. Of course, he wasn't a spy. He wrote a letter of resignation to the radios, but the Americans are hiding the fact. In addition, they trumped up charges against me, and I had to spend six months in jail."

"Why doesn't he go back to Germany?"

"Not now. That's being arranged. But if he goes back now, he will be arrested by Interpol."[6]

Tumanov and Fyodor

In September 1987, Radio Liberty Russian Service employee "Fyodor" found an RFE/RL envelope in his mailbox. The first page of the two-page letter contained mostly personal information already known about Tumanov's life in Moscow. The second page read:

> You already understand that this letter is not an ordinary one. Here at home, I am writing this to you because we have been friends for such a long time that we know each other well. Moreover, most probably we can trust each other.
>
> You know that I will never compromise you, and I would never bring you any harm. Just as you have never done this to me (I know this and I remember).
>
> After you receive this letter, you will be called. Someone will call who will explain all the details. You, of course, are within your rights to drop the receiver. However, you will be within your right to agree. I will tell you one thing — at the present moment, you are needed by our Homeland. OURS!
>
> And it is possible that in the manner you act in the very near future will determine the way you will judge yourself. If everything will be "OK," then you and I possibly will be able to meet in your favorite city.
>
> On my part, I can guarantee you complete safety. In this, you should not have any doubts.
>
> I hope in you and believe in you, in your Russian soul. I embrace you. Awaiting our meeting. Destroy this letter. Oleg (O.T.)[7]

That night, between 6:30 and 7:00, a man called and asked in German for "Herr" Fyodor, who answered, "Yes, I am." The man immediately switched to Russian. He asked if Fyodor had received Oleg's letter.

Fyodor answered, "Yes, I did." The man then identified himself as "Yura." He asked Fyodor what he thought of the letter, saying that he and Oleg "rely on you. We hope you will be able to help us."

Fyodor asked, "How?"

Yura said he couldn't discuss it over the phone; they would have to meet. Fyodor told him he was tired, and he invited Yura to his apartment. Yura refused for "technical reasons," but said he was very near.

He asked Fyodor again, "Will you help us?" Fyodor didn't answer.

Yura then said, "Think it over, and I will call again in a few days."

On September 15, Yura called again and said that he had been in contact with Oleg. Oleg had been told that Fyodor had turned down the offer and was quoted as saying, "That's just like Fyodor: he's too old."

Yura then said, "Tumanov sent his greetings, and we understand the reasons for declining." Their brief conversation continued.

"I can't do anything for you; stop bothering me."

"You think about it; if you change your mind, I will call you up in a couple of months, and you can let me know." "What do you want from me, anyway?" "Oh, just a little thing, let's not talk about it now." That ended their conversation.

Fyodor said, "Yura was not aggressive, in fact, he was very pleasant." Fyodor then added that his wife was very nervous because their grandson was staying with them, and she feared for their grandson's safety. She told Fyodor: "Stay out of it."

Fyodor said he would be going to London and then Ireland for a wedding and would be returning in about two weeks.

A photocopy of the letter and German-language translation was given to the Bavarian State Police Agency (LKA), which still had an open case of possible espionage against Tumanov.

Until then there was no history of KGB direct activity in West Germany against RFE/RL. A control officer would not come to Munich but would meet with our employees in Salzburg or Switzerland. Now the KGB was now dealing directly with Fyodor.

Look in Your Mailbox!

Yura called Fyodor for a third time on Saturday, September 19, 1987, at 10:00 A.M. Yura said: "You asked what we wanted you to do. Look in your mailbox; you will find a notebook; look under the binding (cover)." There were no other messages, according to Fyodor.

Fyodor went to his mailbox and found a large brown envelope with his name written on the outside. Inside was a leather-bound, green-colored, calendar/notebook about five inches by seven inches. There was nothing written on the pages inside; the calendar was for 1985. The binding was thick. However, Fyodor did not open it.

On Sunday, Fyodor flew to London on his way to Ireland with the notebook. On Monday, he met his brother-in-law, who was an officer of the British Air Force, and told him the story of the notebook. The brother-in-law arranged for a meeting with an officer from the special services. Fyodor told this person the story and gave him the notebook. Fyodor was told that another British official would contact him after he returned from Ireland. That happened when he met another officer at the Admiralty, in Whitehall. This officer apparently knew about Tumanov and, after listening to Fyodor, he produced four film sheets, about four by five inches each. One sheet had a list dealing with Radio Liberty:

1. The tasks facing RFE/RL at the present time, and its plans for the near future;
2. New "chiefs" at RL and Russian Service; staffing changes;
3. Struggle of Zionists vs. nationalists (Russophiles), i.e., problems and disagreements;
4. Particulars of the CIA men at RFE/RL;
5. Changes in RL's Budget;
6. RL's links with other ideological centers and publishers;
7. The type of relationships between headquarters in Munich and its bases in the United States, Paris, Rome, Brussels, etc;
8. General conditions at RFE/RL.

The other three sheets dealt with communications and how Fyodor was to correspond with the KGB: instructions on how to use special carbon to write between lines — preferably in German (sheets of special paper were included) and name and address in East Berlin to write to.

The British official told Fyodor that he would be in touch with the Americans who would in turn be in touch with the RFE/Rl security office. He told Fyodor that if Yura called, he was to tell him that he knew no one from CIA at RFE/RL. He should not say that he gave the notebook away but that it is in a "safe place" and that only his wife knew about the notebook.

Yura called Fyodor for the last time on January 27, 1988. After passing on greetings from Tumanov, he asked some general questions about the former Mrs. Tumanov and ended the conversation. Fyodor then requested that RFE/RL transfer him to Brussels, Belgium. RFE/RL did not have a news bureau in Brussels, and his request was denied. Fyodor shortly thereafter resigned from RFE/RL. Yura was never identified.

KGB Agent "Marina"

Referring to the famous espionage case of Melita Norwood, code-named "Hola," who spied for the Soviet Union for over forty years in England, in 1999 journalist Andrew Pierce wrote in the *Times* newspaper, "Until modern times, women have been kept to a limited role by espionage services, and a world away from the seductive beauties of the Bond movies. The reality of the female spy has always been remote from the legend."

He could have been writing about "Marina," who was involved in one of the KGB's most active penetrations of Radio Liberty for over ten years. She was a spy for love, for adventure, for fun, and for the good feeling that belonging to a powerful secret organization gave her.

She was born in France. Her father was a Russian Orthodox priest, and she grew up in the Russian émigré circles of Paris. I know little about her childhood, as this was one subject she hardly ever talked about. She was blond and very pretty as a young woman. French intelligence recruited her for an assignment at a trade fair in Moscow in the 1960s. Her French intelligence handlers called her "Blondie." "Marina" never explained in detail what she was supposed to do or what she did do, but she did say that she met many Russian businessmen and reported her conversations with them to her French handlers. She became bored with working for French intelligence and moved to Munich to join Radio Liberty's Russian-language broadcasting service.

A few years later the man with whom she was having an affair happened also to be a KGB agent at Radio Liberty: Oleg Tumanov. It was he who recruited her to lead the double life of both being a productive employee and a penetration agent of Radio Liberty's Russian Service and staff. "Marina" first learned that Tumanov was a KGB agent in November 1973, when they were vacationing in their apartment in the Grand Canary Islands. They were in bed when he told her that he was in trouble and was working for the KGB. At first she didn't believe him and dismissed his admission as a joke. Some time later he repeated it and told her he was serious, very serious. To convince her, he gave her details of his activities at RFE/RL. She then believed him and agreed to help him.

The KGB officially accepted her sometime in 1974. Tumanov made the arrangements and they flew to West Berlin. After taking two subway lines, they went to the Friedrichstrasse U-bahn stop behind the Wall in East Berlin. They went into a subway shop in the station. Oleg took her to a hallway leading to the restrooms and pushed a button on the wall next to a locked door. The door opened, and they walked outside, where a car and driver were waiting for them. They drove to a small house somewhere in East Berlin. Tumanov was told to go into another room. She remained with two KGB officers. One, called Nicolai (Kolya), who said, "You know too much. Oleg's life is in your hands. If you love him, you must remain silent." She agreed and she and Oleg stayed in that house for three days for training and briefings.

At one point, one KGB officer said, "You need money for your apartment in the Grand Canary Islands. We can give you partial payments. If you keep silent, you will get pocket money from us. You must help Oleg, whenever you can. You must cover for him." She had to sign a receipt: "I have received from the KGB DM 5,000 and I will remain silent about it."

"Marina" developed a form of Parkinson's disease. Oleg had arranged for a trip to Moscow for medical attention. In 1975, they again flew to West Berlin and then made their way to East Berlin. She was given a false Soviet passport in the name "Irina." She flew on to Moscow where the KFB officer

"Kolya" was waiting for her. She had a little trouble at the passport control and couldn't remember her name or details of when and how she was supposed to have been issued the passport. The passport control officer just looked at her and passed her through without questioning her further.

She admitted that one time she went to Vienna and was driven to Melk. While walking along the wall of the monastery, she was asked not to do anything foolish in case "Oleg betrays you." She told them she wouldn't.

As part of their activity for the KGB, she and Tumanov went to different cities in Austria. They always went on Saturdays. Tumanov always gave three consecutive dates for the meeting. During their personal meetings, her handlers asked her questions about specific employees of the Russian Service and its management as well as about the internal organization of Radio Liberty.

Their love eventually faded, and he left her for another woman. "Marina" then continued her double life for the thrill of playing secret agent. From what I learned from my discussions with her, she would have done it for the CIA or another western intelligence service, if she had been given a chance to do so. Ideology and money played no role, "it was simply fun and exciting," she once told me. In addition, the KGB cleverly played on her damaged ego by ensuring that she was made to feel important by what she was doing.

During her active KGB career, she traveled one weekend a month to Austria, mainly Vienna, and passed on her information and documents. She had been tasked with providing internal RFE/RL memoranda, telephone books, etc.

On one occasion "Marina" was asked to try to recruit a particular male coworker in her service. Since the KGB had recruited her through someone in RL's Russian Service, she knew what personal weaknesses the KGB would or would not tolerate. She told them the man in question was unpredictable due to his cocaine habit and the project was dropped. She added that this was the only time she had been asked specifically recruit a Russian Service colleague.

Meetings in Vienna

After her separation from Tumanov, "Marina" usually went to Vienna on one of the last two Saturdays of each month. Tumanov was to go there on Sundays. "Marina" bought a map of Vienna and received signaling instructions from her KGB masters, including the location of the telephone booth to use to leave her identifying mark indicating that she would be making a scheduled meeting. She gave the RFE/RL Security Office a commercial map of

Vienna with various meeting places and routes she used when meeting with
the KGB. These included:

- Marx Park, across from the Stadthalle Hallenbad;
- A small hotel not far from the Westbahnhof near the corner of Stumper
  Gasse and Fuger Gasse;
- A walk along Schloss Allee,
- Across from Schloss Schoenbrunn;
- The famous Johann Strauss statue in Stadt Park;
- Along Landstrasse;
- Airport Air Terminal.

Technical Failure

In various hotel rooms in Austria, the KGB tried to teach "Marina" the
art of "secret writing" by using special ink, prepared paper, and by writing
between the lines of an "innocent" letter. After repeated attempts, she said
she could not do it. She also failed to learn how to use "one-time pads" for
enciphering and deciphering her communications, and she couldn't learn how
to use a radio transmitter/receiver. She was given more special paper for
"secret-writing" but still was unable to master these skills. The idea of technical communications was dropped, and it was decided that she would communicate her information only by personal contact outside Germany.

In addition to the code name "Marina," she was given a code word to
use as an emergency signal: the Russian word for stork (*aist*). She would often
meet her KGB handlers in a safe room in a hotel near the Vienna Westbahnhof—one of Vienna's major train stations. There, her controller would sit in
front of her with a small spiral notebook filled with prepared personal questions on Radio Liberty staffers, which she would answer orally, and she passed
along the documents she had stolen or photocopied.

From the drift of the KGB questions, "Marina" realized that they were
getting information from others in the Russian Service. She was always asked
how she and Tumanov got along, how his drinking problem was coming
along. She was told that even if something happened between the two of
them, she shouldn't do anything and should remain silent. She was told not
to do anything stupid like seek revenge. In the event that she had serious problems, she was to get to the Soviet embassy in Vienna and identify herself simply as "Marina."

"Marina" once said, "Do not forget, people were freer in their talks in the
Radio Liberty building. Give them a drink and they babble, if you are clever
enough to direct or point them in the right direction. We all drank every evening in the canteen. All together, regardless of rank. Information would come

not only from 'Old X' (name withheld), but also from the other heads of services. 'Old X' was dangerous because when awaking from a binge he wouldn't remember the conversation he had had the night before."

She was asked to deliver a gas pistol, or small tear-gas canister, to Vienna for them — she could not explain why they asked for it. She refused to do it.

The KGB paid "Marina" on the average DM 800 per month during her last active years, mostly for reimbursement for her trips to Vienna, and for the KGB to have a record of her signature for payments. At the end, she made three successive weekend trips to Vienna to the prearranged meeting spot: the famous Johann Strauss statue. No one from the KGB showed up to meet her. That was the last time she tried to make personal contact with the KGB, or the KGB tried to contact her. She correctly assumed that someone else had taken over her functions.

Oleg Kalugin said in an interview at RFE/RL in August 1991, "The KGB always had a three-year plan against Radio Liberty, including the placing of bombs near the station to intimidate the staff." KGB officers once asked "Marina" to bring a "fire bomb" disguised as a Coke can into the RFE/RL. She refused to do it. "Marina" said that Tumanov was furious with the bombing. His office directly across from the spot where the bomb exploded was destroyed and at their next meeting in Vienna he vented his rage at the possibility of being injured or killed by the flying glass. The KGB answered that they did not do it and did not know it was going to happen, otherwise he would have been warned.

"Marina" once brought to the security office the paperback book *Breaking the Ring: The Rise and Fall of the Walker Family Spy Network*, by John Barron. She left the following note in the book:

> Tumanov had a Minox camera (found it by mistake a long time before I knew). Even joked about him having a "spy camera." He took it as a joke, too. He took it to the office (1974–76) ... saw him using it once at home, but he sent me away. Then he got a new camera. Olympus something. He had a super Nikon. He would buy a new one every year with all the trimmings.
>
> So we got a new one with instructions on how to use it: distance between objects to the camera (in cm exactly!). Where the light should be, he even bought some special light bulbs. Sometimes I had to help (taking off the clips of the memos [carefully as not to leave traces] then put the clips back, spreading the pages one by one to be photographed. I think memos were administrative or directional/political directives. Did not find them exciting, but he said very useful (he might have taken the Olympus to work but I am not sure).... Memos were of limited circulation. Do not know where he got them. Pinched them in Perouansky's office? (That was until we came to RFE). Do not forget that in 70 or 71 he was appointed features editor. He could stay at work as long as he wanted. If I am not wrong budget was collected in the administrative offices.

There was also the very nice Sony recorder he bought in Las Palmas (guess it might be 1975) with a very special tiny microphone, very sensitive. It made no sound at all and was so small that even I could carry it in a pocket without it being seen and without detection. The microphone could be put so as to appear as a tiny button. Very good. We tried it at a party at home. And then tried it by sticking the microphone to a wall.... He played with it for a while then give it to them (KGB). What in fact he used it for (or not), I don't know because he let me think our "tests" were a kind of joke than anything else. Guess I wanted to think so.[8]

German authorities did not prosecute her due to the statute of limitations on her espionage activities. "Marina" quietly left RFE/RL with her secret life generally intact and died quietly in Munich in 1992; there was no newspaper obituary.

Code Name "Krüger"

"Krüger" was a source for KGB information from 1972 to 1986, but he did not report to or work for the KGB. His story has an interesting twist.

"Krüger" was born in 1922 to Russian émigrés in Belgrade. He graduated from Belgrade High School. During World War II, he went to Berlin in 1941 and studied at the Film Technical School for two years. In 1943, he became an officer of the Russian anti–Soviet army of General Vlasov in Germany. He spoke fluent Russian, Serbian, German, and good English. Because of a war injury, his left leg was amputated at the knee in 1944, and he remained in a military hospital until February 1946. Afterwards while living in various displaced persons' camps in Austria, he was able to get various jobs with the U.S. Army occupation forces as a film projectionist until he successfully got a job as a monitor with Radio Liberty in 1955, because of his language abilities.

He was known to have continuous and serious financial problems in the fifties and sixties until sometime in 1972. While employed in the Russian Monitoring Section, he was also controlled and paid by the former DDR (East Germany) intelligence service (MfS). The MfS was, apparently, operating in behalf of the KGB, since the MfS normally would have had little, if any, interest in RFE/RL. "Krüger" was paid 1,000 DM on the average per month. In return he was to supply personal information about RFE/RL's employees and provide documents especially from his own department, which monitored and transcribed Russian language radio broadcasts.

Also part of his task was reporting on the large and active Ukrainian exile community in Munich. He used his RFE/RL employment to maintain contact with them. "Krüger" met his handler in various locations in Munich and Bavaria. The initial information given to the RFE/RL security office in 1991 did not give concise details of what "Krüger" was to have allegedly done, or what information he might have provided to the MfS, or if he acted alone in the MfS tasking.

The MfS was directly involved in various activities with non–German émigré groups in the West (presumably for the KGB), including employees of RFE/RL. In January 1992, the RFE/RL Bavarian counterintelligence contact finally had the opportunity to meet with the former MfS intelligence officer, Karl-Hermann Mueller, responsible for "Krüger." He said the KGB had originally recruited "Krüger," but in 1972 they turned over the operation to the MfS. The MfS was tasked with gathering information about the CIA, and they wanted to use "Krüger" to gather information about presumed CIA involvement and personnel at RFE/RL. "Krüger" was then given his code name. He was a member of the Works Council and one can assume that this was his prime source of information on RFE/RL: hirings, firings, promotions, demotions, disciplinary action, etc. He provided copies of internal RFE/RL memoranda, the telephone books, and any other written information. In total, the amount of information provided by "Krüger" was about forty inches thick.

The MfS used him to gather materials and information about RFE/RL until February 1986, when Gundarev defected in Athens and was flown to the United States. At the same time, the MfS sent a message to Moscow asking if Gundarev's defection could jeopardize the "Krüger" operation. The KGB answered yes, that Gundarev had knowledge of the KGB's prior control of "Krüger." The MfS thereupon stopped the "Krüger" operation.

"Krüger" met his contacts on a monthly basis in a Wienerwald restaurant in the town where he lived. The MfS and the KGB had conducted a "false flag" operation with "Krüger" as he apparently thought all along that he was providing information to the British Intelligence Agency MI5. Mueller later said that "Krüger" was never told his information was going to the MfS or KGB. He thought that "Krüger" was possibly originally recruited by a KGB agent or officer named Grynov, who also was at one time possibly controlled by the British intelligence agency MI5. Grynov had previously been an officer in "Krüger's" detachment during World War Two, and the two of them maintained contact after the war.

Over the years, "Krüger" was paid in excess of DM 100,000 for his information, which totaled over 2,500 pages. "Krüger" was last known to have met with his MfS contacts in February 1986. The statute of limitations in these cases was five years, thus there was no prosecution possibility.[9]

Agent "Fred"

In September 1991, Vladimir Fomenko, vice consul of the Soviet consulate in Munich, defected. He subsequently identified another KGB agent living in Munich who was the control officer of at least one RFE/RL Russian Service employee, who was identified by the source only to be a male, émigré, Russian, and long-employed at RFE/RL — code-named "Fred." In addition, this employee reportedly had access to a restricted area or secured area of RFE/RL. At that time, he had no further information.

Fomenko said that the Russian Service employee was involved with the Russian Service program "Country and the World." The employee was paid DM 800 per month for years to provide inside information about RFE/RL. "Fred" was controlled by the Soviet embassy in Bonn until after 1989, when he was put under the control of a person living and working in Munich. Fomenko never saw "Fred" and only acted as a spotter for KGB control officer who actually met the employee. Fomenko was to look for any possible German or American counterintelligence activity in the area of the meetings. He never participated in the meetings.

"Fred" was supposedly taken over by the Soviet consulate in Munich in 1989, after having been controlled by the Soviet embassy in Bonn. Yet, all German counterintelligence information showed that the Soviet embassy in Bonn had not run agents in Germany after 1986.

RFE/RL moved to Prague in 1995, and "Fred" by then either had retired from RFE/RL undiscovered, or moved to Prague. In any event, he was never discovered.

Pravda *Interview, February 20, 1989*

Three years after Tumanov returned to Moscow, the Communist Party newspaper *Pravda* published an interesting interview with Oleg Tumanov that was contradictory to anything that had previously appeared in print in the USSR about him:

> I took the elevator to the fifth floor. A short bearded man around 40 years old wearing a blue jogging suit opened the door and apologizing, repeated: "Our lamp has burned out — don't trip over." That's how I met Oleg Tumanov.
>
> "You are, naturally, interested in how I came to be there. And why I am now sitting here?" he asked. In reality, it is a sad story. Long ago, finding myself in Genoa, I requested political asylum. I was 20 years old then. After a while they assigned me to Radio Liberty in Munich. They gave me US citizenship. I very soon realized that I had made an unforgivable mistake. I had to wait an awful long time before I saw my homeland again. When the time came that I could not bear to work any longer at the radio station, I left. Later, I found out that the Bavarian authorities had sentenced me to 25 years imprisonment."[10]

No. He didn't fit the image of "super spy" James Bond, capable of walking through fire and water, especially in this ordinary blue jogging suit.[11]

Oleg Tumanov's memoirs, published in 1993 in English and Germany, succinctly summed up his life and disillusionment in post–Communist Moscow when he wrote:

Today I rarely leave my apartment. I don't have a job and I live on the pension the state pays me. I spend my days reading books and papers. I go to bed early and rise late. I am forty-eight years old, but I sometimes feel like a very old man.

I am alone among strangers and among friends.

Everything is mixed up; everything has changed.

Émigrés who had been working against the Communist regime are now regarded not an enemies but as national heroes.[12]

8. Alpha, Waves, and Hornets

Czechoslovak Intelligence Service Activities

From 1951 to 1989, at least forty Czechoslovak Intelligence Service agents were engaged in activities against the Radio Free Europe, including ten RFE employees.[1]

Agent Toy: The Case of Erwin Marak

In 1975 before a U.S. Senate Subcommittee, former Czechoslovak agent Josef Frolik testified:

> In 1968, the Czech Service sent a man to Germany whose name was Marak. Last year, in 1974, Marak returned to Czechoslovakia with a huge amount of intelligence information from Radio Free Europe. He tapped private telephones of the employees in Radio Free Europe. And he brought some material from the Research Center of Radio Free Europe. This operation of the Czechs created a great deal of chaos in Czech exile circles all over the world.
>
> During his press conference in Prague last year Marak spoke in derogatory terms about his experience in the West. He didn't admit that he was sent abroad as an agent, but when I read this press report, I came to the conclusion that his statement at the press conference was prepared by the Czech Intelligence Service. The standard operating procedure of the Czech Service is to send someone into exile and then bring them back to speak against the country in which they are have been living.[2]

Apparently he had been sentenced to jail in Czechoslovakia in 1956 for undisclosed activities and sometime agreed to work with the Czechoslovak Intelligence Service. In 1966 Marak signed a five-year agreement with the Czechoslovak Intelligence Service. He was paid DM 29,000 and 44,000 Czechoslovak crowns. His assignment was to interview and record the activities of prominent Czech émigrés in Germany. Upon his return to the CSSR, he received a state pension and an apartment. These recordings were summarized six months afterward and serialized on Czechoslovak radio. Unfortunately for the StB, the words and voices of the émigrés criticizing the Communist regime became very popular with the listeners, who sent letters praising the émigrés for their honest and open criticism. The domestic radio programs were therefore stopped.[3]

In March 2004, the Czech Republic's Ministry of Interior forwarded the following information:

> Ervín Marák, a collaborator of the Intelligence Service since 1956 (recruited during the service of his sentence for subversive activities), starting December 1956 taken over under control of the Intelligence Service (under the cover name HRACKA — TOY), sent out to West Germany, returned to Czechoslovakia in December 1973. After his return, he was used for a series of so called active measures, AO REZEDA that met with the best response: a series of radio broadcasts, where Marák published acquired records of telephone calls of Czechoslovak émigrés. However, a few cases only concerned regular employees of the RFE and an illegal phone tapping of private calls did not acquire records. Marák recorded exclusively his own calls to the persons in question. Further it is not altogether true that Marák spoke at a press conference after his return home and that he appeared on mass media in the capacity of a collaborator of the Intelligence Service. Nothing is known about the fact that he could have brought materials from the research center of the RFE, he had no access to the RFE, and he appeared there in the capacity of a visitor only.[4]

Code Name ALPHA

Another Czechoslovak intelligence codeword for RFE as a "spy center of the CIA" was ALPHA. ALPHA files, under Register No. 10081, dealt with employees of the Czechoslovak Service of RFE/RL, divided into five categories:

- Object files: employees not of interest to the StB
- Thematic files: persons of interest because of outside activities (e.g. émigré activities)
- Type files: background files with details of employees, such as date and place of birth, personality traits (alcohol, money, gambling and other problems), jobs at RFE/RL, political attitudes, contacts with foreign "special services"
- "Agent" files
- "Special files" — names sent to Moscow of persons known to have contacts with western intelligence agencies and drug dealers.

Code Name WAVES

RFE had the code name "WAVES" (VLNY in Czech) in the Second Administration of the Czechoslovak Ministry of Interior. This file, under Registration Nr. 9894, started on September 25, 1975. RFE was considered as an espionage main office of the CIA and so treated. The activity of this intelligence section concentrated on mail: all letters addressed to RFE were collected and photocopied. The contents were evaluated before they were sent to RFE.

The officers of the Second Administration of the Ministry of the Interior knew the names and sections of the Czechoslovakia Service from copies of the Radio Free Europe telephone book. For example, the Second Administration received a photocopy of the August 1981 RFE/RL telephone book from the Hungarian Intelligence Service on August 25, 1982. The telephone books contained the real names of the staff, office, telephone, and fax numbers.

The leading officers of the Ministry of the Interior tried to influence public opinion against RFE through two assertions: RFE was a spy center of the CIA and RFE employed former war criminals.

Code Name PLEY

Pavel Minarik, was born June 29, 1945 in Brno, Czechoslovakia. He was trained to be a plumber, worked for the Východočeský Theater in Hradec Kralove for one year, then worked in a steel foundry (Slatina) in Brno for another year. In 1965, Radio Brno hired him as a radio broadcaster.

In 1967 Minarik joined the Corps of National Security of the Federal Ministry of the Interior (SNB-MDV), as a secret agent under the cover name of ULYXES. In the spring of 1968, he underwent special intelligence service training by the SNB and was given the task of getting hired by Radio Free Europe. On September 5, 1968, he "emigrated" to Austria, applied for a job in the RFE office in Vienna and by the end of 1968 was hired as a full-time employee in Munich. Minarik worked under the name ULYXES, and from 1972 as agent PLEY.

In Munich, he supplied his intelligence supervisors, based in Frankfurt, with reports and miscellaneous materials, which he stole or photocopied at the RFE headquarters. Minarik reported on

- RFE directives and regulations,
- The ways Americans controlled the work of the station,
- Activities of different Czechoslovak émigré organizations and individual emigrants,
- Activities of dissident publishing houses and publishers of émigré literature.

Mostly, however, he focused on gossips (who slept with whom, who got drunk, who got in trouble), and other compromising issues, to uncover week spots in RFE employees, and even marked potential intelligence-service collaborators.

He obtained keys to several apartments, and searched them, secretly looking for interesting documents.

Twice a year he would travel to Vienna for three- or four-day long informative meetings, at which he also received more training in encrypting, coding, etc.[5]

Code Name PANEL

Minarik also traveled to Vienna, where he met his supervisor Jarosloav Lis (also known as Necasek). At a meeting in Vienna with Lis in April 1970, Minarik first proposed a bombing of Radio Free Europe, which he would personally execute. The bombing of RFE was given the code name PANEL In November 1971, Minarik again traveled to Vienna and met Lis. They continued with the bombing discussions. In June 1972, prior to the Olympic Games in Munich, Minarik made one more proposal to bomb Radio Free Europe during the Olympics, which he believed would force the German government to close RFE. The Czechoslovak intelligence service did not accept Minarik's proposal. In November 1972, Minarik traveled to Vienna, met Lis, and gave him the floor plan, films, and photographs, and detailed information on where to place the bomb. He brought up the plan with his superiors in 1973, 1974, and for the last time on July 24, 1975.

In July 1975, Pavel Minarik returned to Prague. It was then revealed on Prague Radio that he was "an intelligence officer who had waged a seven-year spy operation inside the Radios." Soviet and Eastern European media gave extensive coverage to revelations which included attacks against both radios, the naming of individual employees, alleged CIA connections, etc. The Czechoslovak StB wrote a short summary justifying his return at that time:

> Top Secret
> Letter of September 30, 1975
> I. správa FMV — odbor 31
> Jaromír Obzina, Minister of the Ministry of the Interior
> A preliminary draft of operations aimed against RFE, Advisory Council, and some Czechoslovak émigrés.
> In September 1968 our agent PLEY was sent to Munich to infiltrate RFE headquarters. The operation was carried out successfully, PLEY familiarized himself with RFE policies, atmosphere and environment, established contacts with almost all 1968 emigrants who worked at RFE. He provided many doc-

uments, including directives of the U.S. management, copies of correspondence of some RFE employees, etc.

During his stay he met prominent Czechoslovak exiles.... According to our
instructions, he was active in different émigré organizations and took part in
important meetings of the top Czechoslovak exiles.

Due to the current cuts and layoffs in RFE and in connection with the
upcoming 15th Congress of the Communist Party of Czechoslovakia, the situation seems favorable for bringing agent PLEY back to Czechoslovakia and
presenting him to the media as a successful communist agent who ... worked
for RFE to uncover and make public the station's hostile activities against the
socialist countries, and disclose bad morale of the RFE employees.[6]

At the end of 1976 he left for the Soviet Union to study at the Institute
for International Relations in Kiev. He returned to Czechoslovakia in 1981
and received his business degree, later PhD in political science, and began
working as a consultant for the Thirty-first Department (ideological diversionist center) of the First Administrative Division of the Federal Ministry of
the Interior. In 1983 he became chief editor of the weekly *SIGNAL.*

He was chosen for the following reasons:

• He was a politically mature and class-conscious member of the Commu-
nist Party,
• He had theoretical knowledge and practical experience in the field of mass
propaganda and journalism corresponding with the required standard,
• He showed initiative and responsibility in his approach to assignments,
• He had political, technical and moral skills needed to perform well.[7]

Minarik was used in the KGB's propaganda offensive against RFE/RL
in the Tumanov case, the Czechoslovak StB for its campaigns, and other Warsaw Pact intelligence services.[8]

After the Velvet Revolution in Czechoslovakia, Minarik was investigated
and eventually indicted in May 1993 for a terrorist act: planning to bomb
RFE/RL. On May 3, 1993, the Czech public prosecutor charged Minarik with

having in the time period between 18 April 1970 and 24 July 1975, as a paid
secret agent of the former First Administration — Czechoslovak intelligence —
of the Federal Ministry of Internal Affairs of the former Czechoslovak Socialist Republic (CSSR), sent to infiltrate Radio Free Europe in Munich, German
Federal Republic, worked out and passed on to the Prague headquarters of
the I. Administration at least three alternative and very concrete proposals on
how to accomplish the destruction of the building of Radio Free Europe in
Munich with the express aim of terminating its broadcasting operation.[9] ·

Minarik was put on trial, found guilty, acquitted on appeal. The prosecutor then appealed, and there was another trial. This cycle continued until
April 2007, when the Czech Supreme Court rejected the last government
appeal and closed the case with his acquittal.[10]

Code Name "Rafan"

One service that Minarik provided to the StB was to recommend RFE staffers who might be subject to recruitment by the StB. One such case is Code Name "Rafan," which started in November 1980. Minarik recommended to the StB that a Radio Free Europe employee named Karel (pseudonym) could possibly be recruited as agent for the Czechoslovak Intelligence Service. A StB agent with the cover name Roman maintained continual contacts with Karel's family. In the late 1970s, he regularly visited the West, Karel in particular. He always reported about his visits with Karel, including Karel's personal life and problems. According to Roman, Karel told him that he was only working at RFE because of the money; he was disappointed that his then wife at RFE was earning more than he was; and, he was also disappointed with his career in the West. Roman told Karel that he had good contacts in Czechoslovakia. Karel asked Roman to help his parents visit him in the West.

In the second half of November 1980, Karel and Roman again met. At this time, Karel asked Roman if he had secured permission for his parents to visit him. Roman then asked Karel if Karel would be willing to earn some additional money, by sending reports about Radio Free Europe.

Karel is reported to have said, "For DM 100 a month, I wouldn't do it. And there is nobody who would pay me DM 3,000 a month."

Roman told him he could pay DM 2,500 regularly.

Karel said, "This is not a joke. There is a risk. I don't want to end as Vajnar in Bonn [a convicted Czech spy]." He added, " I now earn DM 4,000 per month, so the offer is a good one."

Roman suggested another meeting in Vienna for December 7, 1980.

The StB officer in charge of Radio Free Europe, Jaroslav Lis (Necasek) took over the case and went to Vienna to meet with Karel. The StB headquarters decided that Lis would not play the role of asking Karel for anything but would play up to Karel's ego by telling him that he was doing something important as a leading member of a socialist state.

They met in front of Stefan's Dom in Vienna and then drove to the Cafe Post (owned by the Czechoslovak regime) in the Wienerwald outside Vienna. The StB observation team borrowed film cameras from the Soviet KGB and controlled the route to and from the cafe. They filmed all traffic on the road.

Lis was to give Karel DM 2,000, plus DM 300 for his expenses. Lis told him that it was his "duty as an émigré of socialist Czechoslovakia to cooperate with State Security." Lis only gave him DM 1,500, but told Karel that he would receive DM 2,000–5,000 depending on his activities and information.

Karel's conditions were:

- that he have contact with his parents;
- that he not be forced to do anything which was not directly connected with his employment at RFE;
- that he would not be asked to do anything which might bring him under suspicion;
- that he have guarantees (unspecified) if he were endangered.

Karel criticized Minarik for the way Minarik went about gathering material at RFE. He thought that Minarik was too active in émigré activities.

Karel rejected Salzburg as a meeting place, as too many employees of RFE visited Salzburg. He said he even had to be careful in going to Prague, because of the regular visits there by Czech Service employees.

Lis told Karel that if he told anyone about his cooperation with the StB, Karel would be killed. If Karel required a special meeting, he should send two black-and-white postcards to a controlled mailbox in Czechoslovakia. The text was not important, but the date of the meeting should appear along with the initials "K" and "A."

For future meetings in Vienna, the initial contact dialogue would be in German:

> "*Bitte, wo ist hier Weg Haller?*"
> "*Leider, ich kenne nur Maximillianstrasse. Ich vergass alles.*
> *Ich war hier zuletzt fuer 16 Jahren.*"

Karel was then given the code name "Rafan" and he made five trips to Austria to meet with StB officers. Unknown to the StB, he reported everything about these contacts back to his German counterintelligence contact. The last meeting took place in 1982, when the StB did not show up as scheduled, and no further meetings were held between the StB and Karel. Karel did not tell RFE/RL of these trips, since RFE/RL would not approve of such activity.

Case of Premsyl Barak

The 1980s witnessed a new generation of intelligence agents at RFE/RL. On September 18, 1988, RFE's Czechoslovak Service freelancer Premsyl Barak confessed to RFE/RL that he had been spying for the Czechoslovak Intelligence Service (CIS), and that he was under threat from the CIS for refusing to continue doing so. For four years (1984–88), while employed as a freelancer, he reported on all activities of RFE/RL's Czechoslovak Service, and other émigrés living in Germany. He met at least twenty-three times with his handler, who was a diplomat out of the West German Czechoslovak embassy in Bonn. He was paid about DM 25,000 for his information.

In his later sworn testimony to German police, Barak said that he volunteered to work for the StB shortly after the return of former employee Pavel Minarik in 1976. Barak was looking for adventure and was intrigued by the Minarik story about how he had spied at RFE from 1968 to 1976. Barak stated that he was trained in "spy craft " from 1978 to 1982, with interruptions while he traveled abroad as a musician for Czechoslovak musical groups. At one point, to establish his credentials in the West, under the StB supervision, he brought out supposed samizdat documents and handed them over to an émigré writer living in West Germany, who wrote an article from the material he received.

The purpose of Barak's preparations and training in Czechoslovakia, and traveling to meet with émigrés in the West, was to get him ready to join RFE/RL in Munich. From here, he would supply the StB with internal documents, information about personnel, and various émigré groups:

> Besides the previously mentioned documents, which I passed on to my contact officer, I also passed him personal notes and information about people who worked in the Czech. Dept. or belonged to Czech. émigré groups outside RFE. It was part of my tasking to collect all information, personal and professional about these people. Additionally, I received specific concrete tasking from either "Vladimir" or "Ludek" to gather additional information about particular people in whom they were interested.

Barak's trial ended on Friday, June 9, 1989, when was found guilty and placed on probation for two years. The reason for the light sentence was that there was no evidence of any specific damage because of his activities; he had voluntarily gone to the police, and he fully cooperated with the authorities.

It was important that Barak was not encouraged to work full-time for RFE/RL, but only work as a freelancer, and therefore he would not be under any sort of supervisory control. As a freelancer, would be free to come and go as he wanted, including Sundays — when he apparently was most active. Barak admitted stealing RFE/RL stationary and envelopes, and he assisted in the distribution of anonymous letters against the former Czechoslovak Service director and other employees of that service in 1988.

Code Name NIKOLAJ

The Ukrainian minority in Czechoslovakia (mostly in Slovakia) was of concern to the intelligence services of the Czechoslovak Interior Ministry and the Soviet KGB. For example, the 2nd Administration of the SNB's (*Sbor národní bezpečnosti,* or National Security Corps) 12th Division, which was in reality the counterintelligence division of State Security Service (*Státní bezpečnost,* or StB), sent "secret collaborators" (*tajny spolupracovnik,* TS) to contact the Ukrainian Service employees of Radio Liberty and other émigrés in the West. The responsible StB department then sent reports to the Ministry of Interior KGB liaison officer (advisor), identified with the letter "P" (*poradce*), who in turn reported to the Soviet KGB 5th Chief Directorate. One such agent was NIKOLAJ. From one report, we learn the common purpose of this agent to the StB and KGB:

> Fulfilling the tasks of operation NIKOLAJ and in response to your request we would like to inform you that the object conducted the planned visit to the Federal Republic of Germany and France in November 1988; it lasted 19 days. During his trip he personally met with several Ukrainian nationals living in the capitalist countries; after his return he reported on those contacts. His statements were later confirmed by other sources.
>
> Based on the information about the trip of NIKOLAJ to capitalist countries, we ask our Soviet friends to inform us about your possible requests, or directives for NIKOLAJ with respect to individual representatives of the Ukrainian emigration and institutions which were visited by the object during his stay in the USA and Canada.[11]

In a report dated August 28, 1989, the common interests between the KGB and SNB are clear:

> NIKOLAJ also wanted to visit the University of Toronto and the Canadian Institute for Ukrainian Studies at the University of Edmonton where he intended to actively participate in the preparations of a book titled *Ukrainian Games for Children.*
>
> It was expected that he would also be interested in visiting other Ukrainian emigrant institutions and their representatives who are active in Canada and the USA.
>
> This matter had been discussed at the meeting that took place on June 1989 in Moscow. According to the conclusions of the meeting, we [asked] our Soviet friends to conduct an investigation into the activities, the meetings, and the nature of those meetings of the object NIKOLAJ with the Ukrainian emigration and the nationalist institutions during his stay in the capitalist countries.[12]

The next month, on September 25, 1989, the SNB made another interesting report on NIKOLAJ:

> Among the Ukrainian émigrés there is little information on the life and the activities of Ukrainians living in the CSSR. The employees of the Ukrainian section of Radio Liberty are only interested in the situation in the Ukraine and have developed no efforts to obtain information from the CSSR. They consider the CSSR to be a conservative state in which restructuring (perestroika) has so far not gained ground; they believe that the CSSR does not want to introduce (reforms) similar to those in the other socialist countries.
>
> In general, NIKOLAJ learned that RL currently has very reliable and quick

channels to the Ukraine. They receive information on all activities of the internal opposition, on demonstrations, and on the situation in the Ukraine and the USSR in general.[13]

NIKOLAJ actively reported on his contacts with Radio Liberty until just before the Velvet Revolution and end of Communism in Czechoslovakia in November 1989.

Hungarian Intelligence Service: Janos

In October 1986, RFE/RL Hungarian Service employee Janos (pseudonym) reported a visit from his parents from Hungary. This was not their first visit to Munich, or the first visit from any of his relatives. However, this was the first time that he received a message from the Hungarian government.

His father gave him an envelope just before he returned to Hungary. His father was sixty-seven and retired. The father and mother were called into an office after they received their passports to leave Hungary, and they were told to hand-carry a message from the official who interviewed them. They were advised to wait until Janos opened the envelope and wait for his answer.

Janos reported to the RFE/RL security office about the envelope the last day his parents were in Munich. He was advised not to open the envelope in their presence. His father had a history of heart attacks. His father would not have to lie about anything and he could truthfully tell the Hungarian authorities that he didn't know what was in the envelope or Janos's reply.

The next day Janos opened it in the security office. The letter was not signed and contained the following message:

> You have remained Hungarian, your heart remains here, and you never say anything bad against us. Though your work inhibits you, you would like to visit your homeland. I heard you and your wife are having problems. She is German and she hasn't accepted you, or your relatives, because you are a foreigner. We know you earn good money but you have a deep yearning to return. You know there are legal problems of doing so, but you can forget the past and return to a future without worries. Think it over and give me an address where to send a letter and where we can meet. Don't show it to anyone. You can have a rosy future.[14]

Janos said he would not do so and he had no desire to return to Hungary. He and his wife were not having any problems. He added that he would let the security office know if any further attempts were made to "tempt him to return or work for the Hungarian regime." This was the only known attempt.

Tibor

In July 1987, Tibor (pseudonym) met his parents who were allowed to travel to the West. They met in Vienna and he was given the same pitch about working for the regime, returning to Hungary, etc. He called from Vienna to report the message. He was told simply to tell his parents "thanks, but no thanks," and that he had reported their message to the RFE/RL security office. After he returned from his vacation with his parents, he explained what had happened before their meeting. On April 1, 1987, his parents had gone to the Passport Office in Budapest where they were told,

> We were waiting. We know where your son is working. We know everything about your son. He is on a one-year probation. He then went to Monitoring for three months to listen to Hungarian radio. Then there was another year of probation. We have photographs of him at a party. Your son is in the trade union.

A Hungarian intelligence officer using the name Robert Kovacs afterward telephoned the father and asked to meet. They met at an espresso bar, where Kovacs said:

> We will take you to anywhere in Austria. Ask your son to come and then introduce him to me. We don't need a James Bond to look for information. We just want an editorial informant on the editorial line to be taken over the next three months. We will meet him every three months. We want to counter the radio line, to advise the press and organs. We will pay up to DM 1,500 for each meeting. He can then retire to Hungary. No one has been caught in the West. He must answer quickly.

The father agreed to pass on the information to Tibor, and the passports were then mailed out. After the return of his parents to Hungary, they told Kovacs what had happened and said that their son refused to cooperate. There were no further attempts to recruit Tibor.

Jozsef

On November 18, 1988, RFE/RL Hungarian Service employee Jozsef (pseudonym) reported meeting his brother, Laszlo (pseudonym), in Vienna, November 6 and 7. Laszlo had written a letter on October 26, to Jozsef; he had received it on November 1. In the letter, Laszlo wrote all details of how he would travel to Vienna, and he wanted to meet with Jozsef. Jozsef was told to go to a hotel on Maria Hilfestrasse. However, after the train arrived on November 6 at 1:30 P.M., they met and went to another hotel on the Hakengasse (Pension Hotel) to the right of the West Bahnhof.

Laszlo said that he was put under a lot of pressure in Budapest in 1984 because of Jozsef, and he was only a deputy in small department of a Hungarian ministry. He had two boys, ages ten and fourteen, and his wife had Multiple Sclerosis. In September 1984, two secret intelligence officers went to Laszlo and identified Jozsef by his RFE/RL broadcast name.

Laszlo didn't own a shortwave radio and had not heard Jozsef on the air. They then told him that Jozsef belonged to the inner circle in the Hungarian Department and took part in the daily editorial meetings. Recently Jozsef had been having some problems in the department, but his work continued to be excellent. He was told that Jozsef earned about $44,000 per year and was planning to go on vacation in Brazil (a true statement), and that Jozsef was investing in paintings (also true: he'd bought one in New York, others in Munich). They then kept pressure on Laszlo in 1984 to meet with Jozsef, and threatened him with the loss of his job. Jozsef went to the United States in the summer of 1985 and returned to Munich in July. In August, the police again put pressure by meeting with him once a week and in October Laszlo was forced to write the letter (mentioned above) to Jozsef, asking to meet him.

During their meeting in Vienna, Laszlo admitted that he had been asked by the Hungarian Intelligence Service to tell Jozsef the following:

- Jozsef could work for them at RFE/RL for five to seven years.
- He then would be given a professorship of law at Budapest University.
- He will be able to publish books.
- He would be given a three-room apartment in an elegant section of Budapest.
- He would receive 10–15,000 FL per month, to be put into an account for him

Jozsef was to do the following:

- Give a sign in advance on what was going on in the Hungarian Service of RFE/RL, what programs were being planned, so they could set up counterprograms and prepare Hungarian radio and press against RFE/RL,
- Report on all kinds of events, even if Jozsef didn't think they were important, so they could use his reports to confirm other information received,
- Report on radio policy,
- Report on who was preparing overall RFE/RL policy concepts.

Laszlo told Jozsef that another person in RFE/RL's Hungarian Service was also working for them and that if Jozsef didn't want to do it, they would use the other person. If Jozsef agreed, he would get instructions from a man who came regularly from Budapest and returned. If Jozsef refused or reported the meeting, something would happen to him in Munich, that is, his life was endangered. They knew a lot about Ribansky (then director of RFE/RL's Hungarian Service) and said he was a "hard enemy, who is effective and dangerous." Jozsef said he told his brother no on all accounts.

Polish Intelligence Service Activities:
Czechowicz, Lach, and Smolinski

In the 1970, three persons associated with Radio Free Europe supposedly redefected to Poland: Andrzej Czechowicz, Micezyslaw Lach, and Andrzej
Smolinski. All three were then used by Poland in that country's propaganda
campaign against RFE.[15] In addition, the 1976 Joint Action Plan (see Appendix J) contains this paragraph in the "Active Measures" section:

> Examining the question of holding an public tribunal against RFE and RL
> on the territory of a socialist country (CSSR, GDR, or another socialist coun-
> try to be agreed on), under participation of renowned international law
> experts, personalities of society from socialist and Western countries, former
> employees of these centers who were ordered back from the West
> (CZECHOWICZ, LACH, SMOLINSKI — PPR, MARIN — USSR, MIN-
> ARIK — CSSR and others), people who used to work there, selected citizens
> who came under influence of the radio stations, as well as by using documen-
> tary materials from all socialist intelligence services.[16]

One of the best-known Polish Secret Service (SB) agents or collaborators involving RFE was Andrzej Czechowicz, who was evidently recruited
while already in the West and collected information from his desk in the Polish research section for several years before returning to Poland in 1971.

Two other agents returned to Poland in 1974: Mieczyslaw Lach (code-
name "Kumor") and Andrzej Smolinski. They were not only used in internal
Poland propaganda programs but also by the Soviet media in 1975, for example. In a Soviet newspaper (Izvestia) review of a television program in Poland
in March 1975 featuring Smolinski, he was identified as "a former employee
of this subversive center (RFE) [who] exposes the criminal activity of the
radio station and tears the masks from the faces of its present leaders — Gestapo
agents, provocateurs, and spies."

Lach would later resurface in 1983 when a book, *I Trust You, Kilroy*, was
published in Poland. This book consisted of photographs of RFE Polish Service staffers and photocopies of RFE documents, most of which first appeared
in 1975 on Polish television.[17]

In a Hornet's Nest

In 1998, a former Sluzba Bezpieczenstwa (SB) officer gave RFE/RL this
document, which was used in the Polish government's propaganda campaign
against RFE/RL:

Warsaw, 1988–08–15
Secret single copy
N O T E
Re: protection system for the facility code-named Hornets ("Szerszenie")

The unit responsible for the comprehensive program of protecting the facility is the RFE Security Department (Security). Its personnel is made up of US and West German citizens. The Security Department Chief is Richard Cummings — a CIA functionary.

The facility protection consists of:

1. Physical and technical-organizational protection.

- A wall — some 3 meters high — provides the physical protection of the facility running around it, and by guards both outside and inside the building.
- All persons entering it through the reception area are obliged to produce their pass to the guard; since 1987, they must additionally go through a metal-detector gate. Moreover, the guards periodically make random checks of the contents of the staffers' briefcases (hand-bags).
- The technical-organizational side of the protection is provided by rules concerning the circulation of documents; the possibility of taking them out of the building (only with a special permission from the superiors); special passes for the employees (only some of them are authorized to bring in guests from outside). Recently, a special computer-operated system for securing locks on the personnel's rooms has been introduced. They are magnetic card activated. Every opening of a room is computer-registered. That makes it possible to monitor who has stayed in a room [and when and for how long].
- The data-gathering system in the RFE/RL computer center — Arabella Centrum — is secured in a similar way.

2. Operational protection.

- The Security Department conducts operational work among RFE/RL employees with the view to recruiting persons as sources of information. In the case of investigating a suspect, a whole gamut of technical-operational means is employed: telephone tapping, mail checking, observation, etc.

Enclosed: photocopy of a translation of the latest instructions from the RFE/RL Security Department.[18]

French Intelligence Information, 1992

In February 1992, the French government gave the following document to German authorities, who passed it on to RFE/RL as part of their investigation.

Subject: Polish Agents in the Federal Republic of Germany
In answering your message, we inform you that we are not in a position to

pass on a positive result. We would like to draw your attention to two people who live in your country who until 1989 were possibly agents of the former Department 1 of the Polish Intelligence Service, SB. This information
was passed on from a source we consider reliable.

    1. In 1983/84, an officer of Department 1 of the SB, SMEKOWICZ,
       recruited an important agent with Radio Free Europe in Munich. The
       contacts were abroad. The source does not know the name of the agent.
       The source however knows that he is young man from a well-to-do Pol-
       ish family. Before arriving in your country, he had lived abroad for a
       year (US, Canada, and Argentina) from his financial interests.

    2. In the beginning of 1985, an officer of Department 1 of the SB traveled
       to Munich to reactivate a former agent of the SB and to arrange con-
       tact meetings with him in Vienna.

This person, whose name is unknown to source, was a consultant with
Radio Free Europe but the subject is not supposed to have worked in Munich
for ten years. At this time, he was about 60 years old and his wife worked in
the Federal Republic of Germany as a speaker with Radio Free Europe. He
is supposed to have a son who is a scientist at a university.

    At this point in time, this is the only information we have that is of inter-
est to your service. We will be in touch, if we receive more details that are
relevant.[19]

The ensuring German investigation did not uncover who these two
agents were.

The "Sparrow"

RFE/RL employee "Sparrow" (German code name) reported a visit of
his parents in August 1986. His father told him during the last days of the
visit that he brought a message from the Polish authorities, wherein "Sparrow" was advised that he could travel to any place in the world, including a
return trip to Poland. He should think it over and meet the father and "a
friend" in Vienna to discuss more details. "Sparrow" had serious financial
problems but refused to go along with the idea of a meeting in Vienna.

    This approach was reported to the Bavarian Land Security Office (LfV),
and a representative from that agency interviewed "Sparrow." Later "Sparrow" advised that he had received a letter from his parents, and his father was
encouraging him to reconsider his decision. He gave a name of a hotel in
Vienna, and suggested dates for them to meet. "Sparrow" still refused and
another appointment was been made for him to meet again with the Bavarian LfV.

    "Sparrow" had traveled to Vienna twice and once to Berlin, once under
German direction and control, to meet with Polish Intelligence Service (PIS)

officers: the first two meetings took place in Austria; the last meeting took place in Vienna in late 1987. The two meetings in Vienna were made with the approval of their Austrian counterparts, and partially observed by both the Germans and Austrians.

During the last meeting in Vienna, "Sparrow" was asked by the SB if it were possible for him to place a tape prepared in Poland in RFE/RL's master control room for broadcasting. "Sparrow" said it was relatively easy to do so, but also a written summary of the tape would have to be prepared as well, as a tape cannot be played without a written summary. He added that if such a tape was broadcast, he would obviously be caught for doing it, and that would be the end of his tasks at RFE/RL. He was offered DM 30,000, a job and an apartment in Poland, if he did it. The SB officer told him that they would meet him later in Berlin and give him the tape. They also asked questions about Polish Service staff members, etc. At the first meeting, the SB officer knew about the changes in the security instructions and asked him to get a copy, if possible.

In June 1988, he went to Berlin where he thought he would meet the SB officers in Berlin, but only his father showed up. "Sparrow" gave him a copy of the RFE/RL in-house newsletter, apparently as an act of good faith. "Sparrow" did not give the father the security instructions — prima facie evidence of another Polish Service employee in contact with the SB. There was no tape from the SB, but his father gave him DM 3,000.

"Sparrow" was scheduled to be given an easily identified attaché case at the next meeting — which never took place. The Germans presumed that the SB always used a certain attaché case for quick identification. RFE/RL was advised to watch out for any Polish Service employee who regularly came to work with an easily identifiable attaché cases — none were found.

"Sparrow" wrote a letter to his father in August 1988 indicating that he could no longer meet or cooperate with the SB because it was too dangerous for him to do so. He apparently told his father that this was because of his own personal problems (unexplained) and the recent publicity about RFE/RL in Poland, which obviously showed that someone at RFE/RL was leaking information, and all employees of the Polish Service were being carefully watched.

In November 1989, "Sparrow's" parents visited him again. Shortly before the visit, his father met with "Jacek," the Polish Intelligence officer in charge of that service's operation against RFE/RL. Jacek told the father to tell "Sparrow" that the operation was on hold, pending the results of the political changes in Poland. Jacek was not sure what might happen to him, and his department, as a result of the changes.

"Sparrow" agreed to travel to Poland over the Easter holidays in 2000, which he did. "Sparrow" met his control officer in Warsaw; he was not tasked with any future activity at RFE/RL. In fact, the subject of the radios never came up. He was asked by the control officer to keep them informed about West German developments concerning the reunification as it concerned Poland. A meeting between "Sparrow" and the Polish intelligence officer was to have been set up for Salzburg sometime in the future. However, since "Sparrow" was not politically active or interested in West German politics, it appeared that they didn't want to fully break off relations with "Sparrow," but wanted to keep open any options for any future activity. There were no subsequent meetings or contacts.

Gontarczyk Couple

The 1988 Bavarian Counterintelligence Annual Report contained one small item about the former freelancer of the Polish Service named Gontarczyk, who returned to Poland in 1987 and appeared on Polish television denouncing the Polish Service of RFE. It was apparent from all the information we know about them, that the former freelancer and her husband were originally sent to West Germany in 1982, with the task of reporting on the Polish émigré community. Their task ended with the death of a Polish priest, Blachnicki, who was very active in anti-regime activities. He died in a questionable automobile accident, and they returned to Poland in April 1988. The Polish News Agency (PAP) carried this item, quoting the government press relations officer Urban:

> Radio Free Europe journalist Andrzej G. and his wife Jolanda G., a speaker of this broadcasting station, [have] returned to Poland after six years of absence. The G.s were also activists of political structures of the emigration in the West linked with the so-called London Government and the "fighting Solidarnosc." I have said before that part of the Free Europe staff has established contacts here to sound out the possibilities of returning, he said. I think that G.s coming back to the homeland is but a beginning.

Father Blachnicki was a continual thorn in the Polish regime's side. He also was attacked in the Soviet newspaper *Komsomolskaya Pravda*, in Russian, on May 12, 1983:

> Father E. BLACHNICKI, who founded in the Poland the so-called "OASIS MOVEMENT" [is a] "saboteur in a cassock." It is no accident that RFE has become Blachnicki's pulpit, and the émigré rabble have become his flock.

Code Name Lighter

Dr. Zdzislaw Najder was a dissident in Poland and later director of the Polish section of the RFE/RL from 1982 to 1987. He was hired as the director of the Polish Service of RFE/RL in April 1982. Through a routine background check, RFE/RL learned that Najder was alleged to have met 10 to 12 times with agents of the Polish Intelligence Service (SB) in 1957 and 1958. In May 1958, Najder reportedly signed the following agreement with the SB:

> I pledge to provide voluntarily the employees of the Security Committee of the Internal Affairs Ministry with information that is accessible to me with the limits of my personal conviction. I pledge also to keep in total secrecy the content of my talks with employees of the Institution mentioned above.
> I will sign with the pseudonym Zapalniczka (Lighter) the statements that are deposited by me.
> Zdzislaw Najder[20]

Shortly before he traveled to the United States in February 1959, Najder reportedly met with his intelligence contacts. This contact officer wrote a "strictly confidential" memo on January 7, 1959, which gave Najder his tasks and the ways they could have contact with him. Najder remained in the United States until September 1959.

He then went to England in October 1959 and remained there as a student at Oxford University until June 1960. It was then that he signed a receipt, reportedly as "Lighter," on October 25, 1959, for 1,000 Polish zloty he had received from one of his contact officers.

Najder was allowed to return to England in April 1961 and he remained there until June that year, when he received a B. Lit. from Oxford University. He had written in his RFE/RL job application that he had been arrested (or detained) in April 1962 "for smuggling 'subversive' texts ... between Warsaw and frontier."

Years later, during a meeting with RFE/RL senior management, Najder said he had been arrested at Warsaw airport in June 1975 on the charges of intent to disseminate anti-government publications. He added that charges had been dropped after the intervention of the minister of culture. He traveled to the West in years 1976–81.

On May 28, 1983, the Polish military court sentenced Najder to death for treason, in absentia, on espionage charges. RFE/RL issued a press statement that protested the charges of espionage as baseless. The next day, on May 29, 1993, the Soviet newspaper *Izvestiya* reported on the trial with the headline "Turbid Waves in the Air." Commenting on the trial, journalist A. Druzenko wrote:

> A logical end and a just conviction are in store for yet another renegade. In this case it is not important whether he stands trial in person or whether he is tried in absentia. In the army of villains one cannot rise to a higher rank than that of "traitor."
> Najder and the other CIA hirelings who do their work in RFE are certainly

doing a useful job in one respect. By their daily ravings they are making the Poles realize who their true friend is and who does not give a damn about their problems. And so really, it is an ill wind that blows nobody any good.

On June 1, 1983, the U.S. State Department endorsed RFE/RL's position when a spokesman said, "We are deeply shocked by this action by the Polish government."

Radio Liberty broadcast an interview with Najder on June 1–2, 1993, in which he said, "For the first time ever, a man has been sentenced to death without the tiniest scrap of evidence or the slightest proof of his guilt — a man who has never been in government service and never came within a mile of any state of military secrets."[21]

On June 18, 1983, in a broadcast to Romania in Romanian, Radio Moscow broadcast a criticism of Najder, saying that he had "taken the road of traitor of his own people. The road of a CIA agent along which he had been working for many years, since he had been working at Warsaw University."

On February 13, 1987, the Polish News Agency (PAP) reported that Najder was to be fired shortly and that those employees of RFE/RL's Polish Service who wished to return to Poland could do so without risk of punishment. This last act was in gratitude to the U.S. government for "firing Najder." Najder resigned six months later.

After the collapse of Communism in Poland, Najder returned to Poland. He became a politician and advisor to the government officials in the Solidarity government under President Lech Walesa. The Polish Supreme Court declared the death sentence null and void in September 1989.

1992 Polish Media Information

On June 15, 1992, Najder commented on recent Polish media information, saying that he had contacts with the Polish secret police under the communist regime. He told an RFE journalist in a phone interview that in 1958 he had voluntarily met with the secret police. Najder said that the meeting had been at his initiative, a deliberate attempt on his part to mislead the secret police, and turn them away from a prominent group of dissidents and from the Polish association of writers. He also said that the secret police soon found that was misleading them and, in retaliation, he was fired from his job. He added that he had been persecuted many times by the secret police.

Najder was commenting following reports in Polish media concerning a secret police agent with the code name "Lighter." A Polish television commentator said that President Lech Walesa had written a letter to a senior Interior Ministry official, Andrzej Milczanowski, saying that he had evidence that a former police agent called "Lighter" was responsible for orchestrating the embarrassing release in Parliament earlier that month of a list of alleged Polish police informants.

Walesa asked the Interior Ministry to investigate the issue. In Walesa's letter, it was said that "Lighter" had left Poland on Thursday or Friday. In a report on "Lighter," Warsaw Radio quoted the KPN party as saying that Zdzislaw Najder left Poland on Thursday, the same day as "Lighter."

In his interview with RFE, Najder said that he had left Poland for France on Tuesday, on private matters. He said his colleagues in Poland knew of his plans, that he did not know whom Walesa had in mind, and that he had never been a secret police agent.

Appendix A:
East German Intelligence
Report on Carlos

Department XXII/8

Berlin, 10 February 1981
fo-gl
TOP SECRET!

Report

on the activities of terrorist organizations, particularly the "Organization of International Revolutionaries," which is being headed by *the well-known terrorist "CARLOS."*

In the context of its political and intelligence operations aimed at the struggle against and gathering of information about terrorist forces, groups, and organizations, the MfS (the Ministry for State Security) did not learn about plans or intentions of terrorist groups to act against the interests of the Soviet Union and particularly against the preparations and the carrying out of the XXVI party congress of the Communist Party of the Soviet Union (CPSU).

According to the information of the MfS, there is currently no proof of efforts by imperialist intelligence services to use their moles in terrorist organizations to plan and implement anti–Soviet activities, or activities directed against the party congress.

Thorough operational checks of extreme-leftist terror organizations, such as the "Red Army Faction," the "Revolutionary Cells," the "Group of International Revolutionaries" (called: "Carlos" group), the "ETA," and the "Movement 2 June" also revealed no such activities.

As to the so-called "Armenian Liberation Front" which has carried out anti–Soviet activities in the past, we have no information.

It was only possible to learn that "Carlos" personally maintains contact with the organization; he made it clear in a discussion with leading members of the organization, that he succeeded in reducing the anti–Soviet attitudes of the organization.

The MfS has a broad variety of materials on the "Carlos" group at its disposal. As to the queries, we can provide the following information:

1. The current whereabouts of "CARLOS"

Until 2 February 1981, "Carlos" resided in Bucharest. From there he traveled to Budapest to meet at a base of the group (a private apartment) with a member of the group's leadership, the former FRG citizen

KOPP, Magdalena
called: "Lilly"
catalogue No.: 3

The leading members of the group are using this apartment often. According to our information, it is used to store weapons, explosives, and equipment for the forging of passports.

2. Current plans and intentions of the "Carlos" group

The group still considers itself to be a revolutionary organization, whose struggle is aimed against imperialism of all kinds. They are predominantly concentrating on the support of national liberation movements, as they are convinced that these groups are the most efficient in their revolutionary struggle.

The group considers the socialist states to be its strategic allies; it is interested in maintaining a friendly relationship with them, but expects material and logistical support in return.

Currently, the group does not intend to put much emphasis on its own terrorist activities. Based on their recent activities and statements it is reasonable to assume that the group increasingly tries to grow into the role of a coordinator or mediator between various national terrorist forces.

The "Carlos" group wants to strengthen its influence on other terrorist groups by providing weapons, financial means, and passports, which it obtains in other countries, or produces itself at its bases, and by other logistical support.

At the moment, the leadership of the "Carlos" group is of the opinion that it is not possible to establish its own, stable bases in the group's operational areas.

In the long-term (a period of about 10 to 15 years), it thus intends to establish bases in socialist states with the aim to use them for meetings, for updating their technical equipment, and for recreation. The headquarters should be situated in Budapest.

In the case of potential problems with some of the socialist countries, the group intends to accept the Rumanian offer to move its headquarters to Bucharest.

The Romanian intelligence service made the offer already some time ago and has given the group a house in Bucharest. The direct contact between the Romanian intelligence service and Carlos' group is being maintained by

VICESCU, Andre
catalogue No.: 43
Tel. No.: Bucharest 111 969

In the case that, for one reason or another, Romania will have to be abandoned, "Carlos" intends to switch to Syria. Preparations are thus underway to create a base in Syria, reportedly with the help of the Syrian intelligence service.

As far as the socialist countries are concerned, the "Carlos" group has the following preferences:

People's Republic of Hungary

As mentioned before, Budapest is considered the main base of the group. The reasons for this are allegedly

• favorable communications

- the [Hungarian] regime offers ideal conditions (liberal border controls)
- a good relationship with the foreign ministry, and with government and security institutions
- no problems with the renting of private apartments and hotel rooms

People's Republic of Bulgaria

According to the plans of the group, the People's Republic of Bulgaria is also to be used for the creation of a stable logistical base that could be gradually extended. For this purpose, the internal [political] stability of Bulgaria is favorable.

Cuba

A permanent representation of the group's members in Cuba is currently not anticipated. The activities should be limited to logistical support and to the maintaining of contacts between Latin America and Europe. This wish was expressed by the group's leading members

WEINRICH, Johannes	and	ABUL HAKAM
called: "Steve"		catalogue No.: 4
catalogue No.: 2		

during their stay in Cuba (May 1980).

Socialist Republic Romania

As mentioned above, Romania has already pledged to help the group and provide [material] support. In fact, Romania has been greatly helpful so far, and is treating the group's representatives with great kindness (allegedly on a ministerial level). We have proof for the fact that Romania has provided the group with

- three pieces of RPG-type bazookas with special optical devices and
- 18 pieces of ammunition for them

The group has nevertheless certain reservations about intensifying its relationship with Romania due to the direct contacts between Romania and Israel. The possibility of activities by the "Mossad" intelligence service directed against the group cannot be counted out.

Yugoslavia

The geographical position and the regime present good conditions for an operational base. Yugoslavia is, however, less advantageous to serve for recreational purposes or as a residence. Contacts to security institutions have been established.

USSR

The group considers the Soviet Union to be the center of world revolutionary activities.

Because of its distance to the operational areas, the USSR does not offer the conditions for serving as a residence or as logistical base, however.

It is nevertheless planned to continue using the Soviet Union as a transit route from the Arab and African countries.

People's Republic of Poland

Due to its internal instability, Poland does not offer the conditions for establishing bases or logistical centers.

Czechoslovak Socialist Republic

Because of various intrigues by the Iraqi intelligence service, Czechoslovak officials have a rather negative attitude towards the group which, in turn, makes it difficult to establish a permanent residence or logistical bases in the country. [The Czechoslovak territory] is thus only being used for brief meetings and as a transit route.

GDR

It is particularly the capital of the GDR that offers unique conditions for the group's activities. Because of West-Berlin and the general situation in the capital of the GDR, however, the group considers stays in the GDR to be problematic.

It can be noted that the group currently tries to stabilize itself; continues to gather equipment; and tries to attract new members and extend its contacts.

In this context it has proved to be favorable that

- "Carlos" still has considerable financial means, weapons, and travel documents at his disposal
- that "Carlos" and the members of his group have the possibility to temporarily use the territory of the socialist states for their activities. This makes it possible for them to establish contacts to other organizations without any hindrance on the one hand, and to positively influence new members, on the other.

Besides the above-listed information gathered in the context of our operative work, [we] learned that the group's activities have intensified in both quantity and quality on the territory of the socialist states, including the GDR.

Two of the group's leading members

"Steve" and "Lilly"

have since 1980 regularly visited the GDR to meet with the group's members and with contact persons and other foreigners. Their behavior in restaurants, cafes, and the bars of the Interhotel does not follow the rules of conspiratorial activity. Moreover, the spontaneous establishing of contacts with GDR citizens increases the danger of betraying their true identities.

3. The structure and strength of the "Carlos" group

The group headed by "Carlos" is a terrorist organization whose members are citizens of various countries,

The leader of the group is

RAMIREZ-SANCHEZ, Ilich
called: "Carlos"
catalogue No.: 1

The following persons are known to be members of the leadership:

WEINRICH, Johannes
called "Steve"
catalogue No.: 2

WEINRICH is a former member of the "Revolutionary Cells" in the FRG and his responsibility [in Carlos' group] is to direct the group's activities in Europe. He is one of the people who can partly influence "Carlos."

KOPP, Magdalena
called "Lilly"
catalogue No.: 3

Along with WEINRICH, KOPP is responsible for activities in Europe. She is considered to be an expert in the forging of passports. She is the lover of "Carlos."

ABUL HAKAM
catalogue No.: 4

ABUL HAKAM is a former member of the "WADI-HADDAD" group (PFLP special operations). He is currently responsible for the group's activities in the Arab region.

HAYDER, Abdul Kareem
called: ABU KERIM
catalogue No.: 5

He is responsible for the group's activities in the South- and Latin-American regions. The following persons reportedly also belong to the leadership:

AL-AISAWI, Ali   and   FARHAN, Shihab Achmed

This information has not yet been confirmed, however.

The MfS could identify the following persons as permanent members:

SCHNEPEL, Gerd Hinrich
called: "Max"
catalogue No.: 6

KRAM, Thomas
called: "Lothar"
catalogue No.: 7

It could also be established that the group has a large number of supporters, sympathizers, contact persons, and persons who participated in meetings, but it is yet unclear whether they are members of the "Carlos" group or not.

According to unofficial information, the group has some 40 members in Europe and about 200 members in the Arab region. As to South- and Latin-America, we know of seven contact persons.

It can be assumed that the group is constantly expanding.

4. The sources of income of the "Carlos" group

It is an established fact that the group has received financial support from the Libyan and Syrian intelligence services. It is not known, however, how substantial this support was.

Financial support has also been provided by contact persons, for instance by

AL-HAMDANI, Ahmed	and	ABU FERID
called: "Abu Tamur"		catalogue No.: 60
catalogue No.: 34		

There have also been unofficial reports indicating that the "Carlos" group carried out money-procuring operations [i.e. bank robberies] in Italy and France in 1979. No details are known.

5. Connections of the "Carlos" group

It could be learned that the group has a connection to the Spanish terror organization

"ETA/Politiko Militar"

[We] know of six meetings in the GDR in which 5 members of the "ETA/PM" participated, namely:

GROVEN, Luc Edgar called: "Eric"	CECILIA CECILIA, Manuel
catalogue No.: 14	catalogue No.: 16
DIAZ-MIGUEL MASEDA, Ramon	CANAL, Jose Carlos
catalogue No.: 15	catalogue No.: 17
SANTIAGO LOPEZ DE, Monteverde	
catalogue No.: 18	

"Carlos" promised to provide weapons for the "EAT/PM." In return, the "ETA/PM" pledged to provide logistical support for the "Carlos" group.

The promised weapons were transported by the "ETA/PM" in October 1980 with a

"TOYOTA" van with the French registration:
2382 SH 29

via Berlin to West Europe. The vehicle is a standard model of the TOYOTA company used predominantly in Africa. As it is equipped with a double suspension, and it is thus hard to visually judge the car's overall weight. The storage container is positioned in the roof of the car and is well-camouflaged.

The group also still maintains contacts with the representative of a Swiss terror group,

BERTA, Marina
catalogue No.: 20

A transport of weapons was to be organized for her on 3 July 1980. For this purpose, the following Swiss citizens traveled to the capital of the GDR with a customized Volvo car, with the registration number GR 2343:

FURGER, Enrico Francesco	and	SUKKETTI, Lucia
catalogue No.: 24		catalogue No.: 25

Because of security problems, the operation could not be completed, however.

It could also be determined that the group has a connection to

BELLINI, Giorgio
called: "Roberto"
catalogue No.: 21

who lives in France. It is very likely that BELLINI has contacts to French terrorist forces and to the Spanish "ETA."

[The group] also has contacts with a terrorist organization calling itself the

"Arab Organization of 15 May"

The leader of this organization is the resident of Baghdad

ABU IBRAHIM
catalogue No.: 37

Among the organization's leaders is the Iraqi citizen

SHATUB, Adnan
called: "Abu Nadia"
catalogue No.: 36

Although it is known that this organization has been infiltrated by the Iraqi intelligence service, it was initially planned to let it participate in the activities of the "Carlos" group.

Several meetings and discussions took place between the leaderships of both groups with the aim to initiate joint activities.

Because of the armed conflict between Iraq and Iran, the intensity of these contacts has decreased more recently.

There are permanent contacts with terrorist forces in South- and Latin America. Concrete names of these groups could not yet be learned.

The eight existing intelligence reports indicate, however, that the persons [we] know of belong to certain terrorist structures, particularly in Venezuela. As some of these persons were previously members of an earlier, Paris-based group led by "Carlos," it can be assumed that "Carlos" has a certain influence on these forces.

The "Carlos" group maintains a close connection to the

"Revolutionary Cells"

of the FRG. It is basically a reactivated terrorist structure, which includes, among others, WEINRICH, KOPP, and SCHNEPEL. The current activities of this group are designed to attract new members and activate further force for terrorist activities along the lines of the "Revolutionary Cells'" concepts.

WEINRICH and KOPP have a certain influence on these forces.

It is known since November 1980, that the "Carlos" group has established a contact to a previously jailed member of the

"Movement 2 June"

which operates predominantly in West Berlin, namely

DREHER, Eberhard
called: "Jurgen"
catalogue No.: 10

It is planned to maintain this contact in order to win a certain influence over forces that are operating in West Berlin.

"Carlos" keeps up the contact with the "Armenian Liberation Front" personally. The MfS has no details on this.

6. Contacts between the "Carlos" group and Arab states

Syria

Since late 1978, the "Carlos" group has had a contact with the military intelligence service of the Syrian air force. It is known that the immediate contact person on the Syrian side is

Major HAITHAM

The contact was established with the help of the Algerian ambassador to Baghdad. This contact existed in a loose form until 1979. In late 1979, the Syrian side accepted the demands of the "Carlos" group to deliver weapons, travel documents, and a limited amount of financial means.

A crucial role in the maintaining of the contacts with the Syrian intelligence service is played by the member of the leadership of the "Carlos" group

ABUL HAKAM
catalogue No.: 4

He is permanently residing in Damascus. In February 1980, he arranged a meeting between

"Carlos"   and   "Lilly"
catalogue No.: 1   catalogue No.: 3

and a group of leading officials of the Syrian intelligence service, at which weapons and diplomatic passports were handed over. These documents are official passports, issued by the foreign ministry of the Syrian Arab Republic. It was also agreed that the Syrian embassies in the GDR, the People's Republic of Hungary, the Czechoslovak Socialist Republic, and the People's Republic of Bulgaria would grant the "Carlos" group assistance in the case of difficulties or if help was needed. According to our information, the Syrian ambassadors in these countries only know that these persons enjoy the protection of the Syrian intelligence service and that all support has to be granted in the interest of the Syrian intelligence service.

The code word that is to be used in such cases is

ABUL HAKAM

The group's direct contact person in the GDR is the employee of the Syrian embassy

SHRITAH, Nabil
catalogue No.: 41

Recently, the "Carlos" group has intensified its efforts to establish a secure, stable base in the Syrian Arab Republic.

ABUL HAKAM
catalogue No.: 4

plays a special role in this effort.

In support for this plan, "Carlos" was reportedly given two houses in Syria, along with two cars and financial means.

It could also be determined that weapons, equipment, and documents previously stored in the People's Democratic Republic of Yemen were moved to Syria.

Libya

The group's contact to Libya is also being maintained by the intelligence service. According to unconfirmed and unofficial reports, the contact to the Libyan intelligence service was established by the Lebanese citizen

FUAD AWAD
catalogue No.: 40

The contact person in the Libyan intelligence service is Major

ABU SHREDA, Salem
catalogue No.: 42

The financial and material support for the "Carlos" group was granted by the Libyan intelligence service with the obvious aim to turn it into the terror department of the Libyan intelligence service. According to the currently available information, this effort has not been successful yet.

The contact to the Libyan intelligence service is being maintained personally by the group's leading members "Carlos," "Steve," and "Lilly."

Iraq

According to our information, the contacts between Iraq and the "Carlos" group, sponsored and maintained by the Iraqi intelligence service, have either been cut off, or strongly limited due to the military conflict between Iraq and Iran.

There have, however, been confirmed reports that the Iraqi intelligence service tried to hire "Carlos" during his stay in Baghdad in 1977 and 1978. After turning down the offer, "Carlos," along with other members of his group, left Baghdad for fear of persecution.

Thereafter, there have been repeated efforts by the Iraqi intelligence service to reestablish the contact with "Carlos" in order to maintain some influence on him and the group he created.

These efforts have been carried out by employees and agents of the Iraqi intelligence service, among others by

MATROUD, Falah		BASHALAH, Omar
catalogue No.: 44		catalogue No.: 50
AZIZ, Kamil Majid	and	AL KOURAISHI, Hahsim
called: "Fanar Kamel"		catalogue No.: 51
catalogue No.: 45		

"Carlos" is of the opinion that Iraq must first provide financial and material aid before reactivating its contacts with his group. So far, he has refused to travel personally to Iraq because he mistrusts the policy and the promises of the Iraqi government.

People's Democratic Republic of Yemen

"Carlos" and his group maintain a close relationship with the People's Democratic Republic of Yemen.

The help provided by Yemen was highly appreciated by the "Carlos" group. Because Yemen is not very convenient from a communications point of view and because the support for the group has allegedly been reduced lately, the relationship between them has cooled off recently, however.

An expression of the gradually deteriorating relationship between the group of "Carlos" and Yemen is the move of equipment and weapons, previously stored in Aden, to Syria.

PLO

In 1979, the PLO planned to use the "Carlos" group for terrorist activities in its own interest. There had thus been several official meetings with leading officials of the PLO.

Because "Carlos" demanded considerable financial means in advance and because he refused to subordinate his group to the PLO, all official contacts were eventually ended by the PLO.

Currently, there are only contacts with some PLO associates, but they are kept on an exclusively personal level. They involve, among others

AMINE EL HINDI
catalogue No.: 52
ABU HISHAM
catalogue No.: 53

In addition to the information file no. 137/81, the MfS is able to provide further operative information concerning the "Carlos" group. This material will be summarized in an information report and handed over to the KGB as soon as possible.

Enclosed
- 1 catalogue with 61 pages
- 1 graph

Appendix B:
Action Plan in
Noel Bernard's Case,
Code Name the Jackal

HOME MINISTRY   Top Secret
DEPARTMENT OF STATE SECURITY   Single Copy
UM.0544 -
Nr. 225/ f.9/0025323 August 18, 1980
                                                      Approved
                        Action Plan
            in Noel Bernard's case, code name the Jackal

In his capacity as chief of RFE Romanian Department, the Jackal coordinates the hostile propaganda activity against our country, activity for which he has used a series of employees and collaborators of Jewish origin. He also contacts Romanian citizens, especially intellectuals, who travel abroad or have settled there, whom he debriefs or recruits for dissident or protest actions.

Recently, the Jackal has intensified his slanderous and defamatory propaganda against the Socialist Republic of Romania.

Given the danger the Jackal's activity represents for our country, it is imperative we apply more professional and vigorous security measures, in order to:

- Discredit the Jackal, determine his dismissal from his post with RFE, and pave the way for radical steps against him
- Aggravate the discord between the Jackal and Emil Georgescu, and that among other Romanian and Jewish employees of the radio's Romanian Department with the aim of neutralizing them and having them fired from RFE
- Take special steps in order to paralyze the radio's activity and to neutralize some employees by damaging and destroying buildings and facilities of the radio, apartments and personal vehicles of certain employees, and by inflicting bodily harm on the most active employees and collaborators of Radio Free Europe.

I. To discredit the Jackal and have him removed from RFE, we will take the following measures:

1. Informant Martin from Germany, who gets on well with the Jackal, will be asked to show himself solicitous whenever the Jackal asks for help with a personal problem; Martin will thus obtain information and evidence we will resort to in order to bring discredit on him. The same informant will persuade the German authorities that the Jackal has links with the Soviet secret service.   Deadline: 30 Oct. 1980

2. As for the Jackal's wife, rumors will be spread that she has connections with the Soviet secret service and the Romanian security agencies; that she had been trained and sent to Israel with a mission to settle later in Germany and to infiltrate RFE.

   To make these rumors credible, we will use the plan elaborated for both the Jackal and his wife. (Appendix 1)   Deadline: 20 Oct. 1980

3. In order to back up the rumors spread by us, we will train Ilie Ciurescu whose mission will be to get in touch with the Jackal's wife and to arrange a meeting under cover, preferably in a hotel, so that interested parties may later verify the fact.   Deadline: 20 Dec. 1980

4. Reactivation of the informants couple Filip — Florica from Germany, who have direct ties to the American management of RFE; they will spread the rumor that the Jackal and his wife have links with both the Soviet and Romanian secret services.   Deadline: 30 Oct. 1980

5. Recruiting Marcu from Germany, friend and doctor of Jackal's family. His mission will be to get compromising details regarding the Jackal and his wife; he will also pave the way for the radical measures to be taken against the Jackal.   Deadline: 30 Dec. 1980

6. To discredit the Jackal we will also employ the following sources in Romania: Riva and Ionescu Mihai will be trained and sent periodically to the Jackal with whom they have close relations; their mission will be to deepen the conflict between the Jackal and Emil Georgescu and to report their reactions to the measures taken by us in this regard.   Deadline: 20 Oct. 1980

   (1) Eugen, a doctor and Edgar Rafael's cousin, will be sent to learn details of the conflict between the Jackal and Edgar Rafael; these pieces of information will be used to discredit the Jackal.   Deadline: 30 Aug. 1980

   (2) Cristescu (university professor, Jacob Popper's childhood friend) will be sent on a mission to get compromising facts regarding the Jackal and his conflict with Jacob Popper.   Deadline: 15 Sep. 1980

7. Analysis of Gheorghe Popa's case (former editor with Romanian television, living at present in Italy); his case might be used to expose the radio's policy of instigating people to emigrate; it will also be helpful to thwart the political diversions planned by reactionary circles before the Madrid Conference.

   Gheorge Popa left Romania in September 1978, intending to settle in the United States as his brother and the Jackal had counseled him. Popa did not get the American entry visa and had to remain in Italy where he lives with his wife and 3 children in poor circumstances. He intends to complain against the American authorities and the Jackal's instigation. Popa also intends to repatriate.   Deadline: 30 Oct. 1980

8. Security measures (with Directorate's III and Cluj police forces' assistance) against Sora Mariana and Dordea couple from Germany, who have close relations with the Jackal and travel frequently to Romania; the Jackal takes advantage of these travels to collect information about our country, information he uses to disparage Romania. In both cases, we aim to intercept and neutralize these communicating channels and to get information capable of bringing discredit on the Jackal, and the radio's activity on the whole. Deadline: 30 Dec. 1980

9. Verification of rumors that the Jackal intends to come on a visit to Romania: what might be the subtle grounds for such an action? To find out we will resort to informants Riva, Ionescu Mihai, Marcu, Dinca and Pirvu. Deadline: 30 Dec. 1980

Accompanying the measures mentioned above, we will assess the methods and conditions under which radical steps against the Jackal will be taken. The analysis will take into account reports from Marcu (Germany) the Jackal's physician, Pirvu (Germany) restaurant manager, and Radu Crainic (Paris), whose flat the Jackal uses when in the French capital.

The radical steps against the Jackal will be proposed by March 19, 1981.

Bringing discredit on the Jackal will go hand in hand with measures against Emil Georgescu and the Paris group according to separate plans.

II. In order to amplify the discord between the Jackal and Emil Georgescu, and between Romanian and Jewish employees of the Romanian Department, we will take the following measures:

1. Training informant Kraus from Germany — journalist and the Jackal's friend — to instill into the Jackal's mind the idea that Emil Georgescu is determined to undermine his position in order to become director in his stead. With that end in view, Kraus will be asked to suggest that the Jackal should examine if the anonymous letters against him had not been typed on Adelheide Pfeiler's typewriter (Adelheide Pfeiler is Emil Georgescu's mistress). This fact will bring discredit on Emil Georgescu.   Deadline: 30 Sep. 1980

2. Informant Harald from Austria, a Jew, infiltrated into Emil Georgescu's circle in order to get information concerning his actions against the Jackal, will be asked to warn the Jackal of these actions and to convince him that Emil Georgescu should be fired from RFE.   Deadline: 30. Oct. 1980

3. Reactivation of informant Leul (Germany), former social democrat leader, good relations with the Jackal. Leul will be asked to incite the Jackal against Emil Georgescu. With that end in view, we will exploit Leul's aversion for Emil Georgescu and the compromising facts he knows about Emil Georgescu. To cover Leul's action we will send a letter to his German address containing compromising details regarding Emil Georgescu and his actions against the Jackal.   Deadline: 30 Sep. 1980

4. Operation of attracting Vlaicu (RFE employee known for his aversion for the Jackal); his collaboration will aim at discrediting the Jackal and instigating the Romanian employees against the Jewish ones. Deadline: 30 Dec. 1980

5. Rallying the Iron Guard groups from Germany, France, United States and Spain in order to start concerted actions against the Jackal and the Jews of the Romanian Department. With that end in view, we will resort to the following sources: Vlad, Oreste, Vianu and Martin (Germany) Dragos (France), Aldea (Canada) and Ovidiu (Italy).

By recurring to the measures mentioned above, we aim not only to discredit Emil Georgescu and other RFE employees, but also to amplify the discord between the Romanian group and the Jewish one, in order to bring discredit on the Jackal and thus to incite Romanian employees and Iron Guard followers to intensify their struggle to eliminate the Jews from the Romanian Department and replace them with Romanians. The conflict that will break out between the Iron Guard followers and the Jews will be later useful to cover the radical measures we will take against the Jackal, and other employees, and to cover our future special actions designed to paralyze the radio's activity. Deadline: 30 Dec. 1980

III. In order to paralyze the radio's activity and neutralize some of its employees, we will act as follows:

1. Informative penetrations into the objective:
Attempt to reactivate former informant Manole, a technician with RFE. He may be useful for some special measures. Deadline: 30. Oct. 1980

Training collaborator Danciu from Romania, electronic engineer, in order to send him abroad. He will infiltrate RFE with the mission to destroy the radio's facilities and buildings. Deadline: 15 Feb. 81

Informant Barta Geza's reactivation (Germany), mechanic, who repairs cars for some RFE employees; his mission will be to manipulate the cars so that they may become susceptible to making accidents. Deadline: 31 Dec. 1980

2. By using informants: Riva, Protopopescu, Kraus, Barta Geza and others we will analyze the radio's buildings and facilities, its security system, its vulnerable places in order to find the appropriate means to damage and destroy the buildings and facilities by detonating explosives and committing arson. On the other hand, we will select the persons apt to perform these special actions. By Dec. 31, 1980 we will have tabled the proposals concerning the operation.

3. Identification of the employees' homes, examination of possibilities to break into them in order to place containers with explosives, letters and bogus parcels which would cause explosions. For each case there will be a special variant of action. Permanent task

4. Identification of the garages where RFE employees park their cars or have their cars repaired. The aim: placing explosives or manipulating the cars so that they may cause serious accidents.   Permanent task

5. Identification of restaurants and brothels frequented by RFE employees, where we could frame a scandal during which RFE employees may get molested.   Permanent task

In order to achieve our goals, new measures may be added to the present plan in the process of its implementation.

A monthly analysis by management will assess the stage of the plan's implementation and the tasks to be undertaken in the future.

Sector Chief   Chief of Unit

Col. Tiseanu   Col. N. Damian (?)

Single Copy

TI/NV

r.d.983

Appendix C:
Detailed Plan Used to
Bomb RFE/RL

Summary of Notes by Johannes Weinich
at a planning session in Budapest,
presumably on 14 October 1980

The original document apparently included numerous photographs, including 60 of RFE/RL Munich Headquarters. Accurately drawn plans of RFE/RL Headquarters and the sites Biblis, Lampertheim and Schleissheim were also in English. No plans of Holzkirchen site or photographs of Holzkirchen site were included because they couldn't approach the core area without being observed. Also, there are references to both black and white and color films of all location: at least 5 films were taken. The handwriting of Weinrich was partially illegible in the copy I received and thus there are some question marks and gaps in the text that follows.

Conversation on 14 October 1980

1. Discussion of a planned attack at the VOA relay station in Arazbach.

2. Recommendations for a bomb attack of the transformer station ... information about the infrared equipment

"Security information from you"

3. General ... for them: 2 points must be attacked

— Main Building (discuss, whether you agree or are against)

— the possible night, 4 to 5 devices, or 20 Kg each stick

— 2 possibilities

  1.

  2 ... radio control for our use, you give the concept, after a practice period

4. Equipment:

  8 Walkie Talkies

  2 Pistols with silencers

  5 to 7 pistols, prefer 9 mm Makarov

5 Hand grenades

4 ... grenades, and explosives, prefer plastic

- *"Page 14 of the original"*

5. The following steps have to be taken

    a. area around main building

        security system/can (we) reach (target) without meeting anyone, any fence alarm systems

        area around the supposed garage

        opening in the wall ...

        fire alarms

        fence or gate (automatic, remote controlled or hand operated)

- Escape routes....
- Automobile possibilities ... . from the maps, Tivoli, Theodor Park, Oettingenstr, etc.
- Television cameras — schematic

  *5a) RFE/RL–English Garten

6. Transportation   • ... transport large amount of explosives to Munich

                    • walkie talkies

                    • arms

7. Help in logistics: • apartment

                    • automobiles

8. General Plan   • Careful preparing of operational activities, ca. 3 weeks

                    • Preparation of general materials (arms) and the technical questions by their side, ca. 3 weeks

                    • Operational planning sessions and checking of equipment,

                    • from then on, transportation & logistics and training ca. 1–10 Nov

  **5b) Second Target

    Preferably Schleissheim as "Ear" or RFE/RL (e.g. programs from NYC).... possibilities of destruction of the group ... examine from operational ways? you must consult at every step with the technicians. Until Saturday, an expert....

  **5c) Exchange of Materials: Check Places for Receiving them

[There followed discussion of RFE, Munich, Biblis, Lampertheim, Schleissheim, and Holzkirchen — apparently most of it comes from the 1958 book on Radio Free Europe by Robert Holt]

A. Films of Entrance to Bayerischevereinsbank Parking Lot.

    Observation: Gate Arm closed; during the working day, a guard opens it.

*Refers to photograph.
**Refers to photograph; numbers out of sequence.

B. RFE/RL ... from across the street

> including the guard house: at night after 9 P.M. it is empty. [Author's note: they believed that a CCTV camera was located next to the drain pipe at the main entrance.]

C. Maps to be purchased

- Police Stations of Munich
- RFE
- Schleissheim
- RFE and Hilton Hotel

D. [Detailed description of the Munich headquarters building and surroundings]

E. Description of building on a Saturday night at 22:00

> ... again at 01:00
>
> and *nights at 21:00:* 40% of rooms show lights; est. 20% of personnel at work; no guard is seen; taxis come by about every 8 minutes; the main entrance is not always lit up.

Appendix D:
Letter from Carlos
to Johannes Weinrich

Damascus, 19/VIII/83

Dearest Steve:

First of all I want to inform you of the latest news: today I phoned Lybia [*sic*], spoke to Salem, when I told him that I wanted to travel there, he told me that on monday he is traveling to Damascus and that we can meet here. I will use the French intervention in Chad as a pretext to restart cooperation. I have not waited any longer because all my money is finished with Feisals's trip (he takes $2,000 for you and $500 reserve).

There is left only the $15,000 reserve.

Continuing the money questions:

1. What about Sarkis?
2. Bring the 10 new Brownings with you, or send them with Ali from Budapest.
3. Avu Iyad: is there any money in this contact?
4. Get (from Bucharest?) all the papers and photographs regarding the old Jew-ish woman in Rome whom you phoned once. I think we should engage our-selves in this affair next month after her return from holidays. Convince Fina and Kai to prepare it and if possible to execute it. If needed, either Feisal or Farig will go as well. Please remember that this is a one million dollars busi-ness!

Regarding Andrei: 2 days after your leaving Bucharest, Andrei phoned me here himself, to warn us from the Saudis; he spoke in a way nobody else could under-stand: "the Saudis are very angry (with us), they are searching very well all vehicles and luggage coming into the country, specially from Lebanon, we must be very care-ful." When I asked him why he did not inform you, he answered that he had just received the information.

Regarding Barbie's affair: do not discuss it all with the Socialist Camp, just say that I am personally in charge of this question (remember that there are Nazi refugees in Syria!) Do not meet Herzog in these countries for the time being.

Regarding Albert: the name of his Belgian Comrade who accompanied him to Bucharest is: Freddy Antoine Paul *HERCKENS*.

237

Gianni: what news about Murtaza's operation, and what about the other ones? Rifaat: what about the hijacking? [Is] there any other news? "Khalid" new phone number in (?) is: 65 08 35 (uncoded).

For Ali: Al Khouli has received a report informing him that "Abdul Hakam has used Al Khouli's name, and that the fact that he carries a Syrian Diplomatic passport, to try extorting one million dollars from a Lybian [sic] in Budapest about 6 months ago." Kaytham read me a photocopy of the extortion letter written in the name of Abu Nidal.

After I explained what happened, the atmosphere became relaxed again, but still they want a full report from Ali.

It is obvious now that Ali has been entangled in a bigger provocation than we had ever thought. Therefore, he should put down for our own all information regarding directly or indirectly this affair: dates, hours, names, addresses, phone numbers, meetings with security services, gossips, etc.... I want a full picture of the environment in which he moves in Budapest, particularly regarding Syrians and Palestinians. On this basis we will compose together a report for Al Khouli which we will deliver together, him and me, answering any questions which might arise, in order to clarify this matter completely.

After finishing the operation, Ali must come here.

Ask Helmut about a very powerful liquid explosive which, according to Ali Waton al Arabi is made in East Germany, [it] is call[ed] "HARD DE TAI," and was used in the assassination of Badir Gemeyel. Haythan is interested in this information.

What about Yugoslavia, it is necessary to officialize the relation as soon as possible.

If you cannot meet Raul Lemur in Berlin, go with Ali to meet their man in Budapest. Ali knows him, this *shit* man is called Jorge LOREANs. The Embassy in Budapest has the phone No. 214039/037, the Consulate has the No. 324653.

I have found no German photocopiers here!

I have not news from Lucia yet. I enclose a letter for her to be sent EXPRESS from West Berlin.

We need to meet to talk [of] many things, take this into account when you make your plans. Also cut down unnecessary movements.

Best Regards,
Michel

Appendix E:
Stasi Report on "Separat"

Division XXII

Berlin, 28 April 1981
jä-gl
TOP SECRET

Report

on the consultations with the security organs of the Hungarian People's Republic in regard to the "Separat" operation

On 24 and 25 April renewed talks were conducted, as agreed, with the Hungarian security organs in regard to the "Separat" operation.

Participating on the Hungarian side: Comr. Lieut.-Col. VARGA, Head of Division 8 in the 2nd Main Administration.

Present on the MfS side: Colonel-Gen. DAHL, Head, Division XXII. Colonel-Gen. JÄCKEL, Dep. Head, Division XXII. Major-Gen. VOIGT, Head, Division XXII/8. Lieutenant-Gen. PAUL, Interpreter.

The Hungarian visitor was given accommodation in Object "73" of Division XXII, where the consultations also were conducted.

The trip as well as the departure to Budapest on 25 April 1981, at 6:15 P.M. passed without incident.

Main Content of the Talks

The statements of Comr. Lieut.-Col. VARGA focused on:

1. Assessment of the present situation in the "Separat" group.
2. Handing over a documentation, as well as giving an elucidation, in regard to the attack carried out by the "Separat" group against Radio "Free Europe."
3. Information about the measures planned by the Hungarian security organs against the "Separat" group.

Ad 1.:

Continued control and observation of the "Separat" group resulted in no essentially new findings.

Some information was, however, obtained that made possible a more precise definition of the evaluation of the group. Essential factors:

239

At a meeting of leading members of the "Separat" group a renewed evaluation of the socialist states was made. With the exception of the USSR, negative attitudes in regard to the individual states were expressed.

During a conversation within the group, the head of "Separat" stated that he assumes that his activities are being controlled and known in all socialist countries. He also assumes that there is also relevant coordination between the socialist states. He commissioned members of the group to acquire, on the occasion of contacts with the GDR, information about this cooperation, particularly that between the GDR (German Democratic Republic) and the HPR (Hungarian People's Republic).

The "Separat" group has received several assignments from the Romanian secret service. Of these the ones known are:

• The killing of 5 Romanian families living in exile. In realization of this assignment letter-bomb attacks were made on 5 February 1981 in Paris against Romanians in exile.

• Attack against the Romanian Department of Radio "Free Europe," partly realized on 21 February 1981.

In return for these activities leading members of the group were received by the head of the Romanian secret service and help with arms, diplomatic passports, etc. was promised and realized.

A member of the "Separat" group, BELLINI, Giorgio — cover name: "Roberto" — has been imprisoned in the FRG.

According to the findings of the HPR he had been informed about the preparation and execution of the attack against Radio Free Europe." Should he reveal what he knows, great dangers — for the socialist states as well — would ensue.

By way of extensive reconnaissance measures it was possible to determine that the "Separat" group had, beginning with approximately September 1980, had an assignment from the Romanian secret service to burglarize the Romanian Department of Radio "Free Europe" and subsequently to blow it up.

The date was set for 14 February 1981. The documents acquired, as well as a control of the activities, prove that the leading member "Heinrich Schneider" of the group prepared the action and himself obviously also participated in lt.

Although the attack was not realized as envisaged, the head of "Separat" traveled to Romania where he was praised for the action on the highest secret service level.

The documentation handed over proves these findings. The documentation was also given to the security services of the USSR and the CSSR.

Ad 3.:

The new findings of the security organs of the HPR have confirmed the necessity of introducing, in coordination with the fraternal organs, step-by-step and differentiated measures against the "Separat" group. For this reason a relevant proposal was worked out, which was confirmed by the Minister of the Interior of the HPR.

Comrade Janos KADAR also agreed with the conceptions as regards further procedure vis-a-vis the "Separat" group.

The aim of the measures should be:

• to end the permanent stay of the "Separat" group in the HPR and not to permit an alternate stay (of the group) in another socialist country.

- to provoke no confrontation with the "Separat" group, and also to exclude any difficulties with the states standing behind the group, like Libya, Syria, VDRJ (Yemen), etc.

Conceptions in regard to practical procedure:

In the first half of May the head of the "Separat" group will be summoned to the MfI (Ministry of the Interior) of the HPR for a discussion. On that occasion it will be disclosed to him that, due to

- the violations of law committed by him and the members of his group in the HPR, and
- certain activities of the adversary, like Interpol and Western secret services, against his group
- a permanent stay in the HPR and the other socialist states is no longer possible.
- he will be allowed to re-export his materials stored in Budapest.

The setting of dates in regard to leaving the HPR will be handled liberally. (A period of 2–4 months)

However, the permit for his permanent residence in the HPR will be withdrawn. Transit through the HPR and short stays will continue to be permitted.

The discussion is will be conducted in such a way that it should come to no confrontation and that he accepts the measure on the basis of political considerations.

Parallel to the discussion with "Separat" other control and observation measures will be introduced,

- that prevent the continued importation of arms into the HPR,
- that make the group realize that it is under uninterrupted control in the HPR,
- and that guarantee exact customs controls when entering and leaving (the country).

The fraternal organs will be informed about the discussion conducted and about the reaction of "Separat."

So far, the security organs of the CSSR have agreed with the conceptions of the HPR in regard to procedures vis-a-vis the "Separat" group. A general agreement of the KGB of the USSR is also in hand. The agreement of the Bulgarian security organs is going to be obtained on 27 April 1981. It has therefore been requested by Comr. Lieut.Col. VARGA that the MfS also agree to the planned procedure.

The Hungarian comrades, in coordination with the KGB of the USSR, consider a multilateral consultation on the Deputy Ministerial level to be no longer required. What is important, initially, is to start with the measures against the group and to find out (its) first reactions.

The representative of the Cuban security organs in Budapest is also to be informed about the measures taken.

Since there are certain communication difficulties with the Cuban security organs in regard to the "Separat" group, and (since) the Hungarian comrades have no acceptable proposal about the future permanent place of residence of the "Separat" group, Comr. Lieut.-Col. VARGA asked that it be checked out whether the readiness of the

Cuban security organs to provide the "Separat" group with a new field of activities in Latin America still exists. He asked the MfS to continue consultations in this direction with the Cuban security organs.

The material handed over by the Hungarian comrades includes copies of original documents, which were secured in the course of a conspirative search of the Budapest apartment of the "Separat" group and prove without doubt the participation of the group in the attack against Radio "Free Europe" in Munich and in attacks against Romanian emigrants in Western Europe. The handwritten remarks to the plan of action are from the hand of "Heinrich Schneider."

Comrade Colonel DAHL expressed thanks to Comr. Lieut.-Col. VARGA for the documentation handed over and the information conveyed. Information (material) was handed over concerning:

- planned activities of the "Separat" group in Western Europe,
- connections of the "Separat" group with the hijacking of the Pakistani passenger aircraft,
- observation activities in Budapest noted by the group.

In regard to the conceptions of the Hungarian security organs concerning concrete measures against "Separat" the following basic line was upheld, in accordance with the standpoint we have held throughout:

- any move is to be avoided that could result in the slipping over of the group to the enemy camp,
- a confrontation with the group is to be avoided, in order to exclude reactions of defiance,
- acceptable varieties for a solution are to be sought that would make it possible for the group to have a secure place of residence but that would also offer the security organs a certain measure in possibilities for control,
- the (practice of) granting transit travel and brief stays in the socialist countries to the leading members of the group is be continued.

Appendix F:
Letter from Johannes
Weinrich to Carlos

Author's note: Weinrich is German and was writing in English; hence, his English is not perfect. His wording has been retained throughout, but spelling errors have been corrected in most cases and some punctuation has been altered for clarity. Some paragraphs have been combined for space reasons.

Belgrade 29 August 83

Dearest Michel

I start to write this report today and will add continuations according to developments:

1. *OPERATION BERLIN.* Ziad has told you the most; he was behaving excellent (by occasion [?] give him once more my warmest regards). Regarding Helmut, it is clear that we could trick them, mainly on behalf solidarious [?] help given by Nabil. By the way: he knows about the Operation but as he told and suggested me, not officially.... Because he gave me the hand in keeping explosives without informing the Ambassador, who was absent, but came back before the Operation. So officially Nabil doesn't know about the Operation, only the fact that I brought a bag and took it later.

Helmut was always warning us, not to have an operation in West going directly from East and returning. We always denied and kept the cover of only transporting the bag to the West. They seemed to me on Friday — last meeting with them and after? — not to be sure, if we have done it or the ASALA. And I kept the story: telling them in a way that ASALA never claimed an operation, if not carried out by them.

So — unfortunately — there has been no clash in the last meeting, in which I was prepared well. All the time I kept one point hanging: a long time ago they've stamped (!) MARTINE's ID which is completely unusual ... can be called only "they betrayed her to the enemy." We made photos of it, and the prove is always with he [*sic*].

I did not use all the time, clashed always with them on a "minor" scale as l each (?) opening of the bag, I left in hotel always (nothing important inside...). Those clashes were necessary in order to stop their harassment and to keep them far, but a clash on Martine point is the principal ... we can take only one position: that's the most aggressive and obvious point of their continual line to betray us to the enemy....

So I kept the point, but they did not give me a chance in the last meeting.

It would have been wasted only....

Anyway: maybe it is better like this. The point is not lost. We can use it in the future. And I would like to discuss it over with you, before using it.

And on the other hand,

- We did what we wanted, they have tried to sabotage all the time but surely there was no way out
- They will learn (perhaps) their lesson, when they get the news about official confirmation that it was ours....
- And mainly: I do not intend to use Berlin for a very, very long time, which will be the best lesson for them.

I did not intend to report on that in such length, but I think, you can grasp the picture and will agree with the conclusion to plan everything in a way, that we can avoid Helmut.

From my side: I've changed all the lawyer-business, in order not to depend any more on Helmut. All meetings are planned either at "Chez Doctor" or here.

The Operation itself had bigger impact than I've expected. I sent you the pictures for showing to Omar — if you want — but please send them back by next occasion.

2. *Abu Syad.* The meeting with him as by chance, not this time. But 1st Helmut visit, and against Helmut's will. They do not want to let Abu Syad to out.... Anyway: he was very surprised and jumped upon me. Of course, in a way the invitation means you, although they did not insist that you have to be in the delegation.

My opinion: it is clear for them, that Hocey [?] has to be paid, although not mentioned, and they are interested on behalf of their situation:

A. Syad insisted that we have to meet and said, we choose the country:

All Socialist country (except DDR, from him!)
Yemen
Algeria (he offered)

Contact should be through: Zaki Abas (Ali knows), Aden, 423 40 (office), 427 17 (office), 423 17 (home?)

Originally we should contact from beginning on September but as Ali phoned today, I understood from him, that he has met one of them (I met in Berlin), and they do suggest now the 20-25.9 as time of contact. Ask Ali about it.

Discuss all with Ali, I've given him at that time a report about it. And I hope to see you before we move in that.

Two additional points only:

A. Syad has asked me if it is true what he heard that recently you and me (!) had a kind of disagreement and split the organization. I only laughed as an answer ... denying it by saying: it is good for us that the rumors about are growing unlimited. By the way: a similar question was raised by the Yugoslav.

Note: Obviously there are rumors on this kind going around. Think about it, if we can play with it, for example, on behalf of our position regarding socialist countries ... to confuse them ... we will talk about it.

They do think you are in Bucharest. This I learned from their questions about you. My reply was, we are everywhere and nowhere in the same time, one can find us only in the underground....

3. *Cuba.* We renewed the contact in Berlin, Ali was with me and can tell you the details. We send message to Raoul and asked for answer to confirm that the new man is our official contact. The name: Miguel Roque, Embassy 48 00 216, direct 48 25 022. The phone is 24 hours in service. If he is not there, we should tell the person: "enciende la Grabadora y avisa a Rogue...."

Our names are: Aboul WAKAH (?) and Steve. In case he sends us a message, we gave telex Abil and he will sign as "Mike."

We enclosed in the message to Raoul, that our comrades in prison are fine and very tough.... So about 2 weeks I'll call him, just to ask for the "answer" and the new contact in Budapest.

And ask Ali to tell you also the little point, how we played on the question of the 4 Lybian [*sic*] planes seized some time ago.

4. *Hungary.* Ali can tell you better all the contacts he had with them. After he informed me yesterday that they've been not serious, I think. Our line should be to stay out as much as possible, including Ali!

Only for meeting with lawyers or Albert's people we'll use it, instead of Helmut; but that will be always a short visit, and I do intend not to talk with them.

One good development, after visa trouble with Martine and Riad they have "trapped" themselves in that question assuring us, that after announcing our people will get separate visas. I do expect that at least the next 5 times it will work.

5. *Yugoslavia.* The contact was through "NEDA" the ex-secretary of our lawyer. I asked her to introduce me, because I would like to talk with the "Government" but not via diplomatic channels. She knows an officer, who happened to be involved in 76 in the airport, when they "rescued" you. But he is not any more responsible in this kind of affairs. So he promised to talk to those who are in charge. It took some weeks until another officer contacted me via the girl.

I spoke with him of course alone along following points:

• Introduction on mine (with real name) as a responsible of our organization
• that we want — organizationally — to be in contact with them
• out of the political situation and because we are here ... therefore we would like to establish relation....

I talked longer about: political reasons which led us to the decisions to approach them ... and why by this way and not through Palestinians, for example....

He had only one question: If my approach is an individual or organizational one.... The answer is clear: organizational.

We ended that he was not as "powerful" as he (meaning to be in the position of being a responsible...) and that he will contact me once more, after he will have presented everything to his responsibilities....

It took two weeks until he contacted the girl (Neda) once more. But this time only to get from her more details about: how he knew each other, where I live here ... etc. ... and stressing that she should not tell me ... and he told her again: very soon he'll contact her.... What he did not do until recently, when I was out. Now he is in nowadays or coming back these days.

By the way, that NEDA is still in the question in his decisions. When I talked with him I offered my telefon no. and everything. He refused saying: look I came to listen to you what you want from us ... I am not prepared for other things and I do prefer to contact you the next time once again through Neda and than we will arrange it in another way....

I am confident about the contact. That it takes time means to me

- either all questions regarding us are "highly" bound to a high-responsible
- or they want to find out how hungry we are for that relation.

Anyway: until now I did not push, but I think, next week I will move and contact again. I forgot to write above that I spoke about "relation-with-them" can be a "technical contact" or up to "cooperation" whatever they want....

I am waiting now for the next meeting, and according to what they'll answer I have to call one of you for next discussion.

... I'll tell you my schedule, but if can't come to you to talk it over, I thought: the best would be in case somebody has to come and joint discussion with them, that it is you....

From all the things around here: My "feeling" is positive, they take their time, but I think, results will be very encouraging.

I want you to pay attention to the following point:

- The question here is (besides relations with ANDRE) strategical very important for us....
- So the same time this country is quite open and vulnerable, etc.
- So we have to avoid any slip of tongue or mistake which could leak to the enemy that we are here.

Therefore I've told everybody of the comrades, who knows about our staying here, to be very careful and be secret....

I want that you do the same over there. Tell everbody [sic], to forget, that this country exists and please remind Ali once more, not to make his usual mistake when he meets socially and talks about woman or prices in other countries.... (p.s.: for those reasons I do not like that you've transmitted the phone number to LUCIA). Anyway: the first step to officialize the relation is done, and I am expecting their "answer" soon. Living conditions are better and much cheaper than before. The other people as Svetlana and Wille, I do not see them at all, for them I have left to Baghdad....

6. *New Names.* Before going to other points, please note the new names for most of the comrades, changed as well for telex-communications (on behalf the old HELMUT aggression): Lucy =   . Herzog = Gabriel. Duke = Guillaume. Neda = Sonja. Riad = Amin. Ky = Robby

7. *About GIANNI.* The operations was a lot better than we thought. All our explosive has worked, from our car nothing left. Why the two in the first car were not killed on the spot is strange. Maybe — and it seems to me — that George "pushed" a fraction of a second too early. Anyway, perhaps they are killed, since only once in the newspapers was mentioned ..."heavily burnt" ... and the Ambassador visited them in hospital and after nobody was allowed to see them.... Although journalists have tried, they do write in the newspapers about the sounds of people in third and fourth car, but not any word (except once) about the two and not a single word about passengers or driver of second car, also Saudi....

They lie about Ambassador: saying that on behalf of a hint two months ago, he took extra-security step as never going by car to the Embassy, but leaving it 1 km before and approaching embassy by foot ... a clear provocation, this lie....

The Saudis are trying to cover it up and are supported by the Greeks. Political impact goes that far, that Saudi is voting now in the U.N. on the Cyprus question by "card blanch" [*sic*] not any more alongside Turkey.

Whay ALI .... became 2 weeks later responsible for informing King Fahd (like a private information secretary).

Although possibly almost not noticed, the operation had its impact on the "community of those conspiring against Lebanon," I mean on the governmental level. The enemy tried to retaliate through one little bomb exploding in the night about 4 weeks later under a Syrian car in front of the Syrian embassy. And through another one at the same time which was placed at outside wall of a school Lybians are [*sic*] used to bring their children into.

The Operation was well received in "legal sense" according to GIANNI....

I send you some pictures for Omar (deal with them as above mentioned).

Regarding other Operations:

- TANGO — check in work, but as GIANNI has informed me twice, they could not study because of holidays in August where everything is closed ... liberier etc. [*sic*] ... he promised result for September.
- Kuwait in work.
- French Targets: they want us to kill the French representative of "Pechiney," which is a very important French concern and plays a big role in Greece. They want him also for national politics.... I like it, and besides French diplomatic targets they'll work on him.

Weapons I offered, but they have no transportation facility by now. He had asked ELISABETH to do it. Maybe she'll arrange something. Additional: he has called on Thursday 1-08 saying that work continues and promised next contact around 20-08 (?), most likely for arranging (?) at me to discuss results.

8. *Amin.* I enclose some notes and drawings, although you might not be able to read or understand fully without me, you have some material in your hand for the Boys. Keep the notes with you until we meet.

Shortly:

a. Best and nearly only possibility is Dubai. To get the weapons inside departure basement ... by help of a dipolomatic courier (a real one) who's [*sic*] transit is either coordinated with the comrades-movement (he would leave by another plane) or who will store them on the toilets which is possible. Only problem in the case the two wings of departure gates (right and left wing) are not connected. So it has to be found out before in which our flight will leave, and if always the same one is used. Extra security check very unlikely and never observed by now. Bribery: Amin doesn't dare and doesn't want. He says whomever we approach, the one we get double through accepting bribe and betraying it.... Himself he has no way to bring something into departure basement.

b. A good possibility is Bahrain (Map IV) where he says that security controls (= s/c points) are done for luggage by hand. Radios not controlled, simply put by security controller aside, especially if the type of the radio is one of those sold in duty-free shop. For body by usual frame which — according to Amin — does not work. So they should let somebody pass there to study conditions when one of their flights is leaving, I suggest.

Other news about Amin: mainly regarding a money-operation in Athens. I have continued the old line that we are interested. But first he has to bring all informations [sic]. Last time he said he has done it but did not meet the "Boys" who have studied before seeing he [sic].

Anyway the problem seems to be not that but the "Boys" he wants also to collect informations about them.

Walid [illegible]. Mutran (!) [?]

All of them should be known to George. Ask him about them. The problem with Mutran is clear. (my line should be killed and after *you* tell Omar — as a gift...). He was the one who was with Amin in Athens to collect all informations [sic] about the man to be kidnapped and for us, I think, it is clear out of discussion to proceed. Since Mutlan is with Fatah's "Hanari" (security/ you must know the name).

Discuss this point with Ali who suspects a Fatah-trap. Maybe, but I think that Amin is "innocently" unknowingly trapped if it is like that. He stresses. They Boys do not know about us and even if Mutlan would tell Fatah, they would not be able to draw the line: Amin -> Fred -> us.

But note: There was a strange change in behavior of Amin last time regarding the usual impatience, he shows upon money operations.... But maybe it was due to the "abstract" warning Ali has [given] to him, before I've arrived. According to Amin, all 3 boys have been in Leban, somewhere near Basalbeck last time when I met him which was 23-06-83.

Amin was not informed by me about our Athens-Op and I've no sign he knows. The answer of FRED to your letter: "he is prepared to make introduction in case we send somebody there, but we cannot leave."

Amin has send message now that he is ready to meet us or to be picked up at CHTAURA * If you want I can call him. But I think if you are not in urgent need of him, you should wait until we meet.

In any case, if you tell me "call Amin ... I want to see him" I'll try to pick it up for CHTAURA and you should send another comrade to bring him to you.... Do not go there to see him by the way. The problem with you is over. Amin is "ready" to see you again ... so he tried to tell me last time.

Regarding ZAPPASON — Maps: We can get them easily from him you know. The airline — pilot — map ... and in case of concrete plans for hijacking he is ready to calculate flue, etc. ... all those technical points.

To enable me to fix any apointment [sic] with Amin in CHTAURA, please get from George the name of "our" breakfast-restaurant. Transmit just the name by phone or next letter, I'll pass it, in case you want to see him, to Amin.

For money ops. We have the cooperation of the BANKER who is now in CHATAURA "Deputy Manager" and according to Amin the question of a no. account on wrong identity became easier.

By the way, try to find the name of the Canadian-Lebanese HELMUT gave us once. I checked all and think I've destroyed the note after telling you....

9. *Amin Askari and Approach*. This question is different from the talk with Saika. A. Askari talked with us in the name of Rifal Al Assad. Let Ali tell you all the details from the beginning. And do disclose with him, if you can use it for our interest.

I enclose the "letter" we have send [*sic*]. And the name of the officer in Rifal's office through whom the question is supposed to be given to Rifal and whom I should call: Abou Al Arae, Moukaddan Hassan 669 700.

And I was supposed to say something as: "I am (we are) Steve from Carlos.... Best Regards from Amin Askari, Germany."

10. *Regarding TANGO*: It took some time until I've met all the people after receiving your letter regarding that.

I did not move only for meeting one of them ... money. Following is in works:

GIANNI: All of them (except Malaysia) and will inform me when he got first results. (just information was (?) around 10-08, see above)

ROBBY: Ready for work on it in Holland/Belgium. As news from MARTINE (only by phone) are [*sic*] I suppose he did not move until now, because he has not a penney [*sic*] or he moved without result.

JULIA: Works on it in Italy, but informed me that during August no chance of finding out anything because everything closed.

MARTINE: If she raises some pennies, she'll spend some days in Vienna on route [*sic*] to visit me. At home she could not find out anything.

11) *Regard HELMUT*: I've passed the request but did not get an answer until now. They said: they do not know personally but will contact specialist.

12) *Our Comrades*. All of them are well and tough ... main efforts have spent on HEIDI. She will get her trial on 27-09-83. Charged only with import of explosives with maximum penalty of 5 years. The Italians splitted [*sic*] the charge: this one will be judged on 27-09. The second charge of being involved in international terrorism is kept but not brought to trial now. Servello estimates that they do not intend to open trial on that. So the trial on 27-08 will be very short and simple.

We had a lot of trouble find a suitable lawyer for her. The old question we discussed last time we met did not work because of Barbie and other things. I was informed rather late of it. On top the two did not exchange among each other the "stage of affairs" well enough so we lost time for nothing. I was a bit hard on the two, GABRIEL and GUILLAUME recently. Since that I have the impression that they do work well now. After all GUILLAUME has found an Italian who can be trusted. And he really worked hard for it. The man has a good name. Everything sounds well and just two days ago I learned that he has accepted finally. His name: Aldo Berla FORINO [code: *FRANCA*]. (also on this question holidays have been main obstacle). The only problem: he has nearly no time.... about 70 BR cases ... but as I understood from JULIA: he has accepted and will be appointed now. GUILLAUME will prepare him for first visit to HEIDI, which could be by now. Then we've planned that FRANCA and GUILLAUME come to see me to finalize everything for trial ... if possible, otherwise GUILLAUME will come alone.

The line for trial will be what you and he discussed last time...."TRANSIT DECLARATION" ... parallel Gabriel will approach (or has done it already from what all I know about his movement through SONJA he is going this Thursday...) the Italian government. He will visit me on the 10th.

Most likely GABRIEL will stay out of the case "officially" in order to avoid sabotage of a calk [?] solution f. ex. through the "public opinion" (newspapers), but for the trial we might appoint an additional lawyer as "international observer." We have to [sic] candidates: last years [sic] "BATTONYEE" (Chairman of lawyer-association) of Algiers or "MUSTAFA" who was supposed to be lawyer of trust. In case we do that, this lawyer will give the "transit declaration" and say something like : it is not Italian business ... to get involved.

I think it will be a good "scenario." Such a lawyer will make the Italians careful ... and nobody can connect him with Palestinians or so.... But this point is not decided yet. It will depend from the outcoming of GABRIEL's approach.

With FRANCA I am confident now — Finally! — to gain control of the case and to have a direct link with HEIDI.

I see only two problems: Mainly time. If we can arrange all of it before 27-09 sufficiently and money. I could send for FRANCA only $500 and nobody of the three has money. And you know what a single trip only to me costs. Fortunately JULIA told me yesterday that she was successful in borrowing a 10,000 SFR amount in order to help GUILLAUME in his movement. (last time I asked her for that...)

LILLY and PAUOLO are well and they stopped the harassment on PAUOLO after last time when he answered his punishment by a hygienic-strike (as the Irish). The French try to keep the "balance" not to change anything in the situation after the aggression against PAUOLO they conceded "free Pauolo!" and on the other hand: the second consequence out of the forgery of files. The charge of forgery against the judge of appeal trial has been accepted now, which means that they have a good pretext not to touch the first and main consequence. The "Court de Cassation" is now not under pressure to decide in the question, since they can say they have to wait for the outcome of the trial on "forgery charge." (see above).

No contact so far with the government ... but many details, not linked directly to us, which show how chaotic is the situation inside....

One point now: Francois de Grossouvre — responsible in Elysee for security and by now the strong man behind, more than FRANCESCHI is deeply involved in private business (large one) with Amin Gemayel business in Leban. Can you try if we can find out something about that. Maybe we could hit in the future....

From one, who was moving for this business in Leban for Grossouvre and the new about the French Ambassador.

• he is convinced that the Embassy was ours, and with angry with CHEYSSON

• he is trembling on hearing our name.

GABRIEL will come for time being every month one day (his suggestion) and we meet mainly (at least now) here. He will get some cover for coming here.

BARBIE affair is very interesting. For God's sake Gabriel came back from Bolivia alive. Don't worry. I do not discuss about it with socialist camp, but had a clash with HELMUT (longer time ago), when they learned about it, he was furious....

I took your suggested letter-line only that I took the responsibility on me. Since HELMUT had attacked unqualified the shocking answer for him was when I told him a.) to be careful b.) they should learn and be patient c.) that I took the decision. He couldn't comment and never touched it again.

Gabriel can come directly to Damas, without any problem. He was involved in an affair of a Tunesian [*sic*] whom the French wanted to expel to Tunis, etc. Finally the Syrians agreed to let him come. Gabriel did it through the Embassy in Paris. He dealt with the 1st Secretary and was at the end received by the Ambassador who talked with him about Barbie ... under this Tunesian [*sic*] affair-cover he can travel to Damas officially by help of the Embassy.

In case it comes to that: He will register in Meridien and wait for being contacted by the code: ABOU'L HAKAH (of course if would be good if the one who contacts him is Ali or me).

Generally I've invited him, whenever he has 5 days to rest, etc.

My idea: Think about talking with Hasken that they might instruct the Ambassador in Paris to help Gabriel in any question. I do not know now if it's a good idea. Have my doubts and after all it is — at least now — not necessary objectively.

GABRIEL knows the code with which our people have to be equipped in order to enter Damas. I enclose an article of "Canard" brought by GABRIEL (inside Rifa's envelope)

13. *My Schedule.* We lost too many days in Berlin. GABRIEL was prepared to come on 29-08 but since I returned on 27, he got confirmation too late. He'll come on the 10th.

As you see, HEIDI still keeps me busy. I have to take in account another meeting with GUILLAUME and/or FRANCA before the trial. The question must have priority now. All other things as for example a meeting with ALBERT's comrade can wait or I put it in between, but I will not say for it especially.

I've tried with this letter to give you a picture but there are a lot of things we have to discuss. As soon there is a week free, I'll plan to see you.

But since the lawyer question is going on and on the other hand I am expecting that somebody has to join in discussion with the Yugoslav, I thought: as soon as the "answer" from them is suitable. I will tell you the following: "...I would like that you come to visit me...."

You know what it means: relation here proceeds well — and on that background *you decide* according to developments over there and money facility, if you come or if I move to you. Is that clear?

You can travel to Omar. You'll give me the possibility to contact you there. I'll return immediately from Budapest, after sending ALI, nothing is to be done there.

MARTINE will come on 7-09/9-09 for about 14 days, her holidays. She'll stay with me. In case I should send her you tell me. Maybe she could work on "NELLY."

14. *LUCIA.* From what she told me, I grasped some points, where you have to get all details from her.

-> SHEILA/MARIA developments

her story about LUCIA — "Mistake" with her and passport (forgot in hotel).

-> talk with her. Who knows about you ... and explain [to] her why to be careful with it.

➜ She should code my phone no. which you gave, and give her the 2nd phone number 442 452. It is the phone of the 2nd place, which is completely new. I want to keep the no. absolutely cool, since most likely we will keep it for a long time. It was never used internationally and nobody has the no. except you.

That place we can keep as long as we want. Maybe in half a year we have to give up the one where I stay now.

I give the no. to you to explain LUCIA: if she does not find us under "my place: 44 97 73" in that time, when she comes next from Venezuela she should try that second one.

The telex MICHEL we should keep I suggest.

[and behind her if she talks with the owner of my place now. LUCIA knows her — my name is JOSEPH (and not PETER). The owner is called: DUNJA. Note: if you consider it to difficult for LUCIA to remember, just stick to PETER. But tell me by letter what you've arranged with her. I can make a story about "a colleg [colleague] PETER" to the owner so it will work as well.

I do hope it is clear and not confusing. If you do not understand or something is not clear. Write it in the letter with LUCIA, when you send her back. (in case we do not meet in between).

-> Note for planning with LUCIA: her *return ticket to Madrid expires on 24-09*

-> In case you get money: I would like to send LUCIA to study that restaurant in Paris.

p.s. After reading now, I think I have to clarify. The second no. is not in use. It is given to you and LUCIA for the time when she comes back the next time from Venezuela. In the moment you do not get me practically there. When I am here, I stay under 44 07 73. So when LUCIA comes back from you, she'll find me under 44 07 03. Of course, I think I'll know her return and will be in the airport.

15. *Regarding Files.* I have asked you for the copies of the PAUOLO files, lists of names and addresses found in his apartment. I made the copies in Tripoli and I think I left them with you. But since you did not find, I'll check in Budapest.

Note: I checked here (BODA), they are not here so they must be with you, I think. at the end of all copied "JACQUOT" file you'll have them and there must be also copies in French regarding our people. Send me please all you have regarding the two.

16. *Passports:* A stolen Pakistani (1) and Philipines [sic] once you have asked me to collect whatever would be useful for MARTALA [?]

17. *Sarkiss.* Ask Ali, he knows

18. *NELLY— Files.* I send them in envelope "NELLY"

19. *Italian —??.* Once you asked me to get everything regarding "Italian ??" for you. I send it in envelope "Italian Passports" ... but there is no other way.

20: *Money.* I cut all movement which could be avoided, even with the comrades. I no not pay [sic] for their movement, if possible. F. ex. all what ROBBY got was to be able to go back (!) and JULIA borrows for me. Berlin has focked [sic] my "budget" anyway. Sept. is paid the rend [sic] here in Yugo. ALI has paid until the end of the year (except the Dr. who is by paid till (??) And after I "robbed" everybody, I have 900$ with me. It will not last long.

I am thinking to contact my parents and ask for a loan. I count on 50,000 maybe 100,000 DM. MARINE and ROBBY are requested to collect some informations [sic] F. Ex. if both are still alive before I write a letter I should know about it. And I have

asked HELMUT to give a hand in meeting them. According to news from MAR-
TINE and developments on your side, I will think about to proceed with that or not.
20. *with ALI.* I send 10 Brownings, 1 SHG — Beretta with all and 150 rounds 9 mm
para t.n. [Note: last time when we have me, we did discuss that 2 SHG Baretta should
be [sent] to you. Do you still want 1 more, notice in next letter.], 1 Walther 7.65 PPK
with 2 magazines and 5 × 24 rounds 7.65

   Note: this is the one you asked me to get from Bucharest — for the hijacking (or
as a gift to FATHY). The rounds have been in Belgrade, but we do not have 7.65
there.

   ... that I send you: 1 additional part for the camera good for photographing passports; some films which are left and could be useful; Book: "Fil Rouge"; Some old
newspapers to be checked; C-films (I asked JULIA for more); Giger — fat[?] and a
creme from MARTINE.

21. *About ANDRE.* After last visit you must have misunderstood me by phone. Since
ALI came and had the picture that I was bad. Altogether it was good. Although they
did not really open. But more than before: F. Ex. he wants me to visit him during
last week. I postponed. Maybe later.

   You know that before I left I met the "OLD MAN." We had a nice talk and I
got 24 kg plastic.

   ANDRE has told me that a long time ago he asked your for a RPG 75. Do you
remember? I did not answer yet. What do you think, should we give one?

22. *ZIAD.* If you see him please ask him to buy several of the French watches which
we used in Berlin called "JAPY" (Electronic)

23. *Hijacking.* What was left behind what the people? For propaganda only. We were
involved? Anyway, I like it.

   Study the press-cuttings I send you. Note how they deal with the revelation
about "AL SHARIF" (supposed only member) and us. Only "France Soir" mentions
"CARLOS" and the others write about "COMMANDO MOHAMMED BOUDIA"
as if it were not us — also STRUAUS [?] ! I think this not by accident (in envelope:
hijacking). (Please send back by next occasion the cuttings.)

   Finally two questions:

   - What nice things our boys did. I found something about a bomb against Air
     France ... you were enjoying it when you told me on the phone about "that"
     Thursday.

   - By now I think you have send message to the French Ambassador in Beirut
     saying: Berlin is ours and same explosive as in the Embassy attack 82.

   Dear MICHEL, I'll try to keep everything around here under control. I want
to meet you, as sooner the better.

   Please take care of yourself and the comrades. We need everybody. Warmest
regards to ZIAD and GEORGE.

   And a big kiss for you.

Yours,
Peter.

Appendix G:
West German Annual
Report Excerpts

1984 Bavarian Agency for the Protection of the Constitution (LfV) Annual Report

ROMANIA

When an intelligence officer of the Romanian Embassy in Bonn defected to the West in 1984, important information was obtained on the activities of the Romanian Intelligence Service on the territory of the Federal Republic of Germany. The defector presented evidence of the preparation and the actual carrying out of criminal activities with a political background by the Intelligence Service, represented by officers of the Romanian Foreign Intelligence Service (CIE) who had diplomatic status with the Romanian embassy in Bonn.

Case Number One

On May 2, 1984, a tear-gas assault was made on a Romanian-born German citizen residing in Cologne by two Romanian "tourists" who allegedly had traveled from Paris to Cologne. The unidentified culprits escaped from the house of the victim with money, papers and documents. The victim was known as a former Communist, faithful to the regime and carrying out an official mission in the Federal Republic of Germany. After her return to Romania she lost her former position with the Romanian Party because of alleged anti–Romanian behavior in a foreign country; she took advantage of her stay in a Southern European country to remain in the West. Since that time she had been active within the Romanian émigré circles in the Federal Republic of Germany. The attack that had the case name of RITA-CORBU had been organized and directed by the Romanian embassy in Cologne or Bonn respectively. Ion Grecu, Counter Intelligence Chief of the CIE, first secretary and press attaché of the embassy, was the one directing the case. Cultural attaché Lupu had been ordered to deceive the victim, spy on her following the attack and distract the suspicion from the Romanian embassy.

Case Number Two

A Romanian physician, a close relative of a high-ranking member of the Romanian government traveled to the Federal Republic of Germany and applied for asylum.

In June 1984 the counterintelligence unit of the CIE headquarters received the order to find the refugee and forcibly take him back to Romania. The operation was supposed to be concluded by the time of the scheduled party meeting of the Romanian Communist Party in November 1984. In case the operation was unsuccessful and the refugee not returned to Romania, a specialist was supposed to come from Romania to assassinate the asylum seeker. An operating group was formed at the Romanian embassy, acting from the embassy under the guidance of the deputy director of the CIE and the section chief for West Germany. As of June 1984 nine members of a search troop, disguised as tourists, were traveling within West Germany; this group consisted of physicians, representatives of companies, and CIE officers. Numerous contact persons living in the Federal Republic of Germany were activated, federal agencies were — under pretenses — officially included in the search action. Following are the names of the persons who were substantial in directing the case:

Constantin Ciobanu	Ion Grecu	Ioan Lupu
Councillor of the Embassy	First Secretary	First Secretary

Case Number Three

At least since October 1983 preparations had been made by the CIE's diversion unit C-428 for a bomb attack on Radio Free Europe (RFE) in Munich. The below listed persons were responsible for the exploration of the object and its environment:

Constantin Ciobanu	Dan Mihoc	Ion Constantin
Councillor of the Embassy	Second Secretary	Third Secretary
	Chief, Technical Bureau	Chief, Consular Section

In the summer of 1983 Constantin received the order in Bucharest to collect detailed information concerning a bomb attack on RFE. Following his stay in Munich on October 11–12, 1983, he wrote a thirteen-page exploratory report on the "target" RFE. Ciobanu, as a resident, confirmed in a supplement the accuracy of Constantin's report which he (Ciobanu) had checked through an on-the-spot survey. In December 1983 Constantin attended a two-day orders conference in Bucharest. He was given surveillance reports of the objects by Ciobanu and Mihoc for comparison. Thereafter he received the order to obtain yet further information. In 1984 he made two more trips to Munich to gather missing details.

Appendix H:
1992 SRI Report to RFE/RL

Report from Virgil Magureanu, Director SRI

(Translation)
Bucharest 16 July 1992

Dear Mr. Richard H. Cummings,

Concerning your letter, in which you asked us to clear up certain information, obtained by you from foreign Government sources, according to which certain actions were initiated and carried out from Romania against the "Romanian" opposition in the West, particularly against the RFE/RL radio stations, I am privileged to inform you as follows:

Aware of your legitimate concern to clear up information, the significance of those received by you and, simultaneously, also our own interest to explain the shadowy problems of some past affairs, I have started some investigations, but their success remains conditioned by several factors, among which the most important is the ability to identify persons and proofs, which might confirm or invalidate the information that you passed on to us and others that might be of interest to you.

The cooperation with you is also necessary for us, since we are interested in the Anti-Communist trial, among which the exposure of the anti-democratic action of the former Securitate is our number one concern. But this trial could take more time than I first estimated (approximately one year), and during all this time, an exchange of information with you would be necessary.

Starting in 1980, the Securitate was mainly concerned with counteracting the ideological effects of foreign radio stations' activity, especially those of the RFE, which was considered a destabilizing outpost of CIA.

The aims were:

- The restriction of the flow of news to this station;
- The reduction of its possible freelancers;
- The easing of Government criticism;
- The pervading disarray, through agents of the news section of the Romanian Service.

Till now some aspects were uncovered, which might be connected with the request you addressed to us, and which we bring to your notice:

1. After the death sentence, in absentia, was passed on ex-general Mihai Pacepa, formerly deputy head of the General External Information Department, with the rank of State Secretary of the Ministry of Internal Affairs, in 1979, the terrorist Ilich Ramirez Sanches, alias "Carlos," was contacted and approached to help in carrying out the sentence.

Carlos did not offer definite assurances beyond stating "he would study the problem."

The emissaries who contacted him in Prague were carrying $10,000, but because of the opulence displayed by "Carlos," they considered the amount of money they possessed much too modest to tempt a terrorist, and more they could not promise.

It also certain that "Carlos" was interested (a fact evidenced in 1982) in having the Romanian authorities allow the transfer of his logistic base from Budapest to Bucharest, a request which was not taken into consideration; later, when on several occasions he attempted to bring up again this question, it was turned down, the last time in 1987,

Beyond any doubt, in the interval 1979–1985, a group of about 30 persons, under the leadership of "Carlos," had its base in Hungary, where they had secret contacts with several terrorist networks.

2. Although the Securitate External units had the task of neutralizing the most active members of the station, there is no indication that the former Securitate was involved in the attack of 21 February 1981 against RFE.

STASI documents, in your possession, which give evidence that the Ceausescu regime had been involved in that attempt might simply be the result of the habit of attributing to one of the most reactionary regimes in Eastern Europe all crimes that had taken place during that period.

In fact, in these crimes or criminal attempts were involved regimes that when compared to the one in Romania, appeared more liberal, given the limits of Communist regimes.

We should not ignore that Czechoslovakia then sheltered training camps for Left-wing extremists and terrorists from countries outside Europe. It is also proven that the complicity maintained in the last decades (some of it still carried out now) between the Special Hungarian Services and those of the KGB, etc.

Information spread by the mass media in Poland and Czechoslovakia have attributed the "attempt" to the secret services of these two countries, as revealed by people of the respective services who infiltrated RFE.

There were no collaboration agreements between the former Securirate and the secret services of these two countries,

But it was established that the Securitate had, via sections of its External Service, interest in knowing the RFE guard and security service, especially vulnerability of the facilities for penetration.

3. In order to intimidate some RFE freelancers, or other adversaries of the former regime, some explosive postal devices were used, which through detonation produced the known effects. It can be assumed as certain that all compromising information on the staff and freelancers of the RFE/RL Romanian Department have already been "delivered" in different ways to the American authorities.

Given the nature of operations, they were conveyed under cover, until now the persons involved have not been identified.

4. On the attack of the former RFE Romanian Service employee, Emil Georgescu, no information was obtained to invalidate those generally known and accredited: the action was undertaken by the French citizens Layani and Cottenceau, as a revenge for the swindle in which the victim was involved.

In addition, concerning the cause of death of Noel Bernard, Mihai Cismarescu and Vlad Georgescu, nothing else is known beyond what was established in the medical death certificates.

5. There are a few known cases in which persons, who became employees of RFE, had, before their departure abroad, been informers of the Securitate. [Author's note: the names were omitted due to unsubstantiated allegations against certain individuals.]

It was also established that opportunities were used in contacting RFE staff and freelancers, to "moderate their views" mostly by taking advantage to this effect with their close circles in the country and abroad, and relatives or former colleagues.

Such "moderating actions," without being able to ascertain their results, were directed towards Vlad Georgescu, Liviu Tofan, Ion Ioanid, Alexandru Cifarelli, Alexandra Polizu, Ioana Magura-Bernard, Alecu Rene de Flers and possibly others,

6. From the accounts we have, and to the extent to which they are genuine, lead us to the conclusion that the Securitate, in spite of its intentions, did not accomplish such "classic infiltrations" within RFE.

The failures are explained, first, by the insufficient preparation of the respective operations and, second, by realizing the genuine proportions of a confrontation with a counterintelligence set-up for whose penetration there were insufficient means, the more so as no collaboration existed with the Secret services of the other countries within the Warsaw Treaty Alliance.

What is more, after some time it happened that officers meant to carry out such operation became dependent on RFE ideology, which determined them to cross to the other side. This type of occurrences were "far from few," as it is well known.

We would be pleased should the information here communicated be of use. Should you be interested in digging further in some of these cases, we would like to hear from you.

Yours faithfully, with esteem,
ss Virgil Magureanu
Director of Romanian Information Service
L.S.

Appendix I:
1985 Romanian Ether Report

MINISTRY OF INTERNAL AFFAIRS   Strictly Secret
DEPARTMENT OF STATE SECURITY (DSS)   Copy Nr. l.
U.M. 0610-   U.M. 0544/225
(Internal Security)   (External Security)
      CIE
Nr. 0051-304 of 20.05.1985

REPORT

Concerning the stage of fulfillment
of tasks within the "ETERUL" program.

The foreign radio stations with hostile broadcasts in Romanian, especially RFE, supported by Governments, organizations and outside reactionary circles, directed by Information Services, continued to unfold an intensified political and ideological activity against the Romanian Socialist Republic.

The action of these reactionary propaganda dens was mostly aimed at slandering the internal and foreign policy of the Party and our State inciting some people to contestant/dissident demonstrations; at accusing R.S.R. of alleged human rights abuses, with special reference to the cohabiting nationalities, the freedom of religion, speech and foreign travel.

The American Board for International Broadcasting, and also other U.S. decision authorities, have given continuously repeated supplementary financial funds for the modernizing of the technical basis — an increased attention to appointing within RFE of some notorious elements of a profound anti–Communist orientation. Studies were completed concerning the increase of the diversionist contents of programs and broadcasts by RFE. and, as a consequence, it was proposed to expand the structures and duration given to ideological economic, cultural and social broadcasts. At the same time the concern emerges to expand the obnoxious influence to new categories of people, for instance to agricultural workers, workers in the handicraft cooperatives, retired people, etc.

An outstanding attention continued to be shown to the intellectuals, media, youth, people in religious and sect circles and to actions encouraging emigration. Lately, also, were emphasized actions of provocation and hostile instigation of some elements among the former bourgeois land owning parties and among former offenders guilty of crimes against the State security. Measures of improving transmissions and listening conditions, planning the future use of communication satellites are simultaneously being introduced

I. According to the provisions of the program, concerning the problem "ETERUL," and of the decision by the Executive Council of the Department of State Security, of June 1983, for the combating of hostile action unfolded via the radio-stations in 1984 and the first quarter of 1985, the Central and Territorial Security units have acted as follows:

1. Identification of the contact means and ways of the foreign radios and prevention of information data reaching them,
    To this effect, we acted to develop the information potential, which [led] to an increase of 21%. At the same time, better instructions were secured and, as a consequence the transmission abroad of over 3,000 materials, data and information, meant for the reactionary radio-stations were traced and stopped. An important contribution to this was brought by the Passport-Department and the special "S" and "T" units. Also, through combined actions, at influencing and disinformation, some hostile elements of the Romanian emigration were persuaded to renounce the sending of slanderous materials to RFE.
    By analyzing the information received and the solved cases, it emerged that for the transmission abroad of data and materials, of a slanderous character, diplomats accredited in Romania, especially those at the U.S. and West-Germany Embassies, foreign citizens visiting Romania as journalists, students, tourists, family visitors, agents, navigators, people employed on international transport facilities, Romanian citizens illegally settled abroad or traveling in the West and in neighboring countries, telephone calls and postal communications were mostly used.
    Eight foreign people, suspected as intending to gather information or to facilitate links with the reactionary radios, had their stay permits in Romania canceled, and their names were added to the list of undesirable persons.
    It should also be mentioned that some broadcasts, of profound hostile nature, were obtained by enrolling some traitor elements, living abroad, or on the basis of injunctions by foreign information services, by inventing cases and false problems, with an aim at diversion.

2. The enforcement of a more efficient information control on people maintaining or intending to establish links with foreign radios.
    Quick complex information measures were secured concerning the work-basis elements, by special attention being given to the supervising of information reaching the relatives and the country-links of staff members and collaborators of foreign radios, with the aim of preventing their implication in hostile actions and by persuading some of them to influence those abroad, in the sense of renouncing their activity again[st] the R.S.R.
    The special units have enlisted, in an organized manner, a higher number of elements abroad who were recruited more recently by RFE or taken into consideration by this hostile den.
    Thanks to the measures undertaken, a bigger volume of significant information was received, which allowed the closing through practical means of 25% of cases under consideration and the processing in an organized fashion of an important num-

ber of elements. The information secured attest the high number of people who, with an aim at leaving the country, have attempted or succeeded to contact the foreign radios and some international bodies.

At the same time, the interest of some diplomats and of some foreign journalists has increased in some anarchic and contestant/dissident elements, especially in confessional and sects circles, which determined the taking of complex measures in order to prevent the contact-securing and the transmitting of some data, usable by RFE, in its hostile propaganda against our country.

More firmness was shown in the case of elements intending to contact, or those who had established contact with the foreign radios, by using diversified measures. Principally, with the assistance of competent authorities, measures were used to positively influence elements involved and persuasion to gave up their plans of contacting or maintaining the link with the foreign reactionary propaganda agencies. In 44 cases fines were used, according to Statute 23 of 1971 and in others, more outstanding cases, arrests were imposed by the Prosecutor's Office and the Militia, on the basis of Decree 153 of 1970.

More attention was also focused on identifying and neutralizing hostile activities by people listening and spreading news, of harmful contents, broadcast by foreign radios, to this effect over 30 groupings, in their initial phase of existence, were dispersed among young people and, in a wider field, over 1,200 people were officially warned. In most cases these measures were efficient, and those involved gave up their hostile intentions and preoccupation.

3. *The application of diversified measures in order to prevent and counteract hostile propaganda, by reactionary foreign stations and the shattering of their harmful effect.*

Action was taken through combined and diversified measures, against the more hostile staff members and contributors of RFE and against ... some of their links abroad. Thereby, the focusing/secured on some of them by the German authorities, while in the case of others discrediting and isolation methods were applied.

Through the facilities of the special units and of the independent "D" service, an increasing number of replies and of materials, exposing the propaganda diversions initiated from outside against our country, were published abroad.

Coordinated action was initiated to inform the people within the country, using more the means of mass information — the central and local press, radio broadcasts — containing counteraction and exposing materials combating thus the reactionary activity of foreign radios, especially RFE as to the supposed abuses of human rights, the so-called religious persecution or the restrictions on literary and artistic creation and others.

4. *The improvement of the infiltrating informative activity among the staff members and collaborators of foreign stations and the continuing of measures for the misleading, disinformation and disheartening of such people.*

In collaboration with special units, action was initiated to send an important number of sources with tasks abroad, some of them managed to gain access among targeted elements, within the media used by these stations and for other sources new perspectives were opened to the same effect. This year were selected 97 sources — 68 more than in the one preceding, initiating also their verification, directing and the required instruction.

With the aim at disinformation within the hostile media abroad, a great number of foreign people were contacted confidentially, who were supplied with material denying some speculations by the foreign reactionary radios and by other hostile propaganda for our country. Also, some central and territorial units of the Security sent abroad several reply materials and other for the disinformation of the staff members and the collaborators of the foreign stations and of the reactionary organizations using these propaganda dens.

II. In spite of these measures, registering an advance, compared to the previous period, by taking into account the intensity, the virulence and the dangerous degree of the propaganda action, against our country, one must conclude that the preventive action, the replies and the countering have not yet reached the required level. The infiltration of these dens advance with difficulty and not sufficiently deep, not all the sources used were of the required quality and their adequate instruction was not secured in every case. In attempts among the staff-members and of other hostile elements outside, available for these dens, we only managed to obtain, in few instances data, information and documents, which would facilitate an efficient informative combination to denounce and discredit them.

The central and territorial units are insufficiently concerned with acquiring and putting to good use such data. The military units 0544 and 0195 are contributing too little in order to recognize and notify, in good time, the links abroad of the staff-members and collaborators of the foreign radios, who visit R.S.R. with tasks of gathering data and information to be used in the hostile propaganda against our country.

The collaboration between U.M. 0544 and other Security units for the identification and processing of relatives and links within the country of staff-members and collaborators of the radio-stations B.B.C., Deutsche Welle and Voice of America did not attain the required level, given the practical measures mobilized.

The informative control in places, within media, and among potential objectives, of the reactionary circles, as also of the foreigners visiting as journalists, tourists, visitors of relatives, tradesmen, etc., is not rigorously enough carried out in all instances and thus some elements of the working basis, have managed to convey abroad, via such people, hostile materials, of use to foreign radios. It was insufficiently acted in order to determine some personalities, of the artistic, cultural and scientific field, to adopt categorical attitudes, combating the hostile activities of RFE, though such measures should have been imperative, especially in the case of writers eulogized by RFE and of other intellectuals who appeared as the "yoke" of this propaganda agency.

Discrediting, unmasking and neutralizing the hostile propaganda has not yet assumed a systematic, uninterrupted and offensive character, which should lead to the capture of the initiative and to the establishing in the country and abroad of a public opinion current against the work of such dens. The counterinformation actions, now in preparation, are insufficient, their contribution to creating a general atmosphere of dismissal of the Western propaganda is below requirements and the use of mass-information means — both centrally and locally — developed in a clumsy and sporadic way.

In spite of the fact that the executive group "E T E R U L" has better organized its work, during the reference period it failed to exert a more active role in directing and controlling the way the program tasks are being carried out in order to allow the quick solving of some complex cases. Also, it did not act sufficiently to identify and enroll people able to exert their influence on decisive factors in the Western country aiming thus at the decrease of the hostile activities against R.S.R.

III. In order to remove the existing shortcomings and the improvement of the practical informative activity the following aims should be furthered:

1. The improvement of the information control on foreigners, on persons who have requested the final departure from the country, on hostile elements in the religious and sects circles, as well as in the media of arts and cultural elements and youth, in order to identify the potential elements for a contact with foreign radios and the prevention of any sending, by such people, of slandering materials abroad.

2. Directorate 1, together with U.M. 0544 and the other Security units, will act more coherently in selecting, instructing and dispatching abroad of sources with a potential required for the staff-members and collaborators of the foreign radio-stations, in view of information infiltration and counteracting of hostile acts by such people,

3. The prevention of new recruiting by RFE, through more exacting checking and better counterinformative instruction of those leaving for the West. A special attention should be paid to persons within the literary, artistic, media, educational circles, researchers and other categories of intellectuals.

4. The intensified directing and control, by all central units, within the respective sections of the county authorities, as to the carrying out of the program tasks and the granting of necessary assistance for the quick clearance of the cases being handled.

5. The "E T E R U L" group will secure by July 30th, the identification of all relatives and links in the country of the new staff members and collaborators of the B.B.C.–Deutsche Welle–Voice of America–Radio France Internationale, against whom, according to their competence, the Security units will undertake qualified legal measures.

6. The perfecting of collaboration with the responsible factors within the ideological, cultural field and the press, with a view to increasing the efficiency at identifying and combating external reactionary propaganda.

7. The conclusions reached by the Executive Office of the Leadership Council of the State Security, as also the decisions adopted after the analysis undertaken, will be discussed with the heads of the internal information services, at the meeting in June this year.

The head of U.M. 0610
Directorate I- Internal Security
Maj. Gen. Aron Bordea

The head of U.M. 0544/225
External Security
Col. Plesa

Appendix J:
1976 Joint Action Plan
Against RFE/RL

Work Plan

To the discussion at the conference of representatives of the socialist countries*

In the struggle against the centers of ideological diversion of the USA Radio stations LIBERTY and FREE EUROPE, the minimum objective in the near future is their expulsion from Europe.

The following measures need to be completed in order to achieve this goal.

I. Active Measures

1. Continue the measures against LIBERTY and FREE EUROPE, exposing them as centers of ideological subversion centers of the USA, working at the direction of the CIA. For this purpose, deploy the mass media, radio, and TV of the countries of the socialist community with the goal of providing information to the international public and compromise the enemy.

The following is foreseen from our side:

❑ Publish a APN brochures in German and English with publications from the Soviet press on LIBERTY and FREE EUROPE. Distribute these

---

*Multilateral Meeting of the East Bloc Intelligence Services in Prague, Czechoslovak Socialist Republic, February 12–13, 1976. Intelligence officers exchanged experiences on the active measures taken and being prepared against both Radio Free Europe and Radio Liberty. KGB General Oleg Kalugin made an introductory speech — see Chapters 2 and 7 for more details on his various activities involving both RFE and RL. An English translation of the Russian language Draft Plan was presented at the conference on "The Impact of Western Broadcasting During the Cold War," Hoover Institution, Stanford, California, October 14–16, 2004. The full text of the Draft Plan is an appendix to a book of the conference that will be published by the Central European Press, Budapest, Hungary. Appendix J is a summary report prepared by the East German Ministry for State Security Central Analysis and Information Group (MfS Zentrale Auswertungs und Informationsgruppe). There are some minor differences in the original Draft Plan and the East German report, but the thrust of both was clear: force the radio stations out of Europe, or better yet, close them down.

brochures in the West, especially in Federal Republic of Germany, the USA, other NATO countries, and neutral European countries;

❏ Publish a book which uses materials from the American press to expose the activities of the CIA, especially LIBERTY and FREE EUROPE

❏ Produce a film about the subversive activities of LIBERTY

Our Friends plan the following:

❏ Continuation of the publication of articles and public appearances of Minarik, who returned to the CSSR, to expose FREE EUROPE and their support by Right Wing forces of the Federal Republic of Germany in their subversive activities

❏ Publish a book that would compromise LIBERTY and FREE EUROPE as well as the CIA by using the documents obtained by Minarik and other materials.

❏ Production of documentaries and movies that expose the subversive activities of FREE EUROPE

2. Mobilization of international public opinion for the purpose of eliminating the criminal activities of LIBERTY and FREE EUROPE as organs of ideological subversion, whose existence is in contradiction to international law and the Helsinki Final Act.

• For this purpose, it is foreseen that the security organs of the USSR, Hungary, East Germany, Czechoslovakia, Poland, and Bulgaria will be used for the following:

• Realization of Operation "Spider" (East German MfS) in Austria. This Operation serves is designed to make the countries participating in the Helsinki Conference and the international media aware of the legal basis justification of the illegality of LIBERTY and FREE EUROPE;

• Introduction on this question at the Bundestag of the Federal Republic of Germany;

• Organize the sending of letters to American Members of Congress and of statements by progressive groups and press agencies to the U.S. government;

• Concentrate the attention of the international world public on U.S. attempts to force the NATO countries to finance LIBERTY and FREE EUROPE and thereby legalizing the stations as international organs of ideological diversion subversion.

3. Examine the possibilities and conditions of holding a public tribunal against Liberty and FREE EUROPE on the territory of a socialist country. For this tribunal, former employees of these centers will be used who were ordered back from the West (CZECHOWICZ, LJACH, SMOLINSKI,— Peoples Republic of Poland, MARIN — USSR, MINARIK — Czechoslovak Socialist Republic and others). Also former employees of the radio stations, selected citizens who came under influence of the radio stations, as well as by using documentary materials from all socialist intelligence services will be used.

4. Implement respective measures to isolate the radio stations LIBERTY and FREE EUROPE in the international arena (UN, UNESCO, IOC) and national

organizations, centers, societies, and associations as subversive agencies, whose activities in the spirit of the "Cold War" stand in contrast to Détente and the strengthening of cooperation among countries of different social order.

5. In order to disorganize the internal activities of LIBERTY and FREE EUROPE and exert psychological pressure on its employees, the following factors, for example, have to be actively exploited.

❑ Competition between LIBERTY and FREE EUROPE for the dominant position within the system of the "U.S. Board on International Broadcasting;"

❑ Demonstration of nationalist tendencies and statements of hostility between the "national desks;"

❑ Zionization of departments of LIBERTY and FREE EUROPE and the hostile attitudes of members of the stations' employees towards the overwhelming predominance of Jewish forces, primarily towards former Soviet citizens of Jewish nationality;

❑ Preparation and mailing of letters, favorable to us, in the name of employees dismissed from the radio stations to their former colleagues at LIBERTY and FREE EUROPE.

II. Operational Activities of the Network

Coordinated targeted use of existing possibilities for obtaining documentary data and materials relating to such basic questions as:

❑ Objectives, tasks, forms and methods of activities of the stations LIBERTY and FREE EUROPE in their role in uniting all anti–Soviet forces.

❑ Role of the radio stations in the implementation of the political direction policy of the USA and NATO;

❑ Facts on the interference in internal matters of the socialist countries and the violation of the sovereignty of the Federal Republic of Germany.

❑ Falsification of materials. On harsh attacks against the party and government leaders of the countries of the socialist community.

• Role and position of the U.S. intelligence agencies in the activity of LIBERTY and FREE EUROPE: Spies; persons who were confirmed agents or persons suspected to be agents of espionage activities; the system of obtaining incoming information; participation in the development and presentation of broadcasts, in the financing of the stations generally of individual operations.

• The internal situation in the objects: contradictions between LIBERTY and FREE EUROPE, national rivalries and their protagonists, unofficial operative situations as a in connection with new exposures on the part of result of the exposing measures of the intelligence agencies of the socialist countries; control and spying surveillance on of employees and others;

• Mutual help by the fraternal intelligence services in the assessment of the operative targets that come to the attention of the unofficial employees and their agents. Assignment of proven agencies with the task of systematically analyzing all enumerated issues relating to the activities of the radio stations and drafting proposals for their discredit and exposure Assignment of tasks to the verified network in order to systematically project and compile analyses of issues concerning the work of the radio stations, as well as to contribute suggestions on how to discredit and expose them.

- Regular assessments of the reaction of the enemy to our active measures as well as checking the counteractions initiated by the enemy.
- The socialist countries and of the countermeasures undertaken by the counterintelligence agencies, strengthening of the socialist countries by using such possibilities as: expansion of the agency positions within LIBERTY and FREE EUROPE by intelligence organs of the socialist countries in cooperation with their internal organs. The following measures should be taken:
  - Working on employees of the stations by the agencies, including by trusted officials of the counterintelligence services, to effect defection or compromising of the stations through the existing network and active members of the internal organs;
  - Infiltration into LIBERTY and FREE EUROPE from positions of the nationalist emigration, Zionists and dissidents. In this regards existing possibilities are to be examined and additional ones are to be created;
  - Targeted preparation of unofficial employees by the security agencies for prolonged deployment with the objective of penetrating the enemy's centers of ideological diversion.
  - Targeted deployment of intelligence agents with the aim of infiltration into the ideological centers of the enemy;
  - Short-term targeted trips by internal agents to capitalist countries in the short-term, targeted deployment by the security agencies of unofficial employees with the most potential in capitalist countries, with the objective of obtaining information and working on specific persons of LIBERTY and FREE EUROPE.
  - Using the possibilities of the intelligence and counterintelligence agencies of the socialist countries to counter the subversive activity of the enemy on the territory of the countries of the socialist community (uncovering agents, dissidents and persons who have contact to LIBERTY and FREE EUROPE;
  - Organizing persons who will be "set up;" intercepting of communication channels and materials; implementing operative games, etc. If necessary, this work is to be conducted jointly with the interested service units of the respective security agencies of the socialist countries.
  - Regular exchange of generalized summarized and documentary materials, under the obligatory provision that the receiving party coordinates in advance the possibilities and permissible manner of using their use.

III. Measures at the diplomatic level

With the advice of the security agencies of the socialist countries is the question to be discussed with the foreign ministry of each of the socialist countries in order to launch diplomatic steps at a politically appropriate moment against the USA and the FRG regarding the subversive activities of RL and RFE. Representatives of socialist security agencies need to be consulted on the question of the current position of the foreign ministries of each socialist country on taking diplomatic steps against the U.S. and Federal Republic of Germany governments concerning the subversive activities of LIBERTY and FREE EUROPE.

In the case of a public tribunal against RL and RFE, the questions is to be examined as to whether there should be any diplomatic steps by the foreign ministries of the socialist countries to the governments of the USA and the Federal Republic of Germany after conducting a public tribunal against LIBERTY and FREE EUROPE on the territory of a socialist country, joint diplomatic steps against the U.S. and Federal Republic of Germany governments by the foreign ministries of the socialist countries will be considered.

Number 153/1748

Source: The Federal Commissioner for the Records of the Ministry for State Security of the former German Democratic Republic (BStU), Berlin. Mfs-ZAIG 22570 (BstU 000223–000229)

Translation by I. Pentenrieder

Appendix K:
Selected Summary of Threats, Intimidations, Contacts, Intelligence Cases and Notes

1952 *January* Richard Herbert Moschner was sent by the Czechoslovak Intelligence Service to the West in April 1951, to gather information, with the intent to bomb Radio Free Europe sites. He took photographs of the RFE Munich building and the transmitting site at Holzkirchen, south of Munich. On January 31, 1952, the American military court in Nuremberg found him guilty of being a Czechoslovak agent and sentenced him to seven years imprisonment.

1954 *March* Polish intelligence officer Jozef Swiatlo defected in Berlin and was flown to the United States.
From September 30 to December 31, 1954, Radio Free Europe broadcast his story. And his story was sent to Poland via the balloon/leaflet program. He also testified before the U.S. Congress (see chapter 2).

August Radio Free Europe staffer Stefan Kiripolsky was kidnapped in Vienna and returned to Czechoslovakia, where he remained in prison until 1968 (chapter 2).

September The body of Radio Liberation staffer Leonid Karas was found floating in the Isar River in Munich. The circumstances of his death were unknown.

November Radio Liberation Azerii Chief Abo Fatalibey was murdered in Munich (chapter 2).

1955 *September* Helmut Schwan was arrested in Munich and confessed to being a Czech agent, with a mission of sabotage against RFE. He claimed that he had been instructed to purchase a truck and several cylinders of acetylene and oxygen and to drive the loaded truck to the front of RFE, where an explosive charge would set off the cylinders. He also was told to obtain information about a number of RFE employees.

1957 *April–August* Under code name "Pine Tree" ("Borovice" in Czech), there was a Czechoslovak Intelligence Service plot to blow up RFE Broadcast Center in

Munich. The person selected to carry out this operation at the end refused to complete the operation.

1958   In July 1958, a bogus edition of *Ceske Slovo* was prepared and distributed, after unknown persons broke into the Munich apartment of RFE employee Jozef Pejskar, editor of the Czech exile newspaper. *Ceske Slovo* was edited and published in Munich with a monthly circulation of 5,000, with approximately 10 percent of each issue being smuggled into Czechoslovakia.

1959   *November*   Salt Shaker Incident — the Czechoslovak Intelligence Service made a plan to place atropine, a dangerous poison, in Radio Free Europe cafeteria salt shakers. An RFE employee, who was a double agent at the time, using code-name "Jachym," reported details of the plot to CIA.

1960   *November*   Alfred Frenzel, member of the West German Parliament, was arrested in November 1960 on charges of spying for Czechoslovakia. Frenzel had the code name "Anna." Frenzel was sentenced to fifteen years imprisonment but was exchanged for four West Germans agents and returned to Czechoslovakia.

1961   Dr. Aurel Abranyi, a supplier of information to Radio Free Europe in Vienna and co-author with an RFE staffer of a book on the Revolution in Hungary 1956, was kidnapped and returned to Hungary for imprisonment. He was never released and was presumed executed (chapter 2).

1963   *November*   The Polish Foreign Intelligence Service recruited a Radio Free Europe announcer with the code name "Fonda." He provided basic information on RFE, including information on the tasks of individual departments and methods of editorial work, on American management and security at RFE Munich.

1964   *November*   RFE actor/announcer Stanislav Kavan committed suicide in his apartment after Munich police began interrogating him about his activities on behalf of Czech intelligence.

December   Radio Free Europe employee Milan Kout returned to Czechoslovakia, while under investigation by German authorities on charges of espionage, i.e. working for StB while employed at RFE, under code name "Zdenek." He was employed from October 16, 1963 to October 31, 1964.

1965   The Polish Foreign Intelligence Service recruited Andrzej Czechowicz, who worked in RFE's Research and Analysis Department. He returned to Poland in March 1971 and was used for years in Polish anti–Radio Free Europe propaganda campaigns.

1966   *June*   USSR KGB agent Oleg Tumanov joined Radio Liberty. He remained at Radio Liberty until February 1986, providing documentation and information (chapter 7).

1967 *October* Ludwig Kolin, an Austrian citizen, was arrested in Czechoslovakia in October 1967 while attending the wedding of a friend. The Free Europe Committee book distribution program used Kolin, an employee of the State Labor Office in Vienna, for a number of years. He went into Czechoslovakia in an attempt to bring out the son of his friend, Bohumir Bunza, a RFE freelancer in Rome.

1968 The Czechoslovakian Intelligence Service sent Ervin Marak to work at Radio Free Europe.

Under code name "Toy" ("Hracka")), he provided documentation, information, and recordings of conversations with staffers of the Radio Free Europe Czechoslovak Broadcast Service that were used in the anti–RFE propaganda campaigns. He returned to Czechoslovakia in 1974 (chapter 8).

August The Polish Foreign Intelligence Service recruited Mieczysław Lach in Vienna under code name "Kumor." Lach worked in Munich until his return to Poland in November 1974. He was subsequently used in the Poland and Soviet Union anti–Radio Free Europe propaganda campaigns (chapter 8).

September Czechoslovak intelligence officer Pavel Minarik was sent to Vienna; he then joined Radio Free Europe and provided information and documentation under code names "Ulyxes" and "Pley," until his return to Czechoslovakia in July 1975. He was used in the Czechoslovakian and Soviet Union anti–Radio Free Europe propaganda campaigns (chapter 8).

1969 *Summer* Czechoslovak intelligence officer Josef Frolik defected to the West, after seventeen years in the Ministry of Interior. He testified before U.S. Congress in 1975 about Czechoslovak intelligence plans and actions against Radio Free Europe. He was the author of the book *The Frolik Defection. The Memoirs of an Intelligence Agent*, published in London in 1976 (chapter 8).

1973 *September* The Polish Foreign Intelligence Service recruited Andrzej Smoliński, an employee of the Research and Analysis Department preparing economic analyses for Radio Free Europe. Smolinski provided information and documentation under code name "Kryza," until his return to Poland in August 1974. He was used in the Poland and Soviet Union anti–Radio Free Europe propaganda campaigns (chapter 8).

1974 Agent Marak returned to Czechoslovakia. Agents Lach and Smolinski returned to Poland (chapter 8).

1975 *July* Czechoslovak Service employee Pavel Minarik of RFE/RL, who was scheduled for a reduction-in-work-force termination, returned to Prague. It was then revealed by Prague Radio that he was "an intelligence officer who had waged a seven-year spy operation inside the radios." Soviet and Eastern European media gave extensive coverage to revelations which included attacks against both radios, individually named employees, alleged CIA connections, etc. (chapter 8).

November German police arrested two Polish diplomats in Munich while they were attempting to recruit a Polish employee of RFE/RL for intelligence purposes. The diplomats were returned to Poland in exchange for the release of three Germans held in Polish jails.

December   After a two-and-a-half year hiatus, Radio Bucharest renewed its attacks against Radio Free Europe; however, these attacks were directed against RFE personnel, as well as being general in nature. In December, RFE Paris employee Mrs. Monica Lovinescu and Romanian Service Director Noel Bernard were attacked in a broadcast on Radio Bucharest.

1976   *March*

1. Yuri Marin, a former Russian employee of RL, who had redefected to the Soviet Union, was quoted widely in the Soviet press in articles attacking the RL as instruments of the CIA, for violations of the Helsinki Agreement, etc. (chapter 7).

2. Bulgarian press and radio announced the return of Hrisan Hristov, an intelligence agent who had worked for eleven years in the West uncovering "the undermining activity of the CIA, Radio Free Europe and hostile émigrés working against Bulgaria." The man never was employed by the Radio Free Europe. Many media attacks centered on the radios' former Vienna news bureau and opinion research activities in Austria.

April   Both German and U.S. military intelligence agencies advised radio management of their strong suspicions that a Polish refugee living in Munich might be involved in espionage activities. The person's wife was an employee of RFE/RL.

May

1. A Radio Liberty employee was visited at home by an unidentified Russian, who attempted to recruit him for KGB activities. His visitor reminded the employee that he still had relatives living in the Soviet Union. He was handed two rare stamp collectors' books belonging to a relative living in Moscow to prove the authenticity of the approach.

2. The Bulgarian News Service issued the first of a series of articles covering the return of Hrisan Hristov, who described various intelligence channels he had passed through in West Germany. He cited Radio Free Europe and U.S. Army intelligence connections and named radio employees who, he alleged, collaborated with intelligence agencies.

July

1. An employee of the radios received a visit from relatives living in the USSR, one of whom told him secretly that they had been issued passports with specific instructions to ask the employee to work for Soviet intelligence.

2. A Polish employee of the radios was visited by his brother, who identified himself as a Polish military intelligence officer and then attempted to recruit the employee for intelligence purposes. He asked for one of the new RFE/RL identification cards, etc. German police arrested the relative in Munich (see February 1978).

August

1. A Radio Liberty Nationalities Language employee was visited in his apartment at night by a man claiming to be from the same hometown in the USSR, but whose stories of acquaintanceship with the employee's relatives were highly question-

able. The man attempted to get the employee to join him outside. When the employee refused, the man became extremely nervous and quickly went away, never to be seen or heard from again.

2. A Radio Liberty employee was introduced to persons who said they could arrange for her to meet with her mother from Moscow. The employee flew to West Berlin where she saw her mother. Afterward the persons who arranged the meeting attempted to recruit her for Soviet intelligence. She later flew to Moscow and met with KGB officials.

October   Emil Georgescu, Romanian Service, escaped injury when his car was rammed twice on the driver's side by another car. The employee and his wife reported to police that the other driver jumped out and climbed into another car, which was following them. Police ascertained that the car abandoned at the scene was rented two days earlier by a Frenchman, who had checked out of his Munich hotel before police arrived The name and address on the car rental and hotel registration forms proved to be fictitious. In the meantime the employee received anonymous threatening letters and telephone calls (chapter 6).

1977   *January*   During the Christmas holidays, a Polish employee of RFE/RL received a telephone call from a longtime Warsaw friend visiting in Belgium. The caller related that before being issued a tourist visa, she had been summoned to the Polish Ministry of Interior, where officials asked her to convey certain "proposals" to the radio employee.

February

1. The Polish military intelligence officer, who in July 1977 attempted to recruit his brother, a RFE/RL employee, for intelligence purposes, was charged with conducting espionage activities in the Federal Republic of Germany. He pleaded guilty and was given a one-year prison sentence. The seven months he had been in custody were deducted, and the remaining five months were suspended. He returned to Poland.

2. German police advised that a Bulgarian, who had approached an RFE/RL employee previously with an offer to return to Bulgaria, was back in Germany. The man again contacted the radio employee and told him that his parents wanted him to return home, but if this was not possible then he should stop working for the radio at once.

3. By means of a photograph, German authorities were able to identify the man who visited the Radio Liberty employee in his apartment in August 1976. The man was one of a group of twenty Soviet journalists who visited Austria. The group arrived in Vienna and traveled by bus to various Austrian cities. The bus reached Salzburg on August 8, but only nineteen journalists registered in a hotel there. The Austrian intelligence agents watching the group failed to locate the missing one. With the identification of the photograph, it was known that the twentieth journalist crossed the border into Germany and appeared at the apartment of the RFE/RL employee on August 9. The Soviet journalists checked out of the Salzburg hotel on August 10, boarded a bus and waited. The missing man arrived by taxi, climbed directly into the bus, which departed for Vienna, from where the group flew back to the Soviet Union.

March   The Radio Liberty employee who had been contacted previously by an East German woman again was asked to meet the woman, this time in a downtown Munich department store restaurant. The German police monitored the meeting. Among letters turned over to the employee was one that contained appeals to his patriotism, suggested a meeting in West Berlin, and requested detailed information about Radio Liberty. Specifically, he was asked to provide data about strategy and tactics of subversive propaganda against the Soviet Union, Radio Liberty sources and methods of getting information, employment figures and names of the most active staff members. German authorities questioned the woman courier and released her. She returned to East Germany.

November   In November 1977, prominent Romanian dissident Paul Goma arrived in Paris. On November 21, RFE employee Mrs. Monica Lovinescu was beaten in front of her home in Paris. Goma stated at a later press conference that this assault on Mrs. Lovinescu was the work of the Romanian secret police which had warned him just before he had left Romania that the "arm of the revolution is very long and could reach everywhere," and that sign proving this would await him in Paris. The two men who beat up Mrs. Lovinescu were never found and she spent four days in a hospital.

1978   *August* Bulgarian Service freelancer Vladimir Kostov was shot by a Bulgarian intelligence agent using the umbrella weapon in Paris (chapter 3).

September   After two unsuccessful murder attempts earlier in the year, Bulgarian Service freelancer Georgi Markov died in London after being shot by the same method that was used in the Kostov attack — the so-called "Umbrella Murder" (chapter 3).

1979   *Trifa Case:* On April 29 and May 1, 1979, the Romanian Service of Radio Free Europe broadcast a thirty-one minute interview with Bishop Valerian Trifa of the Romanian Orthodox Church of America. At that time, and since 1975, the Justice Department was prosecuting a denaturalization suit against Bishop Trifa for "Nazi collaboration" (chapter 6).

July
1. In early July, various employees of the Romanian Service received this anonymous letter.

Smelly Rotter
You and all your family will pay for the trouble caused our Bishop
The Iron Guard lives
The Iron Guard is living
The Iron Guard will survive
Death Squadron 'Mota and Marin'

2. On July 26, between 6:30 and 7:00 A.M., Bavarian State Police (LKA) agents picked up a RFE Czechoslovak Service actor-producer and a freelancer, Yuri Leitner, separately at their homes. The employee was later freed and not charged. In December, Leitner was tried, found guilty of espionage and sentenced to one year and eight months in prison.

1980   *November* A Czechoslovak Service employee had a visitor from Czechoslovakia, an acquaintance of his parents. The visitor had been several times previously in Munich. The visitor told the employee that he should remember his patriotism and be prepared to do something for his former homeland, Czechoslovakia. The visitor offered to arrange for his parents to visit him in Vienna; offered to arrange payments up to DM 25,000 in exchange for providing certain information.

The visitor said the parents could be brought out of Czechoslovakia and could meet him on the steps of St. Stephen's Church in Vienna at 1:30 P.M. on December 10. The employee said he would think it over, and the visitor left the next morning for Nuremberg (Chapter 8).

1981   *January*   Anti-Semitic and threatening letters were mailed to Romanian Service employees in Munich and Washington. One Romanian Service editor resigned under pressure of the threats. Later evidence points to the Romanian Intelligence Service as being behind the letter campaign (chapters 5 and 6).

February

1. Romanian Service freelancers in Paris and Cologne were injured when book bombs mailed from Spain were opened. Evidence later showed that the Romanian Intelligence Service was behind the attacks (chapter 5).

2. RFE/RL headquarters building bombed, resulting in injuries to four employees and damage of about two million dollars. The famous terrorist Carlos had sent a team to bomb the building, on payment of the Romanian Intelligence Service (Chapter 4).

May   The secretary to the Radio Free Europe central news director was arrested in the building on charges of being a spy for Romania — possible code name "Balthazar." She was not prosecuted for lack of evidence. She resigned from RFE/RL (chapter 5).

July   Romanian Service employee Emil Georgescu was stabbed twenty-two times on his way to work. The police caught his assailants, two Frenchmen, as they tried to escape to Austria. They were tried and found guilty the following year (chapter 6).

1982   *February*

1. With the defection back to Czechoslovakia of Josef Hodic in July 1981, the Bavarian Agency for the Protection of the Constitution (LfV) attempted to put together a history of all his activity in West Germany. They were very interested in any connection Hodic might have had with RFE/RL employees. They supplied a list of names of possible contacts. They also asked for biographical information on some of our employees. There was also fear that one of our employees would be another "Minarik," though they were not sure if this meant that our employee would soon return to Czechoslovakia, or if he was simply supplying information for a future return. A series of interviews was set up with employees (one of whom had already been interviewed), three more to follow. There was no information that Hodic was ever in the RFE/RL building, though RFE/RL did know that he met RFE/RL employees on at least three occasions,

2. A Czechoslovakian living in West Germany was approached by the Czechoslovak Intelligence Service and told to try to get employment with RFE/RL. This man was a refugee living in a with a U.S. soldier somewhere north of Munich. He made

an attempt and completed an employment questionnaire; however, he was never seriously considered for employment, and his application was rejected.

1983   *February*   Information was received from Munich police that a Romanian intelligence agent had defected and revealed information about a serious plot to kill an RFE/RL freelancer in Paris. The State Department was asked to get more information. The plot was reported in French newspapers (chapter 5).

1984   In September 1984 a staff member of the Romanian embassy in Bonn, BRD, defected to the West. To establish his credentials, he presented a copy of a thirteen-page physical surveillance report that was written by a Romanian Intelligence Service officer named Constantin sometime between October and December 1983. This surveillance report was based on two days of personal observation in October 1983 and was presented at a Romanian Intelligence Service headquarters meeting in Bucharest in December 1983. Five Romanian diplomats were expelled from Germany (chapter 5).

1985   *April*   Another letter was received by some members of the Czechoslovak Service, full of details of various internal problems of that service.

May
        1. At about 10:30 A.M., there was an explosion at the RFE/RL transmitting site in Gloria, Portugal. Three plastic charges had been placed on a tower, and one of the three had exploded. There was minor damage, and a group calling itself the "Anti-Capitalist and Anti-Militarist Group" claimed credit for the blast. The police bomb squad disarmed a second charge, and the third apparently malfunctioned and only burned. The police investigated; the gendarmerie, GNR, placed one man in front of the RFE/RL Lisbon office. The GNR stepped up patrols at Gloria, and a meeting was held between the GNR and the contract guard company, Transegur, at Gloria, to recommend further security measures. A report of these recommendations was sent to Munich. Two contract guards were added to the night-shift patrols at Pals, Spain; all sites in Germany were put on special alert.
        2. The West German Ministry of the Interior put out its annual report on espionage activities in the FRG. The Romanian plot to bomb the Munich headquarters building of RFE/RL received special attention in the report. Of particular interest is the part dealing with RFE/RL. The report showed activity directed against RFE/RL, starting in 1982 (chapter 5).
        3. The Soviet media campaign against RFE/RL continued. One published article called "The Black Pearl" dealt with an alleged battle between the Radio Liberty division director George Bailey and the RFE/RL security office. The article demonstrated how the security office won the battle and the war, and George Bailey was forced out of RFE/RL.
        4. Earlier this year a questionnaire was sent to various people and organizations in the West, which was purported to be a RFE/RL document approved by the Polish Service. The questionnaire was an obvious forgery, and the purported sender of the document was an émigré living in Vienna. The Polish Service arranged for a published denial of the authenticity of the document.

5. An RFE Polish Service employee reported to the security office that her brother had arrived from Poland for a visit. Before her departure, she was approached by two members of the Polish Intelligence Service who requested that he talk to her and another female employee of the Polish Service and offer both "good jobs and security" in Poland should they return. In addition, she was to obtain a copy of a Polish-language book recently published, in West Germany, which was written by a recently deceased Polish Service employee.

August

1. Bomb threats received August 15, 1985. A previously unknown group claimed responsibility for the bombing of the U. S. military radio and television network antenna in Munich. The same morning, RFE/RL received a series of bomb-threat telephone calls. This group claimed to be "the Fighting Unit for the Construction of the Anti-Imperialism Front in Western Europe." Apparently, the caller representing the group attempted to give the group an international flavor by claiming to represent a "Front in Western Europe." The caller also called for the release of a West German terrorist member of the Red Army Faction.

2. The Radio Liberty Belorussian Broadcast Service was again the target of a media attack in the USSR. This was the fourth such attack in three weeks.

3. One RFE/RL employee reported that his aunt living in the Ukraine had written a letter to his parents in Great Britain, which the employee believed was at the urging of the KGB. His reasoning was that his aunt had previously visited his parents and indicated that she would not correspond with them in the future. In the letter she sent to them, she wanted to know about him and where he was living in Munich, etc. His aunt would not normally have asked these types of questions in a letter. He was sure that she did not send it on her own accord.

4. One more article in the Soviet media attacked RFE/RL. This one went into detail about Dr. Najder of the Polish Service and his supposed connection to the CIA. Of particular interest was the mention of the security department and one previous director named Kurt Fisher, who was a supposed member of the Nazi SS. There was no information available at RFE/RL showing that such a person ever worked for RFE or RL. Also, the article erroneously said that the security department had duplicate keys to all RFE apartments and that there are thirty armed guards around the building day and night. There were some photographs of the building, taken many years before.

5. An RFE Bulgarian Service employee was mentioned over Radio Sofia as a witness in Rome at the trial of the Bulgarian accused of conspiring to kill the pope. The employee had been the subject of various threats in the past, but he had not taken them too seriously. This article was not taken as a threat against the employee but was an attempt to discredit him as a credible witness. He was mentioned to be working for a "diversionist" radio station financed by "American and other Western Secret Services."

6. A RFE/RL Polish Service Monitoring employee reported a recent visit from his parents who lived in Poland. Prior to their departure they were approached by the Polish Intelligence Service to make contact with him. His sister was first given a travel passport, but this was taken away from her as she apparently refused to cooperate with the authorities.

7. Information received shows that the Polish Intelligence Service was attempting to learn as much as possible about the RFE/RL computer system.

8. Radio Sofia reported on November 8 about a former employee and the RFE Audience Research operation in Vienna. The person had been employed in the RFE Vienna News Bureau until 1974, when he was terminated as a result of a reduction in force. He was not tied into the actual operation of the Audience Research Department. He had some sort of unofficial relationship with the various research institutes that did the actual interviewing of Bulgarians in Vienna. He apparently acted as a spotter for the institutes, and he received a nominal fee for letting the institutes know where the Bulgarians were.

9. An RFE/RL Hungarian Service employee reported that he had met his brother in Vienna and that his brother had told him that he had been sent by the Hungarian Intelligence Service (HIS) for the specific purpose of asking him to work for the HIS. The employee said that he refused to do so (chapter 8).

1986 *January* Another Polish Service employee reported that her brother, living and working in Warsaw, had been called into the office of the Ministry of the Interior recently. She was told that if she continued to work for RFE/RL, he would lose his job, and he would not receive a passport to travel. Both her parents were retired and they had had no problems with the authorities up to then. This was the first time that the brother had been called in to the Ministry of Interior. She had received the information indirectly from the brother through a friend who had traveled to Poland.

February
Radio Liberty Russian Service employee Oleg Tumanov was reported missing (chapter 7).

April
1. Some Russian Service employees of RL received threatening phone calls, possibly from someone living in northern West Germany. The police investigated these calls.

2. The Czechoslovak Service director was criticized through copies of an anonymous letter that circulated within the service. The letters were mailed to staff members in envelopes with the RFE/RL logo. Some envelopes had not yet been opened and were given to German authorities for examination.

3. Oleg Tumanov was shown on Soviet television as an ex-RFE/RL employee in an anti–RFE/RL propaganda campaign (chapter 7).

May
1. RFE/RL gave the U.S. consulate political officer in Munich information concerning the trial in Warsaw, Poland, of a former journalist for the Polish News Agency (PAP). He was sentenced to eight years in jail for supplying RFE with information for a ten-year time period. In fact, the journalist had once traveled to West Berlin, sent materials to RFE, and received payments for his information.

2. Employees of the Russian Service of Radio Liberty received threatening phone calls. One employee who received such a call thought that he could identify the voice of the caller. This information was passed on to the police investigating the calls, and the police interviewed the employee on May 25.

3. RFE/RL learned that an employment candidate had been given the assignment to come the West with an "intelligence" purpose of making contact with RFE as a Bulgarian refugee. After his defection, he did admit having had contacts with Bulgarian embassy officials in Bonn. However, one reliable source claimed that this was a "false confession" to ensure that any reports of said contacts made by others to the agencies could be easily explained as having been already admitted. He was not hired.

4. A new book in the Soviet anti–RFE/RL propaganda campaign appeared on the market: Gennadi Alev and Vassilli Viktorov, *Aggression in the Ether: The Psychological War: Witnesses, Facts, Documents* (Moscow: APN Verlag, 1986).

September

1. The Red Army Faction bombed the Panavia building located across from the RFE/RL Annex located on the Arabellastrasse at 1:45 A.M., September 15, 1986. The next afternoon, the police notified RFE/RL that an anonymous caller had telephoned the police and said that RFE/RL was going to be bombed. The police responded with a team of experts who were sent to the RFE/RL headquarters building. A search of the building and grounds was made, but nothing unusual was found, and there was no disruption of the work in the building. The caller was never identified. What was a little disturbing was the fact that the front page of the *Deutsche Tagespost* in Wuerzburg carried an article on September 16 identifying RFE/RL as being across the street from the site of the bombing. RFE/RL had gone to lengths not to have the Annex identified. None of the Munich newspapers mentioned RFE/RL.

2. News from the RFE/RL New York Programming Center was that a "diplomat" had approached a person associated with RFE/RL in New York. This time a Soviet diplomat apparently directly approached the employee to make contact.

3. Two employees of the Polish Service reported separate recent incidents of Polish Intelligence Service interest in RFE/RL. Information from a father-in-law showed that the Polish Intelligence Service knew about one employee's recent visit to London. She had been employed with RFE/RL since March 1983 and this was the first reported attempt of recruitment or harassment. Another Polish Service employee reported that a visit of his parents had taken place in August 1986. His father told him that during the last days of the visit he brought a message from the Polish authorities wherein the employee was advised that he could travel to any place in the world, including a return trip to Poland. He should think it over and meet the father and "a friend" in Vienna to discuss more details. The employee refused to go along with the idea of a meeting in Vienna.

4. An RFE/RL Czechoslovak Service employee reported that his sister and brother-in-law had visited recently from the CSSR. During the visit, his brother-in-law stated that they had received the visa to leave the CSSR only if he would try to get a photograph of the employee and an original letter written by him, which would include his signature. The employee refused to have his photograph taken. He was sure that no letters or other written material with his signature, had been taken from his apartment. He later heard through a cousin of his that the Czechoslovak Intelligence Service had questioned the brother-in-law about his visit to the apartment, and he was asked for the items. It is not known what happened afterwards to the brother-in-law for the "failure" to bring back the materials he was supposed to.

October   An RFE/RL Hungarian Service employee reported a visit from his parents from Hungary. This was not their first visit, or the first visit from any of his relatives. However, this was the first time that he had received a message from the Hungarian government. His father gave him an envelope just before he returned to Hungary. His father was sixty-seven and retired. The father and mother had been called into an office after they received their passports to leave Hungary and they were told to carry a message from the official who interviewed them. They were advised to wait until the employee opened the envelope and wait for his answer. The employee brought the envelope to RFE/RL, the last day his parents were in Munich. He was told not to open the envelope in their presence. His father had a history of heart attacks. Also, in this way his father would not have to lie about anything and he could truthfully tell the Hungarian authorities that he didn't know what was in the envelope or the employee's reply. This was the first reported contact made with an employee of the Hungarian Service in a long time. The message is exactly the same given to Soviet and Polish émigrés recently.

November   A Hungarian Broadcast employee reported that his mother who was retired and living in Hungary was denied a passport to visit him on grounds of "not [being] in the national interest." She appealed the decision, but it was turned down again.

December   A Czech-language letter was sent to at least two freelancers of the RFE/RL Czechoslovak Service. The handwritten letter told the recipients to ask for DM 2 million from RFE or physical harm would come to them. Included in the letter was mention of copies being sent to RFE, the police, and the newspaper *Abendzeitung*.

1987 *January*

1. An RFE/RL Polish Service employee reported that he had received a letter from a friend who was allowed to travel to Vienna. This friend wrote that the employee's sister wanted him to pass on the information that she was called in to the Polish counterintelligence service concerning her request for a passport and permission to visit the West. She was told that she could have the passport, that she would receive a substantial amount of money, and if she wanted she could get a job at RFE/RL. The officer hinted that they had someone at RFE/RL who could assist her in getting a position at RFE/RL. All she had to do was tell the employee, after she arrived in Munich, that all was forgiven, and he could return to Poland and suffer no consequences, since things were changing for the better in Poland. She refused. The man then said that she could think it over, and if she did not want to do it, that was okay, because they would find another to bring the message.

2. Four employees received a copy of an anti–Semitic letter. Someone at RFE/RL had supplied the post office box numbers within RFE/RL to an outsider, or an employee of RFE/RL had mailed the letters. They were postmarked in Hamburg, Germany.

February

1. An RFE/RL Polish Service freelancer reported that his sister-in-law had arrived in Munich from Poland, two weeks previously. Before her departure she was called

in to the local police department, where she met with a man from Warsaw. This man told her that he knew about the freelancer working at RFE/RL, etc. He then asked her to tell the freelancer that it would be okay for him to return to Poland, that he could get a good job, etc., If the freelancer wanted more information, this man would meet him anywhere in the West the freelancer chose.

March

1. On Friday, March 13, about 6:30 P.M., RFE/RL learned that Swiss intelligence authorities had uncovered a plot to kidnap an employee of the Polish Service of RFE/RL. The RFE/RL security office spoke with her and advised her of procedures to take to detect surveillance, numbers to call, etc. It appeared that the plot was to kidnap her and return her to Poland for political reasons: trial or TV presentation, most likely the latter. Polish Intelligence Service agents were then known to be very active in Switzerland.

2. It was reported that the KGB was making serious inquiries into Tumanov's activities at RFE/RL and his circle of friends.

April A Russian Monitoring employee reported that he had been approached by the KGB, through his cousin, with the request that he work for them at RFE/RL. He now reported a second attempt via telephone, and his cousin said that he would travel to Switzerland sometime in the near future and he would like to meet the employee there.

June An RFE/RL Polish Research Department employee reported that he had traveled to Vienna and met his brother, who had traveled from Poland. They met on Sunday, May 31. He had reported the possible meeting prior to his departure. The brother was a Communist Party member and worked for the State Tourism Agency. The brother made a very low-key approach that the employee could return to Poland, if he wanted to, and go back to his "old job" with no problems. The employee said that he declined the offer, and there was no further discussion.

July

1. An editor of the Hungarian Service reported that his son had visited him from Hungary, for the first time in eleven years. He said that shortly before his son had left, he had been called into the Ministry of Interior, or equivalent, and told that he should tell his father that they would be willing to meet with our employee, have him return to Hungary with no problems, etc. In other words, the standard-approach offers to have an RFE/RL employee return to Hungary. The employee told his son to advise the authorities that he had no intention of meeting any official anywhere, or returning to Hungary for any reason.

2. The trial of a Polish émigré was continuing in Munich. He had been arrested in the summer of 1986 and was alleged to have had contacts with the Polish Intelligence Service and to have reported on émigré activities in the Munich area, including Radio Free Europe.

3. Another employee of the Hungarian Service met his parents, who had been allowed to travel to the West. They met in Vienna and he was given the same pitch about working for the regime, or returning to Hungary, etc. He called the RFE/RL

security office from Vienna to report the message. He was advised to tell his parents, "No, thanks," and that he had reported their message to the security office.

4. A Czechoslovak Service employee reported that his sister had been allowed to leave the CSSR to visit him. The last time she had been allowed out had been four years before. This time she brought the message that he was free to return to CSSR and enjoy a good life there, or he could stay in the West and work for the regime by reporting on Czechoslovak émigré circle activities. He declined both offers; she returned to CSSR with the message.

5. An RL Russian Monitoring employee reported another phone call from his cousin who was presumed to be KGB. The cousin said he was going to be in Switzerland in October and he would like to meet him. He decided not to go.

August   Another RFE/RL freelancer returned to the USSR. There was mention in the German-language press about the recent return of a Soviet émigré named Vladimir Kovnats, whose wife was a freelancer for RFE/RL in New York. She was an announcer who voiced scripts on the average of twice a week. There was no record about her husband ever having been employed with RFE/RL.

October   Austrian counterintelligence officials expressed interest, through West German officials, in the travel of a Radio Liberty employee to Vienna.

November
1. A Polish Service employee reported that she had received a telephone call from her sister-in-law asking that the employee meet her brother in Vienna, at the request of the Interior Ministry. She would receive a letter giving all details of the meeting. The employee stated she would not go and would translate the letter into English as soon as she got it.

2. RFE/RL was told by a reliable source that there was an even chance that a Polish Service employee would return to Poland between then and January 1, 1988, for propaganda purposes. Apparently, the employee had been offered $30,000, an apartment in Warsaw, and a permanent job. One employee was put under German police surveillance but he noticed it and did not leave Germany.

3. A Russian Service employee received a letter from Oleg Tumanov asking specific questions in behalf of the KGB (chapter 7).

1988 *January*
1. A Russian Service employee reported that he received another phone call on January 25, from the KGB officer named Yuri. Yuri passed on more greetings from his friend (Tumanov) and said that his friend was concerned about his family in Munich — Tumanov's ex-wife who was still in jail, and their daughter (chapter 7).

2. The RFE/RL security office received photographs of ex-Romanian King Michael showing blood on his hand and a bullet wound in his head. The photographs were included with a photocopy of a leaflet of a supposed group in New York called "In the Service of the Marshall" (chapter 5).

March
1. RFE/RL received allegations from a reliable source that a Polish Service employee had attended a party or celebration recently and information that was received in Warsaw was now suspected of being the source of information to the Polish Intelligence Sources: there seemed to be a pattern of events/happenings he attended, which were then reported to Warsaw, or appeared in the Polish media.
2. The Romanian Intelligence Service was very interested in the way RFE was reporting on the Hungarian minority in Romania. It was believed that the Romanians might seek a way to influence broadcasting, directly or indirectly, or to counter what was perceived by Bucharest to be a pro-Hungarian attitude by Radio Free Europe.

April There was an attempt from Paris, France, to enter the RFE/RL mainframe computer through the digital network on Easter.

May An RFE/RL Polish Service employee's twenty-two-year-old daughter had recently arrived from Poland. Shortly before she had been allowed to leave Poland, she had been called to the Interior Ministry and met with an intelligence officer named "Jacek Rozdaj," who said that he would like to meet the employee in Austria, Greece, Yugoslavia, or anywhere in the world except West Germany. This was not the first time he was told such information from a family member: he had informed the RFE/RL security office in the past about previous family harassment from the Polish regime. The daughter did not want to return to Poland but wanted to go the United States.

July Another KGB contact approach was made to two Radio Liberty employees.

1989 *March* On March 26, RFE/RL Bulgarian Service employee Pavel Glavousanov returned to Bulgaria.
(On May 3, 2005 the former head of the Bulgarian Intelligence Service, Gen. Vladimir Todorov, confirmed that among their secret agents at RFE Bulgarian section in Munich were Hrisan Hristov and Pavel Glavousanov.)

April Returned RFE/RL Bulgarian Service employee Pavel Glavousanov gave two press conferences in Sofia. In one of them he told about RFE/RL's audience research operation in Vienna.

June A threatening telephone call was received in the Czechoslovak Service of RFE/RL and a threatening letter, mailed from Czechoslovakia, was received by the same service.

July The 1988 annual report of the West German counterintelligence agency was published. Radio Free Europe was listed as one of the major targets of Eastern European/Soviet intelligence agencies.

August RFE/RL had to turn down the employment application of a candidate for the post office. The reason was that he had falsified his application by indicating that he was born in a city in Southwest Africa, went to school there, and his parents lived there. A check with an outside agency resulted in the information that he was actually born in the GDR, went to school there, served in the East German army, and that his parents were still living in East Germany.

September   An RFE/RL Bulgarian Service employee reported further contact with a Bulgarian living in Moscow.

November
1. An RFE/RL employee, with a previous Polish intelligence connection, was visited by his parents. Shortly before the visit his father met with "Jacek," the Polish intelligence officer in charge of that service's operation against RFE/RL. Jacek told the father to tell the employee that all operations were on hold, pending the results of the political changes in Poland. Jacek was not sure what might happen to him and his department as a result of the political changes.
2. A Czechoslovak Service employee reported that his father just visited him from Czechoslovakia, and on three occasions prior to the visit, the father had been visited by a Ministry of Interior official named Dr. Stribrny (intelligence officer), who said he wanted to meet the employee in a neutral country: Hungary or Switzerland. The employee told his father to tell the intelligence officer, "thanks, but no thanks."

1990   *January*   The KGB officer who sometimes contacted RFE/RL employees telephoned from Budapest to say goodbye to one RFE/RL employee as he was being reassigned to Moscow. He said that he had recorded the employee's voice on tape and was leaving it with the KGB in Budapest, in case the employee ever had a need to contact the KGB or visit the KGB in Budapest. The contact officer did not say he was being replaced, just that he was being reassigned to Moscow.

March   A Russian Service employee visited Moscow. During the visit she was called into the visa office (OVIR), Room 25. A young man was sitting in the room. He said, "How was it going through customs this time as last time we checked everything? Hope you're not being troubled this time. We hope your father will visit the USSR, and I would like to meet him." He gave her details she hadn't known about the arrest of her grandfather and uncles during the Russian Revolution. She asked him if he would find out more information about her relatives and what had happened to them. He promised her that he would. He called her every second day to ask how she was doing. She then asked if he could help her get permission to go to Minsk, Byelorussia. He did, but she decided not to go for personal reasons. He asked her to meet him at the Hotel Rossiya. They met for five hours. He asked her about things at RFE/RL to which she answered she didn't know. The meeting ended, and he promised to be in touch with her the next time she visited Moscow. When she went though customs as she was exiting the USSR, the officials "took everything apart," but they had no interest in the books and papers: they were more concerned with perfumes and jewelry.

April   A Russian Service employee returned from a trip to Riga, Latvia, and Moscow. A KGB officer met with him in Riga, and the same officer met him again in

Moscow. The meetings were not adversarial. The officer said that his name was Rashid, and that he was Azeri. The employee had been expelled from the USSR for political activity about thirty years before. The KGB officer told him that his same activities today would not have resulted in his expulsion. However, since he was expelled, under present Soviet law, the employee was told that he had to be put under observation. This KGB officer spoke little about RFE/RL but did say that the KGB was disturbed by two things: (1) The Audience Research Office in Paris which was "nothing but a CIA front for espionage," and (2) RL provocative programming about events in Central Asia, especially the Azeri/Armenian programs.

June   During his recent forty-five-day stay in Romania, a Romanian Service employee had the occasion to meet with a former military intelligence officer, who stated that during his time in the military he had read radio traffic concerning another employee of the RFE/RL Romanian Service. She was highly regarded as an informant for the Securitate, according to this man. He asked the employee to pass it on to the Romanian Service director and to the RFE/RL security office.

October
   1. An RFE/RL Polish Service employee again visited Poland for both personal and professional reasons. He met a school friend, who gave him ripped-up pieces of "Secret" (as indicated on the pieces) reports written by the former Polish Intelligence Service (SB) about the employee in 1978 when he was first employed by RFE/RL. From the pieces put together, one could see that a thirty-page report written in December 1978 listed his salary at RFE/RL; that he would be "confirmed for full time employment; and likes alcohol, girls, and his mother." A four-page report also written in December 1978, gave other details about his work at RFE/RL and his comments at a party in Berlin he attended. It was clear from these pieces of reports on him, that someone at RFE/RL was supplying information about him to the SB. Other pieces show reports written in 1979 about his work and his friends in Berlin.
   2. An RFE/RL employee reported that a friend and sometime source of his information about Yugoslavia was interrogated by the secret police for three hours. One hour was dedicated to questioning this friend about the employee and his activities in both Yugoslavia and Munich. From the questioning and information the agents gave about the employee it was clear to him that was both followed in Yugoslavia and that someone in Munich was reporting details about his professional and personal life.
   3. The RFE/RL Hungarian Broadcast Service director reported that during his last trip to Hungary, he was told by someone in the present Hungarian Interior Ministry that two names popped up as having some sort of connection to the former Hungarian Intelligence Service. Allegations of such activity against both had surfaced in the past.

1993   *September*   RFE/RL received death threats against Slovak Service freelancer Stephan Hrib. He was one of the regular freelancers from Bratislava on temporary duty in Munich. The RFE office in Bratislava received several phone calls with threats: "We will kill Mr. Hrib, when he shows up in Bratislava." What's even more vicious is that an unknown caller called his parents saying: "We succeeded in killing Stefan in Munich!"

1994 *March*   Four journalists, three of them representing RFE/RL in Slovakia, were mishandled by demonstrators in Bratislava. A crowd of about six hundred people demonstrated outside the offices of Slovak president Michal Kovac in central Bratislava. They supported ousted Prime Minister Vladimir Meciar and called for Kovac to resign. Members of the former Meciar government had criticized RFE/RL in the past. Some of the demonstrators turned on RFE/RL correspondent Stefan Hrib. He was kicked and thrown to the ground. His jacket, documents and money were taken. Police were present but did not act to help Hrib, who later went to a hospital for examination. Some of the same demonstrators kicked and punched RFE/RL correspondent Milan Zitny in a separate incident, and destroyed his camera. Zitny said that a policeman had helped him into a police car to escape the crowd. Members of the same crowd tried to pull a recording device from the hands of RFE/RL correspondent Luba Lesna and punched Slovak radio reporter Anna Samelova in the face several times. Samelova said that a policeman watched but refused to help her.

Chapter Notes

Preface

1. A detailed review can be found in the author's article "The Intelligence Underpinnings of American Covert Radio Broadcasting in Germany During the Cold War," *Journal of Intelligence History* 1, no. 2 (Winter 2001). An excellent source for declassified CIA and State Department documents is *Emergence of the Intelligence Establishment, Foreign Relations of the United States, 1945–1950*, U.S. Department of State, 1996, available through the U.S. Government Printing Office, ISBN 0-16-045208-2, GPO Stock #044-000-02413-6. Another prime source is the volume from the Center for the Study of Intelligence, CIA History Staff, Michael Warner, ed., *CIA Cold War Records: The CIA Under Harry Truman* (Washington, D.C.: CIA, 1994). A superb historical summary of RFE/RL, including photographs, is Cissie Dore Hill, "Voices of Hope: The Story of RFE and RL," *Hoover Digest* no. 4 (2001). This article was published for the exhibition of the same name at the Hoover Institution, Stanford University, April 24–28 through December 2001. Many documents on Radio Free Europe's history also can be found at the Open Society Archives, Central European University, Budapest, Hungary: HU OSA 300 Records of Radio Free Europe/Radio Liberty Research Institute (RFE/RL RI), 1949–1994. The records consist primarily of clippings, abstracts of media reports, and monitoring of television and radio broadcasts, with a total of 17,938 archival boxes, 2,322 linear meters.

Chapter 1

1. John Lodeesen, "Radio Liberty (Munich): Foundation for a History," *Historical*

Journal of Film, Radio, and Television 6, no. 2 (1986), 197.

2. "Radio Free Europe and Radio Liberty, Memorandum for the 303 Committee, January 27, 1969," *Foreign Relations, 1969–1976*, Volume 29, Document 28, 81.

3. A photocopy of this directive can be found in Michael Warner, ed., *CIA Cold War Records: The CIA Under Harry Truman*, Psychological Operations, NSC 4-A, (Washington, D.C.: CIA, 1994) 175–177. Also, "Memorandum from the Executive Secretary (Souers) to the Members of the National Security Council, NSC 4-A, Washington, December 9, 1947," in *Foreign Relations of the United States, 1945–1959, Emergence of the Intelligence Establishment* (Washington, D.C.: U.S. State Department, 1996), Document 253, www.state.gov/www/about_state/history/intel/index.html

4. *Ibid.*

5. Cited in Warner, National Security Council Directive on Office of Special Projects, NSC 10/2, Washington, June 18, 1948, 213–216, and *Emergence of the Intelligence Establishment*, Document 292. On May 11, 1971, Richard Helms, director of the Central Intelligence Agency, wrote to President Nixon: "The Agency's role was to provide funding and liaison technique of such nature that any Government direction or control of the Radios could be plausibly denied. These arrangements were successful in the initial period, but in recent years more and more allegations of CIA backing have appeared in the press. The circumstances are such, therefore, that plausible denial has been increasingly difficult." *Foreign Relations of the United States, 1969–1976*, Volume 29, Document 52 (Washington, D.C.: U.S. State Department), 44.

6. *Emergence of the Intelligence Establishment*, Document 269.

7. *Ibid.*

8. *Ibid.*

9. *Ibid.*

10. Full Text of NSC 10/2 can be read in Warner, 213–216.

11. Warner, 215–216.

12. *Ibid*, 216.

13. *Ibid.* 214.

14. *Foreign Relations of the United States, 1948* (Washington, D.C.: U.S. State Department), 428.

15. See full details of Wisner's experiences in Romania in Evan Thomas, *The Very Best Men: Four Who Dared: The Early Years of the CIA* (New York: Simon & Schuster, 1995).

16. "RFE was one of the projects in which Dulles was especially interested." Wayne G. Jackson, *Allen Welsh Dulles as Director of Central Intelligence, 26 February 1953–29 November 1961,* Vol. 3, Covert Activities (Washington, D.C.: Central Intelligence Agency, 1973), 102. In addition to his public role with Radio Free Europe, Dulles also was on the board of directors for the Crusade for Freedom.

17. "Memorandum from the Director of the Policy Planning Staff (Kennan) to the Under Secretary of State (Lovett), Washington, June 30, 1948," *Emergence of the Intelligence Establishment*, Document 294.

18. "Hillenkoetter's Memorandum for the Record, August 4, 1948," Warner, 217.

19. RFE/RL Collection, Hoover Institution, Stanford, California.

20. "The Report of The President's Committee (Jackson Committee) on International Information Activities, June 30,1953: Project Clean Up," *Foreign Relations, 1952–54,* Vol. 2, International Information Activities (Washington, D.C.: U.S. Department of State), 1832.

21. "Memorandum from the Assistant Director for Policy Coordination (Wisner) to Director of Central Intelligence Hillenkoetter," *Foreign Relations of the United States, 1945–1950, Emergence of the Intelligence Establishment*, Document 306.

22. From the National Committee for a Free Europe press release, July 3, 1950, a copy of which can be found in the RFE/RL Collection.

23. Translated copy in RFE/RL Collection.

24. NCFE press release, July 13, 1950, RFE/RL Collection. Excellent sources of information on the history of Radio Free Europe are Arch Puddington, *Broadcasting Freedom: The Cold War Triumph of Radio Free Europe and Radio Liberty* (Lexington, University of Kentucky Press, 2000), Sig Mickelson, *America's Other Voice: The Story of Radio Free Europe and Radio Liberty* (New York: Praeger, 1983), and Alan Michie, *Voices Through the Iron Curtain: The Radio Free Europe Story* (New York: Dodd, Mead, 1963*)*.

25. For details of the Holzkirchen transmitters, see Charles Ruckstuhl, "The Beginning of Electronic Warfare: Piercing the Iron Curtain (Radio Free Europe)," *World and I* 18 (October 2003). After the collapse of Communism in Eastern Europe in 1989, RFE/RL closed its Hungarian Service in 1993, ended Polish broadcasts in 1997, and halted Czech-language broadcasts in 2002. It ended broadcasts to Slovakia and Bulgaria in 2004, and to Romania in 2008.

26. RFE/RL Collection.

27. *Ibid.*

28. "Memorandum to the Executive Secretary of the National Security Council (Lay) Washington," Third Progress Report on NSC 59/1, Foreign Information Program and Psychological Warfare Planning Document, *Foreign Relations of the United States, 1950–1955, The Intelligence Community 1950–1955*, Document No. 57 (Washington, D.C.: U.S. Government Printing Office, 2007).

29. Quoted from a Massachusetts Institute of Technology pamphlet, *Origins of the Center* (MIT Center for International Studies).

30. "Memorandum from Robert J. Hooker of the Policy Planning Staff to the Director of the Policy Planning Staff (Nitze) Washington, March 26, 1951," *Foreign Relations, 1950–1955*, Document 59.

31. *Ibid.*

32. "Memorandum from the Assistant Director for Policy Coordination (Wisner) to Director of Central Intelligence Hillenkoetter," *Emergence of the Intelligence Establishment*, Document 306, Note 2.

33. *Time*, "Winds of Freedom," August 27, 1951.

34. *Ibid.*

35. *Ibid.* See also Allan A. Michie, *Voices Through the Iron Curtain*, 137.

36. More details on these operations, including photocopies of propaganda leaflets, are found in the author's article "Balloons Over East Europe: The Cold War Leaflet Campaign of Radio Free Europe," *Falling Leaf*, no. 166 (Autumn 1999), published by he PsyWar Society — an international association of psycho-

logical warfare historians and collectors of aerial propaganda leaflets.

37. Michie, 136–141.

38. Copies of the "Black Books" are found in the RFE/RL Collection.

39. *Ibid.*

40. Address at Mechanics Hall in Boston, October 27, 1948, Harry S Truman Library & Museum, Independence, Missouri, Document 260. John T. Woolley and Gerhard Peters, *The American Presidency Project* (online). Santa Barbara, CA: University of California (hosted), Gerhard Peters (database). Available at http://www.presidency.ucsb.edu/ws/?pid=13073.

41 John T. Woolley and Gerhard Peters, *The American Presidency Project* (online). Santa Barbara, CA: University of California (hosted), Gerhard Peters (database). Available at http://www.presidency.ucsb.edu/ws/?pid=13768.

42. News Release, April 26, 1950, RFE/RL Collection.

43. The American Presidency Project.

44. *Ibid.*

45. Dwight D. Eisenhower Presidential Library & Museum, Abilene, Kansas.

46. Noel Griese, *Arthur W. Page: Publisher, Public Relations Pioneer, Patriot* (Tucker, GA: Anvil, 2001) 365.

47. *Ibid,* 371.

48. "Memorandum for the Files, November 23, 1951," *Foreign Relations, 1950–1955,* Document 94.

49. "Memorandum of Conversation, Washington, January 17, 1952," *Foreign Relations, 1950–1955,* Document 100.

50. "Second Annual Report, March 1952–1953, The East European Fund, Inc., New York, NY." Copy in the RFE/RL Collection.

51. In the 1950s, Cord Meyer was the CIA chief of the International Organization Division, which had administrative oversight of Radio Free Europe and Radio Liberty, among other organizations. In his memoir *Facing Reality: From World Federation to the CIA* (New York: Harper and Row, 1980), there is a full chapter on RFE and detailed information on his and the CIA's role in Hungary. For one scholar's view, see A. Ross Johnson, "To the Barricades: Did Radio Free Europe Inflame the Hungarian Revolutionaries of 1956? Exploring One of the Cold War's Most Stubborn Myths," *Hoover Digest* no. 4 (2007). For another scholar's view of the CIA's intelligence failure, see the excellent book by Charles Gati, *Failed Illusions: Moscow, Washington, Budapest and the 1956 Hungarian Revolt* (Stanford, CA: Stanford University Press, 2006). Gati was able to obtain the following highly censored but revealing documents under the U.S. Freedom of Information Act from the CIA for his book: (1) CIA Clandestine Services History, The Hungarian Revolution and Planning for the Future, 23 October–4 November 1956, Volume I of II, January 1958; (2) CIA Historical Staff, The Clandestine Service Historical Series, Hungary, Volume I, [Deleted], May 1972; and (3) CIA Historical Staff, The Clandestine Service Historical Series, Hungary, Volume II, External Operations, 1946–1965, May 1972. National Security Archive, George Washington University, Washington, D.C.

52. As reported in *U.N. Review.* United Nations, Report of the Special Committee on the Problem of Hungary, June 20, 1957.

53. George R. Urban, *Radio Free Europe and the Pursuit of Democracy: My War within the Cold War* (New Haven, CT: Yale University Press, 1997). Urban's book contains a detailed chapter on the Hungarian revolution based on his access to the full set of recorded programs.

54. Urban, 228. His book *The Nineteen Days: A Broadcaster's Account of the Hungarian Revolution* (London: Heinemann, 1957) is an insightful and contemporary review of Hungary 1956 and the role of radio broadcasting.

55. James A. Michener, *The Bridge at Andau* (New York: Random House, 1957), 252–253.

56. Project Clean Up, 1831.

57. *Ibid.*

58. Radio Liberty Press Release, January 10, 1964, RFE/RL Collection.

59. *Ibid.*

60. RL Statement in Connection with Change of Name of the American Committee for Liberation, January 10, 1964. RFE/RL Collection.

61. "Memorandum for the 303 Committee, Washington, January 27, 1969," *Foreign Relations, 1969–1976,* Volume 29, Document 28, 93.

62. "Memorandum for the Record," *Foreign Relations, 1969–1976,* Document 147, 457.

63. "Memorandum from the President's Assistant for National Security Affairs (Kissinger) to President Nixon, Tab A," *Foreign Relations, 1969–1976,* Document 149, 463.

64. RFE/RL Collection.

65. *Ibid.*

66. Transcript of Remarks by President Emil Constantinescu, RFE/RL, http://www.rferl.org/content/article/1084085.html (viewed 24 November 2008).

67. Transcript in RFE/RL Collection.

68. *Ibid.*

Chapter 2

1. John Le Carré, *The Secret Pilgrim* (London: Coronet, 1991), 125.

2. Author's collection.

3. The biographical information was extracted from his "autobiography" for employment with Radio Liberation. RFE/RL Collection, Hoover Institution Archives, Stanford, California.

4. *Ibid.*

5. RFE/RL Collection.

6. The MVD was the forerunner of the KGB.

7. RFE/RL Collection.

8. *Ibid.*

9. The full broadcast text is in the RFE/RL Collection.

10. It is estimated that at least twenty Czechs and Slovaks were kidnapped in the early 1950s: Interview with Prokop Tomek, Office for the Documentation and Investigation of the Crimes of Communism (UDV), Radio Prague in English, October 4, 2007. Details of the Kiripolsky story are taken from the author's collection.

11. RFE/RL Corporate Records, Washington, D.C.

12. Alan Michie, *Voices Through the Iron Curtain: The Radio Free Europe Story* (New York: Dodd, Mead, 1963), 278–279. Cord Meyer, *Facing Reality: From World Federation to the CIA* (New York: Harper and Row, 1980), 120.

13. Stewart Steven, *Operation Splinter Factor* (Philadelphia: J.B. Lippincott, 1974).

14. Ted Shackley, *Spymaster: My Life in the CIA* (Washington, D.C.: Potomac, 2005), 79–85. Another CIA officer who had the chance to interview Swiatlo after his arrival in the United States was Tennent H. Bagley. See Tennent H. Bagley, *Spy Wars: Moles, Mysteries, and Deadly Games* (New Haven, CT: Yale University Press, 2007).

15. As cited in Michie, 1963, 165. Also, a listing of his interviews is available at the Open Society Archives, Budapest, Hungary, HU OSA 300-50-6.

16. Flora Lewis, *Red Pawn* (Garden City, NJ: Doubleday, 1965), 239.

17. Stewart Steven, 208.

18. *Operation SPOTLIGHT: Regime, Press and Radio, Western Press and Radio and Internal Reactions, Feb. 12–Mar. 13, 1955* (New York: Free Europe Committee, March 1955), RFE/RL Collection.

19. *Ibid.*

20. *The Inside Story of the Bezpieka and the Party: Jozef Swiatlo Reveals the Secrets of the Party, the Regime, and the Security Apparatus,* English translation, page 2, in RFE/RL Collection.

21. "The Swiatlo Story," *News from Behind the Iron Curtain* 4, no. 3 (March 1955), 3.

22. Full details of the Swiatlo case and its reverberations in Poland can be found in L.W. Gluchowski, "The Defection of Jozef Swiatlo and the Search for Jewish Scapegoats in the Polish United Workers' Party, 1953–1954," *Intermarium* 3, no. 2, http://www.sipa.columbia.edu/ece/research/intermarium/vol3no2/gluchowski.pdf.

23. Memorandum from Robert Lang, director of Radio Free Europe, to the Executive Committee of the Board of Directors of the Free Europe Committee, March 4, 1955. The copy of this letter in the RFE/RL archives was "declassified with deletions" by the CIA on August 10, 1989, and omitted references to "Mr. Dulles' operation." The copy found in the President Eisenhower Library was declassified by the United States Information Agency on May 16, 1997, with no omissions. The author thanks Hugh Wilford, who wrote *The Mighty Wurlitzer: How the CIA Played America*, for a copy of the latter.

24. *Ibid.*

25. Shackley, 85.

26. *Operation Focus, Volumes I–III, Progress Reports on Operation and Program Summary, Regime Reaction, Refugee Reports, and Leaflet Content* (New York: Free Europe, 1954), copies of which are located in the RFE/RL Collection.

27. *Hungary and the 1956 Uprising,* Special Report No. 12, March 1957, Audience Analysis Section, Radio Free Europe, Munich, available in the RFE/RL Archives. This document and many more became available on the Web in November 2006 and are available at OSA 1956 Digital Archive, http://www.osa.ceu.hu/

digitalarchive. This digital archive was dedicated to the 1956 Hungarian revolution and its fiftieth anniversary; the documents of the history of the revolution were publicly available for the first time.

28. Radio Free Europe Internal Memorandum, May 30, 1951, RFE/RL Collection.

29. *Ibid.*

30. Siegfried Kracauer and Paul Berkman, *Satellite Mentality: Political Attitudes and Propaganda Susceptibilities of Non-Communists in Hungary, Poland, and Czechoslovakia* (New York: Frederick A. Praeger, 1956), 143–144.

31. Colonel Bell's Military Analysis 42, The Plan in Secret Warfare, RFE Script No. 48-0951, Project No. 11, September 1951, a copy of which is in the RFE/RL Archives, Hoover Institution.

32. RFE Internal Memorandum from William Griffith to Richard Condon, dated December 5, 1956, "Policy Review of Voice for Free Hungary Programming, October 23? November 1956." It surfaced in 1996 and was reprinted (without supporting appendices) in Csaba Bekes, Malcolm Byrne, and Janos M. Rainer, *The 1956 Hungarian Revolution: A History in Documents* (Budapest: CEU Press, 2002). What were not published. however, are three appendices to this report.

Appendix I contains the summary evaluation of each individual program.

Appendix II evaluates the performance of the individual Hungarian Service broadcasters.

Appendix III contains excerpts of the written RFE policy guidance for the period.

The review covered 308 programs or 70 percent of all non-news broadcast coverage during the period. A copy of the memorandum with all three appendices can be found in the RFE/RL Collection.

33. *Ibid.*

34. *Ibid.*

35. Hlavni Sprava Rozvedky, Main Directorate of the Second Department General Staff.

36. Josef Frolik, Testimony before the United States Senate, Committee on the Judiciary, Communist Bloc Intelligence Activities in the United States, November 18, 1975, page 38. In absentia, Frolik was sentenced to death for his defection and disclosing of secrets.

37. For details on Operation VETO, including a copy of one of the leaflets, see the author's article "Balloons Over East Europe: The

Cold War Leaflet Campaign of Radio Free Europe," *Falling Leaf Magazine*, Autumn 1999.

38. Josef Frolik, Testimony, 39. In his memoirs, Frolik changes the "poison" from atropine to potassium cyanide crystals. Josef Frolik, *The Frolik Defection: The Memoirs of an Intelligence Agent* (London: Lee Cooper, 1975), 33.

39. Uncorrected e-mail sent to the author. Author's collection.

40. Kalman Konkoly, Lajos von Horvath, and Aurel Abrnyi, *Ein Land in Flammen: Der Opfergang Ungarns* (München: Isar, 1956).

41. The author received an e-mail message from Abranyi's niece in December 2007 in which she wrote: "Last year I visited Budapest and found an office in Eotvos utca dealing in missing persons etc. but they would not help me as I was not an immediate relative of Aurel's."

Chapter 3

1. Most of Markov's literary works have not been published in English. The titles are translations from Bulgarian.

2. Georgi Markov, *The Truth That Killed* (London: Wiedenfeld and Nicholson, 1983), 267.

3. Georgi Markov wrote his scripts in London and sent them to RFE in Munich, where RFE's Bulgarian Service employees would read them over the air. The full text of his scripts in Bulgarian can be found at the RFE/RL Collection, Broadcast Archives, Hoover Institution, Stanford University.

4. Markov, 199.

5. *Ibid.*, 197.

6. *Ibid.*, 264.

7. Leonid Katsamunski, then Bulgaria's chief investigator into the death of Markov, gave an interview to the Associated Press in December 1991 and said that the decree "created the atmosphere that freed the hands for individual decisions by ministers, secret services, or other organs."

8. Published in Markov, *The Truth That Killed*, 215–261.

9. *Ibid.*, 236.

10. Kyril Panoff, "Murder on Waterloo Bridge," *Encounter*, November 1979.

11. I had a lengthy meeting in my office at RFE/RL with former KGB general Oleg Kalugin in August 1991. That conversation forms

the basis for the reconstruction of that fateful meeting in Andropov's office. Kalugin has changed his version of his own involvement over years, but the basic story remains the same as he described in the meeting. See Oleg Kalugin, *The First Directorat* (New York: St. Martin's, 1994) for more details.

12. Sterling Seagrave, *Yellow Rain: A Journey Through the Terror of Chemical Warfare* (London: Sphere, 1981).

13. Information in this section taken from the author's meetings with Popov and notes and memoranda from former directors of security, Russ Poole and George LeVaye. Author's collection.

14. Vladimir Kostov, *The Bulgarian Umbrella: The Soviet Direction and Operations of the Bulgarian Secret Service in Europe* (New York: St. Martin's, 1988), 2.

15. *Ibid.*

16. The pellet is on display at New Scotland Yard headquarters, London, England.

17. *POGLED*, no. 47 (November 25, 1991).

18. *Ibid.*

19. "My New Friends in the New Russia: In Search of a Few Good Crooks, Cops and Former Agents," *New York Times,* February 19, 1995.

20. Letter to the Editor, *New York Times,* April 2, 1995.

21. *Ibid.*

22. AFP news agency, Sofia, July 12, 1993.

23. Anthony Georgieff, "The Bulgarian Umbrella," *Vagabond* no. 4 (January 2007), http://www.vagabond-bg.com/?page=live &sub=37&open_news=231.

24. Kalugin, 178.

25. Vladimir Bereanu and Kalin Todorov, *The Umbrella Murder: Georgi Markov,* translated from Bulgarian with amendments by Vladimir Bereanu (Bury St. Edmonds, Suffolk: TEL, 1994).

26. *The Sofia Echo,* January 4, 2001.

27. *Ibid.*

28. "Tramp" (skitnik) was the Bulgarian intelligence service code name for Georgi Markov. The English translation of the title is *Kill the Tramp: The Murder of Georgi Markov and Bulgarian and British Government Policy* (Sofia: CIELA Soft and Publishing AD, 2005). English translation forthcoming.

29. "Secrets of the Dead: Case File Umbrella Assassin," PBS, http://www.pbs.org/w net/secrets/case_umbrella/index.html.

30. *Ibid.*

31. Author's collection.

32. *Ibid.*

Chapter 4

1. RFE/RL monthly newsletter *Inside RFE/RL*, no. 12 (December 20, 2001) contain details of the ceremony, including speeches and photographs. RFE/RL Collection, Hoover Institution, Stanford, California.

2. Two recommended books in English that cover the early years of Ilych Ramirez-Sanchez are Colin Smith. *Carlos: Portrait of a Terrorist* (London: Andre Deutsch, 1976; also, London: Sphere Books, 1976), and Christopher Dobson and Ronald Payne, *The Carlos Complex: A Pattern of Violence* (London: Hodder and Stoughton, 1977; New York: Putnam, 1977).

3. *Washington Post,* August 17, 1994.

4. Magdalena Kopp, *Die Terroristen Jahre: Mein Leben an der Seite von Carlos* (Munchen: DVA, 2007), 127.

5. Appendix A, Top Secret Stasi Report, Department XXII/8, February 10, 1981, translated copy in author's collection.

6. Kopp, 132.

7. Quoted at a press conference of Minister of Interior Balacs Horvath, broadcast on Hungarian domestic radio, June 27, 1990.

8. See Appendix A for full text.

9. Nica's last point referred to Carlos not having anyone in the United States to fulfill the plan; full text of translated copy in author's collection. The Romanian government submitted a copy to German prosecutors investigating the bombing. Nica died in 1995.

10. Appendix B. For this section, the author thanks former RFE Romanian Broadcast Service employee Traian Bratu for his assistance in translating the 1980 action plan. The full text of the action plan was released by the Romanian Foreign Intelligence Agency in the summer 2007 and reproduced in full by various newspapers in Romania.

11. Submitted by Hungarian authorities to German prosecutors. Copy in author's collection.

12. In July 1981, Emil Georgescu was stabbed over twenty-five times in front of his residence by a French criminal who was arrested with another French criminal on their way to Austria. They were found guilty and

imprisoned for this assault. However they did not admit any political motive for the attack, nor was evidence produced showing a connection to Carlos. See chapter 2 for details. A bomb in a book of Khrushchev's memoirs was sent to Goma in February 1981. The bomb exploded when a policeman tried to remove the bomb. He was injured; Goma was not. See chapter 4 for details.

13. Kopp, 136.

14. Transcript of monitored conversation in author's collection.

15. Hungarian Intelligence Monitoring Report included in the document submitted by Hungarian authorities to German prosecutors; translation copy in author's collection.

16. Translation of recorded telephone conversations in author's collection.

17. Kopp, 137.

18. John Follain, *Jackal: The Complete Story of the Legendary Terrorist Carlos the Jackal* (New York: Arcade, 1998), 126, quoting from an article by Robert Fisk in the newspaper *Independent*, August 20, 1994.

19. Appendix E, Stasi Report, April 29, 1981; translated copy in author's collection.

20. Translated report in author's collection.

21. Budapest Television Service, Panorama Program, July 6, 1990.

22. *Ibid.*

23. *Ibid.*

24. *Ibid.*

25. Appendix A.

26. See Appendix D for full text.

27. See Appendix E for full text.

28. *Ibid.*

29. "Operation Tourist," Czech-language magazine *Svet v obrazech*, August 22, 1990; translation in author's collection.

30. *Ibid.*

31. Billy Waugh, *Hunting the Jackal* (New York: HarperCollins, 2004) 198.

32. Author's collection.

33. Translation in author's collection.

34. Translation of letter in author's collection.

35. *Ibid.*

36. Appendix H, translated copy in author's collection.

37. Author's collection.

38. *Ibid.*

39. Kopp, 199.

40. Varga television interview broadcast June 3, 1996, Middeldeutscher Rundfunk.

41. *INTELLIGENCE*, no. 63, New Series

(June 30, 1997). http://www.blythe.org/Intelligence/readme/63sum

42. The film *Cold Waves*, written and directed by Alexandru Solomon, released in November 2007 in Romania.

43. *Ibid.*

Chapter 5

1. From the speech given by the president of Romania, Traian Basescu, on the occasion of the presentation of the Report by the Presidential Commission for the Analysis of the Communist Dictatorship in Romania, the Parliament of Romania, December 18, 2006.

2. Author's collection.

3. Pacepa, Ion, *Red Horizons: Chronicles of a Communist Spy Chief* (Washington, D.C.: Regnery Gateway, 1987). His revelations resulted in her arrest in the RFE/RL Headquarters building in Munich in May 1981. Her office and home were searched but no evidence was discovered. "Balthazar" resigned from RFE/RL. But Pacepa was not allowed to leave the United States to testify, and there was no prosecution for lack of other evidence. Jack Anderson reported her arrest in the *Washington Post*, July 25, 1981 ("The Ante Rises Over Radio Free Europe").

4. Peter Samuel, "Book Exposing PLO-Romanian Intrigue and Scandal Said Targeted by Terrorist" *New York Tribune*, December 29, 1987.

5. Quoted in Ion Mihai Pacepa, "The Kremlin's Killing Ways: A Long Tradition Continues," *National Review*, November 2006.

6. Author's collection.

7. *Ibid.*

8. *Ibid.*

9. Author's collection.

10. *Ibid.*

11. English translation in author's collection.

12. *Ibid.*

13. Author's collection.

14. Nestor Ratesh, "Radio Free Europe's Impact in Romania During the Cold War," Conference on Cold War Broadcasting Impact, October 2004. Publication forthcoming.

15. RFE/RL Collection, Hoover Institution, Stanford, California.

16. David Binder, "Romanian Diplomat Pushed Into Exile in U.S.," *New York Times*, October 9, 1990.

17. Author's collection.
18. *Ibid.*
19. Ratesh, "Radio Free Europe's Impact in Romania During the Cold War."
20. Author's collection.
21. See Appendix B for full translated text.
22. B.I.R.E. was the *Bulletin de Informatie Pentru Romani in Exil* (Information Bulletin for Romanians in Exile), a Romanian-language newsletter published in Paris.
23. Author's collection.
24. Author's collection.
25. More details of the Khrushchev book bombs came to light only in November 2007, when the Institute for the Investigation of Communist Crimes in Romania filed a "penal notification" against those allegedly involved.
26. Author's collection.
27. *Die Welt*, November 9, 1984.
28. Appendix G has the English translation of the relevant section of the annual report plus some details of two other cases of hostile Romanian intelligence activity in Germany.
29. See Appendix H for the complete text.
30. The full text was placed on the Internet by the IICCR at http://www.crimelecomunismului.ro/en.
31. Germina Nagat, "Radio and Punishment: The Communist War Against Our Ears," paper prepared for the Hoover Institution–Cold War International History Project Conference on Cold War Broadcasting Impact, Stanford, October 13–15, 2005. Publication forthcoming. Germina Nagat was a member of Romania's National Council for the Study of the Securitate's Archives (CNSAS).
32. *Ibid.*
33. See Appendix H for the full text of the 1985 Ether Report.
34. Nagat, "Radio and Punishment."

attempted to stir up animosity inside Radio Free Europe in order to have Bernard stripped of his position. Based on evidence from her husband's Securitate file, she also described Bernard's mysterious 1981 death as an assassination. See chapter 5 for more details on the death of Noel Bernard.
2. Author's collection.
3. *Ibid.*
4. "Bercovici" referred to Noel Bernard. The "Captain" referred to Corniliu Codreanu, known as the "Archangel," who was murdered as leader of the Romanian Iron Guard before World War II. Translation in author's collection.
5. Author's collection.
6. *Ibid.*
7. See chapter 5 for details of the hostile Romanian Intelligence Service activity, including threatening letters, against Vlad Georgescu and Noel Bernard.
8. See chapter 4 for details.
9. Securitate code name: Valerian.
10. Author's collection.
11. *Ibid.*
12. *Ibid.*
13. *Ibid.*
14. RFE/RL corporate records, Washington, D.C.
15. Pacepa, Ion, *Red Horizons*, 162–164.
16. His book also created major problems for RFE/RL in 1987 and 1988 with death threats to employees and managers, including the president of RFE/RL. See chapter 5 for details on the FBI investigation into these threats.
17. See Appendix H for details.
18. Ratesh, "Radio Free Europe's Impact in Romania During the Cold War." The book containing this document and others presented at the conference is to be published by the Central European Press, Budapest, Hungary.

Chapter 6

1. Report by Roy Minton and Edward Alexander to John Gronowski, then chairman of the Board for International Broadcasting (BIB), February 19, 1980, page 10, RFE/RL Archives, Hoover Institution. Also, in a 2003 article from the Romanian newspaper *Revista 22*, Noël Bernard's wife, Ioana Magura Bernard, noted that her husband was being targeted by the Securitate, and argued that, especially after the Trifa interview, the communist institution

Chapter 7

1. Oleg Tumanov's memoirs were published in English and contain different information. See Oleg Tumanov, *Confession of a KGB Agent* (Berlin, Edition Q, 1993)
2. Refer to chapter 8 for more details about Czechowicz.
3. Refer to chapter 8 for more details about Minarik.
4. Author's collection.
5. GRU was Glavnoje Razvedyvatel'noje

Upravlenije (Main Intelligence Directorate of the General Staff of the Armed Forces of the USSR).

6. Translation in author's collection. Tumanov made a strange remark about Fyodor not compromising Tumanov or bringing him harm. How could he have done so unless Fyodor knew more about Tumanov's activities than had previously been known? Was it possible that he was "protecting Tumanov" out of friendship? If one wanted to, one could have read various plays on words and hidden meanings in Tumanov's remark. For example, Tumanov wrote that if everything was "OK" than he and Fyodor would be able to meet in Fyodor's favorite city. Fyodor said that this meant Moscow.

7. Author's collection.

8. Author's collection.

9. All the information about "Kruger" comes from the author's collection.

10. Tumanov was never prosecuted in Germany for his spying activities.

11. *Pravda*, February 20, 1989, 7.

12. Tumanov, *Confession of a KGB Agent*, 184.

Chapter 8

1. Prokop Tomek, Office for the Documentation and Investigation of the Crimes of Communism (UDV), "StB Carried Out Actions Against Radio Free Europe," CTK National News Wire, August 25, 2005. Tomek has researched and written extensively in the Czech language on Radio Free Europe and the Czechoslovak Intelligence Services. For example, he is the author of *Issue No. 14 — Czechoslovak Security Services Against Radio Free Europe, "Target ALFA"* Prague, November 15, 2006.

2. Josef Frolik, testimony before the U.S. Senate, Committee on the Judiciary, Communist Bloc Intelligence Activities in the United States, November 18, 1975.

3. Author's collection.

4. *Ibid*. In uncorrected English as sent to author.

5. Author's collection.

6. Jiri Setina Collection, Box 15, Hoover Archives.

7. See Tomek, "Target ALFA" for full details, including photographs and drawings that Minarik submitted to Prague.

8. See Appendix J for the 1976 Joint Action Plan against RFE/RL, which includes references to Minarik.

9. Information provided to the author on April 30, 2004. Author's collection. *Respekt* (weekly magazine in the Czech Republic), May 7, 2007.

10. Translation in author's collection.

11. *Ibid.*

12. *Ibid.*

13. *Ibid.*

14. Interviews of the three from press summaries in Poland and in the West can be found in the Open Source Archives, Budapest, Hungary, under HU OSA 300-50-9, Records of RFE/RL Research Institute, Polish Unit.

15. Author's collection.

16. Appendix J.

17. Mieczyslaw Lach and Zdzislaw Oberman, *ufam ci Kilroy (I Trust You, Kilroy)*, Warsaw, 1983. Includes thirty pages of endpapers consisting of photographs of RFE/RL's headquarters, twenty-six present and former RFE/RL employees, and a map.

16. The photocopy of the latest instructions was in German and only a few persons had requested these instructions in German. The ensuing investigation was unable to discover who within RFE/RL had provided the instructions for use in the propaganda campaign.

18. Author's collection. The last sentence of the document was most interesting as the photocopy of the latest instructions was in German and only a few persons had requested these instructions in German. The ensuing investigation was unable to discover who within RFE/RL had provided the instructions for use in the propaganda campaign.

19. Author's collection.

20. His tenure at RFE/RL was tumultuous. For details, see George Urban, *Radio Free Europe and the Pursuit of Democracy: My War within the Cold War* (New Haven, CT: Yale University Press, 1997), 124–125. Translation in author's collection.

21. *An Interview with Zdislaw Najder*, Radio Liberty Background Report, RL 291/83, August 1, 1983.

Bibliography

Alexeyeva, Ludmilla. *U.S. Broadcasting to the Soviet Union.* New York: Helsinki Watch Committee, 1986.

Bagely, Kenneth H. *Spy Wars: Moles, Mysteries, and Deadly Games.* New Haven, CT: Yale University Press, 2007.

Board for International Broadcasting. *Annual Reports.* Washington, DC.

Browne, Donald R. *International Radio Broadcasting: The Limits of the Limitless Medium.* New York: Praeger, 1982.

Critchlow, James. *Radio Hole-in-the-Head/Radio Liberty: An Insider's Story of Cold War Broadcasting.* Washington, DC: American University Press, 1995.

Dobson, Christopher, and Ronald Payne. *The Carlos Complex: A Pattern of Violence.* London: Hodder and Stoughton, 1977.

Dulles, Alan. *The Craft of Intelligence.* Westport, CT.: Greenwood, 1963.

Follain, Jack. *Jackal: The Complete Story of the Legendary Terrorist Carlos the Jackal.* New York: Arcade, 1998.

Foreign Relations of the United States, 1945–1959: Emergence of the Intelligence Establishment. Washington, DC: Government Printing Office, 1996.

Frolik, Josef. *The Frolik Defection: The Memoirs of an Intelligence Agent.* London: Lee Cooper, 1975.

Gati, Charles. *Failed Illusions: Moscow, Washington, Budapest and the 1956 Hungarian Revolt.* Stanford, CA: Stanford University Press, 2006.

Griese, Noel. *Arthur W. Page: Publisher, Public Relations Pioneer, Patriot.* Tucker, GA: Anvil, 2001.

Grose, Peter. *Operation Rollback: America's Secret War Behind the Iron Curtain.* Boston: Houghton Mifflin, 2000.

Hersh, Burton. *The Old Boys: The American Elite and the Origins of the CIA.* St. Petersburg, FL: Tree Farm, 2002.

Holt, Robert T. *Radio Free Europe.* Minneapolis: University of Minnesota Press, 1958.

Jackson, Wayne G. *Allen Welsh Dulles as Director of Central Intelligence, February 26, 1953–November 29, 1961.* CIA Historical Study, 1973.

Kalugin, Oleg. *The First Directorate: My 32 Years in Intelligence and Espionage Against the West.* New York: St. Martin's, 1994.

Kessler, Ronald. *Spy vs. Spy: Stalking Soviet Spies in America.* New York: Charles Scribner's Sons, 1988.

Kostov, Vladimir. *The Bulgarian Umbrella: The Soviet Direction and Operations of the Bulgarian Secret Service in Europe.* New York: St. Martin's, 1988.

Kovrig, Bennet. *Of Walls and Bridges: The United States and Eastern Europe.* New York: New York University Press, 1991.

Lendvai, Paul. *The Bureaucracy of Truth: How Communist Governments Manage the News.* London: Burnett, 1981.

Lucas, Scott. *Freedom's War: The American Crusade against the Soviet Union.* New York: New York University Press, 1999.

Markov, Georgi. *The Truth That Killed.* London: Wiedenfeld and Nicholson, 1983.

Meyer, Cord. *Facing Reality: From World Federalism to the CIA.* New York: Harper and Row, 1980.

Michener, James A. *The Bridge at Andau.* New York: Random House, 1957.

Michie, Allan. *Voices Through the Iron Curtain: The Radio Free Europe Story.* New York: Dodd, Mead, 1963.

Mickelson, Sig. *America's Other Voice: The Story of Radio Free Europe and Radio Liberty.* New York: Praeger, 1983.

Mosley, Leonard. *Dulles: A Biography of Eleanor, Allen, and John Foster Dulles and Their Family Network.* New York: Dial, 1978.

Muravchik, Joshua. *Exporting Democracy: Fulfilling America's Destiny.* Washington, DC: American Enterprise Institute, 1991.

Nelson, Michael. *War of the Black Heavens: The Battles of Western Broadcasting in the Cold War.* Syracuse, NY: Syracuse University Press, 1997.

Pacepa, Ion. *Red Horizons: Chronicles of a Communist Spy Chief.* Washington, DC: Regnery Gateway, 1987.

Parta, R. Eugene. *Discovering the Hidden Listener: An Assessment of Radio Liberty and Western Broadcasting to the USSR During the Cold War.* Stanford: Hoover Institution, 2007.

Powers, Thomas. *The Man Who Kept the Secrets: Richard Helms and the CIA.* New York: Pocket, 1991.

Price, James R. *Radio Free Europe: A Survey and Analysis.* Washington, DC: Congressional Research Service, Library of Congress, 1972.

Puddington, Arch. *Broadcasting Freedom: The Cold War Triumph of Radio Free Europe and Radio Liberty.* Lexington: University of Kentucky Press, 2000.

Report of the Presidential Study Commission on International Radio Broadcasting: The Right to Know. Washington, DC: Government Printing Office, 1973.

Saunders, Frances Stonor. *The Cultural Cold War: The CIA and the World of Arts and Letters.* New York: New, 1999.

Seagrave, Sterling. *Yellow Rain: A Journey Through the Terror of Chemical Warfare.* London: Sphere, 1981.

Shackley, Ted. *Spymaster: My Life in the CIA.* Dulles, VA: Potomac, 2005.

Smith, Colin. *Carlos: Portrait of a Terrorist.* London: Andre Deutsch, 1976.

Sosin, Gene. *Sparks of Liberty: An Insider's Memoir of Radio Liberty.* University Park: Pennsylvania State University Press, 1999.

Short, K.R.M., ed. *Western Broadcasting Over the Iron Curtain.* London: Croom Helm, 1986.

Starr, Richard F., ed. *Public Diplomacy: USA versus USSR.* Stanford, CA: Hoover Institution, 1986.

Steven, Stewart. *Operation Splinter Factor.* Philadelphia: J.B. Lippincott, 1974.

Thomas, Evan. *The Very Best Men: Four Who Dared: The Early Years of the CIA.* New York: Simon & Schuster, 1995.

Tumanov, Oleg. *Confessions of a KGB Agent.* Chicago: Edition Q, 1993.

_____. *Gestaendnisse eines KGB-Agenten.* Berlin, Edition Q, 1993.

Tyson, James L. *U.S. International Broadcasting and National Security,* New York: Ramapo, 1983.

Urban, George. *The Nineteen Days: A Broadcaster's Account of the Hungarian Revolution.* London: Heinemann, 1957.

_____. *Radio Free Europe and the Pursuit of Democracy: My War within the Cold War.* New Haven, CT: Yale University Press, 1997.

Warner, Michael, ed. *CIA Cold War Records: The CIA Under Harry Truman.* Washington, DC: CIA, 1994.

Washburn, Philo C. *Broadcasting Propaganda: International Radio Broadcasting and the Construction of Political Reality.* Westport, CT: Praeger, 1992.

Waugh, Billy. *Hunting the Jackal.* New York: HarperCollins, 2004.

Wettig, Gerhard. *Broadcasting and Detente: Eastern Policies and Their Implications for East-West Relations.* London: C. Hurst, 1977.

Wheland, Joseph G. *Radio Liberty: A Study of Its Origins, Structure, Policy, Programming and Effectiveness.* Washington, DC: Congressional Research Service, Library of Congress, 1972.

Wiener, Tim. *Legacy of Ashes: The History of the CIA.* New York: Doubleday, 2007.

Wilford, Hugh. *The Mighty Wurlitzer: How the CIA Played America.* Cambridge, MA: Harvard University Press, 2008.

Index